D0302781

CODE-SWITCHING IN CONVERSATION

'Altogether this is a most impressive book. It is a highly integrated collection of current work . . . highly original, containing much unfamiliar but excellent material. Its structure is very simple and helpful. I welcome this book as it is likely to make a range of techniques which focus on conversational interaction available to others . . . a book which focuses on the interactional issues in code-switching is very timely. . . . The presentation of a large amount of material drawn from a number of different language mixing situations is excellent . . . should be of great interest to readers in a wide range of disciplines, particularly anthropologists, social psychologists and linguists.'
Lesley Milroy, *University of Michigan*

'This innovative and in many ways fascinating collection of papers is the first systematic comparative treatment of the communicative import of code-switching. It clearly demonstrates that code-switching, wherever it is employed, counts as a discursive strategy that achieves communicative ends by either building on or violating what are commonly seen as fixed boundaries . . . . Recommended reading for anyone interested in multilingualism, conversational analysis or language use in general.'
John J. Gumperz, *University of California, Berkeley*

Code-switching, the alternating use of two or more languages within conversation, has become an increasingly topical and important field of research.

This volume brings together contributions from a wide variety of sociolinguistic settings in which this phenomenon is observed. It addresses the structure and the function, but also the ideological values, of such bilingual behaviour. The contributors question many views of code-switching on the empirical basis of many European and non-European contexts. By bringing together linguistic, anthropological and socio-psychological research, they move towards a more realistic conception of bilingual conversational action.

Contributors: Celso Alvarez-Cáccamo, Rita Franceschini, Michael Meeuwis and Jan Blommaert, Cecilia Oesch Serra, Yael Maschler, Li Wei, Giovanna Alfonzetti, Melissa G. Moyer, J. N. Jørgensen, Mark Sebba and Tony Wootton, Ben Rampton, Christopher Stroud.

CODE-SWITCHING IN CONVERSATION

Language, interaction and identity

Edited by Peter Auer

London and New York

First published 1998
by Routledge
11 New Fetter Lane, London EC4P 4EE

Simultaneously published in the USA and Canada
by Routledge
29 West 35th Street, New York, NY 10001

First published in paperback 1999

Routledge is an imprint of the Taylor & Francis Group

Typeset in Times New Roman by
The Florence Group, Stoodleigh, Devon
Printed and bound in Great Britain by
Biddles Ltd, Guildford and King's Lynn

British Library Cataloguing in Publication Data
A catalogue record for this book is available from the British Library

Library of Congress Cataloguing in Publication Data
Code-switching in conversation : language, interaction and identity/
edited by Peter Auer.
    p.   cm.
1. Code switching (Linguistics)   2. Conversation analysis.
3. Bilingualism.   4. Discourse analysis.   I. Auer, Peter, 1954–
P115.3.C65   1998
306.44--dc21   97-22664

ISBN 0–415–15831–1 (hbk)
ISBN 0–415–21609–5 (pbk)

CONTENTS

v

CONTRIBUTORS

Giovanna Alfonzetti is post-doctoral Research Fellow at the University of Catania, Italy

Celso Alvarez-Cáccamo is Associate Professor (Professor Titular) at the University of Coruña, Spain

Peter Auer is Professor of German Linguistics at the University of Freiburg, Germany

Jan Blommaert is Professor of African Linguistics at the University of Ghent, Belgium

Rita Franceschini is Lecturer at the University of Basel, Switzerland

J. Norman Jørgensen is Associate Professor at the University of Copenhagen, Denmark

Yael Maschler is Lecturer at the Hebrew University of Jerusalem, Israel

Michael Meeuwis is post-doctoral Research Fellow at the University of Antwerp, Belgium

Melissa Moyer is Associate Professor at the University of Barcelona, Spain

Cecilia Oesch-Serra is chargée de cours at the University of Neuchâtel, Switzerland

Ben Rampton is Reader at the Thames Valley University, UK

Mark Sebba is Lecturer at Lancaster University, UK

Christopher Stroud is Associate Professor at Stockholm University, Sweden

Li Wei is Professor at the University of Newcastle, UK

Tony Wootton is Senior Lecturer at the University of York, UK

ACKNOWLEDGEMENTS

This volume originated from a workshop held at the University of Hamburg in January 1995. The financial support of the Deutsche Forschungs-gemeinschaft and of the City of Hamburg for this meeting is gratefully acknowledged.

The preparation of this volume would hardly have been possible without the help of Karin Brockmann, Barbara Rönfeldt and Ines Lange who substan-tially contributed to the preparation of the chapters for print and carefully read through all the papers.

1

INTRODUCTION

Bilingual Conversation revisited

Peter Auer

1 What this book is about

During the last twenty years, we have experienced a sharp rise of scientific interest in phenomena of bilingual speech, and in particular, in code-switching. Code-switching used to be a matter for a few specialists in the 1950s and 1960s, of peripheral importance for linguistics as a whole. A number of pioneering and now classical publications of the 1970s, both on the syntactic (Poplack 1979 [1981]) and the sociolinguistic (Blom and Gumperz 1972) aspects of bilingual speech, have moved it into the focus of interest of a great number of researchers in syntax, sociolinguists and psycholinguists. The 1980s and particularly the 1990s have witnessed the publication of numerous monographs and articles on the subject, and, in Europe, the establishment of an ESF (European Science Foundation) Network on Code-Switching and Language Contact (cf. Milroy and Muysken 1995). Thus, code-switching has developed from what used to be looked upon as 'possibly a somewhat peculiar ... act' (Luckmann 1983: 97) into a subject matter which is recognised to be able to shed light on fundamental linguistic issues, from Universal Grammar to the formation of group identities and ethnic boundaries through verbal behaviour.

Within this now vast field, the present volume is devoted to the study of code-switching as (part of a) verbal action; as such, code-switching has and creates communicative and social meaning, and is in need of an interpretation by co-participants as well as analysts. The contributors to this volume are united by their conviction that in order to explicate the meaning of code-switching as (part of a) verbal action, the 'alternating use of two or more "codes" within one conversational episode' (thus the usual definition) needs to be taken seriously *as such*, i.e. as a conversational event. Whatever cultural or social knowledge may be necessary to arrive at a full understanding of code-switching practices in a given community, its analysis first and foremost requires close attention to be paid to the details of its local

1

production in the emerging conversational context which it both shapes and responds to (cf. Li Wei, this volume).

The traditions of research in which the articles in this volume are embedded seek to understand verbal actions not by subsuming ('coding') them under pre-established external categories, but by explicating the systematic resources that members of a community, as participants in a conversation, have at their disposal in order to arrive at interpretations of 'what is meant' by a particular utterance in its context. With respect to code-switching, as we shall outline below, this methodological postulate has far-reaching consequences, since what linguists tend to take for granted as 'codes' (and hence classify as 'code-switching') may not be looked upon as 'codes' by members/participants (see Alvarez-Cáccamo, this volume and below, section 3).

Both the insistence on the conversational dimension of code-switching and the insistence on reconstructing participants' categories instead of imposing external linguistic or sociolinguistic ones on them, are relatively recent developments in research on bilingualism and are certainly not shared by all present-day theories of code-switching. They are, in addition to various other interactional/interpretive approaches, indebted to ethnomethodological and conversation analytic thinking about human interaction, even though most contributions in this volume do not subscribe to an orthodox conversation analytic framework. They also provide the two most important theoretical issues running through the chapters of this book: (a) what are the 'codes' in 'code-switching'? and (b) how does conversational code-switching relate to its wider ethnographically reconstructed (social and cultural) context?

In this Introduction, these central themes of the volume will be treated in the following way. Section 2 will outline what the conversational dimension of code-switching looks like; in particular, the relationship between conversational structure and ethnographically gathered knowledge in the interpretation of code-switching will be discussed, which is the topic of the chapters in the second part of the book. Section 3 contains some thoughts on the notion of a 'code' and sketches a possible continuum from 'code-switching' to 'mixed codes', corresponding to the topic of the first part of the volume.

Frequently, the background of the discussion will be *Bilingual Conversation* (Auer 1984a), in which an attempt was made to apply a CA (conversation analysis)-type approach to data in which two or more languages are used alternately and in which this alternation between codes is employed as a resource for the construction of interactional meaning. Since then, a number of highly competent studies using the same or a similar methodology have appeared (to mention just a few: Alfonzetti 1992, Khamis 1994, Li Wei 1994, Sebba 1994). They have broadened our understanding about the organisation of bilingual conversation by investigating in detail the structures of code alternation in a variety of speech communities.

2 The conversational structure of code-switching and its social and cultural embeddedness

From earlier and more recent research we know (a) that code-switching is related to and indicative of group membership in particular types of bilingual speech communities, such that the regularities of the alternating use of two or more languages within one conversation may vary to a considerable degree between speech communities, and (b) that intrasentential code-switching, where it occurs, is constrained by syntactic and morphosyntactic considerations which may or may not be of a universal kind. Accordingly, the dominant perspectives on code-switching taken in research have been either sociolinguistic (in the narrow sense of the term, i.e. as referring to relationships between social and linguistic structure), or grammatical (referring to constraints on intrasentential code-switching). The central research question of the first type of research is how language choice reflects power and inequality, or is an index of the 'rights and obligations' attributed to incumbents of certain social categories. The second tradition usually addresses the question of syntactic constraints from within the framework of a particular grammatical theory.

Yet these two traditions leave a gap which is well known to every linguist working on natural data from bilingual settings. The gap is due to the fact that, on the one hand, macro-sociolinguistic aspects of the speech situation never determine completely language choice, including code-switching and the absence of it. Often, and in many ways, the verbal interaction between bilingual speakers is open to local processes of language negotiation and code selection. Many macro-sociolinguistic investigations of code-switching restrict themselves to analysing the social meaning of the occurrence or non-occurrence of code-switching in an interaction at large, by reference to its participants, topic or setting, but they fail to account for these local processes, and therefore the place *within* the interactional episode in which languages alternate, either because they dismiss the question itself as uninteresting, or because they do not believe that such an account is possible.

On the other hand, the gap is also due to the fact that code-switching is never restricted to the intrasentential case which may be amenable to a strictly syntactic analysis; on the contrary, whenever intrasentential code-switching occurs, intersentential switching is a matter of course, but not all code-switching situations/communities which allow intersentential switching also allow intrasentential switching. This means that neither the sociolinguistic approach (*sensu stricto*) nor the grammatical approach explores the whole range of observed regularities in bilingual speech. The lacuna is precisely in those patterns of code-switching which go beyond the sentence, i.e. code-switching between conversational 'moves' or 'intonation units' each representing full 'constructional units' in terms of their syntactic make-up.

3

In order to fill this gap, it has been claimed in *Bilingual Conversation* that there is a level of conversational structure in bilingual speech which is sufficiently autonomous both from grammar (syntax) and from the larger societal and ideological structures to which the languages in question and their choice for a given interactional episode are related. The partial autonomy of conversational structure in code-switching is shown, for example, by the fact that switching is more likely in certain sequential positions than in others (for example, responsive turns or components are less suited for switching than initiative ones), or that certain sequential patterns of alternating language choice direct participants' interpretation (Auer 1995). It is also shown by the many ways in which code-switching can contextualise conversational activities, for example on the level of participant constellation, topic management, the structure of narratives, etc. (cf. Gumperz 1982, 1994; Auer 1984a; Li Wei and Milroy 1995; Sebba and Wootton, this volume; Alfonzetti, this volume; Meeuwis and Blommaert, this volume; as well as many others).

But the 'partial autonomy' of the conversational level does not imply that 'macro' dimensions are irrelevant for the interpretation of code-switching. Quite on the contrary, the indexicality of patterns such as the ones proposed in Auer (1984a) and schematised in Auer (1995: 125–6) provides a built-in sensibility for these dimensions: conversational regularities (such as the ones found to hold in turn-taking) are both context-independent and context-sensitive. The model's indebtedness to CA, as well as to Goffman's notion of the 'Interaction Order', is particularly visible here (see in particular Goffman 1982). While *Bilingual Conversation* attempts to 'flex the muscles of conversation analysis as much as possible' (1984a: 6), the indexical aspect is still clearly visible. In the following, I want to give some examples of the ways in which the wider social and cultural context of an interactional episode links up with conversational structure.

The first is *discourse-related code-switching* (in the terminology of Auer 1984a), i.e. the use of code-switching to organise the conversation by contributing to the interactional meaning of a particular utterance. Let us consider as an example a very simple conversational pattern of this type in which code-switching is frequent and has been reported in many bilingual communities all over the world: the repetition in the other language of a first pair part which was not responded to ('second attempts', Auer 1984b), as in the following extract:

EXAMPLE 1

Informal conversation among young Spanish–German bilingual speakers of South American origin in Hamburg; W, female; M, male; Spanish in italics.[1]

---

1   (25.0)

2 W *qué hora es?*

```
          ('what time is it?')
3         (2.0)
4 →       wie spät?
          ('what time?')
5   M     zwanzig nach elf;
          ('twenty past eleven;')
6   W     h (2.5)
7   M     wann muß du hoch?
          ('when do you have to go?' [i.e. to the university])
8   W     nö – nich so früh. Ich hab erst um vier Uni.
          ('no – not so early. I haven't got classes until four.')
                              (Tilmann Altenberg, unpublished data, 1992)
```

The non-response in line 3 by the second participant (in this case, after an initial question which reopens this focused interaction after a 25-second silence) is interpreted by the first participant as repair-initiating. Code-switching on the 'second attempt' (line 4) offers a first speaker's account of this 'notable absence' as being due to the 'wrong' language choice, i.e. one not coinciding with that recipient's preferred language. Code-switching in this sequential position, i.e. in order to contextualise it as a 'non-first first', certainly is discourse-related, following

Pattern Ib: . . . A1 // B1 B2 B1 B2 . . .

of Auer (1995) (where letters stand for languages, and numbers for speakers).[2]

Among the younger children investigated in our study of Italian immigrant workers' children in Germany, the same structure was observed. But in addition, switching on such repairs was found to have a constant direction: overwhelmingly from Italian (dialect) into German (dialect) but rarely the other way round (Auer 1984b). This direction indexes the larger context of the children's life-world in Germany, for it evokes the status of German as what one might call the 'in-group' language of peer interaction (the 'out-group' language of the parents and other adults being Italian (dialect); cf. Jørgensen, this volume, for a similar reversal of the 'we-code'/'they-code' distinction of adult migrants in their children): for the second, the 'repaired' version of the activity, the 'right' language is chosen, which concords with the dominant language choice of the children among themselves – German. Code-switching serves a conversational function, but at the same time it links up with 'larger' (ethnographically recoverable) facts about the children's life-world; yet reference to these facts in our analysis is indexed by conversational structure.

Discourse-related code-switching is particularly likely to index elements of the wider context in cases like this in which its direction is constant in a given conversational environment (cf. Alfonzetti, this volume). Similarly, *discourse-related insertions*,[3] i.e. code alternation of the

> *Pattern IV:* ... A1[B1]A1 ...

often evoke episode-external ('ethnographic') knowledge about interaction histories and cultural contexts. Consider the following extract:

EXAMPLE 2

Informal conversation among a group of young Spanish–German bilingual speakers of South American origin in Hamburg; J and U are the hosts, C is a guest; Spanish in italics.

1	J	*qué estás buscando?* [from the distance]
		('what are you looking for?')
2	C	*cigarros*
		('cigarettes')
3	J	*ay por qué?*
		('oh why?')
4		(1.0)
5	C	*por qué?*
		('why?')
6	J	*por qué por qué quieres ir al* flur?
		('why why do you want to go out in the corridor?')
7	C	*para fumar*
		('in order to smoke')
8	J	*aha*

9 L   *a(h)l*   fl(h)ur [*a(h)l a(h)l*   [*a(h)l*
    ('to the corridor to the to the   to the')
10 J   [*y dónde*   [*al* flur? *h h*
                   ('and where   in the corridor?')
11 A *he he he* [*he*
12 U   [*fuerte*
            ('cool')
13   (2.0)
14 L *ahí donde está la bicicleta* [*está*
    ('there where is the bike is')
15 J   [*aquí no hay aquí no hay* nichtraucher=
                   ('here we don't have no-smoking')
16 L =*donde está la bicicle-* he he
    ('where the bike is')

(Peter Giese, unpublished data, 1992/93)

There are four potential insertions in this little conversation about smoking which is basically in Spanish: German *Flur* ('corridor') which is used by J (twice) and by L (once), and German *Nichtraucher* ('no smoking'). Both words are used as descriptions of localities here. The first mentioning of the word *Flur* in line 6 comes without any kind of flagging, and certainly cannot receive a competence-related interpretation. Knowledge about recurrent patterns of language usage in this group of speakers would be required in order to be able to decide if perhaps the word has been borrowed into these speakers' Spanish. In any case, the repeated use of *Flur* in L's and J's subsequent turns, in which they laugh at C's idea of not smoking in the living room but outside in the corridor where the bikes are kept, is a strategy of establishing textual coherence by using several times the same word in the same language: that is, it has a discourse-related function.

However, the important insertion for this discussion is not that of *Flur* but that of *Nichtraucher* in line 15. Sequential analysis of its locus of occurrence offers some hints that a discourse-related interpretation is appropriate here as well. The turn in which the insertion occurs ('here we don't have no-smoking') is an 'account' for a particular act by J and L, i.e. their laughing at C's idea of smoking in the corridor. This account contrasts certain rules of conduct in the present South American household in Hamburg (*aquí*) with those of some other place where smoking and non-smoking areas are strictly separated. According to the rules of conduct of this other place, it would be appropriate or even necessary to leave the living room in order to smoke. J and L distance themselves from this rule which they find ridiculous, and point out that it does not hold in their apartment. What is more, C is laughed at for believing that anything else could be the case and called to order, i.e. requested to follow the rules of conduct which are valid here, and not those of the other place. Now, what is this 'other place'? The choice of German for 'non-smoking' gives the decisive clue: it is a certain segment of German culture which is contrasted with these South American participants' way of living in terms of how it deals with smokers. Yet it seems difficult to establish this interpretation on the basis of the transcript alone. Background information not explicated in this conversation reveals that smoking in German society has indeed been a topic in this group of speakers. It is only on the basis of an analysis of the sequential position of the insertion *together with* this background knowledge, which is indexed by the insertion and thus made relevant for the organisation of the interaction at this particular point, that a full understanding of code alternation can be reached. On the basis of this background information, it is possible to understand that the insertion establishes a link between this episode and these previous ones in the same group; that is, it works 'intertextually'.

A third code-switching pattern found in conversation which regularly indexes extra-conversational knowledge is *preference-related switching*, i.e. the

Pattern IIa: ... A1 B2 A1 B2 A1 B2 A1 B2 ...
(sustained divergence of language choices) or

Pattern IIb: ... A1 B2 A1 B2 A1 // A2 A1 A2 A1 ...
(language negotiation sequence: convergence of language choices).

In *Bilingual Conversation*, the notion of a 'language negotiation sequence' is supposed to capture all those stretches of talk in which participants do not agree on one common language-of-interaction. In contrast with discourse-related switching, where the new language prototypically evokes a new 'frame' or 'footing' for the interaction which is then shared by all participants, preference-related switching results in more or less persistent phases of divergent language choices. This is a marked state of affairs for many bilingual speech communities, though certainly not for all.[4] Thus, the basic difference is that, in discourse-related switching, participants search for an account for 'why that language now?' within the development of the conversation, while in participant-related switching, they search for an account within the individual who performs this switching, or his or her co-participants.[5]

Speaking of individual speakers' 'preferences' for one language or the other in this context should not be taken to imply that any kind of psychological concept is at issue. What the term refers to are rather the interactional processes of displaying and ascribing predicates to individuals. Their exact nature is entirely dependent on the wider social, political and cultural context of the interaction at hand. In the Italian/German data produced by children that were used for *Bilingual Conversation*, these predicates were usually of a very profane kind (competence playing an important role, ideological factors none at all). Adult bilinguals may account for a divergence of language preferences in a much more complex way (cf. Stroud, this volume; Sebba and Wootton, this volume; Rampton, this volume).

But discourse- and participant- (preference-) related switching are not strictly separated. In pattern IIb, the transition from divergent to convergent language choices (i.e. the moment where one common language-of-interaction is found) may take on discourse-related meanings; the same holds for the beginning of a sequence of divergent languages choices, unless it coincides with the beginning of the episode as a whole. Compare the arrowed positions in the schematic representation in Figure 1.1.

As far as the closing of a negotiation sequence is concerned (second arrow), the schematic representation following pattern IIb does not imply code-switching at all at this point, but rather the absence of further participant-related code-switching. It is this non-switching which takes on a discourse-related meaning.

As an example of how the sequential structure of language negotiation interacts with episode-external facts, consider the following extract,[6] taken from the work of Myers-Scotton, a prominent researcher on code-switching

```
...
A1
A2        A = language of interaction (convergent choices)
A1
   B2     ←— language (re)negotiation starts
   A1
   B2     negotiation sequence (divergent choices)
   A1
   B2
   ...
   B1     ←— language (re)negotiation stops
   B2
   B1     B = language of interaction (convergent choices)
   ...
```

Figure 1.1 Language negotiation sequence

who explicitly denies the relevance of a CA-type approach (Myers-Scotton 1993). Closer inspection of the data shows that the opposite is the case.

EXAMPLE 3

Lwidakho–Swahili (italics)–English (bold-face) switching in western Kenya. Reproduced without alterations, but line numbers added. Interaction between a local farmer 'who speaks Lwidakho and also, perhaps, a bit of Swahili' and a local person now employed in an urban centre outside the area in a rural bar. Until now, the conversation was in Lwidakho; 'rather predictably', as Myers-Scotton informs us, 'the farmer is asking the salaried man for money'.

1	FARMER	Khu inzi khuli menyi hanu inzala- ('As I live here, I have hunger-')
2	WORKER	[interrupting:] *Njaa gani?* ('What kind of hunger?')
3	FARMER	Yenya khunzirila hanu- ('It wants to kill me here-')
4	WORKER	[interrupting again, with more force:] *Njaa gani?* ('What kind of hunger?')
5	FARMER	Vana veru- ('Our children-' [said as appeal to others as brothers])
6	WORKER	*Nakuuliza, njaa gani?* ('I ask you, what kind of hunger?')
7	FARMER	Inzala ya mapesa, kambuli. ('Hunger for money; I don't have any.')

8 WORKER	**You have got a land.**
9	*Una shamba.*
	('You have land [farm].')
10	Uli nu mulimi.
	('You have land [farm].')
11 FARMER	... mwana mweru-
	('... my brother-')
12 WORKER	... mbula tsisendi.
	('I don't have money.')
13	**Can't you see how I am heavily loaded?**

(Myers-Scotton 1983: 128, reproduced in Myers-Scotton 1993: 82)

Myers-Scotton analyses this interaction exclusively on the basis of conversation-external knowledge about language use in Kenya, by indicating that Swahili and English are both marked code choices for a place and interaction of this type.[7] This markedness triggers the inference that the worker refuses an appeal to solidarity by using the 'out-group' languages Swahili (unmarked in inter-ethnic communication) and English (unmarked when used by the educational elites). From a conversation-analytic point of view, however, a number of problems with such a broad description remain, some of which are rather substantial for the interpretation of the meaning of code-switching in this extract.[8]

In terms of the conversational structure of code-switching, this interaction is a clear case of language negotiation in which an initial divergence of language choices (Lwidakho/Swahili/English) is resolved by the worker's accommodation of the farmer's preferred variety in line 10. The common language-of-interaction found at this point in the interaction is quickly abandoned again in line 13 by the worker's switching back into English. According to the schematic representation in Figure 1.1, the utterances in lines 10 and 13 are candidates for a discourse-related interpretation of the termination or beginning of a language negotiation sequence.

We may start by noting that it is wrong to say that the worker uses the marked languages English and Swahili in this episode; he does so, indeed, in the beginning and also at the end, but two interactionally very focal activities in between are in Lwidakho, the language used by the farmer throughout. The focal status of the Lwidakho utterances reveals itself on the basis of a sequential analysis (limited by the quality of the transcript but sufficient to make the point clear):

1 FARMER	As I live here, I have hunger-	indirect request
2 WORKER	(interrupting):	clarification
	What kind of hunger?	request
3 FARMER	it wants to kill me here-	elaboration
4 WORKER	(interrupting again, with more force):	clarification

	What kind of hunger?	request/ 2nd attempt
5 FARMER	our children- (said as appeal to others as brothers)	indirect request/ 2nd attempt
6 WORKER	*I ask you, what kind of hunger?*	clarification request/ 3rd attempt
7 FARMER	Hunger for money; I don't have any	answer
8 WORKER	**You have got a land**	indirect decline
9	*You have land [farm]*	indirect decline/ 2nd version
10	You have land [farm]	indirect decline/ 3rd version
11 FARMER	. . . my brother-	indirect request/ 3rd attempt
12 WORKER	. . . I don't have money.	direct decline
13	**Can't you see how I am heavily loaded?**	

The extract starts with an indirect request for money by the farmer. The worker profits from this indirectness when he subsequently starts an insertion sequence (line 2), asking what kind of hunger the farmer is speaking of. Thus, the request for money is neither declined nor complied with at that point of the interaction; instead, a response to the farmer's request is suspended. The farmer, however, does not answer the worker's question directly either. Instead, he elaborates on his previous indirect statement (3), which leads to the worker's first repetition of his question (4). Sequentially, at this point, the farmer insists on his request, though again only indirectly, while the worker insists on an insertion sequence. Both are clearly working on different sequential structures and are, in this sense, out of tune or conversational alignment.

The same sequential derailment holds for the following pair of utterances; the farmer's formulaic exclamation 'our children' (5) seems to be yet another indirect version of his initial request, while the worker repeats his question a second time; this 'third attempt' is typically marked by a performative verb (6). After the threefold exchange of non-matching turns, line 7 finally solves the sequential conflict; the farmer now answers the worker's question and thus closes the insertion sequence. Since the initial request is still awaiting a response (i.e. the adjacency pair is still open), the worker is now under considerable sequential pressure to produce such a response. He does so indeed, and almost as if he wanted to provide a counterweight sufficient to balance the farmer's three unanswered attempts to request money from him, he delivers his response in three versions as well, distinguished only by their language. Language choice in 8–10 starts with English, a language used for the first time here, continues with a repetition in Swahili, the language used by the worker up to now in this passage of diverging language preference, and ends in Lwidakho, the farmer's displayed language of preference in this episode. Symbolically, the passage is from 'no one's language' through 'my language' to 'your language' (in this episode).

Code-switching on these three versions of the declination is an example of 'reiteration' or 'repetition' for emphasis by code-switching, which has been observed in many other studies as well. But in addition, by switching from English into Swahili into Lwidakho, the worker gradually converges to the Lwidakho-speaking co-participant's language preference. It is for this reason that the direction of the transition is not reversible and in itself meaningful: accommodation coincides with emphatic repetition. The worker now is 'with' the farmer on the level of language choice, although through the verbal contents of his utterance he declines his wishes. While Myers-Scotton claims that code-switching by the worker serves to distance himself from the farmer, a closer investigation of the sequence seen as a language negotiation sequence reveals almost the opposite: the focal usage of Lwidakho in the decisive third repetition of the decline could in fact be interpreted as a mitigation of a conversationally dispreferred move (the declination of a request).

The sequence is terminated at this point and the interaction might stop here. However, we observe the farmer to reinstantiate his request one further time, once more using an indirect strategy to ask for money. (Note that he does not argue with the worker by attacking the latter's reasons for declining his request.) Lines 11 and 12 thereby form another request/declination pair sequence, again in Lwidakho, but different from the previous one in that the worker is quite explicit now. The worker's final utterance (13) opens another language negotiation sequence and leaves (for good?) the common symbolic ground he and the farmer have found in their short Lwidahko exchange, i.e. a common language; this time, both the request and the common language are refuted.

Close attention to conversational structure and sequential development can thus lead to a deeper understanding of this piece of interaction. They cast a very different light on the interactional meaning of language choice and language alternation, since it can be shown that the worker accommodates with his language choice the farmer, exactly at the point where the sequence reaches its climax.[9] The point is that even a poorly transcribed extract such as the one discussed here contains a wealth of information which needs to be explicated in order to arrive at a valid interpretation of switching data which goes beyond illustrating a point made on entirely different grounds (i.e. conversation-external knowledge). On the other hand, the discussion in this section also has shown that a sequential approach to code-switching does not exclude linking microscopic aspects of conversational organisation to ethnographically documented wider (macroscopic) structures, but rather serves to ground the former in the latter.

3 The 'codes' of 'code-switching' seen from a members' perspective

If conversational code-switching is supposed to be the juxtaposition of two codes such that participants see it as such (which is a necessary condition for any kind of 'emic' approach to the interactional meaning in code alternation), the question of what counts as a code is not easily answered, for it must refer to participants', not to linguists' notions of 'code A' and 'code B'. It seems that we have no other final authority to turn to if we want to decide whether a given sign is part of the same system as the contiguous signs, or whether it is part of a different system, and takes part in a juxtaposition of two codes. The 'objective' statement by the linguistically or semiotically trained analyst that a given arrangement of signs constitutes a combination of elements of two systems is not only very difficult to make at times (see the discussion on borrowing), it is also irrelevant. There may be cases in which the two systems juxtaposed by the members of a community (and interpreted as such) are 'objectively speaking' very similar, but from the members' point of view completely independent (as in dialect/standard switching; cf. Alfonzetti, this volume), just as there may be systems that are 'objectively speaking' very distinct but nevertheless seen as nondistinct by the users. The question 'Do bilingual participants see and use it?' takes us from structural systems continually referring to each other, to the speakers. It implies a shift from a structural towards an interpretive approach to bilingualism. In fact, while most approaches to the pragmatics of code-switching have started from the presupposition that there are two languages which are used alternatingly, and proceeded to ask what function switching between them may have, it may well be advisable to ask the question in the opposite way: that is, to start from the observation that there are two sets of co-occurring variables between which participants alternate in an interactionally meaningful way, and then proceed to seeing them as belonging to or constituting two 'codes' (cf. Alvarez-Cáccamo, this volume).

But how can we, the analysts, prove that a given set of co-occurring linguistic features is perceived by participants as a distinct code? The only valid answer is: by showing that switching between this set and another is employed in a meaningful way in bilingual conversation. The issue is of particular interest in cases which, linguistically speaking, may be looked upon either as instances of code-switching between closely related varieties, or as one code showing internal variability. For instance, Alvarez-Cáccamo (1990: 164) discusses materials in which the alternating codes (Galizan Spanish and Galizan) are structurally so close that they are separated only by a handful of phonological and morphonological features. The following extract is given here in the phonetic transcription provided by Alvarez-Cáccamo, with minor additions done with his authorisation.

EXAMPLE 4

Telephone call to taxi station, verbatim memory transcript; T, receptionist; C, caller.

1	T	[pa'raða de ta'sis]	neutral
		('Taxi station')	
2	C	['bwenas ke'riamos un 'tasi para'ki para ɤram	
		'bia ðows'θɛntos]	Galizan
		('Hi, we'd like a taxi here at two-hundred Main Street')	
3	T	[para 'ɤram 'bia ðos'θjentos]?	Spanish
		('At two-hundred Main Street?')	
4	C	['si], [paɾa'ki ɔ 'laðo ða kafete'ria **la** 'ðraŋxa]	mixed
		('Yeah, here next to "The Farm" cafe')	
5	T	[paɾ **a** 'ðraŋxa]?	Galizan
		('At the "Farm"?')	
6	C	['si]	neutral
		('Yes')	
7	T	['bweno], ['ʃa βa**i** paɾ a'i **o** 'θɛnto kwa'rentai̯ 'tres]	Galizan
		('Ok, [taxi number] one-forty-three will be going that	
		way in a minute')	
8	C	eh?	neutral
9	T	['**ja** β**a** paɾ a'i **el** 'θf;ento kwa'rentai̯ 'tres]	Spanish
		('One forty-three will be going that way in a minute')	
10	C	ah ['bweno], ['ɤraθjas]	neutral
		('Oh, ok. Thanks')	
11	T	[ta 'loɤo]	neutral
		('Bye')	

(Alvarez-Cáccamo 1990: 164)

Phonological and/or morphonological differences between the two languages are in bold face. All remaining utterance parts are identical for the two varieties in contact. Note that structural convergence has taken place; thus, as Alvarez observes, *bueono/bueonas* has come to replace the older Galizan forms (*bem*), and *ta logo* instead of *ata logo* has been taken over from Galizan into Galizan Spanish.

The linguist's labelling of participants' utterances is given on the right-hand side. The caller speaks either Galizan or in a neutral way not displaying any features of Galizan or Galizan Spanish throughout. (The 'mixed' utterance line 4 is due to the 'quotation' of a place name, *la granxa*.) The taxi-driver, on the

14

other hand, alternates between codes: he starts out in Spanish, paraphrasing the caller's Galizan utterance in that variety in the understanding check of line 3; yet, in the second understanding check of line 5, he reformulates the caller's Galizan utterance in an even more Galizan manner, replacing the Spanish article form in the proper name by its Galizan counterpart. Finally, when the taxi driver uses Galizan himself for an initiative move (line 7), his other-initiated self-repair of line 9 is a reformulation in Spanish.

As Alvarez argues in his analysis of this extract, the latter repair is the most important interactional event: the taxi driver's self-administered repair of code-choice from Galizan into Spanish is, arguably, triggered by the client's repair-initiating *eh?* in line 8. According to Alvarez, the fact that the taxi-driver interprets an unspecific repair-initiator as relating to language choice refers to a set of politeness norms which prescribe the use of Spanish instead of Galizan in a transactional (service) encounter such as this one, where Galizan would be too informal.

The analytic issue of interest to this discussion of the 'codes' in 'code-switching' boils down to the problem of making sure that the linguist's labellings ('Spanish Galizan', 'Galizan' and 'neutral' in this case) are indeed identical to participants' labellings. The move from a purely structural field of analysis into the field of interpretation shows nicely that the interactional analysis of conversational code-switching is not independent of the structural analysis of language contact phenomena, and vice versa. In order to be instances of conversational code-switching, transitions such as between lines 2 and 3, lines 4 and 5, or lines 7 and 9 have to be perceived *by participants* as involving different 'codes'. Yet, in the transition between 4 and 5, at least, there is no indication that participants orient to the Spanishness or Galizanness of the utterances in question. The Spanish or Galizan feature that is in fact changed (article with or without/l/) may not be sufficient for them to recognise the second utterance as being more Galizan than the first. On the other hand, it seems clear from the sequential development of the interaction that, in the transition between 7 and 9, features are employed which turn a Galizan utterance into one which definitely is Galizan Spanish for the participants.

The theoretical point to be made from this and similar examples is that the definition of the codes used in code-switching may be an interactional achievement which is not prior to the conversation (and to be stated once and for all by the linguist) but subject to negotiation between participants. If anything, it is not the existence of certain codes which takes priority, but the function of a certain transition in conversation.[10] From this, it follows that there are many phenomena of language contact other than code-switching which for the linguist may represent cases of the juxtaposition of two languages or varieties, but not for the bilingual speaker (cf. Auer 1990). One such case of language contact which plays an important role in this volume is 'code-mixing', or the emergence of a *mixed code*.

Mixed codes contain numerous and frequent cases of alternation between two languages when seen from the linguist's point of view, but these singular occurrences of alternation do not carry meaning *qua* language choice for the bilingual participants (although they will usually be able to recognise them). That such a mixed code is used at all may of course be a noticeable event for the speakers, just as the absence of mixing may be noticeable; yet the invididual cases of alternation receive neither discourse- nor participant-related interpretations. If the mixed code contrasts with an internally less heterogeneous variety, we may speak of (second-order) code-switching between a code which in itself is mixed, and one which is not (Meeuwis and Blommaert, this volume). (Functional) code-switching and usage of a mixed code often co-occur in a given conversation so that it is analytically difficult to disentangle the two phenomena.

In the remainder of this Introduction, I will sketch a possible continuum from code-alternation[11] to a mixed code. Although mixed codes may come into being in other ways, the continuum from code-alternation to a mixed code seems to represent one possible path of development in the course of time. It may be an example of a 'cline' from pragmatics to grammar, i.e. a case of grammaticalisation (cf. Maschler, this volume).

In the prototypical case of code-alternation as portrayed in *Bilingual Conversation*, speakers orient to a preference for one language-of-interaction which is accepted until language negotiation sets in, or until discourse-related switching changes the 'footing' of the conversation, and with it the language-of-interaction. A first step on the continuum towards a mixed code, still representing code-alternation, though of a less prototypical kind, consists in dissolving this state of affairs; instead, discourse-related code-switching occurs which does not change the language-of-interaction; the preference for one language-of-interaction is thereby relinquished.

Consider extract 5:

EXAMPLE 5

Italian versus Sicilian dialect (italics); telephone conversation during the Berlusconi electoral campaign.

T   Ma l'hai visto? Io mai l'ho vista una campagna elettorale così. Questo oggi dicevamo con A. Neppure nel quarantotto, che era il dopoguerra, che c'erano ... che c'erano proprio umori tremendi. Mai si era verificato. *N'autra cosa t'ai 'a cchièderti*, G. Cambiamo discorso. Io continuo a telefonare a M. Perché è da Pasqua che le voglio fare gli auguri, le cose. Perché non la non la trovo?

('Have you seen? I've never seen an electoral campaign like this one. I was talking about this to A today. Not even in 1948, in the post-war period, when there were ... when there were tremendous emotions. It never happened. *I've got something else to ask you*, G. Let's change topic. I keep on calling M. I've been trying to give her my wishes, and so on, since Easter. Why can't can't I find her?')

(Alfonzetti, this volume: 198)

Here, the code-switched utterance definitely introduces a new footing (indicating, as it does, a metapragmatic comment); it is therefore discourse-related. However, the speaker marks only the contrast between the old and the new context by a change of language; as soon as the new context/footing is established, she returns to Italian. The 'left margin' of the new context coincides with and is signalled by code-switching; yet the usage of dialect is not co-extensive with the duration of this new footing. A definition of code-switching which assumes a new language-of-interaction from the switching point onwards cannot handle this pattern well. On the other hand, the duration of the switched passage is not predictable either, which means that no 'insertion' is involved; the distinction code-switching versus insertion (as defined in *Bilingual Conversation*) is becoming fuzzy.

The same is true, for example, for the data discussed by Sebba (1994) (also cf. Sebba and Wootton, this volume), who observes that switching from London English into London Jamaican English can never result in a complete change of the language-of-interaction for a longer period of talk; rather, London Jamaican is only interspersed for longer or shorter utterances into basically English conversations. In such cases, the only criterion for distinguishing insertions and code-switching is that the switched-to passage is not perceived as a structural unit (which would turn it into an insertion).

Another move towards the development of mixed codes is the frequent use of (nonce) borrowings (instead of (functional) insertions) which may trigger (Clyne 1967) the inclusion of other-language materials around them. Nonce borrowings (in the sense of Poplack and Sankoff 1984, etc.) are often content words, in particular nouns. As an example, see the expression *hunnert* **miles from Chicago**, 'one hundred miles from Chicago', in extract 7 (line 3) below, where the English noun *miles* together with the place name *Chicago* triggers code-alternation in the second part of the noun phrase, including the preposition *from*.[12] The final step on this route towards a mixed code is the use of language B materials to the exclusion of the equivalent forms in the surrounding language A, such as in the case of English numbers which are used exclusively in various East African settings among bilinguals (cf. Khamis 1994).

Other single-word borrowings that often contribute to the formation of mixed codes are language B *discourse markers*, which, in many bilingual communities, occur in conversations in language A (cf. Maschler, this volume and forthcoming; Oesch Serra, this volume). Here are two examples from widely diverging sociolinguistic contexts.

EXAMPLE 6

Mandinka/Wolof (italics)/English (bold face); interview data from Gambia.

---

1   a ka itolu fanaŋ nafaa wo le ñaama-
    ('it is also to their advantage')
2   **because** a si a tara – **you know** – **certain things**-oo-lu be jee itolu
    fanaŋ maŋ meŋ-lu je ì yaa-
    ('because – you know – there are certain things there which they haven't
    got in their countries')
3   *xam nga* – niŋ ì naa-ta jaŋ *rek-*
    ('you know – now if they only come here')
4   niŋ ì taa-ta ǹ la ñiŋ wuloo-lu kono-
    ('if they go into our woods')
5   ì si a tara *suma waay-*
    ('they will my friend')
6   **you know** – ì si wo-lu doo-lu je-
    ('you know – they will see many of them')
7   **you know** – a te ke-la ì bulu baa – **you know**
    ('you know – it doesn't exist at their place – you know')

(Haust 1995: 70)

Speakers are highly competent in all the languages involved, but particularly in English and Mandinka *or* Wolof. In the extract given here, the language-of-interaction is Mandinka, but all discourse markers and 'metapragmatic' activities are either in English or in Wolof.

The second data extract is taken from an interview with a Low German speaker who migrated to the United States in his youth and has now almost completely lost this variety. In the past decades, he almost never used Low German and very little Standard German.

EXAMPLE 7

Low German/Northern Standard German (italics)/American English (bold face); A, interviewer; B, interviewee.

---

1 B   **See**, *wir sind ausnandergegang*, **see**.
       ('You see, we went to different places, you see')
2   *Du gehst hierhin, du machst dein Lebn.*[13]
       ('You go this way, you make your living')
3   **Now** *Kurt, der is ungefähr so hunnert* **miles from Chicago**,
       ('Now Kurt, he is about hundred miles from Chicago')
4   *wo er gewohnt hat da und hat sein Geschäft da* (.)
       ('where he lived and had his business')

5   *und Erwin auch,* **see**.
      ('and Erwin as well, you see')

6   *Erwin kann auch nich viel* Plattdütsch schnacken.
      ('Erwin can't speak much Low German either.')

7 A Nee, aber häi versteht dat.
      ('No, but he understands it.')

8   Dat [hätt häi mi sä[cht.
      ('So he told me.')

9 B   [*ja*/[*ja,*   *er versteht,*   **[because** *er/*
            ('yes   yes he understands because he')

10 A   [aber häi kann dat nich selbst schnacken.
                         ('but he can't speak it himself.')

11 B **see**, äh (.) sin mudder un vadder de hebt ja ümmer tosomm Platt/Plattdütsch schnackt.
      ('you see, ehm (.) his mother and his father always spoke Low-Low German together.')

12 A jo.
      ('yes.')

13 B: **see**, de hebt ümmer tosomm Plattdütsch schnackt.
      ('you see, they always spoke Low German together.')
                         (Sabine Behling, unpublished interview data)

The speaker starts with northern Standard German, but as a consequence of a number of Low German interventions by the interviewer who has displayed his preference for Low German before the beginning of this extract, and facilitated by Low German *Plattdütsch schnacken* ('to speak Low German') in line 6, he later switches to Low German. In both parts of the extract, we find English discourse markers in German/Low German turns (in particular, *see* in lines 1, 5, 11, 13). Yet the speaker's competences are highly unbalanced between English and German/Low German.

These differences of sociolinguistic context and bilingual competences between the Gambian and the American/German example notwithstanding, discourse markers used by the speakers in extracts 6 and 7 have one thing in common: they frame the A-text in a metapragmatic way; that is they jointly establish a second level of metapragmatics which is opposed to the primary (referential) one. It is tempting to analyse these discourse markers as discourse-related insertions.

Yet we may ask whether the discourse markers in the 'other language' are cases of code-alternation at all. In order to ascribe meaning or function to them not only *qua* discourse markers, but *qua* insertions, we would have to prove that this meaning is created by the usage of the 'other' language. Alternatively, and more plausibly, it may be the case that a mixed code has developed to which, diachronically speaking, language B has contributed discourse markers and possibly other metapragmatic structures.

Summarising the argument so far, we may characterise a certain middle position on the continuum between interactionally meaningful code-alternation and a mixed code in the following way: there are numerous (nonce) borrowings which may cause surrounding materials to be switched as well; there are numerous turn-internal switches which, however, do not change the language-of-interaction (i.e. they are non-consequential on the level of language choice); and the distinction between insertions and code-switching thereby gradually loses its force.

Examples of such frequent code-alternation may be found in the present volume in the chapters by Moyer (p. 218–220), Franceschini (p. 59–68) and Meeuwis and Blommaert (p. 86–88). Usually, they contain juxtapositions of the two languages which are text- and discourse-related in addition to others for which such an interpretation is more difficult or even impossible to find. This leads us to a further characteristic feature of this middle position on the alternation/mixing continuum: It seems natural that frequent code-alternation weakens the contextualisation value of this cue. In gestalt-psychological terms, the figure of code-alternation is most salient against a ground which is not in itself mixed, but monolingual. The more frequently code-alternation occurs, the less salient it becomes; as a consequence, the potential for using it in discourse-related ways is diminished. At the same time, the extra-conversational ('social', 'political', etc.) dimensions of code-alternation are generally lost in its individual occurrence, a process which might be compared to semantic bleaching in grammaticalisation.

The final step which moves a case of what linguists classify as a juxtaposition of two languages towards a mixed code, is the emergence of a new structural division of linguistic labour between the elements originally taken from language A and those from language B. In this final step, the elements take on a new grammatical function or lexical meaning which is *not* based any longer on the inferences which are triggered by their other-languageness; rather, it is defined in structural terms, by paradigmatic oppositions and syntagmatic links. Examples for such a grammaticalisation or lexicalisation of code-alternation may be found in the chapters by Maschler and by Oesch Serra (this volume).

In order to argue for a mixed code, questions such as the following need to be asked: (a) Do the candidate insertions compete with discourse markers in the surrounding language or are they the only discourse markers available for the speaker(s)? (b) If there are competing discourse markers in the surrounding language, are they interchangeable with the candidate inserted markers without a difference in meaning apart from that which is created by the alternation, or have the markers rather specialised in function? (c) Have both the candidate insertions and the possible discourse markers of the surrounding language retained their meaning and/or function (apart from what is due to the alternation) when compared to the monolingual usage, or have they specialised in meaning? It seems wise to allow for gradualness here. But if the first alternatives hold in each case, there can be no doubt that we are dealing with insertions (i.e. code alternation); if the second alternatives are the correct answers, there is good evidence for a mixed code. Numerous scenarios in between are conceivable, as Maschler (forthcoming and this volume) and Oesch Serra (this volume) show in their detailed analyses of Hebrew/English and French/Italian bilingual conversations.

4 Conclusion

This volume contains interaction-oriented investigations locating bilingual practices in a wide range of sociolinguistic situations comprising very different language pairs (English/Spanish in Gibraltar, English/Chinese in the UK, London English/London Jamaican English, British English/Hindi~ Urdu, Italian/French and German/Italian in Switzerland, Italian/Sicilian, Turkish/Danish, Swahili/French and Lingala/French in Belgium, Tok Pisin/Taiap in Papua New Guinea, Hebrew/English in Israel). By presenting a variety of possibilities in which conversational code-switching is indicative of and shaped by local and global contexts, they will hopefully contribute to a better empirical understanding of this particular phenomenon of bilingual speech. At the same time, the contributors to this volume raise and discuss a number of important theoretical questions demonstrating that what linguists mean by the term code-switching is itself in need of clarification; this clarification will not be a easy one to give, but it is essential in order to judge its relevance for (socio)linguistic theory at large.

Notes

1 The following transcription conventions are used in the extracts:

[simultaneous talk
=   latching (i.e. no interval between adjacent turns)
(.)   micro-pause
-     break-off/unfinished word
(2.0) length of silence in seconds
h   laughter

The following punctuation marks indicate final intonation contours:

?   rise to high
,   rise to mid
.   fall to low
;   fall to mid

2 Representing achieved conversational structures by schematic patterns certainly is not without problems. They here serve to indicate prototypical surface realisations which are the outcome of those procedures of the production and perception of code-alternation which are outlined in detail in Auer 1984a.

3 The term replaces the earlier term 'transfer', used in Auer 1984a, which has the disadvantage of being used in research on second language acquisition in a different sense. The renaming also agrees with a proposal by Haust 1995.

4 Note that in a community in which a code-mixing style is established as a new variety of its own, the alternating use of the two contact varieties within this code is not ever open to a participant-related interpretation.

5 The latter case is exemplified by switching for the benefit of another participant, for example taking into account his or her (supposedly) insufficient competence in the language spoken so far.

6 Any serious interactional analysis of code-switching working with excerpts of naturally occurring data must conform to certain methodological standards as they have developed in the study of face-to-face interaction over the last decades. Little is to be gained from publishing 'transcripts' (and thereby suggesting a conversational basis of analysis) otherwise. In the present case (and in fact, further examples from other published work are not difficult to find), the transcription surely does not conform to such standards. Instead of representing simultaneous talk in the transcript, the fact of an 'interruption' is simply claimed; there is no single hesitation or self-repair, no discourse marker or particle; pauses are marked ambiguously at best ('. . .' may refer to various things). The whole transcript looks like a purified, stylised version as in a drama textbook, but certainly not like a reliable transcription. This, in turn, makes a controlled sequential analysis difficult. In addition, the section of the transcript presented in the publication does not coincide with the natural boundaries of the interaction; the extract is selected in such a way that decisive aspects have to be paraphrased by the vague description 'the farmer is asking the salaried man for money'. In particular, we do not know if this asking for money is done indirectly in the farmer's first turn, or if it happened before the transcript starts.

7 Myers-Scotton 1993: 83.

8 The classification of this kind of switching in Myers-Scotton's model remains difficult, since it is a marked choice on the part of one participant only (the farmer uses the unmarked language Lwidakho); her four types of switching refer to joint language choice by both participants, however. A similar case of divergent language choices is analysed as a case of exploratory switching in another part of the book (Myers-Scotton 1993: 145).

   A cogent critique of Myer-Scotton's switching types can be found in Meeuwis and Blommaert 1994 and shall not be repeated here.

9 Further 'contextualisation cues' should be included in a thorough analysis of this extract; in particular, the indirect style used by the farmer, which is based on formulaic expressions and hints, and contrasts with the eventually very open and blunt style used by the worker.

10 On the more structural side, the problem is this: very likely, phonological or morphonological parameters do not all play the same role (do not have equal importance) in the members' task of assigning utterances to 'codes'. Some variables may have a more important signalling value in this respect than others. However, what exactly a given variable contributes to this task is hard to say at the present stage of research.

11 In the sense of the term as introduced in *Bilingual Conversation*, i.e. comprising code-switching and insertion.

12 The step from functional insertions to juxtapositions within a mixed code may be what is implied by Poplack's 'nonce borrowing' (cf. Poplack and Sankoff 1984; Sankoff, Poplack and Vanniarajan 1990, etc.). Note, however, that

speaking of 'nonce borrowings' and their 'integration' into the system of the surrounding language presupposes a monolingual framework in which the receiving language accommodates materials from the other language without being affected by it; in contrast to this view, the 'mixed code' view implies convergence between the languages in question.

13 If this is the right meaning, the German expression is a calque on English.

Bibliography

Alfonzetti, Giovanna (1992) *Il discorso bilingue. Italiano e dialetto a Catania*, Pavia: Francoangeli.

Alvarez-Cáccamo, Celso (1990) 'The Institutionalization of Galizan: Linguistic Practices, Power, and Ideology in Public Discourse', Ph.D. thesis, University of California at Berkeley.

Auer, Peter (1984a) *Bilingual Conversation*, Amsterdam: Benjamins.

Auer, Peter (1984b) 'On the meaning of conversational code-switching', in P. Auer and A. di Luzio (eds), *Interpretive Sociolinguistics*, Tübingen, Germany: Narr, 87–112.

Auer, Peter (1990) 'A discussion paper on code alternation', in European Science Foundation, Network on Code-Switching and Language Contact, *Papers for the Workshop on Concepts, Methodology and Data, Basel, January 12–13 1990*, 69–89.

Auer, Peter (1995) 'The pragmatics of code-switching: a sequential approach', in L. Milroy and P. Muysken (eds), *One Speaker, Two Languages: Cross-Disciplinary Perspectives on Code-Switching*, Cambridge: Cambridge University Press, 115–135.

Blom, Jan Petter and Gumperz, John (1972) 'Social meaning in linguistic structures: code-switching in Norway', in J. Gumperz and D. Hymes (eds), *Directions in Sociolinguistics*, New York: Holt, Rinehart & Winston, 407–434.

Clyne, Michael (1967) *Transference and Triggering*, The Hague: Mouton.

Goffman, Erving (1982) 'The interaction order', *American Sociological Review* 48, 1–17.

Gumperz, John (1982) *Discourse Strategies*, Cambridge: Cambridge University Press.

Gumperz, John (1994) 'Sprachliche Variabilität in interaktionsanalytischer Perspektive', in W. Kallmeyer (ed.), *Kommunikation in der Stadt, Teil 1: Exemplarische Analysen des Sprachverhaltens in Mannheim*, Berlin: de Gruyter, 611–639.

Haust, Delia (1995) 'Code-switching in Gambia. Eine soziolinguistische Untersuchung von Mandinka, Wolof und Englisch im Kontakt', Ph.D. thesis, University of Hamburg. Published as Vol. 1 of *Sprachkontakt in Afrika*, Cologne: Rüdiger Köppe Verlag.

Khamis, Cornelia (1994) 'Mehrsprachigkeit bei den Nubi. Das Sprachverhalten viersprachig aufwachsender Vorschul- und Schulkinder in Bombo/Uganda', Ph.D. thesis, University of Hamburg. Published as Vol. 4 of *Hamburger Beiträge zur Afrikanistik*, Münster: Lit-Verlag.

Li Wei (1994) *Three Generations, Two Languages, One Family*, Clevedon, England: Multilingual Matters.

Li Wei and Milroy, Leslie (1995) 'Conversational code-switching in a Chinese community in Britain: a sequential analysis', *Journal of Pragmatics* 23, 281–299.

Luckmann, Thomas (1983) 'Comment [on Breitborde]', *International Journal of the Sociology of Language* 39, 97–101.

Maschler, Yael (forthcoming) 'Emergent bilingual grammar: The case of contrast', *Journal of Pragmatics*.

Meeuwis, Michael and Blommaert, Jan (1994) 'The "Markedness Model" and the absence of society: remarks on code-switching', *Multilingua* 13, 4, 387–423.

Milroy, Leslie and Muysken, Pieter (eds) (1995) *One Speaker, Two Languages: Cross-Disciplinary Perspectives on Code-Switching*, Cambridge: Cambridge University Press.

Myers-Scotton, Carol (1983) 'The negotiation of identities in conversation: a theory of markedness and code choice', *Journal of the Sociology of Language* 44, 115–136.

Myers-Scotton, Carol (1993) *Social Motivations of Code-Switching*, Oxford: Clarendon Press.

Poplack, Shana (1979 [1981]) '"Sometimes I'll start a sentence in Spanish Y TERMINO EN ESPAÑOL": toward a typology of code-switching', *New York, Language Policy Task Force Paper No. 4*. Revised version published in *Linguistics* 7/8, 581–618.

Poplack, Shana and Sankoff, David (1984) 'Borrowing: the synchrony of integration', *Linguistics* 22, 99–135.

Sankoff, David, Poplack, Shana and Vanniarajan, Swathi (1990) 'The case of the nonce loan in Tamil', *Language Variation and Change* 2, 71–101.

Sebba, Mark (1994) *London Jamaican Creole*, London: Longman.

Part I

THE 'CODES' OF CODE-SWITCHING

INTRODUCTION TO CHAPTER 2

Peter Auer

Although loosely based on Celso Alvarez-Cáccamo's empirical research on language use and linguistic ideologies in Galiza, Spain, the chapter which introduces the first part of this volume first and foremost has a theoretical and historiographical orientation. Alvarez takes us back to the beginnings of the use of the term 'code-switching in linguistics', which means to the early 1950s. We learn that in studies in bilingualism, it was not E. Haugen who used the term for the first time (as is often believed), but rather Hans Vogt in an article from 1954. More important for the term's success in linguistics was probably Roman Jakobson, who as early as 1952 drew parallels between language switching, co-existent phonological systems in borrowing, and information theory, where the term was already established usage. (The information theoretical connotation of the compound 'code-switching' is of course easily traceable even today, but many researchers take the term for granted without knowing its origins, or at least without wanting them to be part of its meaning; hence the widespread use of the non-hyphenated form in recent publications.)

Alvarez advocates a return to the Jakobsonian notion of 'switching codes'. The important aspect in Jakobson's early borrowing of the term from information theory is that, in this usage, it does not refer to a switching of languages in *speech*, but rather to the cognitive codes humans or machines must have *stored* in order to process speech in two forms (which may, but need not, correspond to languages in the established linguistic sense). For instance, a computerised speech decoder must be able to switch between the parameter sets of various speakers in order to understand the speech of more than one individual, each of which exhibits characteristic idiosyncratic features (e.g. in the higher vowel formants).

Alvarez-Cáccamo criticises the more recent work on code-switching for equating 'codes' with linguistic 'varieties' (languages, dialects, etc.). This equation is problematic for two reasons: one is that the equation of code-switching with language-switching takes for granted that the alternation of languages as defined by the linguist is indeed meaningful to participants, thereby precluding the alternative possibility of a code-switching style that

27

has developed into a 'code' of its own (the phenomenon referred to as code-*mixing* in the Introduction). In this way, the scope of code-switching is widened to include 'non-meaningful' switching (which is excluded in Jakobson's version because his 'switching code' has to do with expressing intentions and interpreting utterances). This line of thinking will be pursued in the following chapters (in particular, in Chapters 4, 5 and 6).

The other problem with the speech-oriented redefinition of Jakobson's cognitive code theory is that equating 'codes' with 'languages' also restricts the extension of phenomena. In fact, redefinitions of the situation, different 'footings', recontextualisations or reframings, are frequent indeed in all kinds of sociolinguistic contexts, not only in bilingual ones. If Jakobson's notion of switching codes is taken seriously, this means that all sets of co-occurring features (or even a single feature) that can be used for such a purpose must be considered to be a code. In fact, the notion of a 'code' then comes very close to that of a 'contextualisation cue' in the sense of John Gumperz (1982).

A good case in point is reported speech (see Alvarez-Cáccamo 1996) and, by extension, all cases of polyphony in the Bakhtinian sense (see Chapters 12 and 13 in this volume). To the extent that the narrator 'puts on stage' the words of the other, she or he employs certain means to do so, thereby shifting the footing of the interaction. In bilingual conversations, a standard way of staging another person's speech is by switching the language, not necessarily in the direction of the original utterance (see Chapters 8 and 12). According to Alvarez's proposal for a redefinition of 'code-switching', not only the latter case would be considered, but also the former.

Bibliography

Alvarez-Cáccamo, Celso (1996) 'The reflexive power of language(s): code displacement in reported speech', *Journal of Pragmatics* 25, 1, 33–59.

Gumperz, John (1982) *Discourse Strategies*, Cambridge: Cambridge University Press.

2

FROM 'SWITCHING CODE' TO 'CODE-SWITCHING'

Towards a reconceptualisation of communicative codes

Celso Alvarez-Cáccamo

1 Introduction

From its origins in the physical sciences (Fano 1950) until its current circulation in political anthropology (Gal 1987, 1995), the notion of 'code-switching' has experienced the characteristic multiplication, fragmentation and metamorphosis that a conceptually rich term is prone to experience (consider, in this respect, the history of 'diglossia' or 'speech act').[1] The increasing lexicalisation of the expression (from 'switching code' to 'code-switching') indexes its central place in academic fields dealing with so-called bilingual behaviour. However, throughout its history, it is not unlikely that 'code-switching' has lost part of its original meanings at the expense of producing a profitable object for research, one amenable to easy handling as an emblem of disciplinary identity.

In a sense, 'code-switching' research seems to be at a crossroads. On the one hand, ample research has shown that the alternate use of recognisably distinct speech varieties in discourse may have accountable meanings and effects. In this line, speech varieties have been mechanistically associated with 'codes'. On the other hand, some research has shown the impossibility or inappropriateness of assigning specific meanings to some types of variety alternation, and has thus implicitly started to question whether 'meaning-less code-switching' can be called code-switching at all (Auer 1989; Alvarez-Cáccamo 1990; Stroud 1992; Swigart 1992). That is, if codes do not contrast, can we maintain that they are indeed distinct codes? Given the different natures of 'unmarked' and 'marked' code-switching, are we witnessing two distinct phenomena? Or is something missing in the way 'code-switching' is currently conceptualised?

In this chapter I attempt to shed some light on the issue, by tracing back the origin and development of the notion of 'code-switching' from its earliest formulations as connected to information theory, structural phonology and bilingual contact studies, to current conversational and anthropological work on the phenomenon. Briefly, I argue that 'code-switching' may now subsume and globalise a number of possibly unrelated phenomena while excluding others which are clear candidates for being considered switches in communicative codes. The connecting thread in this work is the need to return to a communicative view of codes, here regarded as systems of transduction between two sets of signals: at the one end, communicative *intentions*, and at the other end, linguistic–discursive forms amenable to *interpretation*. In this vein, I suggest that a clearer conceptual distinction between 'linguistic variety' in its broadest sense and 'communicative code' is crucial for explaining conversational conduct.

2 The origins

Three research trends converge in the consolidation of 'code-switching' studies: structural phonology, information theory, and research on bilingualism. The maker of an initial synthesis is, recognisably, Jakobson, not exactly in his 1961 'Linguistics and communication theory', but quite a few years earlier, in his work with Fant and Halle (Jakobson, Fant and Halle 1952). There Jakobson refers to the phenomenon of 'switching code', based on Fano's work (1950) on information theory, and on Fries and Pike's (1949) on 'coexistent phonemic systems'. Fries and Pike attempt to demonstrate, and argue abundantly, that 'two or more phonemic systems may coexist in the speech of a monolingual' (1949: 29). Evidence presented is the existence of phonemes alien to what would seem to be the speaker's system, for example Mazatec phonemes in loanwords into Spanish. Fries and Pike not only deal with bilingual speech, but postulate the existence of four basic types of 'coexistent phonological systems' in vernacular languages.[2] Type (4), 'a vernacular . . . with general differences of quality, style, or speed' (Fries and Pike 1949: 49) is particularly interesting, as it points to Gumperz's (1982) notion of 'changes in pitch register' as a type of contextualisation cue functionally comparable to code-switching. In a similar line, and around the same time, Hoijer (1948) established the pair of concepts 'phonemic *alternation*' and 'phonemic *alteration*', which roughly parallel those of 'code-switching' (where phonological systems 'alternate') and 'borrowing' (where an aspect of the target language's grammar is 'altered'). None of these works, however, refers explicitly to 'code-switching'.

Jakobson (1961; Jakobson, Fant and Halle 1952) integrates with intelligence, boldness and sense of opportunity the foundational block of information theory: the notion of 'code' as a mechanism for the unambiguous transduction of signals between systems, and specifically Fano's application to 'speech communication'.[3] Here 'speech', however, must be regarded in its material, physical dimension. Jakobson adapts the notion of 'switching code' to the change a monolingual *or* bilingual speaker must effect in order to interpret ('decode') another person's system ('code'), or to produce such a change:

> Obviously such a task of deciphering becomes more difficult in the frequent cases called 'switching code' by communication engineers or 'coexistent phonemic systems' by linguists. The Russian aristo-cracy of the last century with its bi-lingual speech – switching continually from Russian to French and vice versa even within a single sentence – provides a striking illustration.
>
> (Jakobson, Fant and Halle 1952: 603–604)

Significantly, Jakobson continues: 'Two styles of the same language may *have* divergent codes and be deliberately interlinked within one utterance or even one sentence' (ibid. 1952: 604; my emphasis). Notice that Jakobson's formulation is that each language style *has* a code, not that it *is* a code. This view is strictly faithful to Fano's discussion of speech codes and communication:

> Spectrographic analysis has indicated that the different speech sounds used by any one speaker have easily distinguishable frequency patterns which are essentially stationary with time. This does not seem to be true for speech sounds used by different speakers. If we consider these frequency patterns as code groups, it appears that different speakers use, in a sense, somewhat different codes. These codes are stored in the brain of the listener who uses in each case the appropriate code. New codes are continually learned whenever new people are met, particularly people belonging to different linguistic groups. This point of view is in agreement with the observation that our ability to understand and the effort required to understand depends on our familiarity with the speaker's voice. In addition, we are often conscious of 'switching code' in our brain, *particularly* when a change of language takes place.
>
> (Fano 1950: 695–696; emphasis added)

Here again, codes are 'used' in order to interpret and produce speech – they are not the speech material itself. In other words, for Fano 'switching code' is a strictly psychological phenomenon consisting of altering one's internal mechanism for the identification of phonemic symbols, i.e. for the trans-duction of speech patterns ('frequency patterns') into the Saussurean 'mental images' of phonemes and vice versa.

As we can see, the works reviewed set the basis for the conceptualisation of code-switching as the alternation not only of languages, but also of dialects, styles, prosodic registers, paralinguistic cues, etc., that is, practically all phenomena later described by Gumperz (1982, 1992) as 'contextualisation cues' and intelligently explored, in the same vein, by Auer (1992). Why and how the lexicalised 'code-switching' has come to subsume a number of forms of presumably bilingual behaviour is a long story, whose complete plot escapes me. But the third thread of scholarly research (bilingual studies) is probably a main protagonist.

3 Studies on bilingualism

Initially, work on bilingualism (Haugen 1950a, 1950b; Weinreich 1953; Vogt 1954; Diebold 1961) seemed to have been oblivious to the incipient conception of languages as 'having' a code. Haugen, for example, in such a pivotal article as 'Problems of bilingualism' (1950b), aimed at reviewing the main questions of bilingual research in order to 'predict in some degrees the behavior of bilingual speakers' (1950b: 271), makes no mention of 'switching codes' alongside phenomena such as 'linguistic pressure, substitution, importation, phonemic redistribution, reborrowing, loanwords, loanblends, loanshifts, and creations' (1950b: 271). In another work (Haugen 1950a) a reference to switching languages appears in the following way: 'They [the speakers] may switch rapidly from one [language] to the other, but at any given moment they are speaking only one, even when they resort to the other for assistance' (1950a: 211). The same view of language-switching behaviour is expressed in Weinreich (1953: 73), and in Mackey as a synonym of 'alternation' (1962: 66–68). For this line of research, it was (and is) crucial to understand *which* 'language' a bilingual was using at a given moment – hence the interest in distinguishing 'switching' from 'borrowing', 'transfer', 'interference', 'integration', etc., which was continued in the conversational analysis of 'code-switching' (Auer 1984).

The first explicit mention of 'code-switching' is found in Vogt (1954): 'Code-switching in itself is perhaps not a linguistic phenomenon, but rather a psychological one, and its causes are obviously extra-linguistic' (1954: 368). Haugen also refers to 'the code switching which occurs when a bilingual introduces a completely unassimilated word from another language into his speech' (1956: 40), and characterises the phenomenon as one of the 'three stages in diffusion', together with 'interference' and 'integration'.[4] Later, 'code-switching' would appear in Diebold (1961) and in Jakobson (1961), where it is used in the sense of 'recoding' (1961: 250).[5] Interestingly, in the French translation 'recodage' is interpreted as 'le passage d'un code à l'autre (*code-switching*)' (Jakobson 1963 [1961]: 95), whereas in the Spanish version 'recodificación' ('recoding') and 'interconexión codal' ('code-switching') are interpreted as different phenomena (Jakobson 1984 [1961]: 89).

Rather than anecdotal academic facts, ambiguities in these works show that at that early stage 'code-switching' did not have a uniform meaning.

The psychological approach, for instance, was present in Jakobson and Diebold, and would continue until Hockett (1987), for whom through internal 'switching-code' 'certain sounds or arrangements of sound in the alien dialect come to be coded automatically into the proper sounds or combinations of sounds in the listener's own dialect, and the intended word is recognised by assembling the latter' (1987: 43). In this view of switching as mono-lingual or bilingual 'recoding', the process consists of the establishment of one-to-one correspondences between elements of two systems which, in semiotic terms, have the same designata (whether referential objects or abstract phonemic entities). In the following diagram, the possible switches are represented by horizontal arrows:

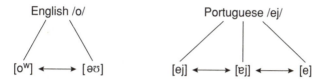

However, the interpretation of 'code-switching' as linguistic action (language alternation in speech, including grammar and lexicon) was to be the foun-dation of most current research on bilingual conversation. Viewed as bilingual behaviour even smooth switching is a potential source of 'inter-ference', in Weinreich's original sense (1953), located in a diachronic and interlinguistic continuum together with 'borrowing', 'integration' and 'transfer' (Mackey 1962, 1970; Clyne 1987).

4 The interactional turn

The turn toward a functional, interactional view of 'code-switching' was initiated by Gumperz in his work on social dialectology in India (Gumperz 1957, 1958, 1961, 1964a, 1964b; Gumperz and Naim 1960). Although Gumperz asserts (personal communication, 1994) that he took the notion of 'code-switching' as a conversational phenomenon from Jakobson,[6] probably the psychological basis of his view of the phenomenon was already present from his work with Pike in Michigan. For instance, Gumperz's account of the allophonic and allomorphic 'alternations' in Hindi–Urdu (Gumperz and Naim 1960) points to this psychological view. In this line, particularly inter-esting is the authors' claim that dialect convergence may lead to individuals sharing the 'allophonic content' while not sharing 'phonemic inventories', as it implicitly questions the categorisation of speech material from highly diverse speech communities into discrete languages.

The need to look at the social functions of these alternations is empha-sised throughout Gumperz's work, and systematised in two of his earlier essays (1962, 1964a). In 'Hindi–Punjabi code-switching in Delhi' (1964a),

Gumperz highlights the fact that standard grammatical rules may be applied to diverse data from a multilingual 'stylistic continuum', and he introduces the notion of 'code-switching style' (later to be cloned by Poplack (1980) as 'code-switching mode') as one of those sets of data amenable to standard grammatical description. In 'Types of linguistic communities' (1962), Gumperz's concern is to relate the functions of specific 'codes' from an integrated societal 'code matrix' to specific 'communication roles' within a society's 'communication matrix'. In this respect, codes or 'subcodes' function as 'linguistic diacritic[s]' (Gumperz 1962: 102)[7] which signal the role being performed. Significantly, the maintenance or disappearance of 'codes' is a function of society's need to maintain roles apart or to collapse them.

The indexical value of 'codes' is recaptured in Gumperz and Wilson (1971), where it is shown that despite broad syntactic convergence between genetically unrelated languages from the Indo-Aryan and Dravidian families, a few morphophonemic and lexical differential markers are maintained to signal different communicative roles and social identities (1971: 162). This may occur, as we will see, in many apparently bilingual situations where 'code-switching' consists mostly of the mobilisation of some lexical, morphological or prosodic markers. But what to say of daily communicative situations where roles and identities collapse? Is it still possible to maintain that those seemingly differential features carry the same symbolic import as they do in monolingual situations?

5 'Code-switching' and language alternation

Practically all research on 'code-switching' has been based on the identification of 'code' and 'linguistic variety' as interchangeable notions. For Gumperz and Herasimchuk (1972) codes are 'clusters of co-occurrent variables'; for Ervin-Tripp,

> [t]he *code* or *variety* consists of a systematic set of linguistic signals which co-occur in defining settings. For spoken languages, alternative codes may be vernaculars or superposed varieties. *Sociolinguistic variants* are those linguistic alternations linguists regard as free variants or optional variants within a code, that is, two different ways of saying the same thing.
> (Ervin-Tripp 1973 [1964]: 90; emphases in the original)

This broadening of the scope of 'code' may represent a departure from its original meaning in communication theory: speaking of 'free variants' or 'optional variants' contradicts the nature of a communicative code as an unambiguous, one-to-one system of transduction between sets of signals.

34

From this structural perspective, if codes are viewed as sets of co-occurrent linguistic signals, 'code-switching' cannot but be the alternation between such sets of signals, or 'linguistic varieties'. In fact, all research on 'code-switching grammars' and 'constraints' has started from the assumption of the pre-existence of two or more distinct languages from which speakers draw in order to produce 'code-switched' or 'mixed' output (Pfaff 1979; Lenneberg's 'code-mixing', 1967; Clyne's 'mixed grammar', 1987), regardless of whether the linguistic input itself is 'mixed' or not (e.g. Spanglish in the USA, or *portuñol* in the Brazilian–Uruguayan border, Hensey 1972).

However, it appears that, both structurally and communicatively, that style of speaking represented by Gumperz's (1964a) 'code-switching style', Poplack's 'code-switching mode', Sankoff and Poplack's 'norm of communication' (1981: 4), or Myers-Scotton's (1976, 1983, 1988a, 1988b) 'unmarked choice' carries in itself the potential to be treated as the output of an internally coherent system.[8] As a matter of fact, the boundaries between such styles and pidgin languages (the bases for creoles) are uncertain, leaving aside the particular social factors leading to pidginisation. The ample and controversial work on 'grammatical constraints' on switching, which escapes the scope of this article, shows, ironically, the difficulty in finding universal patterns (see Clyne's review, 1987); it even puts into question whether 'code-switching' results from the specificity of restrictions in the surface-level combination of elements from two, apparently distinct languages. For instance, Clyne's discussion of a good number of cases from his data on German/English and Dutch/English speech in Australia gives the impression of a forced insistence on preserving the theoretical validity of notions such as 'borrowing', 'head word', 'convergence' or 'transference' vis-à-vis 'code-switching'. Similarly, Nortier explains the systematic 'omission of definite articles in Moroccan Arabic/Dutch code-switching in terms of neutrality strategies, of which "suspension of syntax" is an example, leading to convergence in order to ease code switching' (Nortier 1995: 89).[9] The notion 'suspension of syntax', however, calls for a certain *suspension of disbelief*. What syntax(es) is/are suspended? Is syntax suspended only in order to facilitate 'code-switching', or can suspension be found in other linguistic phenomena? Can there exist a (code-switching or monolingual) sequence of acceptable discourse without a syntax?

At any rate, the nature of 'code-switching constraints', which work in terms of *tendencies* rather than categorical rules, does not seem different from the nature of stylistic co-occurrence constraints on monolingual speech. The language-specific nature of many of these constraints, valid only for a given pair of languages, parallels the language-specific nature of grammatical rules in monolingual speech.[10] If this is so, the psychological mechanism of 'triggering' (Clyne 1967, 1987), which is the basis of co-occurrence constraints between the various levels of structure (lexical, grammatical, prosodic) would be perfectly applicable to monolingual speech as well, and in this sense the notion would lose its explanatory power to unveil the apparently specific nature of 'code-switching'.

In the data presented in the literature it is not clear that the speakers are actively (or automatically) combining elements from two separate systems. The translinguistic flow of speech is evident in such varied sets of data as 'English/Spanish' speech:

> Y en Puerto Rico *he would say* que cortaba caña, *even though* tenía su negocio, *you know*
>
> > (Sankoff and Poplack 1981: 24)

'French/English':

> Example 16 . . . *okay on pratique on pratique? on* move *les* chairs
> Example 17 *arrête de* picke*r le* ear
>
> > (Heller 1989: 386)

or 'Mexicano/Spanish':

> Amo nicpia *pleito, siempre* ni*vivir*oa *en paz* ica in notahtzin huan-nonatzin huan ica nos –, nopilhuan
> ('Not I have lawsuits, always live in peace with my father and my mother and with my –, my children')
>
> > (Hill 1985: 732)[11]

In sum, research on the grammar of 'code-switching' as a specific phenomenon shows a certain circularity of design. Where two or more 'languages' are assumed to pre-exist in a 'bilingual's' speech, it is not surprising that the data are explained as a result of 'switching' in rather circumvoluted ways from one system to another. In order to argue convincingly *for* or *against* the existence of 'code-switching constraints' and 'code-switching grammars' 'based on the two monolingual ones' (Sankoff and Poplack 1981: 10), research should first convincingly prove that (a) speakers who 'code-switch' possess two (or more) identifiable linguistic systems or languages, each with its identifiable grammatical rules and lexicon; and (b) 'code-switched' speech results from the predictable interaction between lexical elements and grammatical rules from these languages.[12] None of these assumptions, I believe, is proven yet.

6 The pragmatics of 'code-switching'

It has been repeatedly emphasised that not all individual alternations of speech varieties carry interactional meaning; rather, often it is the overall effect of using a 'code-switching style' that is tactically exploited for group identification. This is explicit, among others, in Gumperz's work on Hindi/Punjabi and Spanish/English conversation (for instance, Gumperz 1982; Gumperz and Hernández-Chávez 1971), in Poplack's work on Puerto Rican speech (1980), in Sobrero (1992), where the 'parlato mistilingue' or 'codice misto' in Salento 'costituisce una terza varietà a disposizione' (1992: 37), in Swigart's (1992) thought-provoking description of 'Urban Wolof', in Stroud's (1992; and this volume) work on Taiap/Tok Pisin oratorical discourse, in Halmari and Smith's (1994) account of Finnish/English alternation as another manifestation of register variation, etc. But perhaps more significant for unveiling the indexical values of varieties involved in 'code-switching' is the growing evidence that singular occurrences of language alternation, when they can be proven to be interactionally relevant through detailed interpretive analysis, may carry meanings *not directly associated* with the social-indexical values of the varieties which compose the 'code-switched' material. In one of the most interesting examples of tactical manipulation of speech varieties discussed in the sociolinguistic literature, Mitchell-Kernan (1972) reports that, at the end of an ethnographic session with an African-American subject in Oakland, USA, the interviewee suggests it is time for him to go by 'marking' with the expression: *Tempus fugit, baby*. Symbolically, it is not the 'Latin'/'English' contrast that the speaker exploits, but rather 'educated English' versus 'colloquial speech' (contrast, in this regard, the actual example with a hypothetical *Tempus fugit, Ms Smith*). The indexical value of a classical quotation is that of the *communicative code* it springs from, that is, the mechanism that associates frames and activities from the classroom setting with a set of structures, pronunciations, expressions and rhetorical conventions learned through exposure to formal education.

Similar evidence can be found in my own data on Galizan–Portuguese/Spanish conversation (Alvarez-Cáccamo 1990). In one of the cases discussed, taken from a radio interview, the 'we' voice of Galizans associated with a passage constituting a 'complaint' is channelled simply through Galizan prosody partially overlapping a Spanish stretch of discourse, whereas Spanish grammar and prosody channel communicative distance and a 'reporting' tone. In cases such as these, it seems premature to state a priori that the systems in contrast are 'Galizan' and 'Spanish'; rather, interpretive microanalysis reveals that the speakers exploit contrasts between a 'reporting code' and a 'complaining code', or between a 'procedural code', an 'informal code' and a 'joking code' within the same speech event. We might say that at given points speakers seem to be 'speaking Galizan in Spanish', or vice versa; but, importantly, neither 'Galizan' nor 'Spanish' *per se* match strictly any of the communicative codes listed. Instead, lexical, syntactic and prosodic materials from both varieties are fused into an amalgam, the situated meaning of which is not directly computable from the overall meanings (for instance, 'informality' vs. 'formality') commonly associated with each of the 'languages'.

Additional compelling evidence for the need to keep apart the notions of code and speech variety comes from Rampton's work on 'language crossing' (Rampton 1995; and this volume), that is, the enactment of social voices and illocutionary intentions through non-congruent or 'displaced' (Alvarez-Cáccamo 1996) linguistic choices in ethnically mixed groups of adolescents in England. Rampton's careful analysis shows that integrated community repertoires (English/Creole/Black, or English/Standard Asian English/ Punjabi) are tactically mobilised in non-transparent ways for identity-building purposes. The boundaries between the 'codes', however, often remain unclear. It rather seems that particular markers (e.g. [d] for [ð]) may come to represent entire social styles with associated meanings and given status in members' linguistic ideologies. If one, then, may speak 'Creole' in 'London Black English' (or if one may speak 'Galizan' in 'Spanish'), the doubt remains as to *when* exactly the use of a particular marker constitutes a 'switch', or, more importantly, as to why apparently consistent stretches of discourse in what looks like a single variety should *not* contain internal code-switches. In other words, if a communicative code is something systematically associated with activities, identities and interactional meanings, and if at times two or more varieties may carry comparable meanings, why not then speak of 'switches' only at points where activities change or local identities are reconfigured *in spite of* a single language variety being used?

7 'Code-switching' as an alloy

In keeping the notions of communicative code and linguistic variety separate I am trying to recapture part of the original meaning of codes as mechanisms of transduction. A communicative code would then be a mechanism of transduction between intentions (at several levels of generality) and utterances, and then between utterances and interpretations. These intentions include illocutionary forces at the speech act level, turn-construction functions at the sequential level, overall communicative goals at the situational level, social-indexical meanings, etc. While linguistic structures are subject to grammatical constraints, the linguistic shaping of utterances is subject to situational constraints. Thus, we may have a switching of communicative codes with language alternation (Gumperz's 'situational switching'), not-switching with language alternation (most of conversational 'code-switching styles'), not-switching without language alternation (short utterances in monolingual speech), or switching of codes without language alternation (where the same variety is used across an activity boundary). The following is a simplified representation of the four possibilities in discourse:

SG											
SC											
EG1		EG2				EG3			EG4		
EC1		EC2				EC3			EC4		
SA1	SA2	SA3	SA4	SA5	SA6	SA7	SA8	SA9	SA10	SA11	SA12
SC1	SC2	SC3	SC4	SC5	SC6	SC7	SC8	SC9	SC10	SC11	SC12
A	B	A	B	B	A	A	A	A	A	B	A

SG, situational goal; SC, situational code; EG, episode or activity goal;
EC, episode or activity code; SA, speech act; SC, speech-act code; A, B, utterances in alternating varieties

Utterances result from the interaction of various codes operating simultaneously at several levels. Since codes are directly connected to communicative goals, the situational code affects (a) the overall episodal structure, and (b) the overall use of varieties A and/or B. The episodal and speech-act codes affect the specific distribution of these varieties in utterances. For instance, an in-group conversation may need to be coded in both varieties alternately; within the conversation, a given narrative may require the use of one variety predominantly, with possible alternations at speech act boundaries (e.g. for quotations) or even within speech acts.

Therefore, individual alternation points may have a meaning, but not all need to; specific alternation points may be directly determined by the overall situational code requiring a pattern of frequent variety alternation. Where such is the case, in informational terms the value of particular alternation points may be close to zero, as the pattern is quite predictable. Correspondingly, switches of communicative codes effected at the various levels of discourse organisation may be undetectable solely from examining the sequential distribution of material in varieties A and B, since passages in either variety may span across several speech acts or activities.

Thus, many cases of what is known as fluent 'conversational code-switching' (whether 'intrasentential' or 'intersentential') can be envisioned, at the structural level, as an *alloy* of two or more speech varieties, which signals a number of situational and local intentions through a number of codes. At the situational level, prosody, lexis and grammar fuse in variable proportions into a single amalgam whose overall communicative effect is to index the situation type and/or the group's social identity. Each utterance or turn is then the alloyed product of merging A-variety material with B-variety material. Each utterance, turn or entire discourse thus produces a compound communicative effect and it may be effectively interpreted by participants as a coherent whole on the basis of a coherent code. In successful interaction of this type, the code-based process of intention-interpretation is reflected in metalinguistic statements and perceptions of the type 'we mix languages constantly' or 'I don't realise what language I'm speaking'. While atomically (i.e. intra- or intersententially) fragments of the varieties constituting the alloy can be identified, on the overall level utterances and discourses come across as samples of a particular type of alloy.

8 Switching the code as recontextualisation

Undeniably, switching of communicative codes may occur, and the switch may produce a variety-alternation in either direction, which indexes the recontextualisation process by 'indicating otherness', as Auer (1992: 31) thoroughly explains in his discussion of the signalling value of contextualisation cues. In this case, variety-alternation could be regarded as both a 'final' and an 'initial' (1992: 28) contextualisation cue.

But, as stated, switching the code need not always correspond with points of variety-alternation. For example, when repeated alternations constitute a 'recurrent' cue that points to a given episode or invoked social identity, switching the code may entail an *emic* change in the overall composition of the linguistic alloy – typically, a marked obtrusion in the proportions of A-variety and B-variety material in discourse. Some examples of such a 'layering' of speech material in language alloys are: Lingala/Swahili/French speech (Meeuwis and Blommaert, this volume); Urban Wolof (Swigart 1990, 1992); Common Czech/Standard Czech (CC/SC) alternating speech (Sgall *et al.* 1992); often the Galizan/Spanish speech of periurban and urban populations, a variety commonly referred to as *castrapo*; and probably post-creole continua. Switching the code for recontextualisation may entail mobilising a perceptually different amount of material from each variety within a continuum. For Rodríguez-Yáñez (1994; see particularly pp. 171–177), for instance, what matters for signalling identities and accomplishing discursive tasks between buyers and sellers in transactional encounters in a Galizan town market is not the initial variety chosen, but rather the negotiated, 'fluctuating choice of the degree of code fluctuation', which I would rephrase as the relative amount (and formal properties) of material in 'Galizan' and 'Spanish'. Similarly, Heller's data on French/English speech of children in Ontario schools (1989) show that, when two frames (classroom talk and peer-group talk) 'collapse' in a third type of speech activity (classroom presentations in front of the group), a tendency emerges for the resulting style to be an alloy of English and French material. Likewise, Sgall *et al.* (1992: 18ff.) claim that the 'discontinuous' categories of CC and CS correspond actually to a 'continuous' layering of alternating Czech forms.

From this viewpoint, codes *organise* the materials to be deployed as contextualisation cues. The contextualisation value of variety-alternation may thus operate at various levels: (1) the use of a given variety (either structurally homogeneous or mixed) as a 'recurrent' cue indexes how to map linguistic actions and referential contents against overall intentions, including situational goals and the signalling of social identification; and (2) the fluctuating alternations between varieties (in each case simultaneously 'initial' and 'final') cue generically to changes in contextual states at the level of conversational preferences and illocutionary force.

Finally, switching the code may also manifest itself in the mobilisation of a single speech marker within the linguistic continuum, which comes to symbolise a socially recognised variety, such as the use of *¿no?* as a tag question in Gibraltar speech (Melissa Moyer, personal communication) or the [x] variant for /g/ in Galizan *gheada* speech (Alvarez-Cáccamo 1990). Switching the code may also entail an 'ironic' prosodic contour overlaying either grammatical variety (Alvarez-Cáccamo 1991), or the tactical use of 'other-language' lexical items (such as English terms in Tamil vendors' discourse, Canagarajah 1995), or the aspiration of final [s] in certain Spanish dialects, etc.

It must be emphasised that, if switching the code is contrastive by nature, contrasts are not only culturally based but discursively situated as well. Further, if contrasts are marked (recognisable by participants), they must be empirically accounted for, not just taken for granted. Code switches are of course amenable to the analyst's inspection, but in order for the analyst to give account of contrasts and meanings, preconceptions about linguistic systems must be temporarily left aside. The layering of speech may be so subtle that the differences between adjacent sequences of discourse where contrastive switches of codes were intended escape an initial structural (particularly syntactic) inspection. I believe it is about time to steer away from one of the main concerns of the research on 'bilingual behaviour' and 'code-switching', explicitly stated by Haugen:

> Any item that occurs in speech must be a part of some language
> if it is to convey any meaning to the hearer ... The real question
> is whether a given stretch of speech is to be assigned to one language
> or the other.
>
> (Haugen 1956: 39)

Perhaps the real question is, is this the real question? Perhaps more interesting questions are: What is the differential status (if any) of objects such as 'one language' and 'the other' in speech behaviour in relation to activities and identities? To what extent do materials in 'language A' or 'language B' *count conversationally as* materials in 'language A' or 'language B', and not as something else?[13]

9 Conclusion

In this chapter I have refocused on the meaning of 'code' as a productive and interpretive device or 'cipher', and I have suggested that we need to distinguish between the linguistic material present in utterances (linguistic varieties) and the associative mechanisms which underlie their production (communicative codes). Codes transduce communicative intentions into utterances, and utterances into interpretations. Since various codes operate simultaneously and jointly for the production of linguistic material at several levels of discourse organisation (situation, activity and speech act), the resulting utterances are inherently polysemic as to the intentions being encoded.[14]

Thus, while linguistic varieties are held together by structural co-occurrence constraints, the activation of specific codes responds to situational coherence constraints. Consequently, we need to examine closely whether or not samples of variety-alternation are indeed the manifestation of switches of communicative codes (see also Stroud 1992: 149).

In this regard, today's 'code-switching' notion may subsume a number of possibly unrelated phenomena while excluding others which are clear candidates for being considered 'switching the code', in its original formulation. I thus propose that the scope of 'code-switching' be simultaneously (a) narrowed in order to exclude socially or interactionally meaningless variety-alternation, and (b) broadened in order to include phenomena of monolingual speech (such as prosody or the deployment of speech markers) which recontextualise talk by signalling the onset of emerging frames by virtue of the codes associated with them.

At the broader sociolinguistic level, this view points to the need to reassess the validity of outsiders' accounts of the relationships between variety-alternation and social identity. If, as Eastman states, '[w]here people use a mixed language regularly, codeswitching [i.e. variety-alternation] represents the norm' (Eastman 1992: 1), formulations about 'codeswitching in conversation . . . always [being] a systematic and socially meaningful use of contrasting linguistic resources' (Gal 1987: 648), or about the indexical value of this style for signalling an ambiguous or 'dual' group identification (Heller 1982, 1988, 1992; Myers-Scotton 1988a) ought to be reconsidered, as they assume the indexical value of variety-alternation to be a sort of compound of the social-indexical values of the individual 'languages' in use. For one thing, since a single variety may be generated by more than one code, and since two or more varieties may share the same code, the default product of one code may equally be either a 'mixed' style, or, in other situations, 'unreciprocal choices' of the type observed by Gal in Austria (Gal 1979), by Woolard in Catalonia (Woolard 1989), or by Alvarez-Cáccamo in Galiza. These 'unreciprocal choices' occur, for instance, in interactions between educated 'new speakers' (*neofalantes*) who use regularised, monitored Galizan, and non-educated rural speakers who reply to them in monitored Spanish. At least at one level (that of footing), one common code channelling negative politeness produces monitored Galizan for *neofalantes* and monitored Spanish for Galizan-dominants. Usually, when the 'new speaker' switches the code toward positive politeness and produces mixed speech, the Galizan-dominant introduces Galizan material as well. Therefore, symbolically 'Galizan' and 'Spanish' occupy the same socio-semiotic territory vis-à-vis 'mixed speech', and *language divergence becomes the surface-level manifestation of a shared communicative code*.

Undoubtedly, the question of 'what language/dialect are we using now?' is important in terms of the connections between linguistic ideologies, invoked identities, discursive practices and social structures. But only the detailed scrutiny of talk may tell us when exactly what is commonly called 'code-switching' is indeed a manifestation of 'switching the code'. Perhaps we can thus minimise the imposition of our own interpretive codes upon the innocent, unsuspecting data.

Notes

I am very grateful to Peter Auer for his comments on a preliminary version, and to Geert Craps for providing me with some initial pointers and suggestions. This chapter has also benefited from observations by Xoán Paulo Rodríguez-Yáñez, Susan Ervin-Tripp and John Gumperz.

1 Interestingly, both 'code-switching' and 'speech act' span from the physics of articulation ('code', 'speech') to the political economy of meaningful action ('switching', 'act').

2 'Coexistent systems may include, among other types, a vernacular (1) with sounds borrowed from other languages, or (2) with relics or advance elements of linguistic change, or (3) with special segments of an interjectional type, or (4) with general differences of quality, style, or speed' (Fries and Pike 1949: 49).

3 Sketchy references to the language as a 'code' were already present in de Saussure's *Cours* (1993 [1910–11]), where 'langue' is defined as a '[c]ode social, organisant le langage et formant l'outil nécessaire à l'exercice de la faculté du langage' (1993 [1910–11]: 70). However, it remains unclear whether to de Saussure the language *is* itself the 'social code' or *possesses* an internal code besides linguistic units and elements ('code de langue', 1993 [1910–11]: 70, 73), one which individual speakers would use in order to produce 'parole'.

4 'Precision would thus require us to distinguish three stages in diffusion: (1) *switching*, the alternate use of two languages, (2) *interference*, the overlapping of two languages, and (3) *integration*, the regular use of material from one language in another, so that there is no longer either switching or overlapping, except in a historical sense' (Haugen 1956: 40).

5 'Beside the encoding and decoding, also the procedure of recoding, code switching, briefly the various faces of translation, grow to be one of the focal concerns both of linguistics and communication theory here and in Western and Eastern Europe. Only now do such fascinating problems as those of ways and degrees of mutual understanding among speakers of some closely cognate languages, as for instance Danish, Norwegian and Swedish, begin to attract the attention of linguists and promise to give a lucid insight into the phenomenon

known in communication theory under the label "semantic noise" and into the theoretically and pedagogically important problem of overcoming it' (Jakobson 1961: 250).

6 The example Gumperz refers to is Jakobson's account of Russian/French language alternation among nineteenth-century Russian aristocratic families, who would resort to French as a sort of secret code when they needed to talk privately 'devant les enfants'.

7 I am quoting from the reprint in the collection of essays *Language in Social Groups*, Stanford: Stanford University Press, pp. 97–113 (1971).

8 Gumperz, based on evidence from Spanish/English, Hindi/English, and Slovenian/German conversation, emphasises the internal grammatical coherence of 'code-switching' passages, which are 'tied by syntactic and semantic relations apparently identical to those which join passages in a single language' (1977: 3).

9 In Nortier's data, the equivalence constraint is violated and both Arabic and Dutch grammars are 'suspended'. This occurs mostly with Dutch nouns switched (or 'transferred', for Auer, 1984) into Arabic discourse. Not having proven that these 'switched nouns' belong either to Dutch *or* to Arabic, Nortier goes at great lengths to explain the phenomenon as noted.

10 Mahootian claims that '[g]eneral principles of phrase structure, rather than constraints specific to codeswitching produce codeswitched utterances' (1996: 3). Still in keeping with a separate-language view, Mahootian applies X-bar theory to structures from diverse language pairs, and concludes that 'the language of a head determines the syntactic properties of its complements in codeswitching and monolingual contexts alike' (1996: 3), and that 'the linguistic mechanisms involved in the production of codeswitched sequences strongly indicate that bilingual speech behaviour and monolingual behaviour are identical' (1996: 11).

11 Or, what to say of this apparently trilingual (English/**Spanish**/*Portuguese*) switch spontaneously produced by Alvarez-Cáccamo in informal interaction, each segment preserving its phonetic qualities?: 'Ten **es** *muito*' ['tʰɛn 'es 'mujto] ('Ten is *a lot*').

12 Silva-Corvalán's (1983) discussion of English/Spanish 'code-shifting' exemplifies this circularity. The 'Compensate for Lack of Competence' function underlies Chicanos' 'shifting' between the two 'languages' to fill lexical gaps. Alternatively, conceiving of an *integrated repertoire* and a unified grammar is a better way to explain why bilingual or monolingual speakers alike resort to subsets of their lexicons to fill lexical gaps in specific styles or registers.

13 Stroud (1992) convincingly shows that 'switch points' in Taiap/Tok Pisin discourse do not carry particular meanings beyond those of signalling 'code-switching' speech. However, he fails to prove that the materials 'switched' contrast by virtue of *counting as* different varieties. For instance, the 'switched' discourse particle *tasol* 'but', assigned to 'Tok Pisin' on formal grounds alone, is argued to channel a rhetorical contrast (1992: 143). Stretching Stroud's argument, an emphatic **but** in monolingual English would channel a similar contrast and thus constitute 'code-switching': *You can't help me with any old thing, **but**, with this you'll help me*. I would not have a problem with this interpretation, but then Stroud's 'switch' does not derive necessarily from the contrast between the two externally identifiable varieties 'Taiap' and 'Tok Pisin'.

14 Stroud claims that these meanings are inherently 'ambiguous' (1992: 148–149). Sajavaara (1988), in a general discussion of linguistic processing, argues that '[r]ecognition of elements embedded in the interlocutor's speech signal is not simply a linguistic phenomenon', but various types of linguistic cues and knowl-

edge 'interact heterarchically in the process of interpretation in terms of an incremental time-sharing system. There is no possible way to predict which type of cue leads to the right or, preferably, most probable interpretation' (1988: 250–251). For the author, 'potentially [sic] interpretations are accessed through a *multiple-code system*, which adapts to the requirements of each particular incremental bit of the incoming message; processing may be partly speaker-specific, partly personality-type-oriented, and partly dependent on cues available' (1988: 251; my emphasis).

Bibliography

Alvarez-Cáccamo, Celso (1990) 'Rethinking conversational code-switching: Codes, speech varieties, and contextualization', in *Proceedings of the Sixteenth Annual Meeting of the Berkeley Linguistics Society, February 16–19, 1990. General Session and Parasession on the Legacy of Grice*, Berkeley: Berkeley Linguistics Society, 3–16.

Alvarez-Cáccamo, Celso (1991) 'Language revival, code manipulation and social power in Galiza: Off-record uses of Spanish in formal communicative events', in Carol A. Klee (ed.) *Sociolinguistics of the Spanish-Speaking World: Iberia, Latin America, United States*, Tempe (AZ): Bilingual Press/Editorial Bilingüe, 41–73.

Alvarez-Cáccamo, Celso (1996) 'The reflexive power of language(s): Code displacement in reported speech', *Journal of Pragmatics* 25, 1: 33–59.

Auer, J. C. Peter (1984) *Bilingual Conversation*, Amsterdam/Philadelphia, Penn.: John Benjamins.

Auer, J. C. Peter (1989) 'A discussion paper on code alternation', paper presented at the *First Conference of the European Network on Code-Switching on Concepts, Methodology and Data*, Basel, Switzerland, January 1989.

Auer, J. C. Peter (1992) 'Introduction: John Gumperz' approach to contextualisation', in J. C. Peter Auer and Aldo di Luzio (eds) *The Contextualisation of Language*, Amsterdam: John Benjamins, 1–37.

Canagarajah, A. Suresh (1995) 'Manipulating the context: The use of English borrowings as a discourse strategy by Tamil fish vendors', *Multilingua* 14, 1: 5–24.

Clyne, Michael G. (1967) *Transference and Triggering*, The Hague: Mouton.

Clyne, Michael G. (1987) 'Constraints on code switching: How universal are they?', *Linguistics* 25: 739–764.

Diebold, A. Richard (1961) 'Incipient bilingualism', *Language* 37: 97–112.

Eastman, Carol M. (1992) 'Codeswitching as an urban language-contact phenomenon', in Carol M. Eastman (ed.) *Codeswitching*, Clevedon, England/Philadelphia, Penn./Adelaide: Multilingual Matters, 1–17.

Ervin-Tripp, Susan M. (1973 [1964]) 'An analysis of the interaction of language, topic and listener', in *Language Acquisition and Communicative Choice*: *Essays by Susan M. Ervin-Tripp*, Stanford, Calif.: Stanford University Press, 239–261.

Fano, R. M. (1950) 'The information theory point of view in speech communication', *Journal of the Acoustical Society of America* 22, 6: 691–696.

Fries, Charles C., and Kenneth L. Pike (1949) 'Coexisting phonemic systems', *Language* 25, 1: 29–50.

Gal, Susan (1979) *Language Shift: Social Determinants of Linguistic Change in Bilingual Austria*, New York: Academic Press.

Gal, Susan (1987) 'Codeswitching and consciousness in the European periphery', *American Ethnologist* 14, 4: 637–653.

Gal, Susan (1995) 'Cultural bases of language use among German-speakers in Hungary', *International Journal of the Sociology of Language* 111: 93–102.

Gumperz, John J. (1957) 'Some remarks on regional and social language differences in India', in Milton Singer (ed.) *Introduction to the Civilization of India: Changing Dimensions in Indian Society and Culture*, Chicago, Ill.: The College, University of Chicago Syllabus Division, 31–38.

Gumperz, John J. (1958) 'Dialect differences and social stratification in a North Indian village', *American Anthropologist* 60: 668–681.

Gumperz, John J. (1961) 'Speech variation and the study of Indian civilization', *American Anthropologist* 63: 976–988.

Gumperz, John J. (1962) 'Types of linguistic communities', *Anthropological Linguistics* 4, 1: 28–40.

Gumperz, John J. (1964a) 'Hindi–Punjabi code-switching in Delhi', in H. Lunt (ed.) *Proceedings of the Ninth International Congress of Linguists, Cambridge, Massachusetts, 1962*, The Hague: Mouton, 1115–1124.

Gumperz, John J. (1964b) 'Linguistic and social interaction in two communities', in John J. Gumperz and Dell H. Hymes (eds) *The Ethnography of Communication* (*American Anthropologist* 66, 6, Part 2), Washington D.C.: American Anthropological Association, 137–153.

Gumperz, John J. (1977) 'The sociolinguistic significance of conversational code-switching', *RELC Journal* 8, 2: 1–34.

Gumperz, John J. (1982) *Discourse Strategies*, Cambridge: Cambridge University Press.

Gumperz, John J. (1992) 'Contextualisation revisited', in J. C. Peter Auer and Aldo di Luzio (eds) *The Contextualisation of Language*, Amsterdam: John Benjamins, 39–53.

Gumperz, John J. and Eleanor Herasimchuk (1972) 'The conversational analysis of social meaning: A study of classroom interaction', in Roger W. Shuy (ed.) *Sociolinguistics: Current Trends and Prospects* (GURT 1972), Washington DC: Georgetown University Press, 99–134.

Gumperz, John J. and Eduardo Hernández-Chávez (1971) 'Bilingualism, bidialectalism, and classroom interaction', in A. Dil (ed.) *Language in Social Groups: Essays by John J. Gumperz*, Stanford: Stanford University Press, 311–350.

Gumperz, John J., and C. M. Naim (1960) 'Formal and informal standards in Hindi regional language area', in Charles A. Ferguson and John J. Gumperz (eds) *Linguistic Diversity in South Asia*, 92–118 (*International Journal of American Linguistics* 26, 3, Part 3).

Gumperz, John J. and Robert Wilson (1971) 'Convergence and creolization: A case from the Indo-Aryan/Dravidian border in India', in Dell H. Hymes (ed.) *Pidginization and Creolization of Languages*, London: Cambridge University Press, 151–167.

Halmari, Helena, and Wendy Smith (1994) 'Code-switching and register shift: Evidence from Finnish–English child bilingual conversation', *Journal of Pragmatics* 21: 427–445.

Haugen, Einar (1950a) 'The analysis of linguistic borrowing', *Language* 26, 2: 210–231.

Haugen, Einar (1950b) 'Problems of bilingualism', *Lingua* 2, 3: 271–290.

Haugen, Einar (1956) *Bilingualism in the Americas: A Bibliography and Research Guide*, Alabama: University of Alabama Press/American Dialect Society.

Heller, Monica S. (1982) 'Negotiations of language choice in Montreal', in John J. Gumperz (ed.) *Language and Social Identity*, Cambridge: Cambridge University Press, 108–118.

Heller, Monica S. (1988) 'Strategic ambiguity: Code-switching in the management of conflict', in Monica S. Heller (ed.) *Codeswitching: Anthropological and Sociolinguistic Perspectives*, Berlin/New York/Amsterdam: Mouton de Gruyter, 77–96.

Heller, Monica S. (1989) 'Communicative resources and local configurations:

An exploration of language contact processes', *Multilingua* 8, 4: 357–395.

Heller, Monica S. (1992) 'The politics of codeswitching and language choice', in Carol M. Eastman (ed.) *Codeswitching*, Clevedon, England: Multilingual Matters, 123–142.

Hensey, Frederik G. (1972) *The Sociolinguistics of the Brazilian–Uruguayan Border*, The Hague: Mouton.

Hill, Jane H. (1985) 'The grammar of consciousness and the consciousness of grammar', *American Ethnologist* 12, 4: 725–737.

Hockett, Charles F. (1987) *Refurbishing our Foundations*, Amsterdam/Philadelphia, Penn.: John Benjamins.

Hoijer, Harry (1948) 'Linguistic and cultural change', *Language* 24, 4: 335–345.

Jakobson, Roman (1961) 'Linguistics and communication theory', in Roman Jakobson (ed.) *On the Structure of Language and Its Mathematical Aspects: Proceedings of the XIIth Symposium of Applied Mathematics (New York, 14–15 April 1960)*, Providence, R.I.: American Mathematical Society, 245–252.

Jakobson, Roman (1963 [1961]) 'Linguistique et théorie de la communication', in *Essais de Linguistique Générale I*, Paris: Editions de Minuit, 87–99.

Jakobson, Roman (1984 [1961]) 'La lingüística y la teoría de la comunicación', in *Ensayos de lingüística general*, Barcelona: Ariel, 79–94.

Jakobson, Roman, Gunnar, M. Fant and Morris Halle (1952) *Preliminaries to Speech Analysis: The Distinctive Features and their Correlates*, Cambridge, Mass.: The MIT Press. Reprinted in *Selected Writings [of Roman Jakobson]. Major Works, 1976–1980*, Vol. 8, Berlin/New York/Amsterdam: Mouton de Gruyter, 583–646. (Page references in the text are to the reprinted edition.)

Lenneberg, E. H. (1967) *Biological Foundations of Language*, New York: Wiley and Sons.

Mackey, William F. (1962) 'The description of bilingualism', *Canadian Journal of Linguistics/Revue Canadienne de Linguistique* 7, 2: 51–85.

Mackey, William F. (1970) 'Interference, integration, and the synchronic fallacy', in James E. Alatis (ed.) *Bilingualism and Language Contact* (GURT 1970), Washington D.C.: Georgetown University Press, 195–227.

Mahootian, Shahrzad (1996) 'The structure of bilingual codeswitching: Psycholinguistic implications', Paper presented at the *First International Conference on the Linguistic Construction of Social and Personal Identity*, International Sociological Association Research Committee on Sociolinguistics, University of Évora, Portugal, March 1996.

Mitchell-Kernan, Claudia (1972) 'Signifying and marking: Two Afro-American speech acts', in John J. Gumperz and Dell H. Hymes (eds) *Directions in Sociolinguistics*, New York: Holt, Rinehart and Winston, 161–179.

Myers-Scotton, Carol (1976) 'Strategies of neutrality: Language choice in uncertain situations', *Language* 52, 4: 919–941.

Myers-Scotton, Carol (1983) 'The negotiation of identities in conversation: A theory of markedness and code choice', *International Journal of the Sociology of Language* 44: 115–136.

Myers-Scotton, Carol (1988a) 'Code-switching and types of multilingual communities', in Peter H. Lowenberg (ed.) *Language Spread and Language Policy: Issues, Implications, and Case Studies* (GURT 1987), Washington D.C.: Georgetown University Press, 61–82.

Myers-Scotton, Carol (1988b) 'Code-switching as indexical of social negotiations', in Monica S. Heller (ed.) *Codeswitching: Anthropological and Sociolinguistic Perspectives*, Berlin/New York/Amsterdam: Mouton de Gruyter, 151–186.

Nortier, Jacomine M. (1995) 'Code-switching in Moroccan Arabic/Dutch vs. Moroccan Arabic/French language contact', *International Journal of the Sociology of Language* 112: 81–95.

Pfaff, Carol W. (1979) 'Constraints on language mixing: Intrasentential code-switching and borrowing in Spanish/English', *Language* 55, 2: 291–318.

Poplack, Shana (1982) 'Syntactic structure and social function of code-switching', in Richard P. Durán (ed.) *Latino Language and Communicative Behavior*, Norwood, N.J.: Ablex Publishing, 169–184.

Poplack, Shana (1980) 'Sometimes I'll start a sentence in Spanish Y TERMINO EN ESPAÑOL: Toward a typology of code-switching', *Linguistics* 18, 581–618.

Rampton, M. Ben H. (1995) 'Language crossing and the problematisation of ethnicity and socialisation', *Pragmatics* 5, 4: 485–513.

Rodríguez-Yáñez, Xoán Paulo (1994) 'Estratexias de comunicación nas interaccións cliente–vendedor no mercado da cidade de Lugo: As alternancias de lingua galego/castelán e a negociación da escolla de lingua', Ph.D. dissertation, Departamento de Lingüística Xeral e Teoría da Literatura, University of Coruña, Spain.

Sajavaara, Kari (1988) 'Cross-linguistic and cross-cultural intelligibility', in Peter H. Lowenberg (ed.) *Language Spread and Language Policy: Issues, Implications, and Case Studies* (GURT 1987), Washington D.C.: Georgetown University Press, 250–264.

Sankoff, David, and Shana Poplack (1981) 'A formal grammar for code-switching', *Papers in Linguistics: International Journal of Human Communication* 14, 1: 3–45.

Saussure, Ferdinand de (1993 [1910-11]) *Troisième cours de linguistique générale (1910–1911) d'après les cahiers d'Emile Constantin/Saussure's Third Course of Lectures on General Linguistics (1910–1911) – from the notebooks of Emile Constantin*, ed. Eisuke Komatsu and Roy Harris, Oxford: Pergamon Press.

Sgall, Petr, Jiři Hronek, Alexandr Stich, and Ján Horecký (1992) *Variation in Language: Code Switching in Czech as a Challenge for Sociolinguistics*, Amsterdam/Philadelphia, Penn.: John Benjamins.

Silva-Corvalán, Carmen (1983) 'Code-shifting patterns in Chicano Spanish', in Lucía Elías-Olivares (ed.) *Spanish in the U.S. Setting: Beyond the Southwest*, Rosslyn, Va.: National Clearinghouse for Bilingual Education, 69–87.

Sobrero, Alberto A. (1992) 'Paese e città del Salento: Come cambia il cambio di codice', in Alberto A. Sobrero (ed.) *dialetto nella conversazione: Richerche di dialettologia pragmatica*, Galatina: Congedo Editore, 31–41.

Stroud, Christopher (1992) 'The problem of intention and meaning in code-switching', *Text* 12: 127–155.

Swigart, Leigh (1990) 'Gender-based patterns of language use: The case of Dakar', *Plurilinguismes* 2 (*Dynamique des langues au Senegal*): 38–66.

Swigart, Leigh (1992) 'Two codes or one? The insiders' view and the description of codeswitching in Dakar', in Carol M. Eastman (ed.) *Codeswitching*, Clevedon, England/Philadelphia, Penn./Adelaide: Multilingual Matters, 83–102.

Vogt, Hans (1954) 'Language contacts', *Word* 10, 2–3: 365–374.

Weinreich, Uriel (1953) *Languages in Contact*, The Hague: Mouton.

Woolard, Kathryn A. (1989) *Double Talk: Bilingualism and the Politics of Ethnicity in Catalonia*, Stanford, Calif.: Stanford University Press.

INTRODUCTION TO CHAPTER 3

Peter Auer

In the following chapter, Rita Franceschini aims at integrating bilingual speech (including code-switching) into a more general linguistic approach which is based on flexibility and variability rather than timeless stability and situation-transcending constancy. Instead of taking the highly codified standard languages (of Europe or elsewhere) as the starting point, she proposes to move mixed codes, code-switching and other manifestations of linguistic variability and flexibility among bilinguals into the centre of linguistic thinking and theorising, which, up to the present, has been dominated by monolingual views of the human language capacity. One of her arguments for such an approach is similar to the one presented by Alvarez-Cáccamo in Chapter 2: bilingual speech cannot be equated with conversational code-switching, which is functional and therefore presupposes the 'underlying' existence of two 'codes' (languages) seen as as separate entities by the participants.

Franceschini characterises the dominant research on conversational code-switching as being focused on *functional* switching as a strategy which is used mainly by younger, lower-class members of minority groups with a strong ethnic background, who also dispose of the monolingual varieties of the two languages in question. (It may be added that this code-switching is usually a marker of group membership, i.e. it is used *among* the minority speakers.) On the basis of her work on Italian/German bilingualism in Switzerland, Franceschini argues that code-switching is often of another, less 'prototypical' kind. For instance, it may be non-functional (i.e., in the sense of the Introduction, a 'mixed code' rather than code-switching), or it may be acquired at a later age (as shown in her examples (1 and 2) of a code-switching mother in interaction with her non-switching children). Moreover, Italian/German (dialect) switching in Switzerland is not restricted to lower-class speakers, but is a feature of middle-class speech as well. (Similar cases will be discussed in later chapters of this book: see the data presented in Chapters 4, 6, 8 and 9.) It is important to note that in Switzerland, code-switching between Italian and German (dialect) does not imply full competence in the respective languages, but may be found in speakers who do not dispose of the respective monolingual varieties as well (see Chapters 4 and 11 for similar arguments). Code-switching may be employed by bilinguals in order to display their group membership and their multilingualism to outsiders (see Franceschini's discussion of Italian/German code-switching in public transport in Zurich and other large Swiss cities as a fashionable display of Italian ethnic background), which means that it is not only an in-group code, but also a way of defining group boundaries in interaction with non-members. Finally, the code-switchers may be part of the (German-speaking) majority instead of the (Italian-speaking immigrant) minority, that is, there may be 'language crossing' as described by Rampton in Chapter 12. (Note, however, that in contrast to Rampton's data, this crossing is not restricted to 'liminoid' situations; rather, the Italian/German switchers use the same mixed code as the Italians in the same situations, probably copying the latter group's code-switching not so much as an ethnic style, but rather as one referring to a particular youth culture and its lifestyle.)

Of course, the specific status of Italian in Switzerland contributes in important ways to the types of bilingual behaviour reported by Franceschini. The Italian immigrants in Switzerland profit from the fact that Italian is one of the four constitutional languages of Switzerland and the dominant language in the Ticino. In this function, it enjoys an official status which is not reached by any other 'minority language' in Europe. In addition, Italian has behind it a prosperous European country which has an important influence on many prestigious spheres of everyday life (fashion, music, furniture, arts, etc.). Although many Italian immigrants in Switzerland are from the Mezzogiorno (a region which traditionally upholds a critical cultural distance from the north Italian industrial and commercial centres, including the Swiss Ticino), they themselves and particularly their children have developed a cultural identity which makes use of these cultural assets in skilful ways. Against the background of the special status of Italian in Switzerland both as a national and as an immigrants' language, and of the Italophile tendencies in Swiss urban culture today, it is no wonder that code-switching between German (dialect) and Italian proceeds in somewhat different ways than among other migrant minorities. Yet it remains open to further investigation whether the negative prestige and low status usually attributed to European migrant languages is in fact valid when we move from the national and political level down to that of smaller sub-cultures and social milieus within a society; when seen from within these sub-cultures/milieus, and when compared to other 'minority languages', varieties such as Jamaican Creole in England (see Chapters 11 and 12) or Turkish in large German cities (such as Berlin or Hamburg) may turn out to be a good deal more prestigious to the members of the local networks than is presently thought.

3

CODE-SWITCHING AND THE NOTION OF CODE IN LINGUISTICS

Proposals for a dual focus model

Rita Franceschini

1 Introduction

For several decades, code-switching (henceforth CS) has been studied using various linguistic approaches within the frameworks of sociolinguistics, psycholinguistics and grammatical studies, all of which have put greater emphasis either on the descriptive or on the theoretical aspects of the phenomenon. There seems at this point to be more and more evidence that CS is a language universal in the behaviour of multilingual speakers, or – to employ a shorthand definition of CS – using several languages or language varieties in the course of a conversation is based on conversation-internal mechanisms observable in various social contexts all over the world. Furthermore, the functions of CS seem to be widely comparable, even for the most diverse combinations of languages (e.g. ESF 1990a–c, 1991; Milroy and Muyskens 1995).

The analysis of CS presupposes clear concepts of what can be taken as a single code or a single language. However, in dealing with real data, and assuming an emic approach as well as taking the intuition of speakers (or groups of speakers) into account, these distinctions often become blurred. Data from multilingual African contexts particularly support this view. For instance, Meeuwis and Blommaert (this volume) claim that 'the unit "a language" is not always the sole salient and relevant sociolinguistic unit for the speakers'.[1] What is needed are further investigations to develop categories which fit these African – and other – bilingual contexts.

This step is necessary because linguistic research methodology and its underlying assumptions have resulted in long and sometimes tortuous discussions about what should or should not be considered code-switching vs. code-shifting, code-mixing, borrowing, transfer, insertion, transcodic markers – or whatever the concepts in use may be.[2] These debates have tended to obscure the fact that subsumed under the heading of CS is a large number of differently motivated but not clearly understood forms of bilingual behaviour. The 'discovery' of CS has occurred in conjunction with a slow change in perspective which has brought into focus forms of behaviour which were 'new' for linguistic research but not for language practice. Dealing with bilingual behaviour represents a challenge for linguistic theory and can contribute to the modification of its descriptive and theoretical framework.

The point of departure in most linguistic theories continues to be the monolingual, individual speaker who never leaves his or her place of origin and is surrounded by a basically monolingual majority. Of course, it has long been well known that multilingualism is not an extraordinary case in the linguistic behaviour of individuals: approximately half of the world's population use more than one language in their everyday life (cf. Grosjean 1982). However, this important empirical evidence has not yet had fundamental consequences in linguistics. Only the pragmatic tradition in linguistics – especially its conversation-oriented and interpretive branch (see Gumperz 1982a, 1982b, Auer and di Luzio 1984) – as well as typological studies[3] have paid some attention to the implications of multilingual behaviour for descriptive and theoretical categories.

In this contribution, we will not regard CS as a supplementary, additional, peripheral behaviour or as an exceptional possibility, but rather will relate CS to a general characteristic of language, i.e. *variability in use*, and to an extra-linguistic factor, i.e. *flexibility in behaviour*. We shall assume that these two forces fundamentally govern the language system and should no longer be seen as its secondary characteristics. Projected on a single continuum, consistent monolingual practices would then be situated at the ends, as rather exceptional cases, whereas the phenomenon of CS would be situated somewhere in the middle, together with other practices realised in language contact (Figure 3.1).

This perspective is also suggested by our data, which were collected in Switzerland and northern Italy. We shall concentrate on some examples, extracted from actual tape-recorded conversations or based on observation, which can shed light on, for example, CS and its genesis, CS and learnability, CS and loss of functions, etc., all areas which have not received a great amount of attention or perhaps have been considered to be non-prototypical types of CS. We will then widen the perspective by pointing out

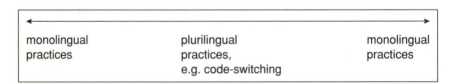

Figure 3.1 Monolingual and plurilingual practices

52

some principles of a theoretical framework of language use based on the multilingual repertoire of the speakers.

2 More and less prototypical code-switching

CS has been analysed largely in adolescents' peer groups. Moreover, these young people have usually been members of minority groups. According to the relevant literature (see note 2), the prototypical CS-speaker can therefore be described in terms of the following individual and social characteristics:

1 young age
2 member of a minority
3 lower class
4 strong 'ethnic' group identity
5 a multilingual social background.

There are, however, many speakers or groups of speakers who produce CS but strongly deviate from at least one of these typical features. We will call them *unexpected code-switchers* and discuss some problems they pose and the consequences which their behaviour has for our framework.

2.1 The genesis of CS

CS is characteristically formed in a specific way. It arises in groups sharing common identities. Consider the following case (based on personal observation):

> At the end of the 1970s, CS could be observed for the first time among Italian adolescents in the suburbs of the mostly Swiss-German-speaking town of Zurich. CS was a topic frequently discussed by the local Swiss-German inhabitants. At the beginning of the 1980s, code-switching adolescents were also observed in Basel and other larger Swiss towns, such as Solothurn and Bern.

It hardly makes sense to claim that Zurich Italian adolescents exported code-switching to Basel or that Basel adolescents imitated Zurich adolescents' code-switching. CS does not originate in a single linguistic centre. It rather emerges simultaneously in various places among multilinguals if similar social circumstances are given, such as:

- a multilingual context
- group awareness
- permeability of cultural and linguistic norms.[4]

Thus, we assume that there is polygenesis under similar social conditions, providing a parallel between CS and pidgin languages.[5]

In the German-speaking part of Switzerland, code-switching speakers born in the 1960s are particularly numerous, much more so than speakers born in the 1950s. Members of the older group of speakers grew up in a social climate of xenophobic anti-foreign-worker campaigns on the one hand and under the political pressure to assimilate on the other. This situation by no means favoured the coexistence of two (or more) languages within an individual speaker. Speakers used their two languages only in socially well-defined situations, if at all. In each situation, only one language was appropriate. 'Threshold bilingualism' was widespread: outside the house or apartment, speakers used the local language, whereas they used the language of origin within the family or ethnic group (Franceschini, Müller and Schmid 1984).

In the 1980s, the political climate changed. The aim of assimilation of immigrants was being replaced by the new goal of integration. Cultivation of the immigrant children's mother tongue was officially encouraged. The gap between local natives and Italian immigrants was based less and less on a perception of 'otherness'. The relaxation of a formerly wide-spread normative, monolingually oriented attitude, as well as the fact that the dividing lines were blurred, led to the development of a linguisti-cally autonomous way of life fed by more than one language – a way of life which was increasingly admired by the indigenous Swiss-German population.[6]

Similar to the ethnic revival movement of 'black is beautiful', there was a growing acceptance and popularity of the so-called *Italos*. They became a new in-crowd, and even in public areas, Italian was now spoken loudly and in a self-assured way. A new, ethnically mixed,[7] plural identity arose. CS could be observed especially frequently in public transport, where Italian adolescents had become virtuosos in loud and fast CS conversations. This brilliant verbal achievement, with frequent intraphrasal CS at its peak of perfection, was strongly marked socially in the early eighties. It excited the bystander's bewildered interest, which, in turn, was pointedly and proudly ignored by the adolescents. Adolescent peer groups, who knew how to differ-entiate themselves by outfit, haircut and gestures, used CS as a code which one of them labelled *italo-schwyz*.[8] It may be that in the early 1980s, a CS culture spread within and beyond adolescents' and children's groups in the urban context. There are, for instance, young speakers who think that CS developed in schoolyards among Italian immigrant children in order to disso-ciate themselves from other immigrant groups.[9] By the 1990s, CS had spread into non-urban contexts, and is now less socially marked; adolescents no longer attract other people's special attention by means of their linguistic behaviour.

2.2 *The acquisition of code-switching and age*

The CS behaviour of the 70-year-old Italian female speaker called M in examples 1 and 2 does not differ from that of a young speaker living in the same area, namely Basel. In example 2, M is speaking to her son.

EXAMPLE 1

Conversation between mother (M) and son (Ma) about governmental decisions in Italy, recorded in Basel in September 1993.[10]

1	M	ha detto che devono pagare i morti – quelli che sono morti fino in giugno (hh::)
		('he has said that the dead have to pay – those who have died by the end of June')
2		*jä* quelli
		('*yes* those')
3	M	[devono pagare le tasse del medico – *das sind* [*(xxx) chaschter*
4	MA	[(xxx) [(xxx)
5	M	*nit vorstelle*
		('they have to pay for the taxes of the doctor – *they are (xxx) you can't imagine*')

In example 2, M is engaged in a discussion with her daughter, Fi:

EXAMPLE 2

Conversation between mother (M) and daughter (Fi) about elections in Italy (recorded in Basel in July 1994).

1	FI	sì ma mamma e se gli italiani lo [ga votà
		('yes, mom but the Italians have voted for him')
2	M	[*chomm hörmer emol uff* – *hei*
3		*goots no* se l'hanno votato
		('*come on, stop it* – *you are crazy* if they had voted for him')
4	FI	sì ma l'hanno votato
		('yes, but they have voted for him')
5	M	*joo* sono d'accordo che l'hanno votato (xxx)
		('*yes*, I agree that they have voted for him (xxx)')
6	M	fascisti [d'accordo? e dopo mettere tutta la la (xx) la
		('fascists, okay?') ('and afterwards put all the the (xx) the')
7	FI	[mamma. (calming) se mi se mi (xxx)
		('mom.') ('if I if I (xxx)')

---

8 M [*jä* che fa dire la messa tutte le [mattine *goots no*
('*yes* who each morning has   the Mass celebrated *it's crazy*')
9 FI [(xx)   [(xx)
10 M (upset) è persino divorziata
('she is even divorced')

In Switzerland, frequent Swiss-German/Italian CS (with or without Italian dialect) has been increasingly observed within the last ten years, also among first-generation immigrants. On the basis of our observations, we presume that they acquired (or allowed) this type of spoken language in the 1980s. What is especially interesting in examples 1 and 2 is the fact that the speaker does not employ CS in convergence with her son (Ma) or her daughter (Fi).[11] Her children, both around age 30, do not use CS at all, either when talking to their mother or when talking to other CS-speakers (personal observation). The opposite case can be more frequently observed in the Swiss-German context: children use CS while their parents answer in code choice, Italian or Italian dialect.

In the German-speaking part of Switzerland, adult speakers' CS can be observed most often in informal situations. These speakers are either members of the second generation mentioned above or persons who have acquired CS late: parents who have given up trying to keep the foreign language off their private territory and now allow for the language to change, to the point of even using CS themselves.

As for linguistic forms, CS speakers of the first generation mostly switch discourse markers, for example when concluding their turns with *joo* ('yes'), or when using final *oder* ('isn't it'), and *weisch* ('you know'). Very rapid intra-sentential CS (cf. example 5) is quite unusual for these speakers (cf. Oesch Serra, this volume).[12]

From our observation of the Swiss-German situation, we conclude that CS can be learnt late, even by older persons. It can be taken over by adult speakers from adolescents, the process of acquisition thus following an unexpected direction, namely from children to adults instead of vice versa.

2.3 CS by majority speakers

There are other CS speakers, at least in the Swiss context, who acquire CS although they do not necessarily share the same ethnic characteristics (see Rampton, this volume, for a similar situation in England).[13] Take the following observation (made in Zurich on 9 January 1993):

In a fashion house in Zurich, I am served by a ca. eighteen-year-old shop assistant in Swiss-German. After about ten minutes, a group of young men, obviously friends of the shop assistant, enter the shop. All of them use the common Swiss-German/Italian CS style, which is certainly not surprising. There is nothing unusual about the scene. The group seems to me to be one of many second-generation immigrant peer-groups.

In order to exchange my purchase, I go to the same fashion house the following day. I am now served by the owner of the shop, a ca. forty-year-old Italian. In the course of our conversation, I am told that the shop assistant I had overheard the previous day is not a second-generation Italian immigrant at all but a Swiss-German. She grew up in a linguistically strongly mixed area of the town and has had Italian friends since her school years.

The way the shop-assistant used CS could not be distinguished from the Italian adolescents' CS. The fact that a difference in the process of CS acquisition does not lead to differences in the surface structure allows us to ask interesting questions previously not considered in depth by CS research, where competence in both languages, and often a good competence, had been seen as a basic prerequisite for CS: CS can be acquired directly, i.e. without a basic competence in both of the languages involved (see also Sebba and Wootton, and Meeuwis and Blommaert, this volume). CS in the case mentioned above can be regarded as an independent language that can be acquired directly. Such CS as a 'mixed code' can, for instance, replace 'pure' Italian.

Another important aspect of this phenomenon should be pointed out: the dimension of identity is not entirely absent, but can be considerably reduced. It is, for example, hardly to be expected that the shop assistant feels like an Italian or like an 'Italo-Swiss' person. Nevertheless, one cannot deny the existence of a general Italophile tendency, not only among adolescents. The adoption of the CS group code by speakers with a Swiss-German background – usage of the minority code from the position of the majority – further blurs the boundaries between an emancipated, self-assured minority on the one hand and a benevolent majority on the other hand.

As far as the strong ethnic group identity mentioned above is concerned, reference to one's own peer group seems to be more important than a nationally, ethnically or linguistically clearly defined identity. Here, too, the traditional distinctions between groups and languages become blurred. Having grown up within a multilingual social environment remains the sole common denominator of all these CS speakers.

Speakers who acquired their CS competence directly without speaking all the varieties involved separately certainly do not constitute the majority of CS speakers. However, their existence suggests that there are scenarios of CS for which the current research paradigm has to be expanded considerably.

2.4 Non-functional uses of CS

The two greatest difficulties in dealing with CS are, on the one hand, the attribution of linguistic elements to two separate codes and, on the other, the attribution of functions to CS.

If two languages are closely related (such as Italian and its related dialects), attributing elements to a particular code is especially difficult, as has been frequently observed by other researchers.[14] Even very elaborate theories such as Myers-Scotton's cannot fully capture the following cases, which are by no means rare.

EXAMPLE 3

Code-switching in Como, Italy (Italian in italics).

ROM eran lur du eh eran lur du Lili Marlen *il* lampiun aah
('there were both of them eh there were both Lili Marleen *the* street-lamp')

(Canegrati 1996: 703)

The use of articles of the other code is quite a common phenomenon in CS between Italian and dialect. In this case, where the Lombard dialect of Monza is the matrix language, the Italian article (ART.), a system morpheme, precedes the dialect noun (N.) representing a content morpheme (Italian in italics):

---

matrix language: dialect

| *il* ART. | lampiun N. |
| M:SING. | 'street lamp': M:SING |

According to Myers-Scotton, only the opposite case would be allowed, i.e. the system morpheme being part of the matrix language, here the dialect. Other combinations of 'codes' may pose similar problems. Consider for instance the following case of CS between Italian and English, which also contradicts Myers-Scotton's theory:

EXAMPLE 4

Code-switching in Canada (English in italics).

MA sono solo italiani *and* i ragazzi di qualche quando io sono arrivata qua
('there are only Italians *and* young people from somewhere when I came here')

(Canegrati 1996: 326)

The system morpheme *and* is used in isolation, but should be part of an embedded language island according to Myers-Scotton. The same applies to other examples in the same Canadian database.

In both cases, Myers-Scotton's assumption of better competence in the matrix language than in the embedded language is also problematic: these speakers have no better competence in the matrix language. Quite often, their competence is equal in both varieties, and sometimes even better in the embedded language. Especially in first case of Italian, where Italian and dialect intermingle in CS, the differences in competence and status of the languages are no longer unequivocal. Thus, Myers-Scotton's very elaborate model proves to be inapplicable in these cases (for more details see Canegrati 1996).

In more functional and interactive approaches, it is, on the other hand, difficult to decide for which functions CS is being used. Especially with intra-sentential CS, where two closely related varieties are used alternatingly (see example 3), the question often remains unsolved. Calling this kind of use code-mixing[15] does not present a satisfactory answer, as the basic problem remains: The speakers do use CS – but what do they do with it? What are the local conversational purposes?

Example 5 serves to illustrate these problems. It is part of a conversation among four 20- to 23-year-old speakers who are all second-generation Italian immigrants. It is also a particularly striking example of CS between Italian (and Italian dialects) and Swiss-German which is typical of the Swiss-German context described above.[16]

Two acquainted couples, who live in Zurich suburbs, discuss various kinds of cheese which are used for the preparation of the typically Swiss *fondue* and *raclette*. Italian elements, as far as they can be clearly distinguished, appear in italics.[17]

EXAMPLE 5

Code-switching in Switzerland: the cheese sequence (Italian in italics). P3, P6, P11 and P13 are abbreviations for the speakers involved.

---

1 P11   *perché* meinsch *che se tu ti mangi* emmentaler *o se tu ti mangi una fontina* isch au en unterschied, oder? schlussändlich *è sempre dentro lì però il gusto* isch andersch.
('*because*, you mean, *if you eat* Emmental cheese *or if you eat Fontina cheese*, there is also there is also a difference, isn't there? Actually, *it's still there, but the taste* is different')

2 P6   *è vero!*
('*that's right!*')

3 P11   du chasch . . . ich han so näs büächli
('you can . . . I have a booklet')

4 P6   *sì e poi qui c'è scritto quello che c'è dentro*
        (*'yes, and then there it is written what's in there'*)

5 P13 ja aber ebä, schlussändlich chunts nöd druffaa *uno gli piace forse
        di più* mitem appäzäller und der ander meh mitem tilsiter so meini
        ('yes, that's right, actually it doesn't matter, *some perhaps like it
        better* with Appenzell cheese and others like it better with Tilsit
        cheese, that's what I mean')

6 P3   ja, ja
        ('yes, yes')

7 P11 es git verschiedeni fondue aso die heisset verschiedä, aso ja das
        isch en himmelwiitä unterschied *se prendi questo o se prendi il*
        chäs normal.
        ('there are different kinds of Fondue, they have different names,
        well there's a huge difference *whether you take that one or whether
        you take the* ordinary cheese.')

8 P6   ehrlich! *beh*, zum biispil *io* raclettechäs *lo prendo sempre fresco.*
        raclettechäs hol ich immer im dings . . . äs git au im migros *così
        implasticato* gits au.
        ('really! well, for instance *me*, Raclette cheese *I always get it
        fresh*. Raclette cheese I always get at what's-its-name . . . they
        also have it at Migros, *wrapped in plastic* they have it, too.')

9 P11 ja guät *implasticato* machts nüüt, aber das isch ebä scho, s'gmisch
        isch ebä ich meinä das isch *congelato.*
        ('yeah, okay, *wrapped in plastic*, it doesn't matter, but that's the
        thing, the mixture is already I mean, it's *frozen* [pre-prepared,
        sic!]')

10 P6   ja im prinzip
        ('yes, basically')

11 P13 ah, isch das scho *congelato!*
        ('ah, it's already *frozen!*')

(Preziosa Di Quinzio 1992: x)

The alternations between the two varieties are functional not only with
respect to changes in participant constellation, turn-taking, topic change,
side remarks, or contrastive devices like topicalisation and reported speech.
In contrast to such functions – which I would label *strong functions* and
which are discussed in almost every study on CS (e.g. Auer 1995: 120) –
there are more subtle ones including almost free variation. We even have
to allow for the case in which CS has no function at all in the local conversational context.[18] Contrastive functions, for instance, are not entirely absent
in the above example.[19] But it is obvious that we are dealing with a type
of CS with diverse, for example, stylistic functions as well. For instance,
it is difficult to assign a function to the switch from Italian to Swiss-German
in the first turn of P13, '*uno gli piace forse di più* mitem appäzäller': after

the prepositional phrase, the turn continues in Swiss-German and no strong function is fulfilled by this CS (the possible contrasted elements, for example 'appäzäller' and 'tilsiter', both appear in Swiss-German). From an external, etic view, CS occurs between the article and the noun in the turn of the speaker P11 later on – '*il* chäs normal' (line 7) – as in the Monza example before. Again, it is difficult to assign a function to the switch. From an internal, emic point of view, grammatical and code boundaries are not treated as pertinent by the speaker. In the last four turns of the extract, we find a double coupled use of the Italian terms *implasticato–implasticato–congelato–congelato* which conveys stylistic functions: see '*implasticato*' ('wrapped in plastic') by P6, repeated by the next speaker P11, who parallels it with '*congelato*' ('frozen'), which, in turn, is repeated by speaker P13, all in a Swiss-German co-text.

In such cases, the global interactional behaviour is based throughout on CS. And it is with respect to these cases that we can say that CS has come to be used as a consistent code of its own, like another focused language, with all its possible variability.[20] The mixture behaves more like a unique code than like two different ones, and they are far from duelling. Or, to use Gardner-Chloros's terms: 'What others call a mixture is the given, the starting point' (1995: 69).

Taking these examples into account, we can broadly describe the phenomenon as a process of grammaticalisation of CS, in which germane and strong functions, which are due for instance to changes in situational contexts, form one end of a continuum, whereas subtle or weak functions are closer to the other end. The acquisition of CS seems to parallel this continuum from more clear-cut functions to more subtle ones.

Functions:
macrofunctions > microfunctions, differences in style > weak to no local function

Forms:
more frequent occurrence of code choice > intersentential CS > intra-sentential CS

When the expansion of CS has reached a maximum, constituting the last stage of the development, it includes the use of all functions on the left-hand side of the scale. In such cases, CS even more resembles a code in itself, a language of its own. In many societies, the development never reaches this end, however.

3 An integrated model of multilingual behaviour

3.1 CS as one possibility of multilingual behaviour

As mentioned at the beginning of this chapter, monolingual speakers represent a minority rather than the majority of the world's population in view of the basic human capability of using various languages and varieties side by side – be they structurally closely related or not (cf. Macha 1991). As a logical consequence, any linguistic theory should take this flexible, fluctuating behaviour as its point of departure, claiming variability as its basis. This should be even more radically postulated than it has been done so far by sociolinguists.[21]

Code-switching is one possible outcome of speakers' acting in a particular situation of language contact; others are, for example, pidgin and creole languages, or interlanguages.[22] But within this wide range of multilingual behaviour, CS in conversation calls into question in a more radical sense how boundaries between languages are established and to what degree they are treated as permeable by speakers. It raises the theoretical problem of what can be seen as a single code with regard to speakers' use.[23]

Of course, CS cannot be taken as a historical language in the sense of being passed on from generation to generation. In this respect, CS resembles interlanguages: both are produced anew in each sociocultural situation and are not stable in time. But in contrast to interlanguages, CS develops group norms and functions, and it expresses group identity. Furthermore, an L2 cannot be as easily distinguished in CS speech as in interlanguage use.

3.2 The linguistic system of a speaker: proposals for a model[24]

From an external point of view, a speaker uses several codes which are then subdivided by linguists into 'languages', 'varieties', 'idiolects', etc. But this does not necessarily parallel the speaker's perception. The linguistic system of a speaker consists of personal linguistic abilities, which have been acquired through interaction in the course of the individual's biography (Franceschini 1996c). In turn, forms of interactions are shaped by the history of societies.

'Languages' are thus formed by groups of speakers who use co-occurring linguistic features in the same way. This conformity is passed on as a tradition to the next generation. Hence, perceived differences between languages originate in speakers' similar linguistic behaviour. Consequently, vowels are regularly used in a certain sequence with particular consonants; sequences of phonemes are used in contrast to others in order to differentiate between categories such as definite versus indefinite, singular versus plural; the position of certain units is employed to create a contrast between foreground and background or between question and statement, etc.

In addition to this and along with other symbolic systems (posture, gesture, clothing, etc.), language serves to differentiate the speaker from others by marking the speaker's belonging to a certain group by means of a similar use of language. Hence, shaping linguistic differences also has an identity function (Gumperz 1982b, Le Page and Tabouret-Keller 1985). By the way we use certain co-occurring linguistic elements, we are able to perceive each other as members of a certain group: 'We create our "rules" so as to resemble as closely as possible those of the group or groups with which from time to time we wish to identify' (Le Page 1980: 15). Converging use of language creates confidence and cohesion, whereas diverging use tends to be ambivalent and dissociative and is easily associated with either 'personal' or 'foreign'.

Speakers have the option of moving around in their repertoire (broadly speaking, the sum of their codes) according to their competence, from more central, i.e. well known, to more peripheral, less fluent forms. A speaker's choice is regulated by his or her aims, interlocutors, biography and traditions, etc. (Franceschini 1996c). In the course of interchanges with other inter-locutors, such as parents, playmates, teachers, friends and superiors, as well as through the media, a speaker has learnt how to use codes. Furthermore, the speaker knows which values, for example values of identity, are trans-ported thereby. Using more or less cognitive effort, she or he can focus on one of the codes.

To put it differently, we can say that one is able to focus on any variety within one's repertoire, to shift one's focus of attention and to highlight other varieties. We use the term *focus of attention* in a weak analogy to its grammatical sense (e.g. sentence focus) to refer to the fact that the speaker has the ability, demonstrated by his or her interactional behaviour, to choose a section of his or her linguistic repertoire for a variable time-span to accom-plish speech activities.

A standard focus of attention can be illustrated as in Figure 3.2.

Any linguistic behaviour which focuses on a single, socially clearly recog-nisable variety corresponds to norms taught at school and thus to more prestigious usage. Many efforts are made in education to render the contours of what in this sense counts as a standard language as transparent as possible. In particular, a variety with the status of a national language has to be used unanimously and cohesively by the major part of the population. We will call this a *monofocus of attention*. It gives rise to monolingual production. This also implies that it represents the marked behaviour, that it is acquired by acculturation and imposed by norms even when it is in opposition to natural tendencies of the system.

By means of focusing, speakers can take on roles such as that of a learner trying to tackle a new language system or, moving towards more periph-eral abilities, the role of a dialect speaker who is deeply rooted locally, the role of a speaker showing off his or her proficiency in languages, the role

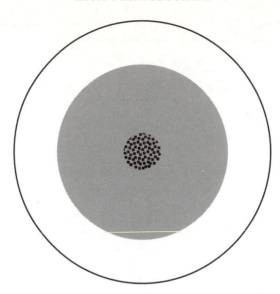

Figure 3.2 Case 1: Standard focus of attention

of a speaker behaving like a native speaker, etc. These roles are also used to convey identities. Speakers are more or less free to vary their roles, reflecting different footings with different interlocutors. In the course of an interaction, the focus can change several times, and speakers can take on various roles.[25] The speaker's focus is thus variable; it can be functionally controlled, it is socially distinguishable and it can be used by interacting individuals to create meaning in a particular social context.

In this framework, CS can be represented as a role a speaker chooses to take on, one role among others. Taking various communicative situations into account, an otherwise CS speaker can also take on the role of a mono-lingual speaker, monofocusing on, for example, Italian or German.[26]

In our model, CS can now be represented as a *dual focus*. In an inter-action, CS speakers use several varieties simultaneously, maintaining this dual focus for a longer period of time, e.g. for the duration of the whole conversation. In other words, a speaker 'can simply let down the mental barriers between the two languages at various different levels' (Gardner-Chloros 1995: 71) and treat them as one (Figure 3.3).[27]

We can specify the abilities of a CS speaker in the following way: (1) the ability to use the dual focus as if it were a unique focus; (2) the ability to maintain the dual focus for a longer time-span (short-term dual focus would result in brief insertions only); (3) the ability to quickly have the dual focus fade into other foci (flexible focusing, e.g. to a monofocus).

Intra-sentential CS is an example of an especially well-mastered dual focus. This also implies that the more a speaker uses CS, the more flexible

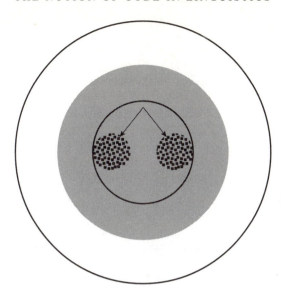

Figure 3.3 The bi-focus of a code switching speaker

and proficient she or he will be. Rare insertions would indicate a small range of CS available to the speaker and/or a low degree of social acceptance of this behaviour.

This framework makes considerable reference to normative aspects at the individual, group and macrosocial level.[28] A certain degree of social and political flexibility of norms at the macrosocial level is necessary for CS to come into being. For instance, the coexistence of several languages and varieties has to be appreciated socially instead of being fundamentally excluded or stigmatised.

The strong association of this framework with normative aspects further-more predicts that socially well-adjusted people do tend not to use CS; moreover, it suggests that CS is less likely to occur in situations of a more official and prestigious character (e.g. ceremonial addresses, speeches in general) and in written language. It also predicts that languages which are not standardised and which exist orally rather than in writing favour the use of CS. Furthermore, the framework predicts that in social situations in which speakers of different languages are hostile towards each other (for social or political reasons), CS is less easy. On the other hand, it pre-dicts that CS is a socially less stigmatised behaviour, even an unmarked choice, in situations where few cultural and identity differences are attrib-uted to varieties. This is for instance the case of Italian and dialect, but it also applies to those cases in which the acquisition of CS overrides the boundary of the original ethnic group (see the example of the shop assistant).

4 Conclusion

code-switching presumably existed in the 17th century as it
does today
Derek Bickerton, Roots of Language, 1981

CS has become a recognised phenomenon only since linguistic theory has
moved towards a pragmatic paradigm and oriented towards language use.
But similar to variability, CS still appears to be rather difficult to handle.
CS therefore reminds us of the need for a *theory of language use in interaction*. Unfortunately, the western European tradition in linguistics presents
an obstacle to the evolution of linguistics as a fundamentally multilingual
field: 'The assumption dominating linguistics continues to be one which
views as the normal or unmarked case the monolingual speaker in a homogeneous speech community' (Milroy and Muyskens 1995: 3). Let us
hypothesise for a moment the utopian idea that linguistics had been developed in Africa or in Pacific countries where multilingualism is more
self-evident: perhaps multilingualism would then have been seen as more
fundamental for the architecture of linguistic theory. And perhaps we could
then agree with the view that discreteness of languages is an oversimpli-
fied construction, to be 'recognised as a myth' (Tabouret-Keller 1995: 351,
with reference to Gardner-Chloros 1995).

Above all, we need to widen our horizons: *variation*, *languages in contact*,
flexibility and the *urge of individuals to differ from each other* could serve
as cornerstones. Within this interrelation of forces, linguistic functions are
developed which shape the platform of everyday interaction. The locally
accomplished interaction is therefore related to the historical evolution of
societies and to the ways in which they tackle the need for (linguistic) differentiation. Thus, CS transports social as well as linguistic information
(Eastman 1992: 1).

What concrete suggestions for future research can we offer? There is, for
instance, the diachronic dimension of CS, its relation to language changes
in individuals (a phase in language attrition?) and in groups and societies
(a step in the process of language loss, a force in language change?), which
has not yet been sufficiently studied. Furthermore, longitudinal studies of
various kinds are needed to look at the learnability of CS and the persis-
tence of its use by groups of speakers. Finally, variation and style of CS
within an individual as well as CS styles within and between groups could
be valuable subjects for future studies.

There is, of course, also a great need for more basic reflection which
would lead to insights into the principles of language use (see the attempts
for a 'unified theory' of CS formulated by Tabouret-Keller 1995). The use
of several different language systems and varieties side by side should no

longer be considered as an exception in the establishment of linguistic theories but as a central potentiality.

In this respect, the phenomenon of CS seems to be on an epistemological threshold, reflecting several facets of the dilemma of modern linguistics: a traditional, monolingually founded concept of *code* treats CS as a peripheral, 'new' phenomenon, but in fact CS displays the underlying linguistic and social flexibility of speakers in conversation.

Notes

1 See Alvarez-Cáccamo 1990 for a similar position.
2 We will not elaborate on the discussion of the literature here, nor on the very heterogeneous definitions. The following volumes and studies, for instance, have been of enormous importance: Blom and Gumperz 1972; Pfaff 1979; Sankoff and Poplack 1979; Poplack 1980; Gumperz 1982a, 1982b; Bentahila and Davies 1983, 1995; Auer 1984, 1995; Lüdi 1986, 1991; Clyne 1987; Heller 1988; Berruto 1990; ESF 1990a–c and 1991 in general; Gardner-Chloros 1991; Eastman 1992; Myers-Scotton 1993a, 1993b; and Milroy and Muyskens 1995.
3 We refer to the theoretical framework of functional–typological studies, cf. Dik 1981, 1989; Givón 1984/1990.
4 In our use, *norm* comprises implicit or explicit rules that speakers and communities refer to in their behaviour. Norms refer to habitual forms of action of groups of different kinds (a peer group, a family, or a professional group, a nation) and are subject to (more or less rapid) change. Permeability refers to the possibility for members to choose between norms, which presupposes that norms can be treated as open to others.
5 Common features of CS and pidgin languages are restricted to external, social factors; the internal systems of CS and pidgins are completely different. For instance, CS does not have a reduced number of vowels, restricted vocabulary and/or a smaller set of morphological possibilities as it is attributed to pidgin languages (cf. Mühlhäusler 1986; Arends, Muysken and Smith 1995) – quite the contrary: CS enormously multiplies the possibilities of expression.
6 It does not follow automatically from the officially multilingual status of Switzerland that Italian gains prestige (it is a national language, beside French, German and Romance). Outside of the Italian-speaking part of Switzerland, the prestige of Italian was negatively affected by its being largely used by immigrant workers.
7 We do not use the term *ethnic* in its biological sense, but in the sense of a self-attribution of identities (cf. Cavalli-Sforza, Menozzi and Piazza 1994).
8 Video recording, Zurich, Bäckerstrasse, December 1989. The range of variation of *italo-schwyz* consists of Swiss-German (i.e. the regional, generally used colloquial language in Switzerland, which in this case is the dialect of Zurich), Italian (mostly of south Italian regional hue) and, quite frequently, Italian dialects (very often southern). Sometimes, standard German is involved, too, and is then mostly used for single, isolated elements or in quotations.
9 Video recording, Zurich, Bäckerstrasse, December 1989, and individual observations.
10 Swiss-German in italics. The following transcription conventions are used:

–   short pause
(xxx)   unintelligible speech

[simultaneous talk
(hh)   laughter

11 In examples 1 and 2, the siblings exclusively use Italian varieties in their two-hour conversation, including some shifts between Italian and Venetian variety (cf. above, Fi: 'lo *ga votà*' and 'se *mi* se *mi*'). Both of them are also fluent in Swiss-German. In contrast to their mother, who freely uses CS at home and in informal situations, the daughter and son prefer a clear language choice. When their mother is not present they seem to speak Swiss-German. The linguistic behaviour of these three speakers could imply that CS had not been the primary code of communication between mother and children, but that it was acquired later on by the mother. Thus, the children, who exclusively use Italian at their parents' home, could be said to continue a pattern typical for the socialisation of Italian immigrants in the 1960s (cf. the 'threshold-multilingualism' mentioned above).

12 For first-generation speakers, CS is clearly not the most frequent linguistic behaviour. Their multilingual speech is characterised by brief insertions from (Swiss)-German into their Italian speech, such as designations of schools (e.g. Swiss-German *Sekundarschuel*, 'secondary school', *Bruefsschuel*, 'college of further education', occupations (e.g. *Putzfrau* 'charwoman', *Packer* 'packer', *Chauffeur* 'driver'), etc. (cf. Franceschini, Müller and Schmid 1984). Known as one of the phenomena of language contact (cf. Weinreich 1953) and often described in extensive taxonomies, which are restricted to single lexemes, these brief conversational insertions can also be regarded as a diachronic phenomenon preceding or even triggering CS. Thus, CS can be seen as a factor influencing the direction of language change (cf. Franceschini 1995 and 1996a).

13 In line with Rampton's observations (see Rampton 1991, 1995 and in this volume) and Hewitt 1986, schoolchildren in the area of Basel and Berlin were heard to sing Turkish songs outside school and use single Turkish words in their speech (personal communications by Rebekka Ehret and Peter Auer, 1995).

14 Cf. Berruto 1990; Alfonzetti 1992 and this volume; Sobrero 1992, 1994; and Giacalone Ramat 1995 with a wide-ranging bibliography on CS within Italian varieties.

15 Or *enunciati mistilingui*, in the sense of Berruto 1990.

16 Cf. Pizzolotto 1991 and Preziosa Di Quinzio 1992, as well as Lüdi 1986.

17 The data were collected in the suburbs of Zurich in January 1990 by Preziosa Di Quinzio (cf. Preziosa Di Quinzio 1992). The transcription of the data, which does not clearly represent overlapping turns, was only slightly changed.

18 Cf. in the same example : '*se prendi il* chäs normal' and '*così implasticato* gits au', among others.

19 An example of a clearly contrastive, topicalising function of CS in example 5 is '*io*, raclettechäs *lo prendo sempre fresco*', with left dislocation of the pronoun *io* and of the object *raclettechäs* in both Italian and Swiss-German.

20 Here, the term 'focused language' means a clearly recognised and institutionally supported language, enjoying prestige by being related to a commonly shared set of traditions and codification. Cf. in a similar sense Le Page 1980: 18 and Le Page and Tabouret-Keller 1985.

21 Even when assuming a sociolinguistic point of view, one may hold that whatever varies within a language is only a small part, the major part of the language being invariable. The concept of contextualisation cues has considerably widened the variable part of a language system however (for an introduction see Auer 1986, and Auer and di Luzio 1992).

22 For learner languages, language acquisition theories and pidginisation, see the introduction to Andersen 1983 as well as McLaughlin 1987.

23 To make it explicit, we use *code* as a superordinate term to designate each systematic co-occurrence of features that speakers use as a consistent vehicle of social behaviour. Thus, a *language* is a particular realisation of a code, used by a large group of speakers (highly focused when elevated to, for instance, a 'national language'). A variety is a subset of any code, variability being a pervasive characteristic of all codes.

24 This view is indebted to previous work on centre-periphery in a functionalist sense and on the notion of code; cf. Travaux linguistiques de Prague 1966; Labov 1971; Le Page 1992, 1994; and also Klein 1974; Dittmar and Klein 1979.

25 Theoretically, a speaker could maintain a single linguistic focus for his or her whole adult life, for instance a dialect variety. As proposed by this framework, this must be regarded as a marginal, highly exceptional case which presupposes interactants who precisely and continually share the same focus. It presupposes, too, isolation from external influences and probably also mental inflexibility. This hypothetical case is rightly put in a marginal place.

26 At the same time, varieties involved in CS are sometimes not completely mastered as isolated varieties by the speaker. This rather extraordinary case is that of the Swiss-German shop assistant discussed above.

27 The languages most likely to be focused by the speaker usually – or prototypically – tend to be situated in the centre of the speaker's system. A language learner producing CS has a dual focus where one language is somewhat more peripheral. For language learners who switch, see Lüdi 1991.

28 See also note 4.

Bibliography

Alfonzetti, G. (1992) *Il discorso bilingue*, Milano: Franco Angeli.

Alvarez-Cáccamo, C. (1990) 'Rethinking conversational code-switching: codes, speech varieties and contextualization', in *Proceedings of the 16th Annual Meeting of the Berkeley Linguistic Society*, Berkeley, Cal.: Berkeley Linguistic Society, 3–16.

Andersen, R. W. (ed.) (1983) *Pidginization and Creolization as Language Acquisition,* Rowley, Mass.: Newbury House.

Arends, J., Muysken, P. and Smith, N. (1995) *Pidgin and Creoles: An Introduction*, Amsterdam: Benjamins.

Auer, P. (1984) *Bilingual Conversation*, Amsterdam: Benjamins.

—— (1986) 'Kontexualisierung', *Studium Linguistik* 19: 22–47.

—— (1995) 'The pragmatics of code-switching: a sequential approach', in L. Milroy and P. Muyskens (eds) *One Speaker, Two Languages: Cross-Disciplinary Perspectives on Code-Switching*, Cambridge: Cambridge University Press, 115–35.

Auer, P. and di Luzio, A. (eds) (1984) *Interpretive Sociolinguistics*, Tübingen, Germany: Narr.

—— (1992) *The Contexualization of Language*, Amsterdam: Benjamins.

Bentahila, A. and Davies, E. E. (1983) 'The syntax of Arabic-French code-switching', *Lingua* 59: 301–30.

—— (1995) 'Patterns of code-switching and patterns of language contact', *Lingua* 96: 75–93.

Berruto, G. (1990) 'Italiano regionale, commutazione di codice e enunciati mistilingui', in A. M. Cortelazzo and M. A. Mioni (eds) *L'italiano regionale* (Atti del XVIII Congresso internazionale di Studi della Società di linguistica italiana), Rome: Bulzoni, 369–87.

Bickerton, D. (1981) *Roots of Language*, Ann Arbor, Mich.: Karoma.

Blom, J. P. and Gumperz, J. J. (1972) 'Social meaning in linguistic structures: code-switching in Norway', in J. J. Gumperz and D. Hymes (eds), *Directions in Sociolinguistics: The Ethnography of Communication*, New York: Holt, Rinehart and Winston, 407–34.

Canegrati, G. (1996) 'Code-switching a Toronto e a Monza: teorie e corpora a confronto', unpublished thesis, University of Bergamo.

Cavalli-Sforza, L. L., Menozzi, P. and Piazza, A. (1994) *The History of Human Genes*, Princeton, N.J.: Princeton University Press.

Clyne, M. (1987): 'Constraints on code-switching: how universal are they?', *Linguistics* 25: 734–69.

Dik, S. C. (1981) *Functional Grammar*, Dordrecht: Foris.

—— (1989) *The Theory of Functional Grammar*, Dordrecht: Foris.

Dittmar, N. and Klein, W. (1979) *Developing Grammars*, Berlin: Springer.

Eastman, C. M. (1992) *Codeswitching*, Clevedon: Multilingual Matters.

ESF (1990a) *ESF Network on Code-Switching and Language Contact: Papers for the Workshop on Concepts, Methodology and Data, Basle, 12–13 January 1990*, Strasbourg: European Science Foundation.

—— (1990b) *ESF Network on Code-Switching and Language Contact: Papers for the Workshop on Constraints, Conditions and Models, London, 27–29 September 1990*, Strasbourg: European Science Foundation.

—— (1990c) *ESF Network on Code-Switching and Language Contact: Papers for the Workshop on Impact and Consequences: Broader Considerations, Brussels, 22–24 November 1990*, Strasbourg: European Science Foundation.

—— (1991) *ESF Network on Code-Switching and Language Contact: Papers for the Symposium on Code-Switching in Bilingual Studies: Theory, Significance and Perspectives, Barcelona, 21–23 March 1991*, Strasbourg: European Science Foundation.

Franceschini, R. (1995) 'Sociolinguistica urbana e mutamento linguistico', *Linguistica e Filologia. Quaderni del dipartimento di linguistica e letterature comparate*, Bergamo, 1, n.s.: 187–208.

—— (1996a) (forthcoming) 'Modelli per lo spazio variazionale dell'italiano all'estero', *Italian Culture*.

—— (1996b) (forthcoming) 'Varianz innerhalb zweier Sprachsysteme: eine Handlungswahl?', in B. Henn-Memmesheimer (ed.) *Varianz als Ergebnis von Handlungswahl*, Tübingen: Narr.

—— (1996c) (forthcoming) 'Sprachbiographien randständiger Sprecher', in R. Franceschini (ed.) *Biographie und Interkulturalität: Diskurs und Lebenspraxis*, Augst (Akten des Symposiums in der Villa Castelen).

Franceschini, R., Müller, M. and Schmid, S. (1984) 'Comportamento linguistico e competenza dell'italiano in immigrati di seconda generazione: un 'indagine a Zurigo', *Rivista Italiana di Dialettologia* 8: 41–72.

Gardner-Chloros, P. (1991) *Language Selection and Switching in Strasbourg*, Oxford: Oxford University Press.

—— (1995) 'Code-switching in community, regional and national repertoires: the myth of the discreteness of linguistic systems', in L. Milroy and P. Muyskens (eds) *One Speaker, Two Languages: Cross-disciplinary Perspectives on Code-Switching*, Cambridge: Cambridge University Press, 68–89.

Giacalone Ramat, A. (1995) 'Code-switching in the context of dialect/standard language relations', in L. Milroy and P. Muyskens (eds) *One Speaker, Two Languages: Cross-Disciplinary Perspectives on Code-Switching*, Cambridge: Cambridge University Press, 45–67.

Givón, T. (1984/1990) *Syntax. A Functional Typological Introduction*, vols 1–2, Amsterdam: John Benjamins.

Grosjean, F. (1982) *Life With Two Languages. An Introduction to Bilingualism*, Cambridge, Mass./London: Harvard University Press.

Gumperz, J. J. (1982a) *Discourse Strategies*, Cambridge: Cambridge University Press.

—— (1982b) *Language and Social Identity*, Cambridge: Cambridge University Press.

Hewitt, R. (1986) *White Talk, Black Talk: Inter-Racial Friendship and Communication Among Adolescents*, Cambridge: Cambridge University Press.

Heller, M. (ed.) (1988) *Codeswitching: Anthropological and Sociolinguistic Perspectives*, Berlin: Mouton de Gruyter.

Klein, W. (1974) *Variation in der Sprache. Ein Verfahren zu ihrer Beschreibung*, Kronberg: Germany: Scriptor.

Labov, W. (1971) 'The notion of "system" in creole studies', in D. Hymes (ed.) *Pidginization and Creolization of Languages*, Cambridge: Cambridge University Press, 447–71.

Le Page, R. (1980) 'Projection, focussing, diffusion or steps towards a sociolinguistic theory of language', *York Papers in Linguistics* 9: 9–31.

—— (1992): ' "You can never tell where a word comes from": language contact in a diffuse setting', in E. H. Jahr (ed.) *Language Contact: Theoretical and Empirical Studies*, Berlin: Mouton de Gruyter, 71–101.

—— (1994) 'The notion of "linguistic system" revisited', *International Journal of the Sociology of Language* 109: 109–120.

Le Page, R. and Tabouret-Keller, A. (1985) *Acts of Identity*, Cambridge: Cambridge University Press.

Lüdi, G. (1986) 'Forms and functions of bilingual speech in pluricultural migrant comunities in Switzerland', in J. A. Fishman, A. Tabouret-Keller, M. Clyne *et al.* (eds): *The Fergussonian Impact, vol. 2: Sociolinguistics and the Sociology of Language*, Berlin: Mouton de Gruyter, 217–36.

—— (1991): 'Les apprenants d'une L2 code-switchent-ils, et, si oui, comment', in ESF, *Network on Code-Switching and Language Contact: Papers for the Symposium on Code-Switching in Bilingual Studies: Theory, Significance and Perspectives, Barcelona, 21–23 March 1991*, Strasbourg: European Science Foundation, 47–71.

Macha, J. (1991) *Der flexible Sprecher*, Köln: Böhlau.

McLaughlin, B. (1987) *Theories of Language Learning*, London: E. Arnold.

Milroy, L. and Muyskens, P. (eds) (1995) *One Speaker, Two Languages: Cross-Disciplinary Perspectives on Code-Switching*: Cambridge: Cambridge University Press.

Mühlhäusler, P. (1986) *Pidgin and Creole Linguistics*, Oxford: Basil Blackwell.

Myers-Scotton, C. (1993a) *Social Motivations for Codeswitching: Evidence from Africa*, Oxford: Clarendon Press.

—— (1993b) *Duelling Languages. Grammatical Structure in Codeswitching*, Oxford: Clarendon Press.

Pfaff, C. (1979) 'Constraints on language mixing: intrasentential code-switching and borrowing in Spanish/English', *Language* 55: 291–318.

Pizzolotto, G. (1991) *Bilinguismo ed emigrazione in Svizzera. Italiano e commutazione di codice in un gruppo di giovani*, Bern: Lang.

Poplack, S. (1980): ' "Sometimes I'll start a sentence in Spanish Y TERMINO EN ESPAÑOL": Toward a typology of code-switching', *Linguistics* 18: 581–618.

Preziosa Di Quinzio, I. (1992) ' "Teoreticamente la firma fa indietro". Frammistione di italiano e schwyzertütsch nella conversazione di figli di emigrati', unpublished M.Phil. thesis, University of Zurich.

Rampton, Ben (1991): 'Interracial Panjabi in a British adolescent peer group', *Language in Society* 20: 391–422.

—— (1995) *Crossing: Language and Ethnicity Among Adolescents*, London: Longman.

Sankoff, D. and Poplack, S. (1979) 'A formal grammar for code-switching', *Papers in Linguistics* 14, 1: 3–46.

Sobrero, A. (1994) 'Code-switching in dialectal communities in Italy', *Rivista di linguistica* 6, 1: 39–55.

—— (ed.) (1992) *Il dialetto nella conversazione: Richerche di dialettologia pragmatica*, Galatina: Congedo editore.

Tabouret-Keller, A. (1995) 'Conclusion: code-switching research as a theoretical challenge', in L. Milroy and P. Muyskens (eds) *One Speaker, Two Languages: Cross-disciplinary Perspectives on Code-Switching*, Cambridge: Cambridge University Press, 344–55.

Travaux linguistiques de Prague, 2 (1966), *Les problèmes du centre et de la périphérie du système de la langue*, Prague: Academia, Editions de l'Académie Tchécoslovaque des Sciences.

Weinrich, U. (1953) *Languages in Contact*, New York. Reprinted 1963: The Hague: Mouton.

INTRODUCTION TO CHAPTER 4

Peter Auer

While the previous chapters of this part of the book have argued from a more theoretical point of view, the following chapter provides ample evidence of the practical difficulties in establishing the 'codes' in 'code-switching'. The topic is 'code-switching' between French and Lingala or between French and Kiswahili in Zaire, particularly in Kinshasa. (Although the data investigated here have been collected among Zairian emigrés in Belgium, the migrant context, for which a detailed description may be found in Meeuwis 1997, is not directly relevant to the argument since the same type of bilingual conversations may be observed in Zaire as well.)

Frequent 'code-switching' between the former colonial language (e.g., English or French), which is now an exoglossic national language, and one of the African languages, is a widespread feature of verbal interaction in the urban centres of many African countries (see, in addition to Zaire, Blommaert 1992 for Tanzania or Haust 1995 for Gambia). This 'code-switching' is found in its most elaborate version among well-educated, urban elites, but the use of the exoglossic language has infiltrated everyday language to such a degree that bilingual elements can be found even among uneducated speakers. The difference is rather in the way in which the two languages are combined. It is natural that 'code-switching' of this type has received some attention by researchers on bilingualism; in fact, whole theories of bilingual interaction have been formulated on the basis of African materials (see Myers-Scotton 1993).

Yet it is also true that this 'code-switching' is only with difficulty subsumed under the usual definition of the 'alternating use of two or more languages', mainly because the presupposition of monolingual codes (and competences) underlying it is hard to make. In fact, and this is the main argument of Michael Meeuwis and Jan Blommaert's chapter, it is only in the eye of the European beholder that bilingual speech in Africa appears to be 'code-switching'. European ideologies of language lead us to look for the same relatively homogeneous, codified language systems we believe to exist in Europe, and which most linguists take as the sole object of study. These relatively homogeneous, codified language systems may be juxtaposed in code-switching in some extraordinary cases (cf. Franceschini's notes on the markedness of bilingual speech in the usual linguistic models, Chapter 3).

A less prejudiced picture is presented by the authors in the following chapter. In the Zairian case, what Meeuwis and Blommaert call a monolectal code-switching style is in itself the code; there are no underlying languages which have some independent interactional reality for a majority of the urban speakers of this 'code-switching code'. In the terminology of the Introduction, we would speak of a mixed code (which shows internal stylistic stratification related to the speaker's education).

In this context one must bear in mind that many of the larger languages of Central Africa (among them the four national languages of Zaire, which are used in addition to the de facto official language French, i.e. Tshiluba, Kiswahili, Kikongo and Lingala) do not have a long history but are the product of deliberate language policies, which started in colonial times and were geared toward superseding the enormous linguistic diversity in the Belgian Kongo (and elsewhere), where more than two hundred vernaculars seriously threatened vertical communication between state authorities and the masses of the people. (See Chapter 13 for another example in which colonialisation imposed a new linguistic superstructure on a formerly extremely diversified linguistic area, i.e. Papua New Guinea.) Thus, Lingala did not exist before the colonisation of the Kongo but was purposefully shaped and propagated by European settlers, missionaries and colonial administrators, and restructured by intermediaries on the basis of their own, partly very different languages (cf. Meeuwis 1997: 107). Its basis was Bobangi, a relatively small language originally spoken north of Kinshasa, but this language had to undergo considerable changes in order to be suitable for use as a lingua franca. For the colonial power, the advantage of an African lingua franca was that French could be reserved for 'horizontal' communication between the elites, while Lingala could be used in 'vertical' communication with the masses. Lingala gained prestige and spread further through its usage within the army and, after independence, through its association with the capital and the politics of President Mobutu (who, however, made no attempt to have Lingala replace French as the national language).

Similarly, Kiswahili was not always present in all of the Belgian Congo but was artificially introduced in certain places by colonizers, again for purposes of vertical communication, but later also adopted by the Congolese as a lingua franca for horizontal communication among themselves.

It is not hard to see that in the given context (with French as the elitist variety, and the vernacular languages usually as the 'home variety') the loyalty towards a 'pure' and homogeneous form of Lingala or Kiswahili is low. This state of affairs certainly supported the emergence of mixed codes as described in this chapter.

Note, however, that classifying the bilingual speech of urban speakers in Zaire as a mixed code does not preclude the possibility of code-switching of the functional kind between this mixed code and another code, as described by Meeuwis and Blommaert in their analysis of alternation between Lingala/French and Kiswahili/French mixing. It is also possible (as we shall see in Chapters 5 and 6) that the same pair of languages is involved in a mixed code and in code-switching.

Bibliography

Blommaert, Jan (1992) 'Codeswitching and the exclusivity of social identities: some data from Campus Kiswahili', *Journal of Multilingual and Multicultural Development* 13, 1 and 2: 57–70.

Haust, Delia (1995) *Codeswitching in Gambia*, Cologne: R. Köppe.

Meeuwis, Michael (1997) 'Constructing sociolinguistic consensus: A linguistic ethnography of the Zairian community in Antwerp, Belgium', Ph.D. thesis, University of Antwerp.

Myers-Scotton, Carol (1993) *Social Motivations of Codeswitching: Evidence from Africa*, Oxford: Clarendon Press.

4

A MONOLECTAL VIEW OF CODE-SWITCHING

Layered code-switching among Zairians in Belgium

Michael Meeuwis and Jan Blommaert

1 Introduction

It is common practice to discuss code-switching as a phenomenon which operates against the background of full bilingualism and, hence, as a phenomenon emerging out of the alternation of linguistic material stemming from two (or more) closed, fixed languages or grammatical systems that are fully known to the speakers who perform code-switching. To give one example, Lehiste's definition of code-switching in her *Lectures on Language Contact* runs as follows: 'a *perfect* bilingual may switch from language to language during a conversation. This phenomenon is called code switching' (1988: 2; emphasis added). Within this view of code-switching as based on full bilingualism, code-switching is commonly approached in terms of 'languages', and the term 'code' in code-switching is the conventional equivalent of 'language'. For instance, Myers-Scotton's ambitious attempt at theorising code-switching, which starts from the catchword-definition of code-switching as 'duelling languages' (the title of her 1993a book), defines the phenomenon as involving 'the use of two or more languages in the same conversation', and further characterises it as 'juxtaposed multiple-language production' (1993b: vii).[1]

The purpose of this chapter is to question this frame of reference and replace it by what we call 'a monolectal view of code-switching'. In this monolectal view, the overall code-switched variant used by speakers is not seen as a product of blending between two or more languages (with its implication of full knowledge of those languages), but as *one code in its own right*. Instead of a split object, a monolectal view allows us to see code-switched speech as a system that operates very much on its own and with a dynamics of its own.

76

This particular dynamics will be illustrated by means of an ethnographic study of 'layered code-switching' among Zairian immigrants in Belgium. Layered code-switching can best be described as 'code-switching within code-switching': different forms and types of code-switching are themselves the object of alternation in one and the same conversational environment. We will argue that in layered code-switching, the alternation of 'languages', as understood from the linguist's perspective, is of little explanatory value, and more attention should be given to forms of linguistic and pragmatic variability *within* code-switched speech, such as style, variety, or even perceived 'quality' of the linguistic material. In terms of sociolinguistic explanation, we will try to demonstrate how these phenomena operate within the universe of a conversation and how the conversational structure generates a number of specific phenomena.

In section 2, we will briefly discuss some of the widespread and deeply embedded views of code-switching as connected to bilingualism and to languages-as-codes. Next, in section 3, we will situate the theoretical and methodological features of our own proposal for a monolectal view. In section 4, we will substantiate this proposal on the basis of empirical analyses of code-switching among Zairian immigrants in Belgium, and discuss the issue of layered code-switching. In section 5, finally, we will summarise our argument and discuss some implications.

2 Problems with languages-as-codes

Treatments of code-switching often start from a perspective in which code-switching is seen as the virtuose alternation of material from two distinct languages, and in which these languages are equivalent to the 'codes' that are 'switched'. There is a whole set of sociolinguistic implications buried in that view: it is implied that these languages are also available and accessible to the speakers in that particular society, and that the code-switching speakers actually 'know' these languages. In this mode of thought, the question as to what particular linguistic knowledge is involved is as a rule evaded, and notions of 'knowledge of language' are highly idealised. Our discussion in the following sections will show that code-switching speakers are not necessarily speakers who would be capable of producing monolingual speech in the languages used in code-switching. From an empirical point of view, a simple connection between code-switching and bilingualism rests on shaky grounds.

The fact that code-switching is commonly anchored in discussions of bilingualism, and seen as conditioned by it, is amply documented in Myers-Scotton's (1993b) *Social Motivations for Codeswitching* (see also Meeuwis 1994; Meeuwis and Blommaert 1994). Myers-Scotton's book, which aims at providing an overall theory of code-switching, starts with a clustering of all the elements we have mentioned so far, and adding another, the 'nation'.

> Everyday conversations in two languages are the subject-matter of this volume. All over the world bilinguals carry on such conversations ... in every nation, successful business people and professionals who happen to have a different home language from the language dominant in the society where they live frequently engage in codeswitching (between these two languages) with friends and business associates who share their linguistic repertoires.
>
> (Myers-Scotton 1993b: 1)

Code-switching is here pictured as an ingredient of mature bilingualism, situated within the sociopolitical space of a 'nation' (usually understood as an equivalent of a 'state').[2]

In discussions such as these, terminologies are slippery and elusive. What does one mean by 'having' a language? When is a language actually qualified as 'a language'? By whom? Myers-Scotton's simple and undoubtedly innocent statement shows how such basic sociolinguistic and pragmatic questions are evaded, their answers taken for granted, and how the arguments sustaining them usually boil down to appealing but unwarranted common-sense reasoning. This common-sense reasoning displays a number of strong ideological biases and idealisations, which deserve to be brought to the surface.

First, the linguistic phenomena discussed as 'languages' are seen as conventional and institutional. They are languages in the textbook sense: things with an identifiable name such as French, English, Swahili, Punjabi, Spanish, Yiddish. The units of discussing sociolinguistic variability are the nation (-state) and its language(s). When a nation(-state) has more than one language – an observation which in itself may hide a tremendous amount of complexity and variability – the nation is bilingual or multilingual. Its speakers are then monolinguals, bilinguals, or multilinguals, depending on the way in which they build their own linguistic repertoires. When they are bi- or multilingual, they are assumed to be able to speak different languages and, occasionally, engage in code-switching between various of those languages.

Second, the norm, or the zero-point of reference, is monolingualism. In Myers-Scotton's example of the successful business people, these business people have a different 'home language' – a concept which should presumably be interpreted as *the* only language one speaks at home. This language is different from *the* dominant language of their society/nation. The background norm is that speakers use one language in each distinct situation or context type; code-switching, then, is merely derived from this situation, but it is never accepted as the starting point of members' multilingual behaviour (see also Meeuwis 1994). Hence, Myers-Scotton's basic question reads: 'what do bilingual speakers *gain* by conducting a conversation in two languages (i.e. through codeswitching) rather than *simply* using one language throughout?' (1993b: 3; emphasis added).

The underlying reasoning pattern runs as follows: since speakers are bilingual and could therefore have monolingual conversations in two discrete languages, why do they resort to code-switching? Not only the question, but Myers-Scotton's answer as well, starts from a monolingual point of reference. She develops a 'markedness model', in which each of the different languages used in code-switching is attributed a 'Rights and Obligations set' (RO set) and is taken to be indexical of a discrete social identity. Monolingual speech signals membership of one identity category; code-switching, then, signals dual or multiple membership. In this manner, Myers-Scotton's analyses become a discourse full of equations: English is 'the language of social mobility', Shona or Swahili is 'the language of nationalism', etc. Both may be combined strategically in a social identity game, *as long as speakers know these languages*. That is, they have to know them in order to be able to use their conventionalised RO sets. So when young Zimbabweans or Kenyans revert to code-switching, full bilingualism is imposed onto them as a prerequisite for knowing how to handle the symbolic load of each of the languages they 'have':

> The young men in [Zimbabwe] and [Kenya] are not satisfied with *either* the identity associated with speaking English alone *or* that associated with speaking Shona or Swahili alone when they converse with each other. Rather, they see the rewards in indexing both identities for themselves. They solve the problem of making a choice by evolving a pattern of switching between the two languages.
> (Myers-Scotton 1993b: 122; emphasis in original)

This view carries a variety of theoretical and empirical problems, more fully discussed in Meeuwis and Blommaert (1994). Suffice it to state here that the suggestion that code-switching speakers would be equally capable of having their 'mixed' conversation in a pure variant of each of the languages they use in their code-switched speech can certainly not be accepted at face value. There are sufficient findings, some of which will be discussed below, that indicate that 'knowledge' of a pure, canonised variety of a language may require some rethinking when it comes to assessing the background of some code-switching speakers. Second, and partially connected to the previous observation, it can also be noted that variability and its connection to indexicality seem to stop at the level of 'languages'. Apparently, what counts in Myers-Scotton's examples is the difference between English and Shona or Swahili. We hear nothing about *what particular varieties* of English, Swahili or Shona are being used, nothing about intralanguage dialectal or stylistic variation, about accents, intonation, conversational structuring, and other proved sense-making pragmatic variables. We hear nothing about more specific identities, about artistic or intellectual speech, about 'strong' or 'weak' language, and so on. And third, it appears as if identity negotiation is the only or at least the most important function of code-switching.

It probably does not require a long exposé to argue that this view, to the extent that it aims at providing an overall theory of code-switching, only accounts for very limited and very specific instances of code-switching (and for those cases, Myers-Scotton's model is certainly valuable). Furthermore, it contains gross idealisations of the sociolinguistic environments in which code-switching appears, stressing – implicitly – the availability and accessibility of linguistic resources to speakers in an apparently bucolic bilingual speech community.[3] In this view, the speakers are rational and calculating actors, who select strategically from a (unspecified and untheorised) range of choices the most appropriate option for the accomplishment of their aims. The range of choices consists of languages, linearly connected to identities via RO sets. These associations between languages and identities have been conventionalised through a (again, rather unspecified) socialisation process, and speakers are aware of them. Code-switching is seen in terms of a combination of monolingual repertoires and competences, and it is judged to bring a semantic and sociopragmatic surplus value to speech behaviour.

3 A monolectal view of code-switching

Let us now contrast this view with a monolectal view of code-switching, and start by spelling out some points that are basic to our proposal. A first point is that code-switched speech can be, for all practical purposes, *one variety of its own*, unconnected to and unconditioned by the full knowledge of two separate languages (i.e. unconnected and unconditioned by conventional notions of bilingualism). The Lingala–French code-switched speech which we will discuss in section 4 operates in very much the same way, under the same constraints, and with the same functions and effects as those usually attributed to 'languages'. Appropriating conventional discourse for the time being, we could say that in this context code-switched speech can be seen as a language in its own right.

This has implications for the notion of 'code'. It is clear that the shift of the analyst's attention away from languages to a wider and more sophisticated set of linguistic varieties is inspired by an urge to include the speaker's view in considerations of 'code' and the way in which codes carry meanings, for 'what looks like a linguistic code for the linguist may not count as a communicative code for conversationalists' (Alvarez-Cáccamo 1990: 11). In the eyes of many users of Lingala–French code-switched speech, the 'code' (i.e. the medium and source of meaning and social indexicality) is exactly that: code-switched speech. Speaking 'Lingala' is equal to producing speech in which abundant code-switching with French appears. A similar argument is made by Swigart (1992: 92ff.) with respect to Urban Wolof, a variety of Wolof containing profuse Wolof–French code-switching and spoken by city-dwellers in Dakar, Senegal. Swigart predicts 'that Urban Wolof, despite the campaigns of certain "purists", will become the native language model of many Dakar children in years to come' (1992: 100). In other words, a situation emerges in which speakers become monolingual in a mixed code.

An analytical consequence of this point is that more and other linguistic and pragmatic phenomena become relevant in the analysis of code-switching. Differences between 'languages' (in the conventional, linguist's sense of the term) may be less salient than differences between *varieties* of languages such as dialects or sociolects, speech styles, specific lexical choices, syntactic patterns, accents, and so on. As a rule of thumb, one could say that all the phenomena which ethnographers, conversation analysts, interactional socio-linguists, Goffmanian symbolic interactionists and others have identified as potentially meaningful elements of communication structure can and do appear as meaningful elements of the structure of communication in code-switched speech. Thus, the analytical reorientation is away from the contrastive role of 'languages' in discourse-structuring to a wider range of pragmatic variables. This is not to say that language contrast would play *no* role in discourse structuring in code-switched speech, for example in marking emphasis, topic, and so on (see de Rooij 1996; Blommaert and Gysels 1990). Nor does it imply that language contrasts could *never* be used in Myers-Scotton's sense as instruments of identity marking and social exclusion. It is just that the range of potential devices in code-switching is much wider, and the kind of dynamics described by Myers-Scotton represents *one particular* way of using code-switching (cf. Swigart 1992: 87; see also Blommaert 1992).[4]

A second point, derived from the first one, is that monolectal code-switching is not necessarily a 'marked' or 'special' way of speaking, with particular functions and effects which make it different or more effective than monolingual speech. In certain speech communities, code-switching is the rule, the default way of speaking; monolingual language use is marked and is perceived by members as special, artificial, or even unintelligible speech. Consequently, not every switch requires a functional explanation, and not every speech event in which people perform code-switching should be seen as a negotiation of identities. Code-switched varieties are often used in a 'relaxed' way, and for purposes – if any – that have more to do with speech elaboration, a desire to speak nicely or artistically, to create humorous effects, and so on (see, for example, Fabian 1982; Woolard 1987; Shields-Brodber 1992). Putting the analysis of code-switching on a track of abnormality, aberrance, and special effects (as in many code-switching studies) may obscure potentially very informative areas of exploration into what code-switching does in discourse and in the society at large.

Analytically, this point may open up a number of ways to reassess the speech repertoires and speech economies of some societies. General sociolinguistic profiles of societies and countries are usually sketched on the basis of 'languages' (at best extended to the domain of 'dialects', i.e. geographical varieties). The distribution of 'languages' is then described in horizontal and vertical patterns which preferably display some clarity and elegance, and which often start from the assumption that one language is associated with one social layer, ethnic category, or (Fishmanian) domain. The problem is that such associations do not necessarily reflect the actual language usage of speakers, and that the unit of 'a language' is not always the sole salient and relevant sociolinguistic unit for the speakers. Linguistic encyclopaedias, atlases, and classifications therefore give us very few clues as to what speech patterns we are actually likely to encounter in the societies they attempt to describe, as their exclusive focus on 'languages' obscures or marginalises an intricate set of 'crossover' phenomena, i.e. mixed, 'impure', and substandard phenomena which may take more crucial places in the speech repertoires and economies of speakers than the 'languages'.[5]

These two points should bring us to a position from which we can more fruitfully analyse particular cases of code-switching. One such case is layered code-switching, i.e. code-switching within code-switching among Zairians in Belgium.

4 Layered code-switching among Zairian immigrants in Belgium

4.1 Linguistic markets in Zaire and in Belgium

Zaire's official language, i.e. the language used in Parliament and in all written legislation, is French. Traditional taxonomies, such as the *Atlas Linguistique du Zaïre* (ALAC 1983), mention 212 African languages spoken in Zaire. Four of these, namely Kikongo, Lingala, Swahili, and Tshiluba, qualify as Zaire's most important languages of wider distribution, in that, as secondly acquired languages but also as mother tongues, they are more widely known and used than any other language in their respective geographical areas of expansion. The areas of expansion look as follows: Kikongo is spoken in the south-western regions, Lingala in the capital Kinshasa and in the western and northern regions, Swahili in the entire eastern section, and Tshiluba in the south-central parts. Zairian laws and official regulations on the language(s) to be used in contexts such as education and jurisdiction are exclusively framed around the opposition between the official language French, on the one hand, and all of Zaire's African languages (called 'national languages', *langues nationales*) on the other, without mentioning the particular African language to be used (Ngalasso 1986; Matumele 1987; Boguo 1988; Sesep 1988). Nevertheless, when African languages may or need to be chosen instead of French (which is the case in the lower and local courts and in the first grades of primary education), preference is mostly given to Kikongo, Lingala, Swahili, and Tshiluba. (This actual practice originates from historical patterns of consuetude and from the *fait accompli* of the four languages' wider spread.) In some contexts, the term *langues nationales* is therefore at times attributed a more restricted meaning, denoting Kikongo, Lingala, Swahili, and Tshiluba *as distinct from* all the other African languages – a terminological frame we also adopt in this chapter.

The relationship between the four national languages in Zaire is only ideally a geographically 'coordinate' one. In addition to their geographical distribution over discrete areas of expansion, there are contexts in which the four national languages actually come into contact with each other. The languages meet, for instance, through the dominance of Lingala in the Zairian army, in Zairian politics, in Zairian music, and in the capital, Kinshasa (see the contributions to Kazadi and Nyembwe 1987). Lingala is used as the medium of communication in the Zairian army throughout the entire territory; it was resorted to by President Mobutu and his officials for the vulgarisation (in public speeches and otherwise) of state politics, decisions, and doctrine (themselves all conceived in French), and is the language in which almost all popular modern Zairian music is composed. For these three factors, Lingala reaches parts of the country outside its own area of expansion and operates, in those parts, alongside (and not in competition with) the other languages.[6] There is also the important role of the capital, Kinshasa, where all of the national services and institutions are centralised. Kinshasa is a typical locus where Zairians from all parts of the country come together, and is thus another context in which Lingala (Kinshasa's dominant language) is complemented with other Zairian languages.

The latter factor is particularly relevant to the Zairian immigrant situation in Belgium (see also Meeuwis 1997). More than Kinshasa and, evidently, more than any other context in Zaire, the immigrant situation in Belgium involves an environment in which Zairians of different regional origins come to live and work together. The possibility of having more than one of the four national languages in one and the same social environment is thus considerably enhanced in Belgium. Since 1991, ethnographic research has been conducted on these and related sociolinguistic issues, both in Zaire and among Zairians in Belgium. This research has particularly been concerned with the relationship between Lingala-speaking and Swahili-speaking Zairians, and Lingala and Swahili are also the main languages dealt with in this chapter. This investigation has revealed that the linguistic market of Zairians in Belgium is to a considerable extent dominated by Lingala (spelled out in Meeuwis 1997; see also Brisard and Meeuwis 1994 for a succinct description). This is partly due to the fact that, given the importance of Lingala in Zaire, the knowledge of Lingala is more widespread among Swahili-speakers than vice versa, and that most Zairian immigrants in Belgium spent an important part of their lives in Kinshasa, a Lingala-dominated city. Very often in Belgium, Lingala, and not French, serves the purpose of communication between Zairians of different regional origins. It is not uncommon in Belgium that an interaction involving a majority of Swahili-speakers and one Lingala-speaker is conducted in Lingala. Within this Lingala-dominated linguistic market, however, there is a secondary linguistic market. Swahili is not only a *possible*, but also an *obligatory* language for ingroup interaction among eastern Zairians, and it is *exclusively reserved* for this type of interaction.

This factor is particularly relevant to the issue of layered code-switching. The scene for that discussion, however, needs to be set by means of a consideration of monolectal code-switching.

4.2 Monolectal code-switching

For many Zairians who were born and raised in urban contexts, the national language of the region is, in actual practice, (one of) the mother tongue(s). But the 'language' these children acquire is from the start a variant marked by profuse code-switching: it is replete with French words and structures and the children do not receive it in its 'pure' variety (Hulstaert and De Boeck 1940; Hulstaert 1953; Kitengye *et al.* 1987; Mayaka 1987). To put it roughly, the only form in which the national languages exist is as code-switched languages. The very few occasions on which 'pure' Lingala, Swahili, etc. occur are some religious services, where the language used is often a legacy of European missionary linguists and their purist campaigns,[7] and some forms of radio and television broadcasting, where the old missionaries' purifications are also adopted as – local – standards. To Zairians, the languages used in both these contexts come across as artificial, highly marked, and, what is more, as nearly unintelligible (cf. Meeuwis 1997). In fact, it is telling that the daily TV newscast in ('pure') national languages does not appeal to and is not understood by many lay Zairians (a point also made in Kazadi 1987: 289). In general, code-switching between the four languages and French is the norm and occurs at all levels, from the language of uneducated youngsters in the streets, over the most intimate contexts at home, to the language use of intellectuals and politicians in official contexts. Even public speeches in Lingala by President Mobutu were characterised by a high degree of code-switching.

It is necessary to stress that, although fossilised and integrated borrowings exist, these crossover codes consist mainly of 'code-switching' in the technical sense, and not of 'loanwords' or 'interference'. The bulk of French words, phrases, structures, etc. are not integrated and/or do not replace their African equivalents at a general level.[8] In different situational contexts, the French elements are readily replaced by African equivalents, and vice versa.

The pervasiveness of code-switching with French is related to the distribution of the knowledge of French. In this respect, the most diverging reports exist. On the one hand, Bokamba (1976: 128) writes that 'less than 10% of the Zaïrian population speak French' and Mutombo (1991: 104) says about French that 'seule une infime portion de la population [constitue] la réserve de ses locuteurs'. Kilanga and Bwanga (1988: 48), on the other hand, maintain that 'il devient difficile à l'heure actuelle de proposer pour le contexte zaïrois une classification pyramidale où seule [sic] le sommet serait le détenteur exclusif de cette langue'. The problem is related to the fact that it is very difficult, if not impossible, to describe the knowledge of French in Zaire in discriminatory terms, establishing either the *absence* or the *presence* of proficiency in French for a given individual. Kilanga and Bwanga (1988) and Ngalasso (1988) convincingly refine this argument, suggesting that the matter should rather be framed in terms of a continuum of proficiency degrees, whereby it is accepted that French is, to some degree or another, known by all members of society, from the most highly educated to the less instructed ones, and in all parts of the country, from the highly urban to the most rural areas. The question is not *whether* a certain proficiency in French can be detected, but rather what level of 'quality' this proficiency attains. The 'quality' is largely a function of formal education, access to which is extremely differential over the several social layers. It can also be noted, at a more general level, that in many discussions of code-switching involving English or French in Third World countries, the issue of indigenised varieties of English and French is rarely touched upon. The varieties observed are often, also in the transcripts of data, reduced to the ideal, metropolitan varieties of these languages.

At one extreme of the proficiency continuum are the members of the small intellectual elite, who have been able to continue their formal instruction to university or other higher levels of education. Their proficiency in French is impeccable, including a more than ordinary eloquence and literary capacities in both indigenised and Ile-de-France varieties of French. The members of this elite exhibit and maintain their sophisticated knowledge of French in their professional environments, which are typically the higher levels of the political, administrative, and academic institutions. At the other extreme of the proficiency continuum, we find the class of the completely unschooled. The ubiquity of French in Zairian society, through its use on radio and television, in public advertising, in official documents, and in the speech of others, which includes code-switching, makes sure that even for the uninstructed, some input of the language is unavoidable. As such, *some* knowledge of French is displayed by these illiterate members of society, too. Needless to say, this knowledge is very limited; mostly it does not transcend the oral production of some words, expressions, and phrases (Ngalasso 1988: 109), and displays a range of (phonetic, syntactic, and lexical-semantic) forms of indigenisation.

As a consequence, the mere *use of* French within speech in a Zairian African language does not constitute the relevant parameter in code-switching with French. It is a nonce-issue for members to socially contrast proficiency in French to the complete lack of such proficiency. Moreover, since all applications of the national languages contain *some* French, the sheer lack of French proficiency is never manifested and can thus not be used as a point of reference by the elite.

What, then, is the significant contrast in code-switching? The code-switched speech must not be seen as a juxtaposition of linguistic elements drawn from two (or more) different 'languages', but as a single and autonomously existing code-switched code. Lingala–French and Swahili–French are all fully-fledged 'languages' in their own right. These 'languages' have their own 'vertical' range of social, stylistic, register-related, and other variants. It is these vertical variants, differentiated on the basis of qualitative criteria such as lexical range, degrees of stylistic elaboration, and so on, which make up the crucial points of reference in the use of code-switched speech.

Let us illustrate this by comparing example 1 with example 2. Example 1 involves Lingala–French code-switching between two graduate students; one of them (A) is a middle-aged man from eastern Zaire and the other (B), who is about the same age, is from north-western Zaire. They are in a car, driving through Brussels on their way to the Zairian embassy, and they are making comments on a mutual friend, Marcel (all names are pseudonyms), who lives together with Stéphane and his wife. Example 2 is also an instance of Lingala–French code-switched speech. Here, three young women from Kinshasa, none of whom has had the opportunity to continue formal education beyond the age of 16, are talking about Paul. Paul was involved in a deal with Nigerians in Brussels before he fled to Zaire with the profits of the deal, leaving his child and wife Mireille behind. Speaker A is upset about the fact that Mireille is still hanging on to Paul.

In these and the subsequent example 3, italics are used for Lingala, French is in bold print, and Swahili is in small capitals.[9]

EXAMPLE 1

---

1 A Stéphane *atéléphoner lobi te*?
   ('Stéphane didn't call yesterday?')
2 B *ngai moto natéléphoner. natéléphonaki na tongo.*
   ('I am the one who called. I called this morning.')
3 A *ye Marcel? azalaki na ndako*?
   ('what about Marcel? was he at home?')
4 B *azalaki na ndako.* (.) **là je ne le comprends plus. il a des problèmes mais il ne fait pas un effort** *po alongwa. a***sedétacher. il aura encore plus d'ennuis**, hein?

('he was at home. (.) that's where I don't understand him anymore. he has problems but he's making no effort to leave. to break away. he's going to have even more problems, isn't he?')

5 A **oui oui, il va en avoir beaucoup plus**.
('oh yes, he's going to have a lot more.')

6 B hein?
('don't you think?')

7 A **il va en avoir beaucoup plus**.
('he's going to have a lot more.')

8 B *asili ye- sik'oyo baini ye* **déjà** *na ndako wana*.
('he's finished- now they already hate him in that house.')

9 A **surtout que** *a*réussir. (.) *esepelisi bango te*, hein?
('especially as he's succeeded [in school]. (.) that doesn't please them, does it?')

10 B *esepelisi bango te. azwi* **bourse**. **et puis** *alongi, azwi, a*réussir *na chick*. **facteur** *ya* **jalousie** *eza na (yango wana)*.
('it doesn't please them. he got a scholarship. and then he's succeeded, he's passed, he's come through in school. there's some jealousy in (that matter).')

11 A **oui oui**.
('oh yes.')

12 B *po na ba*aigris. **parce que moi je peux pas jalouser**. *nakoki kojalouser te epai ya moto* **parce que** (.) *ye azwi. moto na moto aza na ba*capacités *na ye*. (.) **quand tu as négligé les études tu n'as qu'à t'en prendre contre toi-même**. (.) hein?
('as to the embittered. because as far as I'm concerned I can't be jealous. I can't be jealous of someone because (.) s/he's succeeded. each person has his/her capacities. (.) if you've neglected your studies, you only have yourself to blame. (.) isn't that so?')

EXAMPLE 2

1 A *ata* **un franc** *ya kotikela* Mireille. Mireille *aboti mwana. akei ndenge wana. boongo mobali ya ndenge wana nakende kokanisa ye ndenge nini? nakanisa ye na eloko nini. nabosani yo na* **vie** *na ngai, esili. mwana na ngai* **cadeau**, **où est le problème**?
('he [Paul] didn't even leave one franc for Mireille. Mireille got a baby. he just disappeared like that. well then a guy like that, how should I [generic] even think of him? what could remind me of him. I forget you [generic] for [the rest of] my life, and that's it. my child [I simply reconsider it as] a gift, what's the problem?')

2 B *akimaki na mbongo ya mwindo*?
('he really stole the money and ran?')

3 C *ee* [laughs]
    ('yes')
4 B *ya banani?*
    ('whose [money]?')
5 A *ya =ba**Nigériens** moko=*
    ('of =certain Nigerians=')
6 C *=ba**Nigériens**=* [laughs]
    ('=Nigerians=')
7 A *mosusu kutu akufaka.*
    ('one of them actually died.')
8 B *=**Nigérien**?=*
    ('=a Nigerian?=')
9 A *=**Nigérien** wana akufa= likolo ya **souci** wana.*
    ('=that Nigerian died= from those worries.')

In both examples 1 and 2, Lingala–French code-switched speech is used. Rather than considering this code-switched speech as a conversational mingling of two different 'languages', it can be regarded as the manifestation of one linguistic code – indeed, 'a language' in its own right. This 'language', as any other, has different sociolects. In the case of the contrast between examples 1 and 2, three features characterising the range of sociolects may be distinguished. First of all, at the level of sheer density we notice that in the intellectuals' speech (example 1), there is 'more' French. The two students also use French in contexts where the three women simply do not, for example the use of *oui* instead of the Lingala *ee* for 'yes' (lines 5 and 11 in example 1 and line 3 in example 2). Second, the French in (1) is much more 'sophisticated'. Terms, phrases, and expressions such as *se détacher, jalouser, aigris* and *tu n'as qu'à t'en prendre contre toi-même*, as well as the usage of complete French sentences such as in lines 4 and 12, are phenomena which would occur rarely in the code-switched language illustrated in example 2. In that sequence, the inserted French speech is limited to words and phrases (*un franc, cadeau, vie, souci*, etc.) that can be picked up in the streets and from the French speech of others, but the knowledge of which is not conditioned by an advanced level of formal education.

Third, the code-switching in example 1 displays a much higher level of structural pervasiveness than that in example 2. Indeed, much more than in any other instance of Lingala–French code-switching, speech such as in example 1 breaches quite a few of the possible syntactical constraints suggested in the grammatical literature on code-switching. This last observation does not so much amount to an umpteenth critique of the proposed grammatical constraints. Rather, we would like to suggest that the purely linguistic quality of the pervasiveness of code-switching and the related regularity in the application of certain linguistic constraints could regain some analytical value, if approached not from the linguist's perspective but from the perspectives of the social actors, and if removed from the quest for universal properties of the *behaviour of languages* and used within a study of the social *behaviour of language users.*

4.3 Layered code-switching

As mentioned in the introductory sections, 'layered code-switching' is the term we adopt to refer to code-switching within code-switching, i.e. the conversational alternation of languages which are themselves code-switched codes. Example 3, which is a case of code-switched speech in which Lingala–French and Swahili–French are the switched 'languages', illustrates the phenomenon of layered code-switching and its conversational dynamics. The interaction takes place in the living room of B's small apartment, where B and C remain seated while A walks in and out of the adjoining kitchen. The three participants involved are A, a young woman who was born and raised in Kinshasa; B, a middle-aged woman from eastern Zaire; and C, who is the same person as A in example 1: a middle-aged man from eastern Zaire. All three of these interactants are proficient in Lingala–French and Swahili–French, but Lingala–French is the habitual language of A and Swahili–French is the habitual language of B and C.

EXAMPLE 3

---

1 A *ezalaki mokolo ya* **bonne année** *tokutanaki na* Matonge.
('it was on New Year's day, we met in Matonge [a Zairian neigh-bourhood in Brussels].')

2 B *na ndako?*
('at home?')

3 A *na* **Namur** *wana.*
('at [the Porte de] Namur [a well-known traffic junction in Brussels] there.')

4 B *awa na* **Bruxelles**?
('here in Brussels?')

5 A *ee.*
('yes.')

6 B NIKUPATIE *coca?*
('shall I get you a coke?')

7 C HAPANA SAA HII.
('not now.')

8   (.)

9 B NANI- ILE SOKO IKO **fatigue**.
('what- that market is exhausting.')

10 A hein?
      ('sorry?')
11 B *zando wana eza* **fatigue**.
      ('that market is exhausting.')
12 A ah. **heureusement qu'***okei lelo* **dimanche**! mm! [walks into the kitchen]
      ('you're lucky you went today Sunday! I say!')
13 B UKO UNASEMA MUTU ATEMBEE APITE, UKO UNAONA (SAA) VILE
      BIKO BINARUDISHA =TU NYUMA=.
      ('you say someone is walking and moving forward, but you have the impression as if they're just moving back.')
14 A [returns into the living room] =**dimanche** *bato-* =
                                        ('on Sundays people-')
15 C **dimanche** *bato bazalaka mingi* hein?
      ('on Sundays it's always crowded, isn't it?')

The dynamics of this interaction are grounded in an interplay between the two embedded linguistic markets described above, i.e. the overall dominance of Lingala in the Zairian community in Belgium and the compulsory use of Swahili among Swahili-speakers. As mentioned, Lingala very often has the power of veto, as the presence of one Lingala-speaker is sufficient to have the interaction conducted in Lingala. Accordingly, this conversation between one Lingala-speaker and two Swahili-speakers proceeds in Lingala–French as long as the three interactants are conversing together. In line 6, B turns to C, and has to do this in Swahili–French, as this is the obligatory code for in-group interactions among eastern Zairians. In 9, B is still using Swahili–French. Whether it was B's intention to select A or not, A feels, on the basis of the propositional content, that she is being addressed (or she simply wants to be involved in a topic she finds interesting), but is confused because of B's use of Swahili–French. Indeed, to A it is highly unlikely that Swahili–French is used to select her, since that language is reserved for in-group conversations among Swahili-speakers. Lines 10 and 11 are thus the logical consequence: speaker A indicates that she is confused and speaker B restores the misunderstanding by repeating the same proposition in Lingala–French. Line 12, then, which is in Lingala–French, further shows how A is now again fully integrated in the conversation, which was previously limited to B and C.

The dynamics from line 12 onwards are composed of the following features. Lines 12 and 14 are meant by A as one single, continuous utterance. The utterance is A's reply to B's comment in 11. A produces the end of her proposition in 12 while she is walking away from B and C. This makes B think that A is not involved any more and that C is her only interlocutor. The conversation thus changes from an *inter*group to a Swahili *in*-group setting, which imposes the replacement of Lingala–French with Swahili–French, accomplished in line 13. In line 14, A makes her re-entry to the scene of the conversation and continues her reasoning of which 12 was the onset. She sees some disturbing overlap with B's speech and truncates her sentence. C's step in line 15, then, is to abandon the Swahili–French B used before and to heed A's usage of Lingala–French. By using Lingala–French he selects and reintegrates everyone into the conversation.

In general, the dynamics of this stretch are marked by a continuous disambiguating of selected interlocutors. This disambiguating is accomplished against the background of usage patterns of Lingala and Swahili fixed by and within the society – the Zairian community in Belgium – at large. In other words, the alternation of the two intrinsically code-switched languages, i.e. Lingala–French and Swahili–French, throughout the sequential development of the conversation, displays how these socially embedded usage patterns inform the interactional dynamics of layered code-switching. The conversational structure is to some extent pre-given on the basis of an existing and hardly negotiable linguistic market of Zairian immigrants in Belgium. Elements of this market are used to structure the sequence of the conversation, and misunderstanding occurs when the sequential organisation of talk clashes with the way in which the linguistic repertoires of the speakers are manipulated.

The kind of layered code-switching represented by example 3 is a most frequent phenomenon among Zairians in Belgium. On any occasion where Lingala-speaking Zairians and Swahili-speaking Zairians meet, the overall supremacy of Lingala in the linguistic market and the subordinate linguistic market in which Swahili is the compelling code are played off against each other. This generates code-switching between languages that are code-switched languages in the monolectal sense, i.e. layered code-switching.

4.4 Discussion

Two observations are in order here. The first observation is an empirical one. The salience of 'language' in the traditional sense in interpreting what goes on in the conversational sequences presented in the examples is very low. Two reasons may account for this. First, as noted in 4.2, the default code for conversations among Zairian immigrants is code-switching between different varieties of French and Lingala or Swahili. In other words, in terms of speakers' perceptions, French and Lingala or Swahili cannot be separated as two indexical codes in any sensible way. What marks the difference between various forms of speech within this repertoire is based on qualitative criteria: differences in lexical choice, in syntactic, lexical–semantic or stylistic elaboration, density of French elements. The identities of the interlocutors – intellectuals in example 1 and 'common', less-educated people in example 2 – can be retrieved from these criteria, and not from the mere presence of French in their speech. Note that these qualitative distinctions may also count for the *African* language material they use. People may speak 'sophisticated' Swahili or Lingala, and set themselves apart from others who have no access to more elaborate, literate varieties of these languages. In the case of Swahili, for instance, using terms that are perceived as *Bora*, i.e. standard, East Coast Swahili, can be perceived as a form of elaboration or 'language display' (Eastman and Stein 1993). The point is that such small differences between varieties, despite the fact that they are emically more salient to the speakers, often escape the attention of the analyst when the alternation between languages is seen as the paramount feature of code-switching.

The second reason why language differences are hardly salient as explanatory factors for cases such as examples 1–3 is that the languages are indigenised anyway. The French spoken by Zairians is for all practical purposes a Zairian language. As a consequence, perceptions of 'good' or 'bad' French may be based on local criteria for proficiency, and not necessarily on an abstract standard. Thus, even when someone speaks poor French to metropolitan standards, his/her proficiency in French may be judged by his/her peers to be outstanding and a mark of education and elite-membership. The point is that, too often, a distorted picture of 'language contrast' is used in discussing the how's and why's of code-switching, one that fails to question the ways in which 'languages' become the object of power struggles, forms of appropriation, oppression, and resistance in particular societies. Consequently, the standard associations made in the context of Third World societies between European languages and values of high social prestige, upward mobility, and so on, are too simplistic and more likely than not a projection of the values and expectations of metropolitan and local elites (see Parakrama 1995 and Kandiah and Begum, forthcoming, for insightful discussions). They do not, however, reflect the ways in which indigenised varieties are used by speakers in other parts of society. The social indexicality assigned by speakers to their codes cannot be judged or established a priori. It has to be the outcome of an ethnographic search, and the outcome of such a search is often a much more fuzzy and flexible set of indexical values than the ones commonly suggested.

A second observation is methodological in nature. The most informative universe in which language repertoires and their functions can be assessed is that of concrete conversations. Discussing language samples without placing them in the conversational structure from which they are drawn makes too many potentially informative features dissappear. It is clear, in example 3, that the code alternation (Lingala–French/Swahili–French) is a function of conversational structuring and proceeds on the basis of interlocutor selection. There is no local identity negotiation involved, and attempts to explain what happens in (3) in terms of such negotiations are, at best, far fetched. The identities attached to the ingredients of the language repertoire are pre-given, and as noted above, they pre-structure the conversation. The salience of the difference between codes (i.e. Lingala–French and

Swahili–French) is a local, conversational feature, triggered by the peculiar sequential organisation of B's talk. Here, as well as in our first observation, we reach the same conclusion: the dynamics and functions of code-switching have a far wider range than is usually accepted in the literature, and an empirical, close type of scrutiny looks like the most promising approach to uncover these phenomena.

5 Concluding remarks

Let us now summarise our argument. In the first place, many analyses of code-switching seem to have been inspired by a significant degree of idealisation with regard to the nature of codes, as well as with regard to the nature of the sociolinguistic environment in which code-switching occurs. In particular, we have argued against views of code-switching based on the assumption of 'languages-as-codes' and conditioned by the full bilingualism of individuals. The code as seen by the speakers may be quite different from what the linguist may observe as the most salient feature: the difference between languages. Also, competence in the languages involved in code-switching is certainly not a prerequisite for code-switching, as mixed codes are often the norm in the speech patterns observable in a number of societies. We have therefore argued in favour of a monolectal view of code-switching, in which both the notion of language-as-code and that of bilingualism are dissociated from code-switching. Second, we have argued that this monolectal view can open potentially insightful ways of analysing code-switching. The fact that language competence and bilingualism are no longer accepted as givens and thus as a priori elements of explanation, allows for a better and more refined search into the structure, the functions, and the effects of code-switching. In particular, it may allow the full range of pragmatic analyses oriented towards details of conversational or discourse structure to penetrate into research on code-switching, and thereby to reach more satisfactory conclusions with regard to complex and seemingly atypical phenomena such as layered code-switching. A monolectal view restores the integrity of the data. In our approach, the salience of language contrasts or the conditioning nature of bilingualism has been reduced to a possible outcome, rather than an unquestioned point of departure which strongly biases (and distorts) our professional vision of the data.

This view may have some implications in general sociolinguistic terms. It is clear that 'languages' in the usual sense of the term may not be the best parameters for describing and assessing various forms of multilingualism, and that a sociolinguistic description of, for instance, Zaire based on different sociolects of intrinsically code-switched languages could yield a very different picture. At present, code-switching is seen as an almost coincidental by-product of two languages. The two languages usually find their way into the language atlases or sociolinguistic inventories, whereas the mixed codes are usually seen as unworthy of inventorisation. It should be clear by now that such sociolinguistic inventories may miss those ingredients of the linguistic scene that are most salient to the speakers themselves, and that, consequently, they may create a false impression of language problems caused by multilingualism. The multilingualism of a state such as Zaire, when seen from a decontextualised, outsider's perspective, may create an impression of unmanageable diversity, whereas on the ground this Tower of Babel often appears to cause few problems to the members of that society. The practice of multilingualism may to an important extent consist in using crossover codes, mixed variants, and so on, in ways which reduce the massive coexistence of languages to a set of linguistic practices that safeguard the possibilities for communication throughout different layers of society. It is not unlikely that work in the domain of language planning, hitherto strongly focused on idealised views of multilingualism, may contain unwarranted projections of chaos and unmanageability, which could be solved by looking at the language situation in specific societies from the point of view of concrete language practices and members' perceptions of languages and codes.

Notes

The research for this publication was carried out in the context of a program supported by the Belgian National Science Foundation (NFWO/FNRS) and a Belgian government grant (Federale Diensten voor Wetenschappelijke, Technische en Culturele Aangelegenheden, IUAP-II, contract number 27). We would like to thank all participants in the Hamburg workshop on code-switching (February 16–19, 1994) for their useful remarks. The authors and the editor wish to inform the readership that the manuscript for this article was finalised before May 1997, i.e. before Laurent-Désiré Kabila's 'Alliance of Democratic Forces for the Liberation of Congo-Zaire' assumed power in Zaire, changed the country's name into 'The Democratic Republic of Congo', and (knowingly or otherwise) brought about some changes in the language situation of the country.

1   The conventional association between 'code' and 'language' can also be judged from the way in which code-switching is terminologically opposed to other forms of language mixing. For instance, in his discussion of discourse structure in Shaba Swahili-French speech, de Rooij uses the term 'code-switching' to refer to interlanguage switching (Swahili–French), while for intralanguage variation, e.g. between Shaba Swahili and Swahili *Bora* (the 'pure', East Coast influenced variant of Swahili), the term 'styleshifting' is used (de Rooij 1996: 88ff.). Note that elsewhere, de Rooij claims to use the term code-switching 'in Gumperz's sense as including styleshifting' (1996: 37). This claim is not substantiated by his treatment of the data.

2   Note, in passing, the immense amount of idealisation involved in equating societies with nations and nations with states, an equation which Billig (1995: 51–59) would qualify as based on a European nationalist ideological substrate. This unquestioning use of terms which would invoke a massive amount of theoretical and descriptive debate is probably a feature of the kind of sociological naivity in sociolinguistics observed by Williams (1992). It should, however, be stipulated *contra* Williams that some theorising on types of communities and

types of state systems in relation to sociolinguistic phenomena has been done within sociolinguistics, notably in the field of language planning theory, albeit not very successfully (*inter alia*, Fishman 1968; Kloss 1968; Apter 1982, who provides a critique; Blommaert 1996 for a wider discussion).

3 Reflections on the concept of speech community, both theoretical and empirical, are avoided in Myers-Scotton's account. As a consequence, the particular settings from which the data are drawn are the subject of tremendous generalisations, best illustrated by the following statement:

> The urban origin of most of the examples *has no special effect* on the social motivations which apply; *it simply happens* that examples of code-switching are more easily found in urban populations because their multi-group makeup fosters more bilingualism, a prerequisite to codeswitching:
> (1993b: viii; emphasis added)

4 This particular form of usage, in which language alternation is used to situationally mark or construct sociopolitical identities, would also benefit from a more social-theoretically nuanced approach, such as that of Heller (1992, 1994), Gal (1988) or Woolard (1989).

5 Fabian (1986: 82) also notes the obscuring effect of language-based sociolinguistic descriptions, saying: 'Any enumeration of distinct languages will be an artifact of linguistic classification rather than an accurate indication of communicative praxis.'

6 Mekacha (1993) provides a cogent critique of the traditional belief that the coexistence of different languages in Africa also involves their competition and that, eventually, this coexistence is doomed to disappear into monolingualism.

7 Tanghe *et al.* (1940) and Hulstaert and De Boeck (1940) are two papers containing discussions between E. De Boeck, G. Hulstaert, and J. Tanghe, three Flemish missionaries and linguists in the Belgian Congo, on the need for purifying interventions from above. In both discussions, De Boeck admitted and explicated how he wanted to 'change' the code-switched Lingala language. He wrote, referring to Lingala, that 'nous avons fait de nécessité vertu et tâché de corriger ce "jargon"' (Hulstaert and De Boeck 1940: 124) and that he endeavoured to 'former ... une langue plus correcte ... grammaticale et uniforme' (1940: 125). Hulstaert agreed that intrinsically code-switched languages such as Lingala were 'poor' and 'structurally deficient', but fiercely argued against directed interventions, discrediting them as artificial distortions of the natural situation (see also Vinck 1994).

8 Meeuwis and Östman (1995) includes a theoretical discussion of this issue.

9 Other conventional symbols appearing in the transcripts are:

?	rising intonation, question
.	falling intonation
-	truncation, interruption, hesitation
(.)	pause
(text)	guess
=text=	overlap
[information]	extratextual information and transcriber's comments

Bibliography

ALAC (Atlas Linguistique de l'Afrique Centrale) (1983) *Atlas linguistique du Zaïre*, Paris: ACCT–CERDOTOLA.

Alvarez-Cáccamo, C. (1990) 'Rethinking conversational code-switching: Codes, speech varieties, and contextualization', in *Proceedings of the 16th Annual Meeting of the Berkeley Linguistics Society*, Berkeley, Calif.: Berkeley Linguistics Society, 16: 3–16.

Apter, A. (1982) 'National language planning in plural societies: The search for a framework', *Language Problems and Language Planning* 6, 3: 219–240.

Billig, M. (1995) *Banal Nationalism*, London: Sage.

Blommaert, J. (1992) 'Codeswitching and the exclusivity of social identities: Some data from Campus Kiswahili', *Journal of Multilingual and Multicultural Development* 13: 57–70.

—— (1996) 'Language planning as a discourse on language and society: The linguistic ideology of a scholarly tradition', *Language Problems and Language Planning* 20, 3: 199–222.

Blommaert, J. and Gysels, M. (1990) 'On the functionality of English interferences in Campus Kiswahili', *Afrikanistische Arbeitspapiere* 21: 87–104.

Boguo Makeli (1988) 'Situation des langues zaïroises au Zaïre', *Linguistique et Sciences Humaines* 28: 54–58.

Bokamba Eyamba (1976) 'Authenticity and the choice of a national language: The case of Zaïre', *Présence Africaine* 99: 104–142.

Brisard, F. and Meeuwis, M. (1994) 'Variability and code allocation in theory formation on language change', in *Papers from the 30th Regional Meeting of the Chicago Linguistic Society, Volume 2: The Parasession on Variation in Linguistic Theory*, Chicago, Ill.: Chicago Linguistic Society, 13–26.

de Rooij, V. (1996) *Cohesion Through Contrast: Discourse Structure in Shaba Swahili/French Conversations*, Amsterdam: IFOTT.

Eastman, C. M. and Stein, R.F. (1993) 'Language display', *Journal of Multicultural and Multilingual Development* 14, 3: 187–202.

Fabian, J. (1982) 'Scratching the surface: Observations on the poetics of lexical borrowing in Shaba Swahili', *Anthropological Linguistics* 24: 14–50.

—— (1986) *Language and Colonial Power: The Appropriation of Swahili in the Former Belgian Congo, 1880–1938*, Cambridge: Cambridge University Press.

Fishman, J. A. (1968) 'Some contrasts between linguistically homogeneous and linguistically heterogeneous polities', in J.A. Fishman, C.A. Ferguson and J. Das Gupta (eds) *Language Problems in Developing Nations*, New York: Wiley, 53–68.

Gal, S. (1988) 'The political economy of code-choice', in M. Heller (ed.) *Code-switching: Anthropological and Sociolinguistic Perspectives*, Berlin: Mouton de Gruyter, 245–264.

Heller, M. (1992) 'The politics of codeswitching and language choice', *Journal of Multilingual and Multicultural Development* 13: 123–142.

—— (1994) *Crosswords: Language, Education and Ethnicity in French Ontario*, Berlin: Mouton de Gruyter.

Hulstaert, G. (1953) 'Lingala-invloed op het Lomongo', *Zaïre* 7, 3: 227–244.

Hulstaert, G. and De Boeck, E. (1940) 'Lingala.' *Æquatoria* 3, 2: 33–43; 3, 3: 65–73; 3, 5: 124–131.

Kandiah, T. and Begum, R. (forthcoming) 'Minority usage within a new variety of English: Resistance and conformity', in J. Blommaert (ed.) *Political linguistics*, Amsterdam: John Benjamins.

Kazadi Ntole (1987) 'Rapport général', in Kazadi Ntole and Nyembwe Ntita-T. (eds) *Utilisation des langues nationales*. Special issue of *Linguistique et Sciences Humaines* 27, Kinshasa: Centre de Linguistique Théorique et Appliquée, 282–289.

Kazadi Ntole and Nyembwe Ntita-T. (eds) (1987) *Utilisation des langues nationales*. Special issue of *Linguistique et Sciences Humaines* 27, Kinshasa: Centre de Linguistique Théorique et Appliquée.

Kilanga Musinde and Bwanga Zanzi (1988) 'Quelques remarques sur la situation de la langue française au Zaïre', *Africanistique* 16: 46–56.

Kitengye Sokoni, Gidinga Seso and Tshibanda Mamba (1987) 'Impact du métissage linguistique sur l'enseignement du français au Zaïre: Cas des classes du 3e et 4e secondaire', *Annales Æquatoria* 8: 373–390.

Kloss, H. (1968) 'Notes concerning a language-nation typology', in J.A. Fishman, C.A. Ferguson and J. Das Gupta (eds) *Language Problems in Developing Nations*, New York: Wiley, 69–95.

Lehiste, I. (1988) *Lectures on Language Contact*, Cambridge: MIT Press.

Matumele, Maliya (1987) 'Langues nationales dans l'administration publique', in Kazadi Ntole and Nyembwe Ntita-T (eds) *Utilisation des langues nationales.* Special issue of *Linguistique et Sciences Humaines* 27, Kinshasa: Centre de Linguistique Théorique et Appliquée, 186–190.

Mayaka ma Kanda (1987) 'L'utilisation du français dans le discours en langues nationales', in Kazadi Ntole and Nyembwe Ntita-T (eds) *Utilisation des langues nationales.* Special issue of *Linguistique et Sciences Humaines* 27, Kinshasa: Centre de Linguistique Théorique et Appliquée, 248–254.

Meeuwis, M. (1994) (Review of Myers-Scotton 1993b), *Afrikanistische Arbeitspapiere*, 38: 209–214.

—— (1997) 'Constructing sociolinguistic consensus: A linguistic ethnography of the Zairian community in Antwerp, Belgium', Ph.D. dissertation, University of Antwerp.

Meeuwis, M. and Blommaert, J. (1994) 'The "Markedness Model" and the absence of society: Remarks on codeswitching', *Multilingua* 14, 4: 387–423.

Meeuwis, M. and Östman, J.O. (1995) 'Contact linguistics', in J. Verschueren, J.O. Östman and J. Blommaert (eds) *Handbook of Pragmatics: Manual*, Amsterdam: John Benjamins, 177–182.

Mekacha, R. D. (1993) 'Language death: conceptions and misconceptions', *Journal of Pragmatics* 21: 101–116.

Mutombo Hatu-Mukana (1991) 'Les langues au Zaïre à l'horizon de l'an 2000', in J.-J. Symoens and J. Vanderlinden (eds) *Les langues en Afrique à l'horizon de l'an 2000*, Brussels: Académie Royale des Sciences d'Outre-Mer, 85–107.

Myers-Scotton, C. (1993a) *Duelling Languages: Grammatical Structure in Codeswitching*, Oxford: Clarendon Press.

—— (1993b) *Social Motivations for Codeswitching: Evidence from Africa*, Oxford: Clarendon Press.

Ngalasso Mwathi Musanji (1986) 'Etat des langues et langues de l'Etat au Zaïre', in Ngalasso Mwathi Musanji and A. Ricard (eds) *Des langues et des états*, Talence, France: Centre d'Etudes d'Afrique Noire, 7–27.

—— (1988) 'Usage du français dans un milieu urbain africain: Kinshasa', *Présence Francophone* 33: 105–120.

Parakrama, A. (1995) *De-hegemonizing Language Standards: Learning from (Post)colonial Englishes About 'English'*, Houndsmills, England: Macmillan.

Sesep N'Sial (1988) 'Identité nationale, identité ethnique et planification linguistique au Zaïre', *Africanistique* 16: 1–19.

Shields-Brodber, K. (1992) 'Dynamism and assertiveness in the public voice: Turn-taking and code-switching in radio talk shows in Jamaica', *Pragmatics* 2: 487–504.

Swigart, L. (1992) 'Two codes or one? The insiders' view and the description of codeswitching in Dakar', *Journal of Multilingual and Multicultural Development* 13: 83–102.

Tanghe, J., De Boeck, E. and Hulstaert, G. (1940) 'Bestaat er wel in de Congoleesche talen een tegenwoordige tijd?' *Æquatoria* 3, 1: 90–95.

Vinck, H. (1994) 'Correspondance scientifique Hulstaert–De Boeck, 1940–1941', *Annales Æquatoria* 15: 505–575.

Willliams, G. (1992) *Sociolinguistics: A Sociological Critique*, London: Routledge.

Woolard, K.A. (1987) 'Codeswitching and comedy in Catalonia', *IPrA Papers in Pragmatics* 1: 106–122.

—— (1989) *Double Talk: Bilingualism and the Politics of Ethnicity in Catalonia*, Stanford: Stanford University Press.

INTRODUCTION TO CHAPTER 5

Peter Auer

Although Switzerland is a multilingual country, this national multilingualism is not accompanied by widespread individual multilingualism. Apart from the Svizra retorumantscha where bilingualism is the rule, most of the Italian-, French- or German-speaking Swiss grow up monolingually. However, there is a considerable amount of work migration within Switzerland (see Lüdi 1994) and from abroad, of which the Italian immigration into the German-speaking area has received most attention in the linguistic literature (see, among others, Berruto 1991, Pizzolotto 1991, Franceschini, Müller and Schmid 1984). All in all, according to a 1990 census, some 15 per cent of the population in the German-speaking cantons claim to have a language other than German as their 'main language', some 23 per cent in the French-speaking cantons a language other than French, and some 17 per cent in the Italian-speaking cantons a language other than Italian. Since all of them and a part of their children (who may have claimed the majority language of the canton to be their 'main language') are bilingual, the degree of individual bilingualism introduced by work migration is considerable: 4.3 per cent of the informants in the German-speaking area have Italian as their 'main language', and 4.2 per cent in the French-speaking area (see Franceschini 1994: 37).

The following chapter by Cecilia Oesch Serra focuses on the Italian immigrants in the French-speaking areas. The interest in investigating the speech of French/Italian bilingual speakers in the context of this book resides in the fact that the two languages in question are structurally similar and genetically closely related. In the present case, as Oesch Serra argues, this similarity has given rise to the formation of a mixed code of originally Italian and originally French elements.

The chapter follows the same general line of thinking as that of Meeuwis and Blommaert (Chapter 4). However, the kind of evidence against code-switching and for the formation of a mixed code is different: while Meeuwis and Blommaert have argued *ex negativo* for a mixed code, pointing out that mixing Lingala and French or Swahili and French is not functional (while switching between the Lingala/French and the Swahili/French mixed varieties may be), Oesch Serra argues *ex positivo* for a mixed code by showing that in the bilingual speech of her informants, elements of the two source languages have come to take over different structural duties.

Her example is the system of connectives for which she demonstrates that the discourse functions of monolingual Italian *ma* and *però* and those of monolingual French *mais* no longer remain the same in the emerging mixed code. The differences point to a functional specialisation: while *ma* tends to be used as a discourse marker with a metapragmatic meaning, *mais*, which in monolingual French is equivalent to monolingual Italian *ma*, is used with referential meaning only. Also, since there are now three connectives available (while Italian has only two and French just one), a new ordering principle is introduced which places *ma* on the lowest level of a scale of argumentative strength, followed by *mais* and finally *però*, which is used to introduce the strongest argument.

Bibliography

Berruto, Gaetano (1991) 'Fremdarbeiteritalienisch: fenomeni di pidginizzazione dell'italiano nella Svizzera tedesca', *Rivista di linguistica* 3, 2: 333–367.

Franceschini, Rita (1994) 'Das Umfeld der Migration', in Georges Lüdi *Fremdsprachig im eigenen Land*, Basel: Helbing and Lichtenhahn, 23–60.

Franceschini, Rita, M. Müller and S. Schmid (1984) 'Comportamento linguistico e competenza dell'italiano in immigrati di seconda generazione a Zurigo', *Rivista italiana di dialettologia* 8, 41–72.

Lüdi, Georges (1994) *Fremdsprachig im eigenen Land*, Basel: Helbing and Lichtenhahn.

Pizzolotto, G. (1991) *Bilinguismo ed emigrazione in Svizzera*, Bern: Lang.

5

DISCOURSE CONNECTIVES IN BILINGUAL CONVERSATION

The case of an emerging Italian–French mixed code

Cecilia Oesch Serra

1 Introduction

The study I am presenting here analyses an interactive pattern which appears very frequently in the speech of Italian migrants in French-speaking Switzerland. More precisely, it concerns the pragmatic use of three adversative connectives: Italian *ma* ('but') and *però* ('but', 'however', 'yet'), and French *mais* ('but'). As we shall see, these three connectives are used in a particular way within the speech of migrants. When they are used in isolation, they may, in principle, alternate in the same position. Conversational analysis of these occurrences reveals, however, that various factors – such as their discursive function, the importance of the argument they introduce and the base language used at this point in speech – may play an important role in their respective choice. When they are used in combination, they give rise to an argumentative structure which is different from what appears in the languages which contribute towards constructing it. The organisation of the particular argumentative structure in question, its frequency and its regularity provide arguments supporting the emergence of a mixed code.

In this chapter, I shall analyse the use of the three connectives with respect to (a) the argumentative structure they give rise to, (b) variation in structure and use and (c) the emergence of a mixed code.

2 The data

The data are taken from two research projects on Italian migrants in French-speaking Switzerland. The first investigated the use of language choice and code alternation in the speech of Italian migrant workers.[1] The second dealt with the migrants' representations of languages, territories, settlement, integration within the local community, etc., focusing on an important subgroup of the Italian migrant community in Switzerland, i.e. those from the department of *Abruzzi*.[2] Both research projects were similar from a sociolinguistic point of view: they dealt with families settled in Neuchâtel for at least twenty years. Their language repertoire consisted of dialects and regional varieties of Italian and of the Swiss French variety. In both cases, research methods were qualitative, based on individual or group interviews with bilingual researchers, who were often members of the same migrant community.

Even though the second research was carried out ten years after the first, the linguistic analysis of the data reveals the same speech behaviour. It consists of 'bilingual speech' (Grosjean 1982): i.e. the varieties of the repertoire (Italian, Italian dialect and French) alternate within the same speech unit. The migrants' evaluation of such language alternation continues to be negative for the most part, however. The reasons must be found in the 'monolingual' models conveyed by the linguistic norms of both the original and the host communities, to which the migrants refer more or less explicitly. To the migrants, the 'bilingual' way of speaking reflects their social status. They rate it on a social scale, and hold it responsible for the loss of their first language[3] and the poor acquisition of the host language, even calling it *minestrone* ('mixed vegetable soup'). On the other hand, the migrants' conversations show a meta-communicative use of bilingual speech. It is used when making jokes, but also in the linguistic form of 'nonce loans' (Poplack 1990), only flagged by prosody. This confirms that bilingual speech is common in the migrant community and is felt to be a cohesive factor of in-group membership. However, the association between communicative style and group identity is a symbolic one: it does not predict actual usage. There is no direct link between the occurrence of a particular set of linguistic forms and an extra-linguistic context.

The present study is based on audiotaped conversations carried out with sixty migrants. The average length of the conversations was about 160 minutes. The language chosen by the participants – their preferred language (Auer 1990) – is Italian, with many alternations into French.

3 *Mais*, *ma* and *però* in monolingual French and Italian

Before discussing the data, I should like to give a brief description of how the connectives *mais*, *ma* and *però* function in their respective languages. French *mais* is a counter-argumentative connective. These connectives link in interactive acts in a relationship of contradiction, achieved pragmatically by interactive functions such as rejection of an argument, rejection of a fact and confirmation of a contradiction (Ducrot *et al.* 1980; Roulet *et al.* 1985).[4] Given the connection *p mais q*, one could say that the arguments *p* and *q* are anti-oriented. Argument *q* cancels the orientation of argument *p* and has a force which is superior to that of argument p. Let us consider, for example, the following hypothetical case:

EXAMPLE 1

Il pleut **mais** j'ai envie de prendre l'air. Je sors.
('It's raining, **but** I feel like some fresh air. I'm going out.')

In the speech of a speaker belonging to a given cultural context, argument p: 'it's raining', is oriented towards the implicit conclusion 'stay at home'. Argument q: 'I feel like some fresh air' is, on the contrary, oriented towards the implicit conclusion 'don't stay at home'. It therefore contradicts argument p. The conclusion, 'I'm going out', supports the implicit orientation of argument q and cancels that of argument p. In this sense, q has a greater argumentative force than p. Thus *mais* can structure the relation between the two arguments, i.e. it transmits to the recipient the 'instruction to understand': (a) that the arguments it connects are anti-oriented and (b) that the argument which follows is stronger than the preceding one. In fact, if we reverse the position of the arguments under example 1:

EXAMPLE 1A

J'ai envie de prendre l'air **mais** il pleut.
('I feel like some fresh air, **but** it's raining.')

---

their relation will be organised in the opposite way, and will lead to a conclusion of the type 'I won't go out.'

Mais can also have a more general value as a discourse marker. This usually happens when it is placed at the beginning of an answer and suspends the adversative 'instructions' (Roulet *et al.* 1985: 94) linked to its argumentative use. Here, it acts as an anchor within the preceding discursive unit. Used in this way, it is often preceded by *non*: *non mais* ('no but').

EXAMPLE 2

X   si on sélectionne les étudiants sans pitié que faire des professeurs?
    ('if we are merciless about choosing students what should we do about the professors?')
Y   **non mais** ce que je voulais dire c'est qu'il faudrait procéder à des contrôles plus rigoureux.
    ('no but what I meant to say was that we should have stricter controls.')

In example 2, *non mais* ('no but') does not serve to refute or contradict a preceding argument. It does, however, serve to refute the thematic framework proposed. The clause introduced by *non mais* may be considered as a rejection of the preceding thematic framework. *Non mais* authorises this framework to be shifted.[5]

Italian *ma* is a homologue of *mais* (Giuliani and Zonta 1983) and has the same structural and argumentative properties, both as a connective and as a discourse marker. *Però* shares the argumentative properties of *ma* and may be synonymous with it; however, unlike *ma*, *però* has a free distribution, that is, it may stand either to the right or to the left of its argument. *Però* has no univocal French equivalent and may be translated by *mais*, *cependant*, *pourtant* ('but', 'however', 'yet'). It should be stressed that in Italian, the two connectives may be combined in a series *ma + però*. In this case, *però* has a higher argumentative power than *ma*: that is, the orientation of the argument it introduces influences the orientation of the conclusion. The outcome is that when the two connectives form a series, they give rise to a counter-argumentative system on three levels:

argument $p \rightarrow ma$ argument $q \rightarrow però$ argument r

In this case, the argument connected by *però* will be even stronger than the ones connected by *ma*:

EXAMPLE 3

Questa foto è bella **ma** sfocata, **però** ha un suo fascino. La pubblichiamo.
('This photo is good **but** blurred, **yet** it has a certain charm. We'll publish it.')

Here, the first argument, 'is good', is anti-oriented in relation to that introduced by *ma* 'is blurred'. As we have seen above, this latter argument is stronger than the former and could lead to the negative conclusion 'not to publish the photo'. The third argument, 'has a certain charm', introduced by *però,* contradicts, in its turn, the orientation of the second argument and results in the positive conclusion 'publish the photo'. If we change the organisation of the arguments in the example, the argumentative coherence of what is said is no longer guaranteed, for the two arguments introduced by *ma* and *però* then have the same positive orientation and the two connectives are no longer in contradiction with each other:

EXAMPLE 3A

? Questa foto è sfocata **ma** bella, **però** ha un suo fascino. La pubblichiamo.

(?'This photo is blurred **but** good, **yet** it has a certain charm. We'll publish it.')

4 Discussion of the bilingual data

The categories of connections I shall comment upon appear in the speech of migrant informants with average or high frequency. To show the importance of the phenomenon considered and its systematic character, I shall first present the categories in relation to the global production of a single informant. Subsequently, the categories will be illustrated by examples taken from other speakers in the corpus.[6]

Italo N. comes from the *Abruzzi* and has been living in Neuchâtel for over twenty years. I had a discussion lasting nearly two hours with him, his wife and his two children. The base language was Italian. Nevertheless, Italo is the informant who produces the highest occurrence rate of *mais*, rather than of *ma* as one might expect. In Italo's 129 turns, we observe:

19 connections with *mais*
8 connections with *ma*
5 connections with *ma + mais*
2 connections with *mais + però*
2 connections with *ma + mais + però*.

It is clear that this list can serve only as an illustration, and that the connectives cannot be compared with one another in terms of frequency. In particular, the complex forms depend on the organisation of the argument at a precise point in the conversation. However, values are comparable in the two first categories, i.e. connections with *mais* and those with *ma*. Before analysing them, a comment on *ma* in isolation is necessary. In fact, where the base language is Italian, this category may appear superfluous. However, the existence of complex connections, where *ma* alternates with *mais* and with *però*, and the frequency of the connections with *mais*, make it necessary to analyse the argumentative structure in a global manner and not only when code alternation is involved.

One might ask whether *mais* and *ma* are exchangeable. Discursive analysis reveals that they are not always so and that they present a certain degree of specialisation. In Italo's production, *ma* is always used as a *discourse marker*, while *mais* is used as an *argumentative connective*. Example 4 illustrates the use of *ma* as a discourse marker.

EXAMPLE 4

(E, interviewer; I, Italo; Fs, his son)[7]

1	E	e quando i figli fanno un errore in italiano li corregge?
		('and when the children make mistakes in Italian, do you correct them?')
2	I	in italiano? beh se lo sbaglio è proprio grosso. forse lo capisco
		('in Italian? well if it's a really big mistake.　　maybe I understand it')
3	E	per esempio?
		('for example?')
4	I	**ma** non　[so
		('**well**　I don't know')
5	FS	le sucre
		('the sugar')
6	I	come dovrei dire mettere una E al posto di una A capita anche a me
		('how should I say put an "E" instead of an "A" I often do that too')

In this example, *ma* does not connect arguments. On the contrary, it provides conversational structure and acts as an anchor for Italo's reply. Asked to give an example of the mistakes he corrects when his children speak Italian, Italo hesitates. This hesitation is based on *ma* and *non so* ('I don't know'). After his son breaks in, Italo completes his answer by framing it with a modal expression *come dovrei dire* ('how should I say'). From a conversational point of view, the sequence is structured as follows:

E　question: requests information X
I　answer: gives information X
E　question: requests clarification of X
I　*ma* preface: I cannot clarify X
FS　repairs I and gives information Y
I　repairs and gives information Z

As we can see, the function of *ma* is not to introduce an argument, but to resolve an interactive problem. *Ma* prefaces the repair activity when the reply cannot provide the information requested.[8]

In the following example, we observe another case of the interactive use of *ma*. This is an extract of a conversation between M, a migrant woman who has returned to live in Italy and P, the interviewer.

EXAMPLE 5

1	M	nel paese c'era una ragazzina che mi faceva tanto pena sì perché stava sempre sola con la nonna ('in the village there was a kid I was always sorry for, because she was always alone with her grandmother')
2	P	e come cercava di aiutarla le parlava di Neuchâtel o cercava di farci [com– ('and how did you try and help her did you talk to her about Neuchâtel or did you try to keep her comp–')
3	M	[**ma** di farci di far fare compagnia andavamo sempre a trovare i parenti ('**well** to keep her to keep keep her company we always used to go and see the family')

In example 5, P asks M a disjunctive question, taking the form of two proposals combined by the conjunction *o*: 'did you talk to her about Neuchâtel *or* try to keep her comp–'. M interrupts P and produces a completion to the second disjunct, before reformulating it in her own words: '*ma* to keep her to keep keep her company'. In this case, *ma* prefaces an intervention which is not unproblematic, since M takes over from what P is saying before the latter has finished formulating her question. The value of *ma* is once more interactive and not argumentative, since it does not serve to contrast two arguments.

This tendency to use *mais* as an argumentative connection and *ma* as a discourse marker is valid for all migrant informants. However, unlike Italo, they may at times also connect arguments with *ma*.

4.1 Argumentative connections

Mais *as a single connective*

In the argumentative structure we shall examine, the connection by *mais* is the basic form. It is widely found in all contexts and used by all informants. Here is one example, in which S speaks of the various stages of his migration.

EXAMPLE 6

S   prima sono andato in Germania . non ho fatto un'esperienza diciamo . pfh: come posso dire: . positiva . positiva forse dal lato economico ***mais*** moralmente no . perché quello che si sente adesso qui con i Turchi succedeva con gli Italiani . tempo addietro esisteva anche in Germania ('first I went to Germany . it wasn't what you could call an ehm : how can I put it . a positive experience . maybe positive on the economic side **but** not morally, because what you hear here now about the Turks was happening to the Italians . at the time that was also happening in Germany')

In example 6, *mais* organises the opposition between two arguments and strengthens the one which supports the conclusion. It should be noted that the fact of stressing the 'moral' argument has a reason: although S is today a wealthy entrepreneur, he seeks to present himself as a person who attaches no importance to questions of money throughout the interview. From an argumentative point of view, the sequence is structured as follows:

(a) conclusion: 'no positive experience in Germany'
(b) *forse* ('maybe') [concessive] + argument 1 'positive economic experience': attenuates (a)
(c) *mais* ('but') [adversative] + argument 2 'negative moral experience': supports (a)
(d) *perché* ('because') [explicative] + example: 'Germany and Switzerland have the same negative attitude towards foreigners': supports (c) and (a)

The question arises whether the use of the connective *mais* triggers the alternation into French of longer discursive segments, and if this is the case, what the function of these segments is. Analysis of the data reveals that if there are such segments, they appear either to the left or to the right of the connective, with different discursive functions:
1 The switched segment is to the left of the connective. In this case, it is a meta-discursive comment on the connective:

EXAMPLE 7

---

1   E   e succede che ci sia gente che rifiuta invece di parlare italiano?
         ('and on the other hand there are times when there are people who refuse to speak Italian?')
2   I   rifiuta direi no . certo c'è della delle persone italiane che si trovano meglio a parlar francese che italiano . io un esempio *je regrette mais* è . che io mi trovo meglio a parlare il francese che l'italiano[9]
         ('I wouldn't say refuse . of course there are some Italians who feel happier speaking French than Italian . me an example *I'm sorry but* . it's just that I feel better speaking French than Italian')

E asks I for information on the language practices of migrants. As in example 4, the sequence is organised as a question/answer adjacent pair. The answer is again problematic. Unlike example 4, however, I does not preface it but gives an account, i.e. the reason for which the second part cannot correspond to the expectations expressed by E in the first part. I's reply is therefore articulated as follows :

E   requests information X
I   (a) negotiates the expression used by E 'refuse to speak Italian'

(b) other-correction: reformulates E's request as 'prefer to speak French'
(c) gives information X as reformulated in (b) → 'there are some Italians'
(d) announces an example: → 'me an example'
(e) apologises, given Es preferred language: *je regrette* mitigates the following information
(f) specifies the information already given in (b), (c), (d): → '*mais* I feel better speaking French than Italian'

2 The switched segment is to the right of the connective. In this case, the connected argument is a globalising formula which evaluates the previous speech activity and/or the recipient's response to it.[10]

EXAMPLE 8

GP mia figlia è cresciuta molto indipendente . ha preso l'indipendenza della famiglia svizzera che la guardava durante il giorno . è tutta un'altra mentalità eh . tuttora va a mangiare i spaghetti dai svizzeri della famiglia svizzera eh ((laughter 0.3)) . *mais c'est quand même bien* . resta sempre la . la sua seconda mamma
('my daughter has grown up to be very independent . she has become independent from the Swiss family who looked after her during the day . it's a completely different mentality uhm . she still goes to eat spaghetti with the Swiss family, at their home . ((laughter 0.3)) . *but that's okay anyway* . she's still her . her second mum')

In example 8, Gp speaks of the education of her daughter, who was cared for during the day by a Swiss family when she was a child. Here, the segment introduced by *mais* is opposed to an inference concerning the daughter's 'Italian identity'. In fact, Gp says that her daughter, who is now adult, continues to take meals with her host family and that she 'goes to eat spaghetti with the Swiss at their home'. This behaviour contradicts a stereotype[11] valid within the migrant community, and numerously attested in the data, which asserts that only Italians know how to cook pasta. The contradiction is evidenced here by laughter from the participants, which triggers a repair. In moment, Gp reorientates her preceding argument. The repair *mais c'est quand même bien functions*, from an argumentative point of view, in the following way:

laughter from the participants interpreted by Gp as evidence of imminent misunderstanding
(a) *mais* marks opposition to the handling of the preceding information: → 'to eat spaghetti with the Swiss at their home'
(b) *c'*: (in *c'est* – 'it's') [anaphoric]:

→ 'to eat spaghetti with the Swiss at their home'
(c) *quand même* ('anyway'): [argumentative connective][12]
(d) *est bien* ('is okay') positive evaluation of (b)
(e) confirmation of (d): 'Swiss family = second mother':
→ expansion of the parental network of Gp's daughter,
therefore
→ neutralisation of the misunderstanding

In the examples discussed here, code-switching serves different conversational functions. In 6, *mais* is the only element in French within the argument of the present speaker. In this case, *mais* marks more clearly the type of argument it introduces. In 7, the expression *je regrette mais* ('I'm sorry, but') initiates a self-repair (Schegloff *et al.* 1977). The use of French attracts the attention of the addressee to this activity (Auer 1995), which is thus distinct from the preceding other-correction in Italian. From this point of view, example 8 is close to 7, except that the repair is other-initiated by means of laughter, but carried out by the speaker herself.

Ma and *però* as single connectives

As indicated above, a certain number of informants also use *ma* as an argumentative connective. From this point of view, their production is different from that of Italo, who uses *ma* only as a discourse marker. Examples 9 and 10 illustrate this argumentative use of *ma*. Example 9 is taken from a dialogue between a couple who are at this moment discussing the advantages of the Swiss way of life compared to that in Italy.

EXAMPLE 9

L   la pulizia qui è una cosa bella *voilà* nei ospedali se vai in un ospedale
è più pulito dei appartamenti
('cleanliness here is fine *you see*, in the hospitals if you go to the hospital it's cleaner than in the apartments')
T   **ma** in Italia non sono puliti perché perché non c'è educazione
('**but** in Italy they aren't clean because because there's no education')

In example 9, L is arguing in favour of 'cleanliness' in Switzerland and gives an example. She does not compare Switzerland with Italy explicitly. However, her example is one of the stereotypes very frequently used by migrants to compare one country to the other. In addition, the presence of the deictic *qui* ('here') indicates that the cleanliness in question only applies to Switzerland: the conclusive *voilà* ('you see'), code-switching into French, separates this assertion from the example. T then reacts to L's implicit comparison, i.e. Italian 'non-cleanliness'. The use of *ma* makes explicit L's opposition: '*ma* in Italy they aren't clean'. He attenuates the opposition by adding a justification: 'because because there's no education'. In this case, *ma* is used to explain the argument of the other with an intention of mitigating it.

Example 10 is taken from a conversation with another migrant family. Of interest is the use of *ma* within a French context. At this moment, A is opposing the plans of her husband who, unlike herself, does not wish to return to Italy.

EXAMPLE 10

M   *il faut dire que mon mari il aime beaucoup aller dans les autres pays.*
      beaucoup **ma** *pas rester chez . dans son pays . j'sais pas pourquoi*
      (*'I must say that my husband he really likes to go to other countries .*
      really **but** *not to stay at . in his country . I don't know why'*)

By the use of *ma*, M is contrasting two arguments: 'to go to other countries' and 'not to stay at . in his country'. The connective introduces and supports the second argument, which becomes the focal element in the words of this speaker.

This use of *ma*, within a discursive exchange in French, is the counterpart of the same use of *mais* within an Italian exchange. It should be stressed that these occurrences are rare, however, since most interviews took place in Italian. Yet, the fact that these occurrences do exist confirms an important finding, namely that the opposing use of the connective is highlighted by code alternation.

Example 11 is an illustration of *però*. In isolation, *però* takes on the meaning of *ma*, of which it becomes a synonym.

EXAMPLE 11

DF   mia madre stava sempre in campagna lei . mio padre lui non c'era mai
      a casa . si è messo a fa' politica . insomma non è che non lavorava
      però era quasi tutti i giorni da qualche parte . era consigliere comunale
      sette anni
      ('my mother always stayed in the country . my father was never there
      . he started to get into politics . well I don't mean that he didn't work
      but he was almost always going somewhere else . he was a communal
      counsellor for seven years')

In Df's speech, the use of *però* may be compared to that of *ma* in example 9. Here, however, the element introduced by *però* is opposed not to the argument but to the conclusion the recipient could infer. In fact, Df is describing the life of his parents and, at the beginning of his account, he establishes an opposition between his mother who 'always stayed in the country' and his father, who 'was never there'. This way of formulating things could lead to misunderstanding, i.e. that Df's father did not work. Df clarifies the misunderstanding: 'I don't mean that he didn't work' and introduces his repair by *però*: '*però* he was almost always going somewhere else'. In this way, Df guides the recipient's interpretation, since he dissociates the argument 'not to be there' or 'to be away' from a conclusion 'not to work'.

The connections ma + mais *and* mais + ma

When *ma* and *mais* are combined, each of them can be in first or second position. Generally speaking, *mais* supports a stronger argument than *ma*. Therefore, in the sequence *ma – mais*, the force of the arguments increases, but when the direction is *mais – ma*, the argument supported by *ma* functions to specify the argument marked by *mais*.

In the following example *ma* is in first and *mais* in second position:

EXAMPLE 12

FE il francese mi esce più facilmente . diciamo che non lo faccio neanche apposta **ma**: è la mia lingua ***mais*** da quando ho finito la scuola . cerco di frequentare più italiani possibili per . imparare la lingua e leggo molto

('French comes more easily . let's say I don't even do it on purpose **but**: it's my language **but** since I finished school . I try to mix with as many Italians as possible . to learn the language and I read a lot')

In order to understand example 12, it is essential to know that for Fe, the investigator represents the Italian norm. The organisation of Fe's argument is such as to confirm the supposed expectations of the investigator.

(a) conclusion: 'French comes more easily'
(b) attenuation of (a): (a) is not intentional
(c) *ma:* argument which supports (a): 'it's my language'
(d) *mais*: two arguments which prove Fe's good will to speak Italian:
    argument 1: 'I try to mix with as many Italians as possible'
    argument 2 : 'I read a lot'. These arguments attenuate (a).

This type of connection is extremely frequent. The conversational use of *ma* and *mais* makes it possible to deal simultaneously with turn-taking and topicality. Thanks to the combined use of *mais* and *ma* it is, in fact, possible to:

1   quote the prior speaker's argument with *ma* and oppose to it a stronger argument introduced by *mais*;
2   quote the prior speaker's argument and oppose to it two stronger arguments introduced by *ma* and *mais*.

In both cases, *mais* is the connective chosen to establish a contrast with a prior speaker's argument.

EXAMPLE 13

---

1   E   trova che sia una cosa buona che i figli sappiano differenti lingue straniere?
          ('do you think it's a good thing for children to know several foreign languages?')
2   I   anzi io . mi piacerebbe di più darei anche una spinta d'imparare anche non so il tedesco . beh non andrei sull'inglese perch[é
          ('more than that . I prefer I would even push them to learn I don't know German . well I wouldn't go for English because')
3   T   [beh .
          piuttosto l'inglese .   [sinceramente
          ('well I'd prefer English .   really')
4   I   [sì d'accordo **ma** tu l'inglese ***mais*** io son contro di mandare la ragazza diciamo sono un po' freddo dihmandare la ragazza un po' .
          ('yes, OK **but** you English ***but*** I'm against sending the girl let's say I'm a bit cool on the idea of sending the girl a bit .')
5   E   in Inghilterra?
          ('to England?')
6   I   sia . sia in Germania sia in Inghilterra . o fuori
          ('maybe . either to Germany or England . or further')

In example 13, Italo (I) is in the process of answering the investigator's (E) question: 'is it a good thing for children to know several foreign languages?' His daughter (T) breaks in and tries to influence her father's opinion. Italo interrupts once more, reformulating his daughter's argument and keeping the floor. The sequence evolves as follows:

E   asks I to evaluate the proposition (X)
I   (a) ratifies the positive orientation by (X)
     (b) gives the information (X) by two contradictory arguments:
          1 positive: 'learn German'
          2 negative: 'do not learn English'
     (c) *perché* ('because'): introduces support for (b)2

T   (self-selects as a speaker) *piuttosto* ('I'd prefer') positive orientation to (b)2 'learn English'

I   (d) (self-selects as a speaker) marks the end of T's turn: 'yes OK'

    (e) chooses T as addressee: *ma* reformulates T's argument

    (f) chooses E as addressee: *mais* supports (b)2

E   (self-selects as speaker) question: produces a possible completion of (f) supporting (b)2

I   answer: ratifies E's conclusion and cancels argument 1.

In the following example, the sequence of connectives is inversed. We find *mais* in first position and *ma* in second. The function of *ma* is to specify an argument introduced earlier by *mais*.

EXAMPLE 14

---

1 Z   eh! mia moglie è protestante . in Italia quella volta
           ('hey! my wife is protestant . in Italy at that time')

2 Y   non è importante dai!
           ('come on that's not important!')

3 Z   non è importante? ((laughter)) te lo dici che non è importante .
           mais se era protestante di quelli che non vanno mai in chiesa è una
           cosa **ma** se è una di quelle che vanno in chiesa è un'altra cosa .
           sono proprio due cose ben distinte
           ('it's not important? ((laughter)) you might say that it's not impor-
           tant . **but** if she was the sort of protestant who never went to church
           that's one thing **but** if she was one of those who did go, that's
           another . they're really two quite different things')

The topic under discussion is religious differences within mixed couples. Z has just taken the turn; he has a protestant wife and is in the process of opening a narrative structure 'in Italy at that time'. Y, who is his rival for leadership of the conversation, breaks in and challenges Z's story preface by a comment which devaluates it: 'come on, that's not important!' Z repeats Y's argument as a question, and then provides the reply to it himself by opposing two arguments: 'protestants who don't go to church' vs. 'protestants who do go to church', to which latter category his wife belongs. In this case *mais* connects the weaker of the two arguments. However, it is still *mais* which opens the argumentative chain and which is opposed to Y's negative comment.

The connections mais + però *and* ma + mais + però

The importance of segmental order is even more evident when we consider the more complex forms in which *però* is involved. Analysis of the data reveals a tendency to place *però* in final position. The occurrences of this connective are few, but the tendency can nevertheless be verified in the connection *mais + però*. Here, *però* often is in the dominant position,[13] as shown by the following example:

EXAMPLE 15

---

1   E   effettivamente c'è poca partecipazione elettorale . [diciamo a::
       ('it's true that not many voted . for instance in::')

2   W   [vabbè ci sono
       diversi motivi .
       ('but there are various reasons')

3   Z   qui la gente e poi uno dice non sono non sono io che decido penso
       che sia per quello poi non è motivato
       ('people here and then somebody says it's not me it's not me who
       decides I think that's why he's not motivated')

4   W   ecco!
       ('absolutely!')

5   Y   forse anche perchè il cittadino italiano è . si sente considerato un
       cittadino di serie B anche per quello dice **mais** insomma *bon* mi
       invitano a votare **però** so benissimo che non ne tengono conto che
       conto per niente che conto qui che conto là insomma
       ('maybe because Italian citizens are . feel they are second-class
       citizens that's why he says **but** after all *OK* they ask me to vote
       yet I know perfectly well that they don't take it into account that
       I count for nothing')

The investigator (E) and a group of migrants are discussing the participation of foreigners, and migrants in particular, in Neuchâtel's communal elections. E notes that the participation is low. Her co-participants, W, Y and Z, self-select one by one as speakers, but construct an argumentative structure *together* aimed at justifying E's assertion.[14] The direction of the argument moves from the general to the specific:

E   assertion X: 'not many voted'
W   (self-selects)
     (a) announces an argumentative structure which justifies (X):
         → 'there are various reasons'
Z   (self-selects)
     (b) argument 1: makes (a) explicit and justifies the lack of motivation
         to vote
W   (self-selects) ratifies (b)1
Y   (self-selects)
     (c) conclusion of (b): → 'Italians are second-class citizens'
     (d) argument 1: contradicts (c):

→ *mais* + *insomma* ('after all') + *bon* [flag]:
→ 'the Swiss ask the Italians to vote'
(e) argument 2: supports (c) and cancels the orientation of 1d:
→ '*però* I know perfectly well that they don't take it into account'

The sequence remains the same when the three connectives *ma* + *mais* + *però* are combined. This is above all true within a speaker's turn, such as in the following example:

EXAMPLE 16

Z   conosco degli Italiani che dicono eh noi dobbiamo andare in Italia dobbiamo tornare in Italia . passa 'na vita e rimangono sempre qui e si ha questo eh questa sensazione di provvisorio cioè non si è integrati **ma** io non posso pfh diciamo non so diciamo bisognerebbe misurare cosa vuol dire integrazione no ***mais*** diciamo io vivo bene . ci ho un accento non posso dire di essere Svizzero perché quando apro la bocca non parlo come gli altri no? **però** io qui vivo come vivessi in qualsiasi altro posto i miei figli no – non abbiamo mai parlato di andare abitare in . altri posti
('I know some Italians who say hey we should go to Italy we should go back to Italy . a lifetime goes by and they are still here and you have this – uhm this feeling of being temporary I mean we're not integrated **but** I can't pfh let's say I don't know let's say you should be careful about what you mean by integration don't you think ***but*** let's say I live well here . I've got an accent I can't say I'm Swiss because when I open my mouth I don't speak like the others, do I? **yet** I live here like I'd live anywhere else my children and I have never talked about living . anywhere else')

In example 16, Z discusses the problem of integration. First of all, he quotes the opinion which prevails in the migrant community: 'we are not integrated'. On the discursive level, the use of *ma* marks the limit between the quotation of collective speech and what is Z's own opinion. On the argumentative level, *ma* introduces Z's opinion opposed to the collective opinion '*ma* (. . .) you should be careful about what you mean by integration.' A first opposing argument is then introduced by *mais* '*mais* let's say I live well here'. The content of this argument is attenuated by the subsequent: 'I have an accent I can't say I'm Swiss'. Finally, *però* introduces a reformulation of the first argument '*però* I live here like I'd live anywhere else' which, this time, directly opposes the collective opinion mentioned at the beginning of his turn.

When produced within an exchange, the order *ma* + *mais* + *però* can be changed for the needs of interpersonal negotiation. Thus, *ma* can appear at the end of the series, usually with the function of specifying and supporting the argument proposed by *però*. Example 17 is typical of this case:

EXAMPLE 17

---

1   I   io non riesco a capire perché noi ci impariamo la lingua di qua e loro non si imparano la lingua nostra
('I can't understand why we learn the language they speak here and they don't learn ours')

2   M   **ma** loro dicono che sono a casa sua
('**but** they say that they're at home')

3   I   beh non fa niente . ***mais*** sapere una lingua in più . è meglio o no? . va- vanno tanto in vacanza in Italia . perché la lingua italiana no?
('OK then . **but** it's better to know an extra language, isn't it? . They often go to Italy on holiday . why not Italian?')

4   M   eh lo so . vaglielo a far capire a loro
('I know . try and make them understand')

5   I   **però** gli svizzeri tedeschi tanti e tanti che parlano italiano eh . più di qua
('**yet** there are lots of German-speaking Swiss who speak Italian uhm . more than here')

6   T   **sì ma** il svizzero tedesco si dà pena a parlare anche s- sanno . tutti quasi il francese . invece il contrario non c'è
('yes **but** German-speaking Swiss make more of an effort to speak nearly all . of them know French . on the other hand the opposite isn't true')

In example 17, Italo's family are discussing the reasons why French-speaking Swiss do not learn Italian. The organisation of the sequence is the following:

I   assertion by X: 'Italians learn French; the French-speaking Swiss don't learn Italian'

M   (self-selects)
     (a) argument which justifies X:
        ma + reported speech from French-speaking Swiss:
        → '*ma* they say they're at home'

I   (self-selects)
     (b) ratifies M's argument: 'OK then'
     (c) *mais* + a common sense argument opposing (a):
        → '*mais* to know an extra language is better, isn't it?'

M   answers I's question:
     (d) agrees with I's argument: 'I know'
     (e) asserts the fact that it is impossible to change (a):

→ 'try and make them understand'
I   answers M:
  (f) *però* + stereotype:
    → '*però* the German-speaking Swiss learn Italian'
T   (self-selects)
  (g) *sì ma* + stereotype: confirmation and explanation of (f):
    → 'yes but Swiss Germans make an effort to speak'
  (h) example which confirms (g): 'nearly all of them know French'
  (i) *invece* [adversative] + implicit stereotype which explains the
      assertion   by X:
    → '*invece* ('on the other hand') the opposite isn't true'

In this example, the connectives fulfil various discursive and conversational functions. The first *ma*, on the part of M, presents the point of view of the French-speaking Swiss in reported speech. *Mais* and *però* introduce thematic developments and arguments by I. *Mais* marks an argument which reorientates the topic of the sequence 'learn foreign languages'. *Però* develops this topic further and introduces a new agent: the German-speaking Swiss. The second *ma (sì ma)* used by T specifies and supports the preceding argument, which was introduced by I, with the help of *però*. From a conversational point of view, the conjunction '*sì ma* + argument' legitimates T's self-selection as the next speaker. Moreover, the use of *sì ma* attests that the speaker accepts the factual framework, but refuses its inferential relevance (Roulet *et al.* 1985: 109). In fact, T expands the framework proposed by I: German-speaking Swiss do not restrict themselves to learning Italian, but they also learn other languages, for example French.

In this sequence, the use of stereotypes strengthens what the speakers are saying. These formulae, and particularly those used by T, are extremely common in French-speaking Switzerland, where they serve to describe, and not always positively, the language behaviour of the German-speaking Swiss. Italian migrants who acquired the stereotypes of the host country use the oppositions which exist between the two groups of Swiss in order to support their own point of view.

5 Conclusion

The analysis I have presented shows that bilingual (Italian/French) migrant speakers have developed an argumentative system on the basis of two monolingual systems, which is not identical to either of them. In such a system there are three adversative connectives, rather than two as in monolingual Italian or one as in monolingual French. From this point of view the system constitutes a case of an *emerging mixed code*, which has no equivalent in the source languages.

The system uses the Italian adversative connectives *ma* and *però* and the French *mais* with their own rules for application in order to organise argumentative patterns. The patterns are variable, ranging from the most simple (the connection with a single *mais* or *ma*) to the most complex (the connection with the three connectives *ma* + *mais* + *però*). Moreover, each pattern presupposes the existence of the others. Single *ma* tends to specialise as a discourse marker, single *mais* as an argumentative connective. Even though we find cases where single *ma* is used as an argumentative connective, there is nevertheless no example where single *mais* serves as a discourse marker. In the combined use of *ma* + *mais*, *mais* can support an argument which is stronger than that introduced by *ma*; while in the connection *mais* + *ma*, *ma* often specifies the argument introduced by *mais*. This makes sure that *mais* is in a stronger position than that of *ma*. In the more complex pattern, which employs all three connectives, *però* assumes the dominant position.

The status of *mais* could lead us to believe that in this system it has acquired an extra argumentative value. This is not the case. A sequential approach (Auer 1995) shows that *mais* is used in a variety of ways on the conversational level. In turn-taking, *mais* can support the argument of someone who takes the turn. By the contrast which *mais* builds up between the arguments of the present and the preceding speaker, it may also *account* for turn-taking (examples 13, 14 and 17). Within a turn and in the second part of an adjacency pair, *mais* allows the speaker to mark an argument which responds to the presumed expectations of the recipient (examples 6 and 12).

On the other hand, the use of *mais* can also contrast with the expectations of the recipient. In this case, *mais* may trigger switched elements in French (examples 7 and 8), which are usually modal forms or sequences of connectives. They attenuate or emphasise the pragmatic function of *mais*. Given their cohesion with *mais* they seem to have become, in this environment and in the usage of the migrant speakers, formulaic elements of speech. We can therefore assume that these switched elements are also part of the mixed code.

On the conversational level, *mais* (used in an Italian conversation) introduces a contrast with the base language, thus marking the speech activity which it prefaces. (The same applies to example 10, where the connective *ma* alternates in a French context, under the same conditions as those in which *mais* alternates within an Italian context.) Code-alternation highlights the pragmatic function of the connective and might be described as a contextualisation cue (Auer 1995: 124). However, the alternation cannot be interpreted in relation to the speech event and does not necessarily refer to a conversational–external opposition, such as 'we-code – they-code'.

But moreover, the alternation of *mais* and of *ma* is also part of an emerging mixed code. This code has to be accounted for on the basis of bilingual rather than of monolingual parameters: the connectives in French or Italian are not borrowed elements enlarging the (monolingual) Italian or French argumentative system, and therefore more or less integrated into them. Rather, all the connectives involved in the new system form a specific linguistic configuration, using and exploiting the dynamic relationship between the two languages from which they are taken.

Notes

A shorter version of this paper was published in *ESF Network on Code-Switching and Language Contact: Papers for the Symposium on Code-Switching in Bilingual Studies: Theory, Significance and Perspectives.* Barcelona, March 21–23 1991. Strasbourg: European Science Foundation, vol. I, 141–56.

1 *Aspects du bilinguisme dans le Canton de Neuchâtel. Approche linguistique des migrations externes et internes* (1981–1983). In addition to Italian migrant workers, this research was also concerned with Spanish and Swiss German migrants living in Neuchâtel (del Coso-Calame *et al.* 1985; Alber and Oesch Serra 1987; Oesch Serra 1990).

2 *Migrants et migration entre la région des Abruzzi et le Canton de Neuchâtel: discours et représentations relatives aux territoires et aux langues* (1990–1993). This research was undertaken by a team of linguists, geographers, sociologists and ethnologists. A linguistic outcome of the research was an investigation of the use and functions of stereotypes in discourse (Oesch Serra and Py 1993a, 1993b).

3 'First language' here refers both to dialect and to regional Italian. When the migrants consider these varieties as distinct, the reasons they given for their loss are quite different. Dialect is thought to be lost because of its contact with French. Another reason is said to be the natural change of this variety, which occurred while they were outside the country. However, they come to the conclusion that even if their dialect is now 'poorer' than before emigration, it is still the 'purest'. In fact, many lexical items that have disappeared in today's dialect have been retained in their language. Concerning regional Italian, the loss of competence seems to be greater. The point is that the migrants never felt at ease in this variety, even when they were living in Italy.

4 The theoretical approach followed here is basically that of pragmatic linguistics, as developed particularly in the work of O. Ducrot. The argumentative role of connectives has been studied in depth by other researchers as well, of course. For example, Schiffrin writes with regard to English *but*: '*but* marks an upcoming unit as a contrast with a prior unit and this meaning is part of every use of *but*' (1987: 176). Schiffrin describes the various conversational uses of *but*, but argumentative aspects are not analysed extensively. It should be added that the English *but* seems to have an essentially argumentative use, whereas *mais* or *ma* also fulfil a role as discourse markers, corresponding, for example, to the English *well*.

5 Contrary to *non mais* ('no but'), the follow-on with *oui mais* ('yes but') confirms that the speaker accepts the factual framework, but refuses the inference. Therefore, we can apply the description of *mais* given by Roulet *et al.* 1985: 109. This case is illustrated by examples 13 and 17.

6 The total number of examples studied was 99.

7 In the transcripts, a single dot (.) denotes a short silence, and a hyphen a break-off or unfinished word; square brackets indicate simultaneous talk; double colons indicate lengthened vowel sounds; and transcribers' comments are enclosed in double round brackets.

The son's (Fs) code-switching into French in turn 5 of example 4, giving an example of the mistakes his father corrects, is a facilitation strategy arising from linguistic insecurity in Italian. The mistake corrected can be reconstituted easily: *lo zucchero* instead of *il zucchero*, the latter being the form the son is likely to have produced. This form is a consequence of the over-generalisation of the Italian article *il*, following the pattern of French *le*. Nevertheless, the example given by the son is fairly subtle, and as such contradicts his father, who under-estimates his own competence in Italian by saying he only corrects 'big' mistakes.

8 This concerns the linguistic marking of a 'dispreferred second pair part' (Levinson 1983: 307). Li Wei points outs that in his data, 'dispreference markers' such as *well* and *but* do not occur when contrastive language choices are used to mark dispreference' (Li Wei 1994: 165).

9 The meta-discursive comment also has a meta-communicative effect: conversational analysis of the sequence reveals that at this point, the speaker perceives the investigator as guaranteeing loyalty towards Italian, the language or origin.

10 It is important to note that the formula *mais* + borrowings also appears in this position. The borrowings are, in this case, connectives such as: *mais malgrado tutto*, *mais altrimenti*, *mais se no*, *mais li allora*, followed by arguments in Italian. It may appear arbitrary to call them 'borrowings', since these connectives are also part of standard Italian. However, their use in French, in these same combinations, is so frequent in daily discursive practice that it seems justified to use this term. Moreover, many years of observation of bilingual speech (Italian/French) among Italian migrants has led me to conclude that when two connectives have a similar discursive use, preference will be given to the one closest to French. A typical example is that of the pair *appunto*, *giustamente*, in which preference is given to *giustamente*, which is close to French *justement* ('exactly').

11 Stereotypes often signal identity. They are the subject of research currently in progress.

12 *Quand même* ('anyway') has the pragmatic characteristic of 'referring to an institutional norm'; its discursive characteristic is to link 'directly to the illocutory act or enunciation in dialogue' (Roulet *et al.* 1985: 136–38).

13 In the whole data, there are two argumentative sequences in which *però* precedes *mais*. Analyses of these 'exceptions' reveals that they occur with the second part of an adjacency pair (answer) and that the argument connected by *mais* is that which responds directly to the question asked.

14 This pattern is frequent in all conversations and reminiscent of the pattern of 'conversational completion' as described by Gülich 1986.

Bibliography

Alber, J.-L. and Oesch Serra, C. (1987) 'Aspects fonctionnels des marques transcodiques et dynamique d'interaction en situation d'enquête', in Lüdi, G. (ed.) *Devenir bilingue parler bilingue. Actes du 2e colloque sur le bilinguisme, Université de Neuchâtel, 20–22 septembre 1984*, Tübingen, Germany: Max Niemeyer Verlag, 23–56.

Alfonzetti, G. (1992) *Il discorso bilingue. Italiano e dialetto a Catania*. Milan: Franco Angeli.

Auer, P. (1984) *Bilingual Conversation*. Amsterdam: Benjamins.

—— (1990) 'A discussion paper on code alternation', in *ESF Network on Code-Switching and Language Contact: Papers for the Workshop on Concepts, Methodology and Data. Basel, 12–13 January 1990*, Strasbourg: European Science Foundation, 69–88.

—— (1995) 'The pragmatics of code-switching: a sequential approach', in Milroy, L. and Muysken, P. (eds.) *One Speaker, Two Languages: Cross-Disciplinary Perspectives on Code-Switching*, Cambridge: Cambridge University Press, 115–35.

del Coso-Calame, F., de Pietro, J.-F. and Oesch Serra, C. (1985) 'La compétence de communication bilingue. Etude fonctionnelle des code-switchings dans le discours de migrants espagnols et italiens à Neuchâtel (Suisse)', in Gülich, E. and Kotschi Th. (eds.) *Grammatik, Konversation, Interaktion*. Tübingen, Germany: Max Niemeyer Verlag, 377–98.

Ducrot, O., Bourcier, D., Bruxelles, S. and Diller, A-M. (1980) *Les mots du discours*, Paris: Editions de Minuit.

Giuliani, M.V. and Zonta, B. (1983) 'Inferenze, persuasioni e valori nell'uso di ma', in F. Orletti (ed.) *Comunicare nella vita quotidiana*, Bologna: Il Mulino, 279–300.

Grosjean, F. (1982) *Life with Two Languages: An Introduction to Bilingualism*. Cambridge, Mass.: Harvard University Press.

—— (1995) 'A psycholinguistic approach to code-switching: the recognition of guest words by bilinguals', in Milroy, L. and Muysken, P. (eds.) *One Speaker – Two Languages*, Cambridge: Cambridge University Press, 259–75.

Gülich, E. (1986) 'L'organisation conversationnelle des énoncés inachevés et leur achèvement interactif en situation de contact', *DRLAV* 34/35: 161–82.

Gumperz, J. J. (1982) *Discourse Strategies*, Cambridge: Cambridge University Press.

Levinson, S. C. (1983) *Pragmatics*, Cambridge: Cambridge University Press.

Li Wei (1994) *Three Generations, Two Languages, One Family: Language Choice and Language Shift in a Chinese Community in Britain*, Clevedon, England: Multilingual Matters.

Lüdi, G. (ed.) (1987) *Devenir bilingue parler bilingue. Actes du 2e colloque sur le bilinguisme, Université de Neuchâtel, 20–22 septembre 1984*, Tübingen, Germany: Max Niemeyer Verlag.

Maeschler, Y. (1994) 'Metalanguaging and discourse markers in bilingual conversation', *Language in Society* 23, 3: 325–66.

Oesch Serra, C. (1990) 'Italiens vendus ou Suisses à quat'sous?', in Centlivres, P., Kreis, G., Bois, P. *et al.* (eds) *Devenir Suisse. Adhésion et diversité culturelle des étrangers en Suisse*, Geneva: Georg Editeur SA, 211–28.

Oesch Serra, C. and Py, B. (1993a) 'Dynamique des représentations langagières dans des situations de migration. Etude de quelques stéréotypes', in Lüdi G., Py, B. *et al.* (eds.) *Approches linguistiques de l'interaction, Bulletin CILA* 57: 71–83.

—— (1993b) 'Il crepuscolo dei luoghi comuni o gli stereotipi tra consenso, certezza e dubbio', in Di Nicola, G. P. and Py, B. (eds.) *Alterità al quotidiano. Migrazioni Abruzzo – Neuchâtel*. Pescara: Università G. D'Annunzio, Collana del Dipartimento di Teoria dei Sistemi e delle Organizzazioni, 155–79.

Poplack, S. (1990) 'Variation theory and language contact: concepts, methods and data', in *ESF Network on Code-Switching and Language Contact: Papers for the Workshop on Concepts, Methodology and Data. Basel, 12–13 January 1990*. Strasbourg: European Science Foundation, 33–66.

Roulet, E., Auchlin, A., Moeschler, J. *et al.* (1985) *L'articulation du discours en français contemporain*, Bern, Frankfurt am Main, New York: Peter Lang.

Schegloff, E. A., Jefferson, G. and Sacks, H. (1977) 'The preference for self-correction in the organization of repair in conversation', *Language* 53: 361–82.

Schiffrin, D. (1987) *Discourse Markers*, Cambridge: Cambridge University Press.

INTRODUCTION TO CHAPTER 6

Peter Auer

The linguistic situation in Israel dealt with in the following chapter on English/Hebrew code-switching is quite complex. Israel has only one official language (Hebrew) but is de facto extremely multilingual with almost everyone speaking at least one additional language, 80 per cent of the population two additional languages, and 49 per cent even three or more additional languages according to census data (Ben-Rafael 1994: 111ff.). These additional languages are often those of the first-generation immigrants or (usually to a lesser degree) their children and grandchildren. Thus, the situation is not stable but characterised by a transient individual bilingualism to Hebrew, which is rarely spoken before immigration but acquired in the country. However, although Hebrew has been gaining speakers throughout the history of immigration into Palestine and later into Israel, the transition to Hebrew monolingualism has never been achieved completely, since new immigrants continue to bring with them their first languages.

Within this extremely multilingual context, English is one of the many minority (and immigrant) languages spoken by immigrants not only from the USA, but also from South Africa, Australia and other countries. (It should be remembered that about 50 per cent of the Jews in the world live in English-speaking countries.) However, the status and prestige the language enjoys cannot be explained by the number of immigrants from English-speaking countries (nor, incidentally, by the fact that it was one of the official languages alongside with Hebrew and Arab in the times of the British Mandate (1922–1948)). On the contrary, the distribution of knowledge and use of English in the population is very different from that of other immigrant languages: the younger the speakers are the more likely they are to have English as their first language or (if born in Israel) as their first language after Hebrew. (The opposite holds for languages such as Arabic, Yiddish or Polish; cf. Ben-Rafael 1994: 113). If English today 'constitutes the most honoured linguistic resource besides Hebrew', 'holds the upper position in the market of languages' and 'constitutes a status symbol, a power asset, and a boundary marker, the importance of which can be measured by the efforts Israelis invest in its acquisition' (Ben-Rafael

1994: 188–189), this attitude reflects its status the most important *second* language acquired in addition to Hebrew (and not just of an immigrant language 'left over' from the parents or grandparents). As in many other parts of the world, knowledge of English is linked to professional success, to higher social status, and to a cosmopolitan orientation.

For English-speaking immigrants, this high status means that the pressure to adapt to Hebrew is relatively minor, and English is even used outside the home with children and among adults. Field notes by Ben-Rafael (1994: 186 and *passim*) in English-speaking settler communities emphasise the increasing 'mixing' of English and Hebrew.

In the following chapter, Yael Maschler investigates a situation of informal interaction between first-generation American immigrants. Very similar to Oesch Serra's analysis of Italian/French mixing, her chapter analyses the emergence of a mixed code in the structural field of discourse markers and connectives. Her main finding supporting the mixed-code hypothesis is a separation of conjunctions and discourse markers through language: discourse markers overwhelmingly are in Hebrew, but conjunctions overwhelmingly in English. (Only structural discourse markers are in English.) The parallel with the findings in the preceding chapter will be noted, where Oesch Serra argued for a functional differentiation of (originally) Italian *ma* as a discourse marker versus (originally) French *mais* as a conjunction in the speech of her Italian/French bilinguals in Switzerland.

In addition, Maschler shows that the emerging Hebrew/English mixed code may be used side by side with code-switching between Hebrew and English; i.e. the grammaticalisation of code-switching into a mixed code has not yet been completed.

Bibliography

Ben-Rafael, Eliezer (1994) *Language, Identity, and Social Division: The Case of Israel*, Oxford: Clarendon Press.

6

ON THE TRANSITION FROM CODE-SWITCHING TO A MIXED CODE

Yael Maschler

1 Introduction

This chapter is concerned with two types of language alternation phenomena in bilingual conversation and with transitions and interactions between them. On the one hand, we find the case of code-switching[1] – using two languages for ad hoc, interpretive purposes, as a typically bilingual contextualisation cue (Gumperz 1982). On the other hand, we find the case of a mixed code – using two languages such that a third, new code emerges, in which elements from the two languages are incorporated into a structurally definable pattern.[2] First, I offer a diachronic perspective on language alternation phenomena by examining the emergence of a new, mixed code from ad hoc cases of code-switching (section 3). I then examine the interaction of this mixed code with ad hoc motivations for code-switching (section 5). An underlying, new theme in this study will be criteria for deciding when a particular case of language alternation constitutes a code-switch and when it can be said to constitute part of a new, mixed code (section 4).

The mixing versus switching issue has a tradition in syntactic research (e.g. Pfaff 1979, Poplack 1978, 1980, Myers-Scotton 1986), but the issue is not resolved there. In any event, in an interpretive approach to the study of code-switching in conversation, we will see that the basic questions which present themselves are very different.

2 Data and methodology

The study is based first on a corpus of a 40-minute audiotaped conversation chosen from a corpus of 18 hours of recorded conversation among Hebrew–English bilinguals in Israel. The conversation was transcribed in full and segmented into its intonation units, following Chafe (1994). This is a conversation about men which took place between two Hebrew–English bilingual women, named here Shira and Grace, who are family relatives in their early thirties, married and mothers of one young child each. Grace's eight-month-old baby, Tamar, is also present in the interaction, and the women meet in Shira's apartment in Jerusalem which is undergoing renovation in preparation for Shira's second child, with whom she is pregnant at the time.

The study is also based on a corpus of 20 hours of audiotaped playback sessions which I, also a Hebrew–English bilingual, conducted with the participants of this interaction a year later. This database provided many more examples of language alternation.

Shira immigrated to Israel from the US in early adolescence and had been living in Israel for seventeen years at the time. Grace immigrated from the US much later – six years before the conversation took place – but began her Hebrew language studies fifteen years earlier, in college. She nearly completed a Ph.D. in Hebrew literature, and currently teaches Hebrew as a second language in a major Israeli university. While the speakers in this corpus are all quite fluent in the two languages, the nature of their bilinguality differs. I focus here on aspects of Shira's bilinguality and support my qualitative findings with data from other bilingual situations. The quantitative findings, however, are based on the 40-minute corpus alone.

3 From code-switching to a mixed code

One of the clearest motivations for code-switching in this data is the beginning of a new conversational action (Ford and Thompson 1996) in the discourse (Maschler 1991, 1994b; cf. Alvarez-Cáccamo 1990). For instance, the following example begins with Grace elaborating her theory concerning men's *inability to compliment*.[3] (In this and all following examples from the corpus, italics are used for Hebrew and bold face is used for the identification of the specific portion discussed. Underlining is used for Yiddish.)

EXAMPLE 1

	GRACE	.... nó but you kno:w,
		... see Í think,
		... that the ínability to còmpliment,
		... nòt á:ll men have that inability,
5		... but má:ny .. men .. have that inability,
		... to cómpliment, =
	SHIRA	='*at rotsà smartút?*
		('YOU WANT A RAG?')
	GRACE	... right there,
		... Ì'll get it,
10		... Ì'll get it,

```
       SHIRA    [no (          )
       GRACE    [(          )
       SHIRA    ... here you go. {pp}
       GRACE    ... thánk you. {p}
15              ... thánk you! {pp, baby-talk intonation}
                ... say thánk you! {pp, baby-talk intonation}
                ... hás to do with the fà:ct, {mf, non-baby-talk intonation}
                ... that a lòt of mén,
                ... néed to feel,
20              ... that they're bé:tter than,
```

The conversation about men is interrupted in line 7 by something that has been going on with the baby meanwhile (a video recording would have provided more information here), and Shira offers Grace a rag for the baby. The offer is made in Hebrew. The women then leave the main topic of men to deal with getting the rag for ten English intonation units, after which Grace returns to the main topic in line 17. We see that the move to the new conversational action of dealing with the baby's needs is made in Hebrew.

A move to a new conversational action can also be made by the use of a discourse marker (Schiffrin 1987). In this study, in order to be considered a discourse marker, the utterance in question is required first of all to have a metalingual interpretation in the context in which it occurs (that is, rather than referring to the extralingual world, it must refer metalingually to the realm of the text or to the interaction between its participants; see Maschler 1994b for an elaboration of this). The second requirement has to do with structure: the utterance in question must appear at intonation-unit initial position, either at a point of speaker change, or in same-speaker talk, immediately following any intonation contour which is not continuing intonation (i.e. not after a comma in the transcription). It may occur after continuing intonation or at non intonation-unit initial position only if it follows another marker in a cluster.

Examine, for instance, the following example, following a generalisation made by Shira that men do not usually form close friendships:

EXAMPLE 2

```
       GRACE    .... wó:men .. you think are dìfferent?
       SHIRA    ... for women it's just
                .. it just is
                .. it's cúlturally more accè:ptable t:o
5               .. tir'ì there áre men, {change of tone}
                ('LOOK')
                .. who .. c::an .. form ... clóse relationships,
                ... and there àre women who cá:n't, {accel.}
```

Shira does not complete her line of thought in intonation unit 4. Instead, she moves on to a new conversational action of conceding the generalising character of her previous statement, that men do not usually form close relationships. The move to this new conversational action is accompanied by a change in pitch and amplitude (line 5). It also begins with the utterance *tir'i* ('look'), which is considered a discourse marker here because it has a metalingual interpretation in this context (i.e. it is not something in the extralingual world which Grace is instructed to look at), and occurs at intonation-unit initial position following a fragmentary intonation unit (line 4). As in example 1, the move to the new conversational action motivates language alternation. Whereas in example 1 the switch involved the entire first intonation unit of the new conversational action, in example 2 it involves only the discourse marker opening the new conversational action. What results is a structural contrast between the *English* discourse and the *Hebrew* discourse markers segmenting it.

Often, the language alternation strategies illustrated in examples 1 and 2 are combined. For instance, in the following example Shira expresses her amazement at how early boys realise that they should behave like men.

EXAMPLE 3

	SHIRA	... it's amázing,
		... hów quickly it còmes down on them,
		... that thèy have to be *gvarìm* .[4]
		('MEN')
		... *'axshav tagídi li,*
		('NOW TELL ME')
5		... *má hahevdel bein Alon ve:Nìra.*
		... ('WHAT'S THE DIFFERENCE BETWEEN ALON AND NIRA')
		... what's the gréat <u>gròise metsie</u> *hevdèl.* {f, high pitch}
		('BIG FIND') ('OF A DIFFERENCE')
	GRACE	... that one's a bò:y and one's a gí:rl you mean?
	SHIRA	... *naxón* I mean,
		('RIGHT')
		... but I mea:n=
10	GRACE	=in their personálities?
		[( )
	SHIRA	[they're bòth .. yóu:ng, {f}
		.. *ráx,* {f}
		('TENDER')129
		... six
15		.. you know síx year olds.= {high pitch}

GRACE = [yéah.
SHIRA [what's the gréa:t *hevdel* here.
('DIFFERENCE')

In line 4 Shira begins a new conversational action of asking Grace to compare a boy and a girl in their family. The move begins with a cluster of two Hebrew discourse markers *'axshav* ('now') and *tagídi li* ('tell me') verbalised within the same intonation unit (line 4). This cluster is followed by a switched intonation unit (line 5: *má hahevdel bein Alon ve:Nira,* 'what's the difference between Alon and Nira'?). She then continues in English.[5] We see that the strategies of language alternation at discourse markers and at the first intonation unit of a new conversational action are combined.

Altogether 49 different Hebrew discourse markers are found in Shira's speech during the 40-minute conversation. They are presented in Table 6.1 in a classification based on Becker's contextual realms (1988) shaping discourse. In other words, markers are classified according to the realm of context in which there are maximal shifts in aspects of context when the marker in question is employed (see Maschler 1994b for an elaboration of this). The number listed in parentheses by each marker gives the number of tokens found for that marker in the data. The first number at the top of each column indicates the number of different markers (types) in that column, and the second number (n) indicates the total number of tokens in that column.

In a quantitative study of this database, 162 discourse markers are found in Shira's speech during the 40-minute conversation. Of these, 107 or 66 per cent, are Hebrew markers.

If we examine discourse marker clusters, the pattern is even more striking. For instance, returning to example 3, in line 8 we find the next conversational action beginning with the Hebrew discourse marker *naxon* ('right'). This Hebrew discourse marker is followed by three English discourse markers in the same cluster (*I mean, but I mean*, lines 8–9).

Of the remaining 55 English markers, about half the markers – 27 of them – occur in a cluster with at least one Hebrew marker (as do the English markers in lines 8–9 of example 3). Table 6.2 presents the distribution of Hebrew and English discourse markers.

We see that 83 per cent of all markers are either Hebrew markers or occur in a cluster involving a Hebrew discourse marker. Only 17 per cent of the discourse markers in Shira's speech occur in clusters which are *unac-*companied by a switch to Hebrew. (An example would be Shira's *you know* in line 15 of example 3.) What is crucial about the *English* discourse markers in the latter category is that when they *are* used, *the surrounding discourse also takes place in English.* For example, *you know* of example 3, line 15, segments *English*, not Hebrew, discourse: *six you know six year olds.*

Another instance is found in the following example, in which Grace returns to discussing the two children, Alon and Nira.

Table 6.1 Shira's Hebrew discourse markers in the 40-minute conversation

Interpersonal (28, n=66)	Referential (8, n=21)	Structural (11, n=13)	Cognitive (2, n=7)
Perception verbs: *ti'ri* ('look') (8) *tishme'i* ('listen') (1) *ta'amini li* ('believe me') (1) *'at mevina?* ('you see?') (2) *bo'i navin* ('let's understand') (1) *ted'i lax* (lit. 'you should know', 'let me tell you') (1) *'at yoda'at* ('you know') (1) *'at yoda'at 'et ze?* ('you know this?') (1) *lo y'dat* ('don't know') (1) *leda'ati* (lit. 'according to my knowledge', 'in my opinion') (3) *bo'i naxshov 'al ze* ('let's think about this') (1) **Verbs of saying:** *tagidi li* ('tell me') (1) *ma 'ani 'agid lax* ('what shall I tell you') (1) *'ani lo yoda'at ma lehagid lax* ('I don't know what to tell you') (1) *bo'i nagid kaxa* ('let's put it this way') (1) *'ani 'omeret lax* ('I'm telling you') (1)	Deictics: *'axshav* ('now') (4) *kan* ('here') (1) **Causal:** *ki* ('because') (1) *biglal she . . .* ('because') (1)	Conjoining conversational actions: *ve . . .* ('and') (3) *gam* ('also') (1) **Organising the order of conversation actions:** *'alef* ('a') (1) *kodem kol* ('first of all') (1) *kodem 'al ha'inyan haze* ('first about this matter') (1) *texef* ('just a sec') (1) *xaki* ('wait') (1) *xaki shniya* ('wait a sec') (1)	Realising new information: *'a* ('oh') (2) **Taking time to process information:** *e:* ('uh') (5)

130

Table 6.1 continued

Interpersonal (28, n=66)	Referential (8, n=21)	Structural (11, n=13)	Cognitive (2, n=7)
Agreement: ken ('yeah') (14) naxon ('right') (9) ze naxon ('it's true') (4) bidyuk ('exactly') (1) betax ('sure') (1) 'ani betuxa ('I'm sure') (2) 'o key ('okay') (1) yaxol lihyot ('could be') (1)	**Consequential:** 'az ('so') (4)	**Introducing side actions:** 'agav ('by the way') (1) davka (introducing a side comment contrary to immediately preceding discourse) (1)	
Disagreement: lo ('no') (3) lo naxon ('not true') (1)	**Contrastive:** 'aval ('but') (5)	**Introducing a conversational action:** kaxa ('like this') (1)	
Other: bo'i . . . ('let's . . .') (2) ma ('what') (1)	**Concessive:** tov ('all right') (3) beseder ('alright') (2)		

131

Table 6.2 Shira's discourse markers in the 40-minute conversation

Hebrew	English (with Hebrew markers)		English (no Hebrew markers)
107 (66%)	27 (17%)		28 (17%)
		83%	17%
Total		162 (100%)	

EXAMPLE 4

GRACE	... but .. whát were you gonna sày,
	... whát do you think is the .. difference,
	... between Alon a:nd .. and .. Nira .. is.=
SHIRA	**=no but I'm sáying,**
5	... they shòuld not be tréa:ted so differently.

Here we find a cluster of three English discourse markers at a conversational action boundary, the beginning of a response, and the pattern of use of English discourse markers is very different from the pattern by which Hebrew discourse markers are used. Unlike the former case, in which the markers appear in one language and the surrounding discourse in the other (except for, perhaps, the immediately following intonation unit or so), here, *both* the markers *and* the surrounding discourse appear in the same language – English. Thus, except for two cases throughout the conversation (see Maschler 1997), English discourse markers are not used to highlight the contrast between the discourse and its frame of markers in the same way Hebrew discourse markers function in this text.

The pattern of switching languages at discourse markers can be seen also in studies of bi/multilingual discourse involving other languages, although these studies do not generally focus on this issue, and do not employ the term 'discourse marker'. Auer (1995), for instance, mentions the following example from German–Italian bilingual conversation (German is given in italics, Italian is underlined, and the specific portion discussed is given in bold face):

EXAMPLE 5

wenn ä Italiener kommt gell – sofort äh:
('when Italians come you know – immediately (they say):
guardate *Ittakerstinker und so*
look spaghetti heads and so on')

The Italian perception verb *guardate* ('look') is used to mark the beginning of the conversational action of constructing dialogue (Tannen 1989).

In Stroud's data from Taiap–Tok Pisin bilingual conversation (1992) we find a similar case (Taiap is given in italics, Tok Pisin is underlined, and the specific portions discussed are given in bold face).

EXAMPLE 6

	KRUNI	*Uh huh.*
	KEM	**Olsem** *ŋa/ŋa nambar ŋayar ɛnda.*
		('**like**, I/I'm really alone').
		yimɛn ɔrɔmnt kut.
		('I'm in your midst')
		yumana.
		('For you all')
5		**Na** *ŋa ŋayar ŋa sindɛr ida.*
		('**And** I'm truly, I'm without support')
		Na *ŋa ginana inda yumana prukakut.*
		('**And** therefore I'm working for you all')

Stroud notes the function of these Tok Pisin elements 'to maintain the floor, and structure information into bounded units . . . a means of segmenting . . . talk and signaling the introduction of new information' (ibid.: 141–2).

Tao and Thompson (1991) discuss examples of Mandarin 'interference' in the English talk of Mandarin–English bilinguals (Mandarin is given in italics, English is given in regular style, and the specific portion discussed is given in bold face. Other transcription conventions remain as in Tao and Thompson 1991: 219).

EXAMPLE 7

	MEIHUA	*Keshi ta –,*
		('But the–')
		zheige baishu ne,
		('the white yam')
		buhao cun.
		('is not easy to store')
		Ni chun zai jiao limian,
		('Even if you keep them in the cellar')
5		*you de shihou ye hui,*
		('sometimes they may also')
	MICHAEL	**Uhm**= *shi.*
		('Uhm right')

[*Hui lan.*]
('May rot')

MEIHUA   [*Ye hui huai .*]
('May also go bad')
Ye hui lan .
('May also rot')

Tao and Thompson find that when these speakers use Mandarin, their backchannel behaviour is strongly influenced by English. The *uhm* in Michael's talk here is similar to the *naxon* ('right') of example 3, line 8, at the beginning of the conversational action of agreeing.

In the studies presented at the Hamburg workshop, this pattern can be seen in the data of Oesch Serra (this volume), Alfonzetti (this volume) and Moyer (1995). For a more complete survey of the literature in which this strategy was found, see Maschler (1997).

Returning now to the present data, we find here a statistically significant pattern in the employment of discourse markers. Schiffrin (1987) and other linguists studying discourse markers have shown that the need to create and reflect conversational action boundaries in monolingual discourse motivates the employment of discourse markers. In Shira's talk, an additional structural pattern concerning discourse markers emerges: whereas the discourse takes place mostly in English, the discourse markers framing it involve Hebrew for 83 per cent of the markers. This statistically significant structural pattern is viewed here as indicating an *emergence of a mixed code* in Shira's talk: one in which the discourse is separated from the markers framing it in language.

Another, even more statistically significant structural pattern involving discourse markers in Shira's speech is their separation in language from sentence-level conjunctions. In this study, in order to be considered a conjunction, the utterance in question must follow non-sentence-final intonation (transcribed by a comma) or appear following another conjunction in a cluster.

The following example illustrates the contrast between conjunctions and discourse markers. In a discussion about whether differences between boys and girls are innate, Grace asks Shira whether she has read what Brazelton has written about the issue. Shira answers and brings the example of her own three-year-old son, Yo'av.

EXAMPLE 8

GRACE   ... did you ever read Brázelton's bòok?
SHIRA   ...   [*kén*.
                     ('yes')
GRACE   [([   )
SHIRA   [*'aval ted 'i la:x,*
                   (lit. 'but you should know', 'but let me tell you')

134

```
5              ... that dávka Yo'av,
               (PARTICLE INDICATING CONTRASTIVENESS,'YO'AV AS
               OPPOSED TO OTHER BOYS')
               ... was always the quíet bàby,
               ... the òne who would sít there,
               ... and wátch things,
               ... and /táke/ it i:n,
10             ... and=
     GRACE          =yéah.
```

Whereas the cluster of the three Hebrew markers (lines 2, 4) *ken* ('yes'), *'aval* ('but') and *ted'í lax* ('let me tell you') involves a *conversational action boundary* (the beginning of Shira's response to Grace's question), the conjunction *and*, occurring three times in this example (lines 8–10), does not involve a conversational action boundary. All three instances of this conjunction follow non-sentence final intonation and add information about the same referent, Shira's son, Yo'av, who is an exception to a previous generalisation in the conversation, that boys are more active and less introspective than girls.

Furthermore, the conjunction *and* of example 8 contrasts with the discourse marker *ve* ... ('and') example 9. In this example, which occurs shortly after example 1, Shira opposes Grace's opinion that men's 'inability to compliment has to do with the fact that' they 'need to feel that they're better than' women (example 1). According to Shira, men are 'afraid of being rejected'.

EXAMPLE 9

```
     SHIRA   ... lí:sten to the tò:nes of voice,
             ... with which they tá:lk,
             ... sómetimes,
             ... these shéepish little
5            ... they are afrài:d of being rejécted!
             ... mén.
     TAMAR   {whines}
     SHIRA   ... ve'ani
             ('AND I')
             ... 'ani ló be'àd lesaben 'otam lemala velemata,
             ('I'M NOT IN FAVOUR OF (LIT.) "SOAPING THEM UP AND
             DOWN" ', I.E. 'GIVING THEM WAY TOO MANY
             COMPLIMENTS')
```

In line 8 Shira begins a new conversational action of telling what she thinks is not an appropriate response to this problem of men: one is not to give them too many compliments. This conversational action begins with the bound

Table 6.3 Shira's use of discourse markers and conjunctions

Discourse markers			Conjunctions	
Hebrew	English (with Hebrew marker)	English (no Hebrew marker)	Hebrew	English
107 (66%)	83% 27 (17%)	28 (17%) 17%	2 (3%)	56 (97%)
Total	162 (100%)	58 (100%)		

morpheme *ve* . . . ('and') functioning here as a discourse marker (along with a switched first intonation unit of the new conversational action (line 9), as in example 3), in contrast with the English conjunction *and* of example 8.

Altogether, 58 conjunctions are found in the 40-minute conversation. Of these, 56 (97 per cent) are English conjunctions. Apart from *and*, 8 other different conjunctions were found in this conversation: *(be)cause, since, so, if, then, but, or* and *even though*. From examining Table 6.1 it can be seen that *and, (be)cause, so* and *but* have Hebrew 'equivalents' which function in this conversation as discourse markers. (They are found in the referential and structural columns of Table 6.1)

Table 6.3 summarises the quantitative facts illustrated so far concerning discourse markers and conjunctions.

Thus, while 83 per cent of the discourse markers in Shira's talk involve the use of Hebrew, *97 per cent of the conjunctions are verbalised in English. This is viewed here as additional evidence for the emergence of a mixed code in Shira's talk*: one in which discourse markers are separated from conjunctions in language, such that discourse markers generally involve Hebrew, while conjunctions are verbalised in English.

We have seen that motivations for language alternation at discourse markers originate from the need to mark conversational action boundaries. When no conversational action boundary is involved, as in the case of conjunctions, there is no language switch. This suggests the emergence of a new, mixed code in which two structural patterns at the textual level of grammar can be discerned: (1) the discourse is separated in language from the discourse markers framing it, and (2) discourse markers are separated in language from conjunctions.

4 Criteria for constituting part of a mixed code

Du Bois studied the process of grammaticisation,

> the shifting from relatively freely constructed utterances in discourse, whose idiosyncratic form is motivated only by the speaker's goals for the immediate speech event . . . to relatively

fixed constructions in grammar, seen as arbitrary (though *ultimately* not necessarily unmotivated) constraints on the speaker's output.

(1985: 346)

In the bilingual context, the 'relatively freely constructed utterances in discourse' are the cases of code-switching. The 'relatively fixed constructions in grammar', on the other hand, are those switches which are part of the mixed code. Just as Du Bois's relatively fixed constructions are *ultimately* not necessarily unmotivated', similarly, the switches which form part of the mixed code are ultimately not unmotivated: we have seen that they are motivated by the need to mark the beginning of a new conversational action.

One would like to know more about when a case of code-switching is said to have been grammaticised into part of a new, mixed code. So far we have seen that the answer has to do with two issues. The first is statistical: if the ad hoc switch repeats itself in a statistically significant way, we are concerned with a recurring pattern. The second issue concerns the nature of the switch: it must result in some *structural* pattern which can be discerned in the new code. In this case, we have seen two structural patterns concerning discourse markers, which appear at the textual level of the grammar of the mixed code.

A third issue relevant to characterising a case of language alternation as having been grammaticised into part of a mixed code has to do with the functions of the switched elements in the mixed code. In the case of the Hebrew discourse markers, if we could show that they are used exclusively and that there is no English marker with the same function in the data, that would provide an additional argument supporting the emergence of a mixed code. This is because in the course of grammaticisation there is a narrowing down of options.[6] Ad hoc alternatives (employing either an English or a Hebrew discourse marker) would be ruled out because there is a grammatical structure instead of a contextually induced variety of options. Thus, variation between English and Hebrew for the same purpose (employing a particular discourse marker) should decrease in the course of grammaticisation.

In order to investigate to what extent the Hebrew discourse markers are used exclusively here, let us compare the English and Hebrew sets of discourse markers employed by Shira in this conversation. Table 6.1 shows the distribution of the 49 different Hebrew markers in the text. Table 6.4 shows the distribution of the 20 different English markers.

Many interesting points arise from comparing the two tables. First let us look at the similarity between them. They both exhibit the same columns. Thus, the discourse markers of the two languages function within the same four realms – interpersonal, referential, structural, and cognitive. Apart from the structural column, on the whole, both tables generally exhibit similar categories within each column. Furthermore, the two tables are comprised

Table 6.4 Shira's English discourse markers in the 40-minute conversation

Interpersonal (8, n=19)	Referential (4, n=12)	Structural (6, n=21)	Cognitive (2, n=3)
Perception verbs: *you know* (3) *you see* (1)	Deictics: *now* (2)	Conjoining conversational actions: *and* (10) *also* (1)	Realising new information: *oh* (1)
Verbs of saying: *say* (1) *I'm saying* (3)	Causal: *since* (1)	Organising the order of conver-sation actions: *first of all* (5) *that's number one* (1)	Explaining oneself: *I mean* (2)
Agreement: *yeah* (2) *right* (5)	Consequential: *so* (3)	Introducing conversational actions serving as examples: *like* (3)	
Disagreement: *no* (3) *well* (1)	Contrastive: *but* (6)	Repeating conversational action: *again* (1)	

of similar elements of language: perception verbs, verbs of saying, agreement and disagreement tokens, conjunctions expressing similar relationships (cause, result, contrast, coordination), deictics, 'fillers'. The most marked difference is found in the column of structural markers – markers providing information concerning the ways successive conversational actions are related to one another in terms of conjunction, order and hierarchical rela-tions.[7] Here, besides the basic functions of conjoining conversational actions and marking the first conversational action in a series, the elements consti-tuting the Hebrew structural discourse markers and their functions differ significantly from those of the English markers.

Now to other differences between the two tables. The number and variety of Hebrew markers in this corpus is indeed much greater, but this is true to varying degrees for the different columns. Comparing Tables 6.1 and 6.4, we see that the greatest difference in quantitative employment of discourse markers is found in the interpersonal category. This category includes markers whose use facilitates the negotiation of closeness versus distance between participants. There are over three times as many Hebrew inter-personal discourse markers as there are English ones – this is true for types as well as for tokens (28 Hebrew vs. 8 English types, 66 Hebrew vs. 19 English tokens).

In the referential realm, the ratio is closer to 2:1. This category includes two types of markers: the deictics, whose functions in the text parallel their deictic reference in the world narrated by the text, and other markers, whose functions are to mark relationships between conversational actions (e.g. cause, consequence, contrast, concession). These relationships mirror the semantic properties of the expressions employed as discourse markers. We find that there are about twice as many Hebrew referential markers (types as well as tokens, again), as there are English referential markers (8 Hebrew vs. 4 English types, 21 Hebrew vs. 12 English tokens).

In the structural realm the picture is again very different. While there are about twice as many Hebrew, as opposed to English, types (11 vs. 6), there are almost twice as many *English* tokens (13 Hebrew vs. 21 English tokens).[8]

Finally, in the cognitive realm, each set exhibits two types, but there are about twice as many Hebrew tokens (7 Hebrew vs. 3 English tokens). This category includes markers providing information about cognitive shifts occurring at conversational action boundaries which are often revealed in the spoken medium of discourse.

We see that indeed there is a narrowing down of options in the employment of English versus Hebrew discourse markers. A discourse marker is about three times as likely to be in Hebrew if it is an interpersonal marker, about twice as likely to be in Hebrew if it is a referential or cognitive marker, and more likely to be in English if it is a structural discourse marker. This suggests that grammaticisation of Hebrew discourse markers in the mixed code occurs most of all in the interpersonal dimension of discourse, to a noticeable degree in the referential and cognitive dimensions of discourse, but not as much in the structural realm. In other words, the negotiation of closeness versus distance between participants is accomplished through discourse marker employment three times as often in Hebrew by Shira. Relationships between conversational actions mirror the semantics of Hebrew expressions about twice as often as they do those of English expressions. Another way to say this is that most of the iconicities (Becker 1982, Maschler 1993) involving discourse markers are Hebrew iconicities. Cognitive shifts at conversational action boundaries seem to occur about twice as often in Hebrew as they do in English.[9] But the ways successive conversational actions are related to one another in terms of conjunction, order, and hierarchical relations are more often English ways. In other words, the organisation of the structure of the text is mostly an English organisation, but all other aspects of it – interpersonal relations, iconicities with the extralingual world, and cognitive aspects – are accomplished mostly in Hebrew.

It is also revealing to examine those markers in the data which are found along with their 'equivalents' in the two languages. Table 6.5 shows that this happens for only 12 markers in the data. Thus, there are 37 Hebrew markers with no English equivalent and 8 English markers with no Hebrew

Table 6.5 Markers with equivalents in both languages in the 40-minute conversation

Interpersonal	Referential	Structural	Cognitive
Perception verbs: *you know* (3) *at yoda'at* (1) *you see* (1) *'at mevina?* (2)	Deictics: *now* (2) *'axshav* (4)	Conjoining conversational actions: *and* (10) *ve . . .* (3) *also* (1) *gam* (1) Organising the order of conversation actions: *first of all* (5) *kodem kol* (1)	Realising new information: *oh* (1) *'a* (2)
Agreement: *yeah* (2) *ken* (14) *right* (5) *naxon* (9)	Consequential: *so* (3) *'az* (4)		
Disagreement: *no* (3) *lo* (3)	Contrastive: *but* (6) *'aval* (5)		

equivalent in the 40-minute conversation.[10] This in itself is strong evidence that many Hebrew discourse markers are used exclusively and that there are no English markers with the same functions in the data. Hence, additional support for the emergence of a mixed code.

We see that the markers appearing with their 'equivalent' in the other language tend to be the most basic markers for the particular category: *ken* and *yeah*, *naxon* and *right* for agreement, *lo* and *no* for disagreement, *'axshav* and *now* for deictics, *'az* and *so* for consequence, *'aval* and *but* for contrast, *ve . . .* and *and*, *gam* and *also* for conjoining conversational actions, *kodem kol* and *first of all* for organising the order of conversational actions, and *'a* and *oh* for realising new information.

The most basic markers tend also to be those used most commonly in the particular category. Thus, in the interpersonal dimension the most commonly used Hebrew agreement (*ken*, *naxon*) and disagreement (*lo*) tokens have English 'equivalents' in the corpus (*yeah*, *right* and *no* respectively). (However, this is not the case with perception verbs and verbs of saying.) Similarly, the most commonly used Hebrew referential markers (*'axshav*, *'az* and *'aval*) have English 'equivalents' (*now*, *so* and *but* respectively). In fact, these markers are used about as often in the two languages. In the structural realm, which, as we have seen, is English dominant, the most commonly used markers (*and* and *first of all*) also have Hebrew 'equivalents'. However, the most commonly used cognitive discourse marker, *'e* ('uh'), does not have an English 'equivalent' in the data.[11]

On the other hand, the more specialised the marker within a particular category, the less likely it is to have an equivalent. So, for example, while *ken*, in the agreement category, has an English 'equivalent' (*yeah*), *bidyuk* ('exactly') does not. Furthermore, when a more specialised category is concerned, there is no equivalent category in the other language in this corpus. For example, the more specialised category of concession[12] (in comparison to the less specialised categories of cause, consequence and contrast, for instance, within the referential realm) is found only for Hebrew here; and the more specialised categories of introducing conversational actions serving as examples, or repeating a conversational action (in comparison to the less specialised categories of conjoining conversational actions or organising their order, within the structural realm) are found only for English here.

From this we learn that options for choosing either an English or a Hebrew marker decrease also the more specialised a marker is. In other words, the more specialised the marker, the more likely it is to be used exclusively in only one of the languages (usually Hebrew), and therefore the more we would expect it to have undergone grammaticisation in the mixed code. The extreme cases are, of course, markers which are specialised to such an extent that they simply have no equivalent in the other language (not just in this data), such as English *well* or Hebrew *davka* (used to introduce a side comment contrary to immediately preceding discourse).

Still more support for the mixed-code argument comes from examining the exact functions of markers appearing with their 'equivalents' in the data (those found in Table 6.5). This will explain the use of quotes at the above mentions of the concept of equivalence. I surmise that the functions of the Hebrew discourse markers in my data must be somewhat different from the functions of the 'equivalent' English discourse markers, as well as from the functions of these Hebrew markers when they are employed in monolingual Hebrew conversation. If this is the case, then we can show that a third, mixed code has indeed emerged: aside from the two existing codes, one involving English, the other Hebrew utterances (such as line 7 of example 1: *'at rotsà smartút?* 'you want a rag?'), there would be elements fully belonging neither to Hebrew nor to English.

It seems intuitively correct that the Hebrew discourse markers in Shira's talk do not fully belong to either language. First of all, if we consider the full prior-text (Becker 1979) of utterances, and this must include poetic usages (Friedrich 1979) in which they are often involved, we know that there are no *exact* equivalents across languages. Thus, Hebrew *'at yoda'at* and English *you know* (as in example 3, line 15), are not absolute equivalents of each other. The mere grammatical fact (let alone poetic usages) that one varies according to gender and number of addressee and one does not should suffice to make this point.

Second, the switched Hebrew markers gain new meanings from their bilingual contexts, which are absent when they are employed in monolingual Hebrew discourse, and so the switched Hebrew markers must have somewhat different functions than when they appear in monolingual Hebrew discourse. Returning to our example, Shira's *'at yoda'at* in this conversation must be different in some, perhaps very subtle, way from *'at yoda'at* in monolingual Hebrew discourse. One difference has to do with the fact that *'at yoda'at* occurs here as an element which varies according to gender and number of addressee in the midst of discourse which does not generally exhibit these categories grammatically. This *'at yoda'at*, then, might call attention to the specific components of the immediate interaction (specifically, the identity of the addressee) in a different way than it would in monolingual Hebrew discourse. This question, however, exceeds the boundaries of the present study, as additional data is needed in order to investigate the exact differences.

5 The mixed code and new cases of code-switching

If there is indeed a new, mixed code emerging in Shira's talk, a question arises as to why the mixed code does not exhibit the patterns described here in 100 per cent of the cases. We have seen that the patterns by which discourse markers are employed form two structural contrasts in the new, mixed code, at its textual level: (1) the contrast between the discourse and its frame, and (2) the contrast between discourse markers and conjunctions. However, language alternation phenomena can be motivated by many types of contrast in discourse, not just structural contrasts: contrast between different social groups, between different voices in a discourse, between contrasting propositions, between contrasting conversational actions, between preferred and dispreferred responses, and between direct and indirect speech, among others. This can be seen in many studies of bilingual conversation (e.g. Gumperz and Hernandez-Chavez 1971, Blom and Gumperz 1972, Myers-Scotton and Ury 1977, Gal 1979, Gumperz 1982, Heller 1982, Hill 1985, 1986, Hill and Hill 1986, Myers-Scotton 1986, 1988, McConvell 1988, Olshtain and Blum-Kulka 1989, Romaine 1989, Kulick and Stroud 1990, Stroud 1992, Maschler 1994a, 1994b, Auer 1995, Li Wei and Milroy 1995). Because of the situation of competing motivations (Du Bois 1985) for the strategy of highlighting contrast via language alternation (Maschler 1995), the patterns described in section 3 are not always observed.

By examining the exceptions to those patterns one can see that when the structural patterns of the mixed code are not observed, there is usually ad hoc motivation for code-switching in which another type of contrast is involved. Since I have written at length about this matter elsewhere (Maschler 1995), I will examine only two exceptions here.

In the case of the pattern of separating discourse markers from conjunctions in language, we have seen that 97 per cent of the conjunctions are verbalised in English. There are only two exceptions throughout the 40-minute conversation. One exception involves a conjunction of contrast. This happens in the midst of Shira's story about her husband's role in initiating the apartment renovation.

EXAMPLE 10

	SHIRA	... first of all,
		... it's really
		... it's thánks to hì:m,
		.... that the who:le
5		... that the whòle thing *mitbatsé'a* .
		('IS TAKING PLACE')
		... reálly it is,
		... **'cause** Í thought of the idea a long tìme ago,
		... **'aval** /mi:/
		('BUT')
		...... [I dismíssed it ... I dismíssed it
10	GRACE	[/you/ didn't dó it.
	SHIRA	... I còuldn't dó anything ab[out it,
	GRACE	[yeah.

There are two conjunctions in this example, English *'cause* and Hebrew *'aval* ('but') (both following continuing intonation). Although no conversational action boundary is involved, we find here a switch to Hebrew. Not coincidentally, this Hebrew conjunction expresses *contrast* between two propositions: Shira had thought of renovating 'a long time ago', but she 'dismissed it', because she 'couldn't do anything about it'. The contrastive conjunction is separated in language from the English propositions it contrasts. This creates an exception to the pattern by which conjunctions are verbalised in English in this corpus.

Contrast between contrasting propositions is of a different type than contrast between discourse markers and conjunctions. In the former case we are dealing with semantic contrast pertaining to the immediate speech situation, in the latter with structural contrast in the new, mixed code. In other words, here we find local motivation for code-switching, not an 'across the board' pattern, recurrent in the mixed code. In the terms used by Meeuwis and Blommaert (this volume), this case illustrates 'layered code-switching': the ad hoc code-switch related to expressing semantic contrast is layered upon one of the patterns of the mixed code.

One of the follow-up interviews exhibits the use of another Hebrew contrastive conjunction, *mitsad sheni* ('on the other hand'). Talking about the experience of the conversation they had recorded, Shira tells Grace and me how on the one hand she just wanted 'to get it over with' ('it' being the recording task which she had promised me to do), and on the other hand she was actually having a good time; because, being relatives, she and Grace almost always meet with other people present, and this was their first chance to have a real conversation with each other.

EXAMPLE 11

SHIRA   ... I was .. *belibí*,
                      ('IN MY HEART')
    ... *ktsát bekivùn* of,
                      ('A BIT IN THE DIRECTION')
    ... *yálla* ,
                      (INTERJECTION (FROM ARABIC), 'OKAY, LET'S GO')
    ... lét's get it òver with,

5   .. ***vemitsàd shení:*** ,
                      ('AND ON THE OTHER HAND')
    ... it was e
    ... *káxa* ,
                      ('KIND OF')
    it was the fírst tìme,
    ... and the ónly tìme,

10   ... you eve:r .. cáme òver, {i.e. Grace}
    ... and we spènt the afternóon *bidiyùk* [*kaxa*,
                                        ('JUST   THIS WAY')

GRACE   [ríght.
SHIRA   ... and it was fún!=
GRACE   =yéah.

Again, no conversational action boundary is involved and the contrastive conjunction *mitsad sheni* ('on the other hand') appears in Hebrew, in a cluster following the Hebrew coordinative conjunction *ve* ... , expressing referential contrast in the immediate speech situation between two propositions. As in the previous case, when ad hoc motivation for code-switching is present, we find an exception to the patterns of the mixed code.

6 Conclusion

In this chapter I have argued for an emergence of a mixed code from ad hoc cases of code-switching. I have supported my claim in three ways: presenting quantitative data, illustrating structural patterns in the emerging mixed code, and showing that the elements which I argue to be part of the mixed code have exclusive functions in the data (to varying degrees, depending on the contextual realm in which they function and on their degree of specialisation), with no equivalents in the other language. I have then demonstrated that the patterns of this mixed code are 'deferred' in the presence of new, ad hoc motivation for code-switching.

An avenue for further research which ties to other studies in this collection presents itself at this point. We have already seen that the separation of discourse markers from the discourse they frame is a pattern common to many situations of bilingual conversation, not just the one studied here. The question is whether the patterns in the differential use of discourse markers (those described in section 4) are particular to Shira's talk, or whether we find them in other Hebrew–English bilingual conversations as well. If we find, for example, that interpersonal markers consistently occur significantly more in Hebrew than do other markers, we may be able to conclude something about the relationship between ethnography and conversation analysis in the Israeli Hebrew–American English case. However, if we continue to find the same differential patterns in the employment of discourse markers in bilingual conversations in other language pairs – for example that the structural columns in the new tables we compare show consistently different patterns compared with the other columns – we will have to conclude that we are dealing with something particular to the nature of structural discourse markers, unrelated to the ethnographic context in which interaction takes place.

Notes

I wish to thank the participants of the Colloquy on Codeswitching in Conversation for suggesting a new angle on this research to me, in particular Peter Auer, Melissa Moyer, Celso Alvarez-Cáccamo and Jan Blommaert.

1 In previous studies I have avoided this term so as not to evoke the code metaphor of language (Maschler 1991). With these reservations in mind, I use the term here for the sake of consistency with the rest of the studies in the volume.

2 Meeuwis and Blommaert (this volume) take a 'monolectal view of code-switching' in this case.

3 Transcription basically follows Chafe (1994), changing a few conventions and adding some conventions of musical notation. In this transcription method speech is segmented into what Chafe calls intonation units – 'a sequence of words combined under a single, coherent intonation contour, usually preceded by a pause' (1987: 22). In my transcription, each intonation unit begins in a new line. Other transcription conventions are as follows:

...	half second pause (each extra dot = another half second)
..	perceptible pause of less than half a second
(3.22)	measured pause of 3.22 seconds
´	primary stress
`	secondary stress
"	particularly marked primary stress
,	comma at end of line: clause final intonation ('more to come')
.	period at end of line: sentence final falling intonation
?	question mark at end of line: sentence final rising intonation
!	exclamation mark at end of line: sentence final exclamatory intonation

#	no punctuation at end of line: fragmentary intonation unit
:	colon: elongation of preceding vowel sound
[	square brackets to the left of two consecutive lines indicate overlapping speech, two speakers talking at once
=	equals sign to the right of top line= =and to the left of bottom line indicates latching, no interturn pause
( )	transcription impossible
/ /	words within slashes indicate uncertain transcription
accel.	accelerando, speeding up
decresc.	decrescendo, progressively softer in volume
p	piano, spoken softly
mp	mezzo piano, spoken fairly softly
f	forte, spoken loudly
mf	mezzo forte, spoken fairly loudly
{ }	transcriber's comments are set off by curly brackets.
(' ')	translations are set off by single quotes within parentheses.

4 Of course, not all language-alternation phenomena in this text are motivated by the beginning of a new conversational action. The switch at *gvarìm* ('men') is motivated by prior-textual factors (Becker 1979). The prior text of the Hebrew word is much richer in 'machoism' than its English equivalent. See Maschler 1991 for more on prior-textual constraints on language-alternation phenomena.

5 The Yiddish words in intonation unit 6 are borrowed into this East European variety of English, and Hebrew *hevdèl* ('difference') in line 6 is repeated from intonation unit 5. The motivation here is cognitive: it is less time-consuming to repeat a word mentioned previously than to translate it (Maschler 1991). Hebrew *hevdèl* ('difference') is then used again in Shira's next conversational action (in line 17), which also begins with a Hebrew discourse marker, *naxon* ('right') (line 8).

6 I thank Peter Auer for bringing up this point and encouraging me to develop it.

7 Maschler 1994b provides a more thorough discussion of the functions of the markers in the various categories.

8 However, if we disregard the discourse markers *and* and its Hebrew equivalent *ve* ..., the ratio is 10 Hebrew vs. 11 English tokens. We might like to disregard them, because *ve* ... is a bound morpheme, and therefore less likely to be switched (Poplack 1980) and separated in language from the discourse it frames. Indeed, in its three occurrences it is employed either with a first switched intonation unit of the new conversational action (as in example 9, line 8), or between two Hebrew discourse markers in a cluster. In any event, even if we do disregard these discourse markers which consist of the coordinative conjunctions, the structural markers still show a different pattern in the number of tokens (about an equal number of English and Hebrew tokens), as compared with the other discourse markers in the data. This, coupled with the fact that the structural columns show different categories and elements for the two languages, suggests that the case of the structural discourse markers is different from the rest of the markers in this conversation.

9 This suggests that cognitive processes during verbalisation are language-dependent.

10 These figures change, of course, upon examination of the 20 hours of follow-up interviews. In the interest of keeping the database manageable, I have limited the quantitative study, as noted earlier, to the 40-minute conversation. However, my general impression from this additional data is that more types are found for the two languages, but the proportions of the tokens remain similar.

11 For a discussion of this marker, see Maschler 1994b.
12 Another reason concessive markers might occur in Hebrew here has to do with their interpersonal component. In conceding a statement, one is also agreeing with something which, often, was said by the interlocutor. Agreement is one of the quintessential matters in the negotiation of closeness vs. distance with the addressee, and, as we have seen, interpersonal markers are three times more likely to be Hebrew markers.

Bibliography

Alvarez-Cáccamo, Celso (1990) 'Rethinking conversational code-switching: Codes, speech varieties, and contextualization', *Proceedings of the Sixteenth Annual Meeting of the Berkeley Linguistics Society* 16: 3–16.

Auer, Peter (1995) 'The pragmatics of code-switching: A sequential approach', in G. Lüdi, L. Milroy, and P. Muysken (eds) *One Speaker, Two Languages: Cross-Disciplinary Perspectives on Codeswitching*, Cambridge: Cambridge University Press. 115–135.

Becker, Alton L. (1979) 'Text-building, epistemology, and esthetics in Javanese shadow theater', in A. L. Becker and A. Yengoyan (eds) *The Imagination of Reality*, Norwood, N.J.: Ablex. 211–43. Reprinted in Alton L. Becker (1995) *Beyond Translation*, Ann Arbor: University of Michigan Press.

—— (1982) 'Beyond translation: Esthetics and language description', in H. Byrnes (ed.) *Contemporary Perceptions of Language: Interdisciplinary Dimensions (Georgetown University Round Table on Languages and Linguistics 1982)*, Washington D.C.: Georgetown University Press. 124–38. Reprinted in Alton L. Becker (1995) *Beyond Translation*, Ann Arbor: University of Michigan Press.

—— (1988) 'Language in particular: A lecture', in D. Tannen (ed.) *Linguistics in Context: Connecting Observation and Understanding. (Lectures from the 1985 LSA/TESOL and NEH Institutes)*, Norwood, N.J.: Ablex. 17–35. Reprinted in Alton L. Becker (1995) *Beyond Translation*, Ann Arbor: University of Michigan Press.

—— (1995) *Beyond Translation*, Ann Arbor: University of Michigan Press.

Blom, Jan-Petter and John J. Gumperz (1972) 'Social meaning in linguistic structures: Code-switching in Norway', in J. J. Gumperz and D. Hymes (eds) *Directions in Sociolinguistics: The Ethnography of Communication*, New York: Basil Blackwell. 407–34.

Chafe, Wallace (1987) 'Cognitive constraints on information flow', in R. S. Tomlin (ed.) *Typological Studies in Language, Vol. 11: Coherence and Grounding in Discourse*, Amsterdam: John Benjamins. 21–51.

—— (1994) *Discourse, Consciousness, and Time: The Flow and Displacement of Conscious Experience in Speaking and Writing*, Chicago, Ill.: University of Chicago Press.

Du Bois, John W. (1985) 'Competing motivations', in J. Haiman (ed.) *Iconicity in Syntax*, Amsterdam/Philadelphia: John Benjamins. 343–65.

Ford, Cecilia (1993) *Grammar in Interaction: Adverbial Clauses in American English Conversations*, Cambridge: Cambridge University Press.

Ford, Cecilia and Thompson, Sandra, A. (1996) 'Interactional units in conversation: Syntactic, intonational, and pragmatic resources for the management of turns', in E. Ochs, E. Schegloff and S. Thompson (eds) *Interaction and Grammar*, Cambridge: Cambridge University Press, 134–84.

Friedrich, Paul (1979) 'Poetic language and the imagination: A reformulation of the Sapir hypothesis', in *Language Context, and the Imagination: Essays by Paul*

Friedrich, selected and introduced by A. S. Dil, Stanford: Stanford University Press. 441–512.

Gal, Susan (1979) *Language Shift: Social Determination of Linguistic Change in Bilingual Austria*, New York: Academic Press.

Gumperz, John J. (1982) *Discourse Strategies*, Cambridge: Cambridge University Press.

Gumperz, John J. and Hernandez-Chavez, E. (1971) 'Cognitive aspects of bilingual communication', in W. H. Whiteley (ed.) *Language Use and Social Change*, London: Oxford University Press. 111–25.

Heller, Monica (1982) 'Negotiations of language choice in Montreal', in J. J. Gumperz (ed.) *Language and Social Identity*, Cambridge: Cambridge University Press. 108–44.

Hill, Jane (1985) 'The grammar of consciousness and the consciousness of grammar', *American Ethnologist* 12, 4: 725–37.

—— (1986) 'The refiguration of the anthropology of language', *Cultural Anthropology* 1, 1: 89–102.

Hill, Jane and Hill, Kenneth (1986) *Speaking Mexicano: Dynamics of Syncretic Language in Central Mexico*, Tuscon: University of Arizona Press.

Kulick, Don and Stroud, Christopher (1990) 'Code-switching in Gapun: Social and linguistic aspects of language use in a language shifting community', in J. Verhaar (ed.) *Melanesian Pidgin and Tok Pisin (Studies in Language Companion Series 20)*, Amsterdam: John Benjamins. 205–34.

Li Wei and Milroy, Lesley (1995) 'Preference marking and repair strategies in bilingual conversation: Evidence from a Chinese–English bilingual Community', *Journal of Pragmatics* 23: 281–99.

McConvell, Patrick (1988) 'Mix-im-up: Aboriginal code-switching, old and new', in M. Heller (ed.) *Codeswitching: Anthropological and Sociolinguistic Perspectives*, Berlin: Mouton de Gruyter. 97–169.

Maschler, Yael (1991) 'The language games bilinguals play: Language alternation at language game boundaries', *Language and Communication* 11, 4: 263–89.

—— (1993) 'Iconicity in discourse: The story of Echo', *Poetics Today* 14, 4: 653–89.

—— (1994a) 'Appreciation *ha'araxa 'o ha'aratsa?* ("valuing or admiration"): Negotiating contrast in bilingual disagreement talk', *Text* 14, 2: 207–38.

—— (1994b) 'Metalanguaging and discourse markers in bilingual conversation', *Language in Society* 23, 3: 325–66.

—— (1995) 'Competing motivations for iconic contrast in Hebrew–English bilingual conversation', *Texas Linguistic Forum* 34: 29–39.

—— (1997) 'Emergent bilingual grammar: The case of contrast', *Journal of Pragmatics* 28, 3: 279–313.

Moyer, Melissa (1995) 'English–Spanish code-switching in Gibraltar: The quest for bilingual conversational structure', paper presented at the Colloquy on Codeswitching in Conversation, February 16–18, University of Hamburg.

Myers-Scotton, Carol (1986) 'Diglossia and code-switching', in J. Fishman, A. Tabouret-Keller, M. Clyne, Bh. Krishnamurti and M. Abdulaziz (eds) *The Fergusonian Impact, Vol. 2: Sociolinguistics and the Sociology of Language*, Berlin: Mouton de Gruyter. 403–16.

Myers-Scotton, Carol (1988) 'Codeswitching as indexical of social negotiations', in M. Heller (ed.) *Codeswitching: Anthropological and Sociolinguistic Perspectives*, Berlin: Mouton de Gruyter. 151–86.

Myers-Scotton, Carol and Ury, W. (1977) 'Bilingual strategies: The social functions of code switching', *International Journal of the Sociology of Language* 12: 477–94.

Olshtain, Elite, and Blum-Kulka, Shoshana (1989) 'Happy Hebrish: Mixing and switching in American Israeli family interaction', in S. Gass, C. Madden, D.

Preston and L. Selinker (eds) *Variation in Second Language Acquisition: Discourse and Pragmatics*, Philadelphia, Penn.: Multilingual Matters. 37–59.

Pfaff, C. W. (1979) 'Constraints on language mixing', *Language* 55: 291–318.

Poplack, Shana (1978) 'Syntactic structure and social function of code-switching', *Centro de Estudios Puertorricuenos Working Papers* 2: 1–32.

Poplack, Shana (1980) ' "Sometimes I'll start a sentence in English Y TERMINO EN ESPAÑOL": Toward a typology of code-switching', *Linguistics* 18: 581–618.

Romaine, Suzanne (1989) *Bilingualism*, New York: Basil Blackwell.

Schiffrin, Deborah (1987) *Discourse Markers*, Cambridge: Cambridge University Press.

Stroud, Christopher (1992) 'The problem of intention and meaning in code-switching', *Text* 12, 1: 127–55.

Tannen, Deborah (1989) *Talking Voices: Repetition, Dialogue, and Imagery in Conversational Discourse*, Cambridge: Cambridge University Press.

Tao, Hongyin and Thompson, Sandra A. (1991) 'English backchannels in Mandarin conversations: A case study of superstratum pragmatic "interference" ', *Journal of Pragmatics* 16, 209–23.

Part II

CONVERSATION AND BEYOND

INTRODUCTION TO CHAPTER 7

Peter Auer

The second part of this volume, which centres around questions of the conversational vs. extra-conversational (ethnographically recoverable) meaning of code-switching, starts out with those authors who favour an approach along the lines of conversation analysis (Li Wei, Alfonzetti). We then move on towards studies which take a more eclectic stance, combining methods of classical conversation analysis with those of a different background (such as Jørgensen, Moyer, Sebba and Wootton). The final two chapters (by Rampton and Stroud) explicitly criticise the use of conversation-analytic methods in the investigation of code-switching, although their own approach is still based on the close analysis of transcribed interactional materials.

Of course, the choice of a methodological framework is partly a consequence of the sociolinguistic setting under analysis. Li Wei, the author of the following chapter, has done extensive ethnographic and conversation analytic research on the Chinese community in Newcastle, England (see Li Wei 1994). On the basis of this research, he argues that conversation-internal functions of code-switching play an important role in the community, while extra-conversational knowledge may (but need not in each and every case) be 'brought about' to be of relevance as well. Li Wei's conversational approach brings out the limitations of the 'rights-and-obligations' approach of Myers-Scotton, by looking upon code-switching as a 'contextualisation cue'.

The Chinese population in the UK is dominated by emigrants from Hong Kong (some 122,000 according a census in the 1980s), speaking Cantonese as their home language. Although Britain (as many other European countries) had small Chinese communities (mainly sailors) in the major harbour towns even before World War I, the Chinese communities today mostly came into being between the mid-1950s and mid-1970s as a consequence of an economically motivated emigration from the Hong Kong New Territories. The Chinese in Britain typically make their living in small family business, in catering (restaurants, take-aways) and supporting business.

Li Wei (1994: 49) distinguishes three sociological generations not congruent with the genealogical ones: (a) first-generation migrants of the 1950s, including some pre-war emigrants; (b) sponsored migrants who came as immediate kin of the first-generation migrants or through personal contact with people already in Britain; and (c) British-born Chinese. Li Wei underlines that although the third generation are considered well adjusted to British mainstream culture by the British, their way of living causes considerable friction with the older generation(s) of Chinese for whom they are anglicised to the degree of losing contact with traditional Chinese culture. (The derogatory term 'bananas' – 'yellow outside, white inside' – refers to this perceived cultural shift.) Part of the friction is language, since Cantonese is the everyday language of the first and second generation, but English that of the third.

In the following chapter Li Wei argues that, on the one hand, there are reasons to view code-switching between English and Cantonese in this community as contextualisation cues geared toward organising the conversational exchange at hand, i.e. as a technical device similar to other resources such as prosody or gesture. For instance, code-switching is used for announcing (prefacing) activities, as in his examples 1 and 2, and since it is used for this purpose in both directions (English–Cantonese and vice versa), there is no reason to resort to extra-linguistic knowledge in order to explain it. Its function is purely conversational. On the other hand, Li Wei demonstrates that in other cases of switching, such as his examples 7 and 8, certain aspects of the wider context, i.e. knowledge not confined to the interactional episode in which participants are involved, enter into its interpretation, but unlike in other models which content themselves with stating a certain 'meaning' of code-switching (such as given set of rights-and-obligations in Myers-Scotton's approach), he stresses that these aspects need to be 'brought about' in specific ways by co-participants in order to become relevant. In the present case, instances of code-switching are linked to divergent language choices by first- and third-generation speakers, which in turn index (and indeed, iconically symbolise for the former) the loss of respect for the older generation, and hence of their authority in the migrant community. Yet these extra-conversational meanings can be captured only by a sequential analysis of the conversation.

Context as a 'brought about' feature of an interaction is a notion advocated in particular in Schegloff's writings on the subject (Schegloff 1987). It reflects a sound scepticism of the dash to context as the *deus ex machina* which justifies whatever interpretation the analyst wants to give to a particular linguistic act. Following this doubtlessly restrictive notion of context puts the analyst under the obligation of explicating exactly how it is that an extra-conversational element of knowledge enters the realm of interactional meaning construction.

Bibliography

Li Wei (1994) *Three Generations, Two Languages, One Family*, Clevedon. England: Multilingual Matters.

Schegloff, E.A. (1987) 'Between micro and macro: contexts and other connections', in J.C. Alexander, B. Giesen, R. Münch and N. J. Smelser (eds), *The Micro–Macro Link*, Berkeley: University of California Press, 207–234.

7

THE 'WHY' AND 'HOW' QUESTIONS IN THE ANALYSIS OF CONVERSATIONAL CODE-SWITCHING

Li Wei

1 Introduction

One of the perennial questions in bilingualism research is: 'Why do bilingual speakers switch from one language to another in conversational interaction?' With few exceptions, sociolinguists who had studied code-switching before the 1980s directed our attention to extra-linguistic factors such as topic, setting, relationships between participants, community norms and values, and societal, political and ideological developments, all of which were thought to influence speakers' choice of language in conversation. The oft-cited study by Blom and Gumperz (1972), for example, introduced the distinction between 'situational switching' and 'metaphorical switching'. Situational switching, as the term implied, was triggered by a change in the situation. The underlying assumption was that only one of the co-available languages or language varieties was appropriate for a particular situation and that speakers needed to change their choice of language to keep up with the changes in situational factors in order to maintain that appropriateness. Metaphorical switching, on the other hand, referred to changes in the speaker's language choice when the situation remained the same. For the speaker to code-switch in this case was thought to convey special communicative intent. For the conversation participants (and analysts for that matter), however, the interpretation of the speaker's communicative intent in metaphorical code-switching depended on the association between a particular language or language variety and a particular situation which had been established in the case of situational switching. In other words, one must know first of all what the appropriate choice of language would be for the occasion before any deviant choice could be interpreted (see Auer 1984b for further comments). Despite differences in emphasis, sociolinguistic work that focused on the meaning of code-switching did not generally challenge this line of argument.

The publication of Auer's *Bilingual Conversation* (1984a) marked a turning point in the studies of code-switching. Auer questioned the way *situation* was defined and used as an analytic concept in the existing work. For Auer, situation was not a predetermined set of norms functioning solely as a constraint on linguistic performance. Rather, situation was seen as an interactively achieved phenomenon. Using the terminology and analytic framework of ethnomethodology and conversation analysis, Auer argued that participants of conversational interaction continuously produced frames for subsequent activities, which in turn created new frames. Every utterance, every turn, therefore, changed some features of the situation and maintained or re-established others. In bilingual conversation, 'whatever language a participant chooses for the organisation of his/her turn, or for an utterance which is part of the turn, the choice exerts an influence on subsequent language choices by the same or other speakers' (Auer 1984a: 5). The meaning of code-switching must be interpreted with reference to the language choice in the preceding and following turns by the participants themselves. Auer called for a conversation-analytic approach to code-switching which would focus on '*members* procedures to arrive at local interpretations' (1984a: 3; original italics).

More than ten years later, the conversation-analytic approach to code-switching which Auer called for has attracted some attention in the research community (e.g. Sebba 1993; Li Wei and Milroy 1995). Nevertheless, analyst-oriented, theory-driven, top-down approaches continue to proliferate and dominate current studies of code-switching. A comprehensive review of the competing theories and models that have been proposed over the last decade is beyond the scope of this chapter. Instead, I shall discuss the question 'why do bilingual speakers switch from one language to another in conversational interaction?' at a more basic methodological level, as it emerges from our on-going work with the Cantonese–English bilingual speakers in Newcastle–upon–Tyne.

The chapter is structured as follows: I begin with a discussion of the 'markedness' theory of code-switching, which is arguably the most influential theoretical model of the social and pragmatic aspects of code-switching that has been proposed since Gumperz's situational versus metaphorical switching distinction. This theory places its emphasis on the analyst's interpretation of bilingual conversation participants' intention and explicitly rejects the idea of local creation of meaning of linguistic choices. The 'markedness' theory contrasts sharply the conversation-analysis (CA) approach to code-switching which focuses specifically on the *members' procedures* of arriving at local meaning of language alternation. I shall look at the key claims made by analysts of conversational code-switching who adopt the CA approach and the way they address the question of *why* bilingual speakers switch from one language to another in conversation. I shall then present an application of this approach to Cantonese–English code-switching, drawing upon our research in the Chinese community in Tyneside. On the basis of this analysis, I shall discuss, in the last section of the chapter, the 'brought along' and 'brought about' meanings of conversational code-switching.

2 The 'markedness' theory of code-switching

The objective of the 'markedness' model, as its proponent Myers-Scotton points out, is to explain the social motivation of code-switching. It claims to have universal, predictive validity for all bilingual and multilingual communities. Although her own studies have concentrated on code-switching, especially in the African context, Myers-Scotton explicitly wants her theory to be applicable for all phenomena of linguistic choices beyond code-switching. In-depth critiques of the 'markedness' theory of code-switching and its implications for sociolinguistics and pragmatics generally have already appeared (e.g. Meeuwis and Blommaert 1994) following the publication of Myers-Scotton's 1993 monograph. Here, I want to focus on one of the key arguments put forward by Myers-Scotton, namely the social indexicality of code-switching.

In the 'markedness' theory of code-switching, Myers-Scotton repeatedly suggests that code choices are indexical of the rights-and-obligations sets (RO sets) between participants in a given interaction type. An RO set is 'an abstract construct, derived from situational factors' (Myers-Scotton 1993: 85). Myers-Scotton argues that interaction types are to a large extent conventionalised in all communities and carry relatively fixed schemata about the role relations and the norms for appropriate social behaviour including linguistic behaviour. These schemata are the unmarked RO sets for specific interaction types. Knowledge of the unmarked RO set for each interaction type is a normative device that not only unites the speech community as a whole but also gives the linguistic varieties of the community's repertoire their indexicality. Indexicality therefore is 'a property of linguistic varieties', which 'derives from the fact that the different linguistic varieties in a community's repertoire are linked with particular types of relationships, because they are regularly used in conversations involving such types' (Myers-Scotton 1993: 85). Myers-Scotton further suggests that speakers have an innate knowledge of this indexicality or mental representations of a matching between code choices and RO sets. In other words, speakers know that a certain linguistic choice will be the normal, unmarked realisation of an expected RO set for a particular conventionalised exchange, while other possible choices are more or less marked becaused they are indexical of other than the expected RO set.

In many ways, Myers-Scotton's model is similar to Gumperz's distinction of situational versus metaphorical switching. In particular, the way in which the meaning of code-switching is generated and interpreted is monodirectional in both Myers-Scotton's and Gumperz's models. As Auer (1984b: 91–2) points out, in Gumperz's model meaning is generated by situational switching, becomes associated with the two codes, and is then used in those cases of language alternation that cannot be interpreted situationally, i.e. metaphorical switching. In the 'markedness' theory of code-switching, meaning is the accumulation of the associations between linguistic varieties and conventionalised conversation exchanges. Linguistic codes come to index a particular RO set because they are regularly used in a particular interaction type. In Myers-Scotton's theory, as Meeuwis and Blommaert (1994: 399–400) point out,

> the correspondence of unmarked RO sets to conventionalise inter-action types, the indexical values of linguistic codes, and the overall social meaning of code-switching strategies in a specific community, are all a-priori given factors that are simply brought into a conversation where they are exploited to fulfil communicative needs ... The normative indexical values of codes, as well as the normative rules for appropriate code-switching production and interpretation are constant elements in a theory in which intention and contextual conditions are the variables. In this sense, code selection is a predictable. Interaction merely consists of the repro-duction or reification of pre-existing social meaning, and itself is not creative.

The notion of 'indexicality' in Myers-Scotton's 'markedness' theory of code-switching may be a convenient tool for the analyst to predict code choice and assign some social value to particular instances of code-switching. It is, however, hardly the way conversation participants themselves inter-pret each other's linguistic choices and negotiate meaning. In conversational interaction, either bilingual or monolingual, speakers are often faced with the fact that the situation is simply not defined unambiguously. The partic-ipants do not always have 'similar precedents' with which they can compare the current interaction. Even when the situation is fairly clear to the co-participants, they simply do not have the time to inspect the current case for common features with similar precedent cases. Instead, their attention is paid first and foremost to the 'new case' itself and each and every new move by their co-interactants. Psycholinguistic research on on-line discourse processing provides evidence that in conversational interaction speakers constantly check each other's understandings of what is going on and give out complex verbal and non-verbal cues to indicate whether they have under-stood each other's previous moves and what their next moves will be (see Ellis and Beattie 1986 for general references). While their experiences in other situations may be useful in helping them achieve mutual understanding, speakers' on-line focus is on the local production of meaning.

To illustrate the point, let us take a look at two short examples of conversation which were recorded in a Cantonese-speaking family in Newcastle, England.

EXAMPLE 1

Two teenage girls are talking about school life in A's room. 'He' in the conversation refers to one of the teachers.[1]

	A	... he's bor[ing
	B	[mm
	A	I don't know (.) don't like him
		(2.0)
→A		*Ah ngaw jau yau di mafaan gelak*
		('I'LL HAVE SOME TROUBLE')
5	B	*Dimgaai a?*
		('WHY?')
	A	Yesterday right ...

EXAMPLE 2

A, male, and B, female, both in their twenties, have been talking about an event which had happened the day before in a Chinese take-away where A works and which A does not wish a friend of his ('him' in the first line) to know.

	A	... *m hou gong koei tengji*
		('BETTER NOT TELL HIM YET')
		(2.0)
→		Did you see Kim yesterday?
	B	Yeah.
	A	*Mou* [*mat si...*
		('NOT SERIOUS ...')
5	B	[*Yau di tautung je. Mou mat si ge.*
		('(SHE) ONLY HAS A LITTLE HEADACHE. NOT SERIOUS.')
	A	*Ngaw jing yiu man nay.*
		('I WAS JUST ABOUT TO ASK YOU.')

In the first example, A's utterance is overlapped with B's back channel, which indicates B's continued attention without attempt to take over the floor. A's next turn is responded to with silence. At this point, A switches from English to Cantonese. Notice that what exactly she intends to talk about is not made clear by this code-switched turn, although it appears to be a different topic from the one A was talking about in previous turns; rather it seems that A is bidding to attract B's attention before continuing. Indeed, her code-switched utterance succeeds in eliciting a response from B. A then switches back into English for her subsequent talk – a narrative of an event involving the 'boring teacher' she referred to in her earlier turns – and the conversation continues happily in English.

The second example is comparable to the first in that the two-second gap following A's turn indicates a possible end to the current conversational episode. Since B does not take up the following turn, A continues. However, his utterance 'Did you see Kim yesterday?' is not an elaboration on his previous remark, but is a question checking the precondition for his subsequent enquiry about their friend's health, thus constituting a pre-sequence in conversation-analytic terms. The only *demonstrable* reason for A to change his language choice from Cantonese to English at this particular point seems to be that he wants to draw his co-participant's attention so that the conversation can continue. Indeed, once A has achieved this goal, as demonstrated by B's response 'Yeah', he switches back to Cantonese to continue with the conversation.

The similarities of the two examples are striking: both instances of code-switching occur after an interactive episode evidently comes to an end,[2] and both are marking pre-sequences – turns which are built to prefigure the specific kind of activity that they potentially precede. While the languages used in the two cases are different – in (1) the speaker uses Cantonese to code the pre-sequence and in (2) the speaker uses English – both speakers choose a language which is different from the one they use in the immediately preceding turn.

Examples such as these are by no means rare in the research literature. It seems rather far-fetched to suggest that the speakers are trying to 'index' some predetermined, extra-linguistic RO sets, even if these RO sets could be empirically defined. What can be demonstrated, however, is that by using 'another' language, the speaker builds up a contrast which serves to restart the interaction which otherwise is in danger of being abandoned. The fact of the matter is that in bilingual and multilingual communities, many speech activities like restarting a conversation or introducing a new topic are not tied to one particular language (see Meeuwis and Blommaert, this volume). Even for those activities which have a tendency to be realised more often in one language than in another, the correlation is never strong enough to predict language choice in a more than probabilistic way (see Auer 1984a and 1995 for further comments). The significance of code-switching, as far as the participants themselves are concerned, is first and foremost its 'otherness'. Bilingual speakers change from one language to another in conversation not because of some external value attached to those particular languages, but because the alternation itself signals to their co-participants how they wish their utterances to be interpreted on that particular occasion.

It is important to emphasise that we are not saying that code-switching has no macro-level social value. The question is how that social value is generated. The 'markedness' theory of code-switching explicitly rejects the idea of local creation of social meaning and places its emphasis on the analyst's perception of the correlation between one linguistic variety and a particular interaction type. The indexical value of the code-switching is derived from the analysts' perceptions. Code-switching itself is not understood to have any interactional significance. The result is a static, and mistaken, view of the indexicality of code-switching in particular and of the sociolinguistic behaviour of bilingual speakers in general.

In order that the meaning of code-switching is studied adequately, code-switching itself must be taken seriously as a conversational activity. As Auer (1984b: 92) points out, 'the proper locus at which semantic values may be assigned to the codes are the very same situations in which language juxtaposition is used for communicative purposes'. From a methodological perspective, what is required is an analytic procedure which focuses on the sequential development of interaction, because the meaning of code-switching is conveyed as part of the interactive process and cannot be discussed without referring to the conversational context. Such a procedure is provided by conversation analysis, to which I shall now turn.

3 The CA approach to conversational code-switching

With regard to the study of the meaning of code-switching, the CA approach has at least two advantages. First, it gives priority to

> the sequential implicativeness of language choice in conversation, i.e. the fact that whatever language a participant chooses for the organisation of his or her turn, or for an utterance which is part of the turn, the choice exerts an influence on subsequent language choices by the same or other speakers.
>
> (Auer 1984a: 5)

Second, it 'limits the external analyst's interpretational leeway because it relates his or her interpretations back to the members' mutual understanding of their utterances as manifest in their behaviour' (Auer 1984a: 6). For those who adopt the CA perspective, there are three fundamental points about how we approach conversational code-switching: relevance, procedural consequentiality, and the balance between social structure and conversation structure.[3]

Given that code-switching can be, and indeed has been, described and interpreted in so many ways, how do we show that our analysts' descriptions and interpretations are relevant to the participants themselves in an on-going interaction? As has been pointed out earlier, there is a tendency in code-switching research to attribute macro-social value to individual instances of switching and to assume that speakers intend such meaning to be understood by their co-interactants. Analysts who adopt the CA approach argue that while code-switching is indeed a socially significant behaviour, the task of the analyst is to try and show how our analyses are *demonstratively relevant* to the participants.

The point of procedural consequentiality involves demonstrating whether and how extra-linguistic context has determinate consequences for conversational interaction. We cannot just import our intuitions about, say, the family or work like character of the interaction. Instead, we must demonstrate what gives a particular piece of interaction its specific family or work character (see further Heritage and Drew 1992). In Auer's words, context is not something given a priori and influencing or determining linguistic details; rather it is shaped, maintained and changed by participants continually in the course of interaction (Auer 1990: 80; also 1992).

This relates to the third point, the balance of social and conversational structures. Those who adopt the CA approach to code-switching argue that we must not assume that, in any given conversation, speakers switch languages in order to 'index' speaker identity, attitudes, power relations, formality, etc.; rather, we must be able to demonstrate how such things as identity, attitude and relationship are presented, understood, accepted or rejected, and changed in the process of interaction.

These three points imply an important shift of analytic interest. They suggest that any interpretation of the meaning of code-switching, or what might be called the broad *why* questions, must come *after* we have fully examined the ways in which the participants are locally constituting the phenomena, i.e. the *how* questions. In Auer's words, we need to look for the procedures

> used by participants in actual interaction, i.e. that they are supposed to be interactionally relevant and 'real', not just a scientific construct designed to 'fit the data.' So there is an analytic interest in *members'* methods (or procedures), as opposed to an interest in external procedures derived from a scientific theory. In short, our purpose is to analyse *members' procedures to arrive at local interpretations of language alternation.*
>
> (Auer 1984a: 3; original italics)

The best example of the CA approach to code-switching to date is of course Auer's study of Italian migrants in Germany (see especially 1984a, 1984b, 1988, 1995). The conceptual apparatus upon which Auer builds his analysis is Gumperz's notion of *contextualisation*. In general terms, contextualisation refers to the strategic activities of speakers in varying their communicative behaviour within a socially agreed matrix of conventions, which are used to alert participants in the course of the on-going interaction to the social and situational context of the conversation (Gumperz 1982: 132–5; 1992: 42–3). Conversation participants appear to exploit variable spoken language elements at all linguistic levels (prosodic, phonological, morphological, syntactic; see, for example, Local 1986; Local *et al.* 1984; 1986) and at the non-verbal level (gestural, kinesic and proxemic; see for example Duncan 1969, 1972; Kendon 1977) as procedures for signalling contextual presuppositions. In Gumperz's terms, these are contextualisation conventions or *contextualisation cues*, their chief function being to signal participants' orientation to each other. Sometimes they are used primarily to contextualise imminent completion of a turn at talk or topic shifts, but at other times they have the capacity to signal meanings such as irony or seriousness, and social identities and attitudes of the participants. Auer (e.g. 1984a, 1991) argues that bilingual code-switching should be analysed as a *contextualisation cue*, because it works in many ways like other contextu-alisation cues. Nevertheless, code-switching has some characteristics of its own in addition to those it shares with such elements as gestures, prosodies and phonological variables. In particular, the *sequential organisation of alternative choices of language* provides a frame of reference for the inter-pretation of functions or meanings of conversational code-switching.

Let us now exemplify the CA approach to conversational code-switching by analysing some examples of Cantonese–English data which have been collected as part of a larger, on-going project of language shift in the Chinese community in Tyneside.[4]

4 Applying CA to Cantonese–English code-switching

Details of the social and demographic structure of the community, and of the fieldwork methods, can be found in Li Wei (1994). Our attention here is focused on how Cantonese–English bilingual speakers in the Tyneside Chinese community use code-switching as a contextualisation cue.

The first example we consider is an exchange between two women, one in her early thirties (A) and the other in her mid-twenties (B).

EXAMPLE 3

A   ... you go (.) you got another one?
B   *Yatgo dou mou a?*
      ('THERE ISN'T EVEN ONE (THAT SATISFIES YOU)?')
A   (2.0) *mou a* (.) they [look
      ('THERE ISN'T')
B   [For who? *Waiman a?*
                        ('IS IT WAIMAN?')

5   A   *Hai a.*
         ('YES.')
     B   *Nigo le?*
         ('WHAT ABOUT THIS ONE?')
     A   (Looking at the one B gives her.)

In this exchange, A is choosing a T-shirt for her son Waiman from a supply brought from Hong Kong. A's request in English for more T-shirts from B from which she could choose one constitutes a first part of an adjacency pair, which sets up an expectation that the selected next speaker, B, must respond. But rather than complying by offering more T-shirts, B responds with a question, and remarkably the language she chooses for this unexpected second pair part is Cantonese. A's following turn is very interesting. It comprises three parts – a two-second pause, a confirmation in Cantonese that she does not like any of them, and a beginning of an English sentence which seems to offer an account of why she is not satisfied with the ones she has seen. In the CA literature, it has been suggested that pauses and hedges before delivery often indicate the so-called 'dispreferred' second-pair parts. These second parts are usually structurally more complex than the preferred ones, which tend to latch on smoothly to the first parts of the adjacency pair (Levinson 1983; Pomerantz 1984). Giving elaborated accounts is another dispreference marker in monolingual English conversation. What is interesting about the present example is that bilingual conversationalists seem to combine both the more usual monolingual discourse marker, such as pause, and code-switching to contextualise various components of the adjacency pair and preference organisation. A's pause before the short reply indicates a dispreferred second. Her choice of language complies with B's choice in her question. A then elaborates on it by beginning to offer an account. But in the meantime she switches from Cantonese to English to tie back with her choice of language in an earlier turn. B's response in the following turn consists of two further elliptical questions, 'For who? Waiman a?', to which A answers *Hai a.* ('Yes.'). Only then does B offer another T-shirt to A. Notice that B's elliptical questions are in English first, which converges with A's previous choice of language, and then Cantonese, again tying back to her own choice in earlier turns. A's final reply is in Cantonese, which corresponds to B's choice.

This example demonstrates in detail how bilingual speakers work collaboratively at the meaning of each conversational turn and how code-switching is closely associated with conversational structures. While analysts who work with broad functional or social categories may conveniently assign symbolic values to language choices, a fuller understanding of the mechanism whereby bilingual speakers interpret each other's moves and negotiate codes can only be gained through fine-grain analysis of the kind proposed by conversation analysts.

If we look at the sequence as a whole, we will see that the second part of the first adjacency pair is delayed and separated from its first part by embedded exchanges. The following is a schematised pattern:

A	English	Request
B	Cantonese	Question 1
A	Cantonese–English	Answer 1 (+ Account)
B	English–Cantonese	Question 2
A	Cantonese	Answer 2
B	Cantonese	Offer

The embedded sequences are clearly marked out by a series of code-switches, while the final compliant offer aligns with the language of the previous turn.

Let us now turn to another example in which three teenage girls are talking about buying a study guide.

EXAMPLE 4

	A	*... maai m do a.*
		('CAN'T BUY IT.')
	B	[*Ngaw seunggoh*
		('I LAST')
	C	[Did you (.) d'you go to Dillons?
	A	Dillons?
5	C	Yeah. The new one.
		(1.0)
	C	(To B) *Nay ji-m-ji a?*
		('DO YOU KNOW?')
	B	*Hai.*
		('YES.')

Here, A wants to buy a study guide but has failed to find it in the book-shop. She completes her turn without selecting the next speaker, and the turns of B and C accidentally overlap as they self-select. B uses Cantonese to align with A's choice of language, while C's choice involves a contrast. Interestingly, B abandons her turn and gives way to C, and A subsequently responds to C in English. Although there may be more than one reason for B to give up her turn, C's choice of English, which builds up a contrast with the language choice in preceding turns by A and B, seems to have contributed to her success in attracting A's attention.

Research on monolingual English conversation shows that speakers deploy various kinds of prosodic, lexical and syntactic cues in competing for turns in conversation. Example 4 illustrates how bilingual speakers use code-switching in a similar fashion in turn competition. They constantly check each other's contribution and design their own moves accordingly.

Consider now another example.

EXAMPLE 5

A	*mo (.) ngaw mo gin (.) jung mei gin gwoh Cheung saang* ('HAVEN'T ... I HAVEN'T MET ... NEVER MET MR CHEUNG')
B	[mm
C	[*junglai mo* [*a* ('NEVER?')
D	[Y'what?
5 C	*Koei mo gin gwoh Cheung saang.* ('SHE HASN'T MET MR CHEUNG.') (1.5)
D	Maybe you are too busy.
B	(LAUGH) *M dak haan a.* ('NOT FREE.')
C	Maybe both (.) either of you (.) *m dak haan a* ('NOT FREE')
A	No, no. I'm not busy. My sis (.) sister-in-law come Monday.

In this example, four women in their late twenties and early thirties are talking about a Mr Cheung. Speaker A first makes a statement, in Cantonese, that she has never met the man. We can locate a turn Transition Relevance Place (TRP) at the end of her utterance, by virtue of grammatical completion. Because she has not selected the next speaker and there are three other people present, this gives an opportunity for self-selection. C has made use of this opportunity. B's acknowledgement token *mm* overlaps C's self-selection. There is no code-switching up to this point. D then asks 'Y'what?' in English, to which C replies in Cantonese on A's behalf in the following turn. After a 1½ second pause, D makes the assertion 'Maybe you are too busy', again in English. B laughs and reiterates D's utterance in Cantonese. The most notable feature so far is the contrasting choices of code by different speakers in consecutive turns. All the participants self-select and after B's first turn their choices of language are different from the one in the immediately preceding turn. Such contrastive choices of language by different speakers in consecutive turns are not always clearly distinguished in the existing literature from the changing of language by the same speaker in the same turn (either inter- or intra-sentential). The distinction is nevertheless important, because both discourse and social meanings contextualised by, and hence the inferences drawn by participants from, the two types of code-switching may be very different. In the present example, the participants seem to be negotiating the language-of-interaction through a series of competitive self-selection.

The following turn by C is particularly interesting, not only because it is the only intra-turn switching in this example, but also, from the point of view of language negotiation, because it integrates lexical/syntactic choices with language choice and brings together B and D's contributions in preceding turns. The example ends with speaker A, who has kept quiet while the others are competing and negotiating with each other, switching from Cantonese to English. A new language-of-interaction has been established.

Let us now look at another example of how bilingual conversationists negotiate their choice of language.

EXAMPLE 6

Two teenage girls in B's family sitting-room. A suggests that they go out with some school friends.

   A   Can you take the camcorder?
   B   (1.0) I don't know.
   A   You can't?
       (2.5)
   A   *Jong yau gei yat jau fan hokhau.*
       ('NEED TO RETURN TO SCHOOL IN A FEW DAYS.')
5 B   *Hai a. Ngaw dou mou yausek.*=
       ('YEAH. I HAVEN'T HAD A REST.')
   A   =Where do you want to go?
   B   I don't know.
   A   Do you want to take the camcorder?
   B   *Ngaw m ji la.* Me brother doesn't like me taking it.
       ('I DON'T KNOW')

A's initial question 'Can you take the camcorder?' receives a dispreferred response, marked by B's one-second hesitation. A clearly interprets it as a negative response, as she seeks to confirm it. B makes no response at all this time. After a 2½-second silence, A tries to restart the conversation. Noticeably, she has chosen to use Cantonese, and the topic seems to be a different one as well. This particular use of code-switching as a cue to restart a conversation is very similar to what we have seen in the earlier examples 1 and 2. A has successfully elicited a response from B with this Cantonese utterance. But she then switches back to English and asks B where she would like to go, which brings both the language choice and the topic of discussion back to where their previous exchange ended. Following B's 'I don't know', A reiterates the question about taking the camcorder. B's response this time constitutes a code-switching. It is particularly interesting to compare B's response this time to her earlier response to A's question. In the earlier response, B's 'I don't know' in English is 'hedged' with a one-second hesitation. This time B says 'I don't know' in Cantonese, which contrasts A's language choice for the question, and then offers an account in English. It seems that the code-switched *Ngaw m ji la* ('I don't know') serves the same function as the one-second hesitation in B's previous response.

The general point here seems to be that code-switching contextualises turn-taking, pre- and embedded sequences and preference organisation, parallel to the way in which various kinds of prosodic, phonetic and indeed non-verbal marking contextualise such material in monolingual conversations. We can therefore argue that code-switching constitutes a linguistic resource available to conversation participants, especially bilinguals, to 'indicate the status of parts of their talk' (Local 1992: 220); it can help the speaker to restart a conversation at the end of an interactive episode, or to change conversational direction; it also helps the participants to keep track of the main 'drift' of the interaction by mapping out complex nested structural patterns in the conversation.

5 The meaning of code-switching: 'brought along' or 'brought about'

As has been mentioned earlier, the CA approach to conversational code-switching has been developed against the background of an overwhelming tendency in bilingualism research to explain code-switching behaviour by attributing specific meanings to the switches, and by assuming that speakers intend these meanings to be perceived by their listeners. As Stroud (1992) points out, such tendencies can misrepresent and obscure the complexity and dynamics of code-switching. In Stroud's words, 'the problem of intention and meaning in code-switching is the problem of knowing to what extent the intentions and meanings that we assign to switches can in fact be said to be intended by a speaker or apprehended by his or her interlocutors' (1992: 131). The CA approach to conversational code-switching avoids an imposition of *analyst-oriented* classificatory frameworks, attempting rather to reveal the underlying procedural apparatus by which conversation participants themselves arrive at local interpretations of language choice. In contrast to Myers-Scotton's (1993) 'markedness' model, the CA approach dispenses with motivational speculation, in favour of an interpretative approach based on detailed, turn-by-turn analysis of language choices. It is not about what bilingual conversationalists may do, or what they usually do, or even about what they see as the appropriate thing to do. Rather, it is about *how* the meaning of code-switching is constructed in interaction.

The CA approach to code-switching does not in any way deny the fact that code-switching as a contextualisation cue carries more social meaning in bilingual conversation than gestural or prosodic cues in monolingual conversation. Because of the differences in historical development and political status of the languages, different speakers and speaker groups in the same community may acquire the languages for different reasons and at various rates. Consequently, their preference for and attitude to the languages co-available in the community may be different. Nevertheless, we must be extremely careful about assigning meanings to individual instances of code-switching simply on the basis of our (analyst's) knowledge of the community's social history and of the individuals' language attitudes, especially when the analyst is an *outsider* to the community and individuals in question.

Accepting that the co-existing languages in the community repertoire have different social significance for different speakers, the methodological question then is how much of the meaning is 'brought along' and how much of it is 'brought about' in interaction (Auer 1992). The 'markedness' theory of code-switching emphasises the 'brought along' meaning. The languages involved in code-switching have distinctive social, symbolic values, which merely have to be indexed in the interaction in order to become, or to remain, relevant. Consequently, the communicative act of code-switching itself is not seen to have any interactional meaning. In contrast, the CA approach to code-switching stresses the 'emergent' character of meaning. Meaning emerges as a consequence of bilingual participants' contextualisation work. It is 'brought about' by the speakers through the very act of code-switching.

To illustrate the point, let us look at two more examples. The following exchange took place in B's family dining room. A is a man in his late twenties, and B is a 40-year old woman. They are having dinner. Also present is B's teenage daughter, C.

EXAMPLE 7

	B	*Sik gai a.*
		('EAT CHICKEN.')
	A	mm.
		(5.0)
	A	Haven't seen XXX (NAME, THREE SYLLABLES) for a long time.
		(2.0)
	A	Have you seen him recently?
5	B	No.
	A	Have you seen XX (NAME, TWO SYLLABLES)?
	B	(2.0) (To C) *Ning ngaw doei haai lai.*
		('BRING MY SHOES.')
		(To A) *Koei hoei bindou a?*
		('WHERE WAS SHE GOING?')

The conversation up to the beginning of this example has been mainly in Cantonese. When B, the mother, offers A chicken, A gives a minimal response. The pause that follows indicates an end of the current interactional episode. After a five-second silence, A attempts to introduce a new topic (the whereabouts of a friend). This topical change is accompanied by the choice of English, which contrasts B's choice in previous turns. B gives no response; so A reinitiates the topic, this time with an interrogative. The response from B is in English, but negative and minimal. A continues by asking about a different person, again in English. After a short pause, B selects a different addressee (C) and switches from English to Cantonese, temporarily excluding A from the conversation, before she turns back to address him in Cantonese again.

In some of our earlier papers (e.g. Milroy, Li Wei and Moffatt 1991; Milroy and Li Wei 1995), we have suggested that the reason B in this exchange selects a different addressee and switches to Cantonese was that she did not like to be addressed in English by another adult, and the reason B did not like to be addressed in English by another adult was that she belonged to a generation whose language choice and language preference were both clearly Chinese-dominant. Such an interpretation, however, told us little that we did not intuitively know already about bilingual speakers' language behaviour. What seems to be needed is a detailed, turn-by-turn analysis of the participants' conversational work, which can demonstrate how such issues as attitude, preference, community norms have been 'brought about' in the actual contributions of the participants. For instance, the woman B in the above example did actually use English, albeit a single-syllable word, in responding to A's first question. It is only after A has asked the second question and after two seconds have elapsed that B has chosen to switch to Cantonese and a different addressee. Her language alternation, together with her strategic use of the turn-taking mechanism as a way to shift topic and to change addressee, helps to 'bring about' her language attitude and preference.

Similarly, the following example demonstrates how the language preference of speakers of different generations and the authority structure of Chinese families have been 'brought about' in the language choices of the participants.

EXAMPLE 8

A is an 8-year-old girl, and C is A's 15-year-old brother. B is their mother who is in her forties.

A	Cut it out for me (.) please.
B	(2.5)
A	Cut it out for me (.) mum.

```
     C   [Give us a look.
 5   B   [Mut-ye?
         ('WHAT?')
     A   Cut this out.
     B   Mut-ye?
         ('WHAT?')
     C   Give us a look.
         (2.0)
     B   Nay m ying wa lei?
         ('YOU DON'T ANSWER ME?')
10   A   (To C) Get me a pen.
```

The exchange takes place in the family sitting-room. A is making a folder from pieces of cardboard; C, the brother, is looking on, while B, the mother, is knitting in a chair nearby. A's initial request for help to the mother receives a null response. A then repeats it, using a vocative on this occasion to specify her mother as the next speaker. B's subsequent question *Mut-ye?* ('What?') overlaps with C's turn as he self-selects. A then issues her request for the third time, but B repeats the same question as if she hasn't heard A's request properly or she hasn't understood it. Again A fails to amend her request.

The lack of cooperation between the speakers is salient, as is the lack of alignment between the language choices of A and B. A's three repeated requests are in English and show no sign of change in form, while B's questions are in Chinese which could be described, in conversation-analysis terms, as repair initiators offering A opportunities to amend her utterances. A fails to repair her turns, which B apparently expects, and changes little her form of request. At the end of exchange, we find something close to a communicative breakdown, in the sense that B offers no response at all to A's repeated requests. After a 2½-second silence, B asks A why she does not respond to her. A then turns to C, abandoning the exchange between herself and B.

As has been suggested earlier, Chinese adults in the Tyneside community in which our examples were collected generally preferred to speak and to be spoken to in Cantonese, whereas Chinese children in the community preferred English. In the meantime, the authority structure of the family in the Chinese culture expects children to comply with their parents. They are expected to behave in a manner appropriate for their specific status in the family, which means that they should do as their parents (or adults generally) tell them to. These two aspects of the background context have been 'brought about' by the participants in the exchange in example 8 through their insistence on divergent language choices. From the mother's point of view, she believes she has the authority over her children, and when the daughter asks her to do something, she can decide whether the request is reasonable or not; if she thinks it is not, then she can either reject it or request an alternative. Her repeated use of the repair initiator *Mut-ye* ('What') and her use of Cantonese, which contradicts the daughter's language choice, help to 'bring about' her role as the authority figure in the family. In the meantime, the daughter's insistence on her non-convergent language choice highlights the inter-generational differences in language attitude and preference. While it is not possible to predict on an 'if only' basis a possible alternative outcome of A's requests, we can note that A's failure to achieve the desired compliant response from B has contributed to the eventual communication breadown. (See Gumperz 1982: 133 for a comparable case, where failure to read contextualisation cues by the interactants gives rise to a similarly unsatisfactory interactional outcome.)

6 Conclusion

The main purpose of this chapter has been to make a case for the conversation-analytic approach to code-switching which was pioneered by Auer over ten years ago, but which, in the face of vigorously advocated theoretical models such as the 'markedness' theory, has been accepted by only a small number of students of conversational code-switching. It has been argued that the analyst-oriented approaches like the 'markedness' theory tend to use intuitive categories as a basis for the description of code-switching. While such models may be convenient for those working in communities where a rigid diglossia obtains, their methodological validity and applicability are questionable. The CA approach to code-switching which has been taken in this chapter relies on the responses of the participants in a conversation to warrant claims about the work which a particular code-switch is doing. Rather than focusing on the perceived, symbolic values of the different languages, the CA approach tries to establish the meaning of code-switching by examining in close detail the types of interaction which involve the very act of language alternation.

It is important to remember that code-switching is only one of many linguistic resources available to bilingual speakers. They may, and indeed do, select alternative cues in the sequential contexts which we have studied in this chapter. Thus, the fact that a bilingual speaker has chosen to code-switch invites a more detailed, perhaps multi-layered analysis which can demonstrate that in addition to its capacity of highlighting the status of the on-going talk, code-switching as a contextualisation cue has the capacity to 'bring about' higher-level social meanings such as the speakers' language attitudes, preferences, and community norms and values. While the need to avoid the wider contexts overshadowing participants' procedures is apparent, it is equally important to prevent entanglement in over-detailed description of conversation structures without making any sensible inference. The CA approach to code-switching has broken new ground and provided us with the mechanisms to examine and understand bilingual conversationalists' procedures of locally creating and interpreting the meaning of code-switching. Our task in the next ten years or so is perhaps to develop a more coherent model which integrates the fine-grained conversation analysis of code-switching and the macro-level analysis of social and cultural context in which code-switching is used as a community practice.

Notes

Versions of this chapter have been presented at the Hamburg Colloquy on Code-Switching in Conversation, February 1995, and at a research seminar in the Department of Linguistics, University of Manchester. I am grateful to the participants of both events whose comments helped to improve the paper. I am especially grateful to Peter Auer and Yael Maschler for their detailed, positive criticism. David Silverman offered thought-provoking comments on the different approaches to the role of 'context' in analysing social interaction from a sociological perspective, which provided the initial impetus for my writing this chapter. Paul Foulkes acted once again as my proof-reader. I am grateful to them both.

1   In this and all subsequent examples, italics are used for Cantonese. The following transcription conventions are used:

[simultaneous talk
=   latching (i.e. no interval between adjacent turns)
(.)   micro-pause
(2.0)   length of silence in seconds

2   An interactive episode is understood to have come to an end when no participant takes up the floor within the maximum acceptable silence of one second (see Jefferson 1989). It is not defined in terms of 'topic' or what the participants are talking about. For a discussion of the problems associated with the notion of 'topic' in conversation, see Schegloff 1990.

3   These three points were originally made by Schegloff (see especially 1992) in relation to analysing 'context' of social interaction in sociology. Silverman and Gubrium (1994) offer a critique of Schegloff's arguments.

4   The data presented in the chapter have been collected as part of two ESRC-funded research projects (R000 23 2956 and R000 23 5869). I thank the ESRC for their continued financial support. My co-workers on the two projects include Lesley Milroy, Kay Mogford-Bevan, David Walshaw, Sherman Lee, Christine Raschka, Pong Sin Ching and Huang Guowen. Their contribution to the research has been invaluable.

Bibliography

Auer, P. (1984a) *Bilingual Conversation*, Amsterdam: John Benjamins.
Auer, P. (1984b) 'On the meaning of conversational code-switching', in Auer, P. and Di Luzio, A. (eds) *Interpretive Sociolinguistics*, Tübingen, Germany: Narr, pp. 87–112.
Auer, P. (1988) 'A conversational analytic approach to code-switching and transfer', in Heller, M. (ed.) *Codeswitching: Anthropological and Sociolinguistic Perspectives*, Berlin: Mouton de Gruyter, pp. 187–213.
Auer, P. (1990) 'A discussion paper on code alternation', in European Science Foundation *Papers for the Workshop on Concepts, Methodology and Data*, Strasbourg: ESF, pp. 69–87.

Auer, P. (1991) 'Bilingualism in/as social action: A sequential approach to code-switching', in European Science Foundation *Papers for the Symposium on Code-Switching in Bilingual Studies* Vol. II pp. 319–52, Strasbourg: ESF

Auer, P. (1992) 'Introduction: John Gumperz's approach to contextualisation', in Auer, P. and di Luzio, A. (eds) *The Contextualisation of Language*, Amsterdam: Benjamins, pp. 1–38.

Auer, P. (1995) 'The pragmatics of code-switching', in Milroy, L. and Muysken, P. (eds) *One Speaker, Two Languages: Cross-Disciplinary Perspectives on Code-Switching*, Cambridge: Cambridge University Press, pp. 115–35.

Blom, J.-P. and Gumperz, J. (1972) 'Social meaning in linguistic structure: Code-switching in Norway', in Gumperz, J. and Hymes, D. (eds*) Directions in Sociolinguistics*, New York: Holt, Rinehart and Winston, pp. 407–34.

Duncan, S. (1969) 'Nonverbal communication', *Psychological Bulletin* 72: 118–37.

Duncan, S. (1972) 'Some signals and rules for taking speaking turns in conversations', *Journal of Personality and Social Psychology* 23: 283–92.

Ellis, A. and Beattie, G. (1986) *The Psychology of Language and Communication*, London: Weidenfeld and Nicolson.

Gumperz, J. (1982) *Discourse Strategies*, Cambridge: Cambridge University Press.

Gumperz, J. (1992) 'Contextualisation revisited', in Auer, P. and Di Luzio, A. (eds*) The Contextualisation of Language*, Amsterdam: John Benjamins, pp. 39-53.

Heritage, J. and Drew, P. (eds) (1992) *Talk at Work*, Cambridge: Cambridge University Press.

Jefferson, G. (1989) 'Preliminary notes on a possible metric which provides for a "standard maximum" silence of approximately one second in conversation', in Roger, D. and Bull, P. (eds), *Conversation: An Interdisciplinary Perspective*, Clevedon, England: Multilingual Matters, pp. 156–97.

Kendon, A. (1977) *Studies in the Behaviour of Social Interaction*, Lisse, The Netherlands: Peter de Ridder.

Levinson, S. (1983) *Pragmatics*, Cambridge: Cambridge University Press.

Li Wei (1994) *Three Generations Two Languages One Family: Language Choice and Language Shift in a Chinese Community in Britain*, Clevedon, England: Multilingual Matters.

Li Wei and Milroy, L. (1995) 'Conversational code-switching in a Chinese community in Britain', *Journal of Pragmatics* 23: 281–99.

Li Wei, Milroy, L. and Pong, S. C. (1992) 'A two-step sociolinguistic analysis of code-switching and language choice', *International Journal of Applied Linguistics* 2.1: 63–86.

Local, J. (1986) 'Patterns and problems in a study of Tyneside intonation', in Johns-Lewis, C. (ed.) *Intonation in Discourse*, London: Croom Helm, pp. 181–98.

Local, J. (1992) 'Continuing and restarting', in Auer, P. and Di Luzio, A. (eds) *The Contextualisation of Language*, Amsterdam: John Benjamins, pp. 273–96.

Local, J., Wells, W. and Sebba, M. (1984) 'Phonology for conversation: Phonetic aspects of turn delimitation in London Jamaican', *Journal of Pragmatics* 9: 309–30.

Local, J., Kelly, J. and Wells, W. (1986) 'Towards a phonology of conversation: turn-taking in Tyneside English', *Journal of Linguistics* 22: 411–37.

Meeuwis, M. and Blommaert, J. (1994) 'The "markedness model" and the absence of society', *Multilingua* 13: 387–423.

Milroy, L. and Li Wei (1995) 'A social network approach to code-switching', in Milroy, L. and Muysken, P. (eds) *One Speaker, Two Languages: Cross-Disciplinary Perspectives on Code-Switching*, Cambridge: Cambridge University Press, pp. 136–57.

Milroy, L., Li Wei and Moffatt, S. (1991) 'Discourse patterns and fieldwork strategies in urban settings', *Journal of Multilingual and Multicultural Development*
12: 287–300.

Myers-Scotton, C. (1993) *Social Motivations for Codeswitching*, Oxford: Clarendon
Press.

Pomerantz, A. (1984) 'Agreeing and disagreeing with assessments', in Atkinson,
J.M. and Heritage, J. (eds) *Structures of Social Action*, Cambridge: Cambridge
University Press, pp. 57–101.

Schegloff, E. (1990) 'On the organisation of sequence as a source of "coherence"
in talk-in-interaction', in Dorval, B. (ed.) *Conversational Organisation and Its
Development*, Norwood, N.J.: Ablex, pp. 51–77.

Schegloff, E. (1992) 'Reflections on talk and social structure', in Heritage, J. and
Drew, P. (eds) *Talk at Work*, Cambridge: Cambridge University Press, pp. 44–70.

Sebba, M. (1993) *London Jamaican*, Harlow, England: Longman.

Silverman, D. and Gubrium, J.F. (1994) 'Competing strategies for analysing the
contexts of social interaction', *Sociological Inquiry*, 64.2: 179–98.

Stroud, C. (1992) 'The problem of intention and meaning in code-switching', *Text*
12: 127–55.

INTRODUCTION TO CHAPTER 8

Peter Auer

In the first part of this book ('The "codes" of code-switching') it was argued that alternation between stretches of talk that doubtless belong to two different 'languages' for linguists may not always be perceived as such by conversationalists, and that in such a case it might be misleading to speak of code-switching. It seems natural that such a state of affairs should be particularly likely for varieties such as Galizan and Castilian (see example 4 in the Introduction, as well as Chapter 2) which are genetically and structurally very close, and whose status as languages is a matter of dispute even among linguists. The following chapter by Giovanna Alfonzetti shows that this is not necessarily true: just as mixing may occur between genetically and structurally very distinct languages (cf. the examples in Chapters 4 – Lingala/French – and 6 – Hebrew/English), clear cases of conversationally meaningful code-switching may be found in a context in which two closely related varieties are in contact. Alfonzetti's example is Sicily, or more precisely the city of Catania.

Although the dialect has traditionally held a very strong position in Sicily, most Sicilians today are equally competent in Italian (or *italiano regionale*). In addition, Sicily is today characterised by code-switching between Sicilian dialect and Italian in almost all situations. According to a recent survey, the vast majority of Sicilians use both varieties in their everyday life; only 5.63 per cent of the population are pure dialect speakers, and 3.56 per cent speak only Italian (Lo Piparo 1990: 36). According to findings reported in Alfonzetti (1992) on the basis of a conversation analysis of a wide array of situations, only very formal, ritualised situations 'mandate' the exclusive usage of Italian, while dialect is never obligatory. In most situations, including formal and semi-formal ones, code-switching is possible and does indeed take place. Language choice is therefore 'situationally under-determined' to a very large degree, if we use the term 'situation' to refer to gross parameters such as the type of activity or the social roles of the participants involved.

Within an encounter, code-switching may be recurrent, not only between but also within turns. Given the structual resemblance of Italian and Sicilian dialect, intra-sentential switching is also possible. It is usually smooth, without any hesitations accompanying it.

Another important feature which distinguishes the Sicilian situation (or that of Catania) from, for example, the Galizan one is the ideological 'innocence' of switching. The use of dialect within a conversation is neither a strong social class marker (in this sense, Catania is reminiscent of many South German dialect areas and of Switzerland), nor is it fraught with political questions of anti-centralist movements (as in Galiza, or, for that matter, in Catalonia). The two varieties co-exist, and although, of course, one has significance as the national language of Italy, and the other significance as a regional marker of identity, Alfonzetti refuses to grant the status of a 'they-code' to the first, and of a 'we-code' to the second; in fact, she argues (Alfonzetti 1992) that the urban language use in Sicily is not a case of diglossia at all. This is clearly different from the Galizan or Catalan which (at least today) are looked upon as languages (and clearly we-codes) by their L1 users.

Under these conditions, at least two scenarios of bilingual speech are conceivable. The first is the emergence of a mixed code (in the sense of Chapters 4–6 in this volume). According to Alfonzetti, there is no indication that such a development is taking place. Although there is some structural convergence between the type of Italian spoken in Sicily, and Sicilian dialect, this convergence does not include the juxtaposition of the two varieties such that they merge into one. Nor is there a continuum of forms between dialect and Italian which would make it difficult to decide (for analysts and participants) which variety is being spoken at a given point in time, as one might suspect under the given circumstances in which the varieties in question carry such a small ideological weight. (In this respect, the situation in Sicily is different from that in other parts of Italy or, for that matter, in Germany, where such continua exist; see Auer, 1997)

The other possibility is the purely discourse-related use of the two varieties as a contextualisation cue which indexes certain changes in footing or conversational structure. This is the picture presented by Alfonzetti.

The most convincing evidence one can find for the independence of code-switching from conversation-external factors, and for its almost exclusive functioning within the realm of conversational structure, is its directional indifference. If code-switching from Sicilian dialect into Italian serves the same conversational functions as code-switching from Italian into dialect does, then it cannot index any kind of stable conversation-external knowledge attached to the varieties as such, but rather its direction must be entirely dependent on the variety that happens to have been spoken last. In fact, Alfonzetti finds directional constancy only in a limited number of functions (self-corrections of language choice and accommodation to others' preference for Italian in semi-official encounters) while the majority of functions such as code-switching to mark self-repair, preclosings, sequential subordination, etc., are shown to be indifferent to the direction the switching takes.

If one wanted to place the Catanian case on the continuum between code-switching and code-mixing sketched in Chapter 1 (see p. 16f), it is clear that it must be very close to the switching pole, since almost all cases of the juxtaposition of the two varieties are functional and thus perceived by participants as juxtapositions. However, it does not quite reach the polar end of the continuum, for there is little orientation to 'one language at a time' (apart from short convergences of language choice towards Italian in semi-formal situations such as in a shop). Otherwise, prolonged sequences of divergent language choices seem to be possible (Alfonzetti 1992: 249). Therefore, code-switching in Sicily may be less marked (and less salient) than in a context in which it is more related to gross changes in the situation.

Bibliography

Alfonzetti, Giovanna (1992) *Il discorso bilingue. Italiano e dialetto a Catania*, Milano: Franco Angeli.

Auer, Peter (1997) 'Co-occurrence restrictions between linguistic variables: A case for social dialectology, phonological theory and variation studies', in F. Hinskens and R. van Hout (eds) *Variation and Linguistic Theory*, Amsterdam: Benjamins.

Lo Piparo, Franco (ed.) (1990) *La Sicilia linguistica oggi*, Vol. 1, Palermo: Centro di studi filologici e linguistici siciliani.

THE CONVERSATIONAL DIMENSION IN CODE-SWITCHING BETWEEN ITALIAN AND DIALECT IN SICILY

Giovanna Alfonzetti

1 Introduction

This chapter will deal with the following topics: (a) the necessity to postulate – in order to provide a more comprehensive explanation of code-switching – an independent dimension for conversational structure, i.e. a 'third domain' between the grammatical component and the macro-sociolinguistic context (Auer 1995: 132); (b) the possibility for code-switching to be viewed as a con-textualisation strategy, the main function of which is that of creating a contrast exploited by bilingual speakers to mark the constant change of 'footing' occur-ring in natural speech (Goffman 1979) and, in particular, to carry out several conversational activities, thus contributing to the pragmatic interpretation of utterances in context; and (c) the fact that code-switching *can, but need not*, call into play the social and symbolic values of the codes in the repertoire.

Empirical evidence for the theoretical statements made above will be drawn from an analysis of some conversational structures and functions which can be identified in code-switching between Italian and dialect in the urban community of Catania, a town on the eastern coast of Sicily. Attention will be paid both to patterns more closely linked to the social context (section 3) and to others where the autonomy of the conversational dimension shows up more clearly (section 4).

2 Sociolinguistic background

In order to establish the possible connection between conversational patterns of code-switching and broader macro-sociological conditions, a short outline of the sociolinguistic situation in Italy, with particular reference to Sicily, is required.

The linguistic repertoire of the Italian speech community has a complex bipolar internal structure: in every geographical region Italian is spoken together with a local Italo-Romance dialect. Although the local dialects belong to the same Romance subgroup as Italian, they must be considered separate systems rather than mere varieties of the same linguistic system. This is true both from the point of view of mutual intelligibility and from that of structural differences at the phonological and morphosyntactic levels.[1] Each of the two compartments of the linguistic repertoire consists of a set of varieties, which are the result of a prolonged and close contact between Italian and dialect. Within the dialectal subset, the local dialect, for instance, can be opposed to the urban dialect and sometimes also to a regional koine. Within the Italian subset an even higher internal differentiation is to be found, which is first of all based on geographical grounds. The label *standard Italian* refers to a literary, mostly written variety, historically based on the Florentine dialect, 'which forms the traditional bookish linguistic norm the textbooks refer to' (Berruto 1989: 9). Besides standard Italian, which can hardly be identified as a spoken variety (Trumper 1989), each region has its own *regional standard* or *regional Italian*, which is in turn internally differentiated from a social point of view into *educated regional Italian* and *popular regional Italian,* i.e. a substandard variety of Italian spoken by uneducated people.[2]

Such a complex repertoire has often been described as a diglossic one, with the Italian language and the dialects playing the role of the high and low varieties respectively. And yet the diglossia category as defined by Ferguson is not strictly applicable to Italy (Sgroi 1994; Sornicola 1977; Varvaro 1978). In order to better identify the main features which distinguish the Italian situation from a real diglossic one, Berruto (1987) suggests the notion of *dilalìa*. These features are:

1   A wide use of the high variety even in everyday, informal conversation. Italian has been progressively invading domains which were in the past exclusively confined to the use of dialects, like for instance the family and friendship domains.
2   A great amount of overlapping between the two codes in a wide range of domains and communicative situations. The functional differentiation between the high and the low variety is indeed not as sharp and clear-cut as in real diglossia.

Another functional model, proposed by Trumper (1977, 1984 and 1989), is based on the division of diglossia into two basic regional types: macro-diglossia and micro-diglossia. Sicily in particular seems to belong to the macro-diglossic type (Mioni 1979: 109), at least according to some of the criteria proposed by Trumper: as for example the distribution of both codes over a large number of domains, whereas in micro-diglossia one code is used in very few domains; a great amount of both code-switching and code-mixing, rarely to be found in micro-diglossia; and, above all, the presence of code-switching of both the situational and conversational kind, the latter almost unknown in micro-diglossic situations, where a more clear-cut functional separation between codes is found (Trumper 1984: 41).[3]

The macro-sociolinguistic conditions in the use of Italian and dialect in Sicily may indeed account for the widespread diffusion of code-switching in everyday communication. Only in a very restricted set of highly official and formal situations is Italian the only permissible, unmarked choice, while in the great majority of cases Italian and dialect seem to reach a sort of sociolinguistic neutrality, being endowed with an almost interchangeable social role (Alfonzetti 1992a). Referring to the different kinds of code-switching distinguished by Myers-Scotton (1988 and 1993), one could identify the prevailing pattern in Sicily as 'overall switching as the unmarked choice', i.e. a type of code-switching which does not necessarily correlate with a negotiation of interpersonal relationships or with other gross changes in the situation. It is the general pattern which has social meaning, in so far as it may be said to express a double cultural identity, shared by most members of the community. This does not necessarily mean, however, that individual switches do not have meaning or function, as Myers-Scotton's model seems to imply. The point is that in order to grasp the communicative and pragmatic function of single instances of code-switching, suitable methods and theoretical approaches are required. We have to go beyond the predictive macro-sociolinguistic framework which, in linking code-switching to a change in one of the situational components, presupposes too simplistic and deterministic a relationship between code choice and external, social factors. What is needed are adequate micro-level techniques of conversation analysis and a differentiated model in which three dimensions need to be taken into account: the speakers' linguistic preferences and competences, the conversational context and the socio-symbolic values of the two codes in the repertoire (Auer 1990 and 1995). In each individual instance, all three dimensions or only one or two can be relevant. In any case, code-switching as an unmarked choice can also be given a conversational, sequential analysis (see Auer 1995: 127), as we will try to demonstrate in the following sections.

Examples will be drawn from a corpus of about fourteen hours of naturally occurring speech tape-recorded in Catania. The data refer to a wide range of communicative situations, including both formal and official events – such as, for instance, a union meeeting of university researchers, a condominium members' meeting or some interviews on the Italian taxation system – and informal conversations among friends, family members and colleagues at work.

3 Conversational code-switching in which the direction of switching matters

In this section cases of code-switching will be analysed where its direction is relevant; their interpretation requires all the three dimensions mentioned above, i.e. the speakers' linguistic preferences and competences, the conversational context and the social values of the two codes, to be taken into account.

3.1 Accommodation and diverging preference

A very common pattern in the data occurs within larger negotiation sequences, where the use of a different code by participants signals their divergent linguistic preferences and/or competences (see Auer 1984 and 1995). It consists of a sequence of two switches: in the first, the speaker accommodates to the language of the co-participant, whereas in the second, he or she switches back to his or her preferred one. As for the conversational dimension, the pattern of two subsequent switches regularly involves structures characterised by a strong inner cohesion: the accommodation switch occurs in the second-pair part of an adjacency pair, in back-channel responses or in the conclusive segment of a 'joint production' or 'collaborative sentence' (Jefferson 1973: 50). These are conversational contexts which are closely linked to the previous turn, the language of which seems to strongly influence the language used in the turn component affiliated to it. The second switch – in which speakers shift back to their preferred language – occurs immediately afterwards in the following turn component, that is, in a position where the influence of the previous turn is much weaker.

Example 1 illustrates this phenomenon in a question–answer pair. The fishmonger addresses one of his customers in dialect, which is strong evidence of his linguistic preferences. He then switches into Italian in answering the customer's question, thus accommodating to her linguistic choice. In the second turn component, however, he goes back to his preferred language, which will be maintained in his following turns, while the customer will continue speaking Italian.[4]

EXAMPLE 1: AT THE FISHMONGER'S

    FISH.   *Cchi vvuleva, signora T?*
    CUST.   Merluzzi ce ne sono?
→   FISH.   No! Niente, gioia! No lupi e no melluzzi. *C'èranu na para i*
           melluzzeddi a stamatina e ssi ... si nni eru.
5 CUST.   E che prendo pesce per me, insomma che non sia grasso, va'?
    FISH.   *E cchi ssàcciu, si vvoli pigghiari na para i trigghi. Macari ca*
           si fa scaddati.

    FISH.   *What would you like, Mrs T?*
    CUST.   Is there any cod?
    FISH.   No! nothing, my dear! No cod and no bass. *There was a bit*
           of cod this morning but ... but it's all gone.

| 5 | CUST. | And what fish could you suggest for me that is not fatty? |
| | FISH. | *I don't know, some mullet if you want. You can eat it boiled.* |

Example 2 is an example of a joint production, within which the link between turns is even stronger: even if produced by different speakers, they can be considered components of one single utterance. Mr R, the buyer of a billiards hall, is listing to Mrs M, the seller, all the expensive restructuring he has to do in the hall, in order to lower the price she is asking. In his first turn, he speaks his preferred language, i.e. dialect, but he switches into Italian in his second turn (*ci vogliono, parliamo* 'are necessary, let's talk'), where he completes the utterance that Mrs M had started in Italian (*Certo, un po' di spese* 'Of course, some expenses'), thus accommodating to her linguistic choice. He then switches back to dialect in a less cohesive position.

EXAMPLE 2: THE SALE OF A BILLIARDS HALL

MR R	*Chiossài di quaranta miliuni non ci pozzu rari. Ma no ca non c'i vògghiu rari. M'u bbissassi u locali e cci nni rugnu cinquanta.* [. . .] *Ai' a cchiamari* l'idraulico, *u stagninu, o chiddu ca è. Cci vulissi:*
5→MRS M	Certo, un po' di spese::
→MR R	ci voglio, parliamo: . . . *Non ni:. . . . Lei s'u po vvìnniri, ggioia mia!*
MR R	*I can't give you more than forty million. But it's not that I don't want to give you more. Put the place in order and I'll give you fifty million.* [. . .] *I need* a plumber, *a plumber, or whatever it is. We would need*
5 MRS M	Of course, some expenses
MR R	are necessary, let's talk . . . *Don't let's . . . You can sell it, my dear!*

The direction in this group of examples is generally from dialect into Italian in the first switch and from Italian into dialect in the second one. This regular pattern suggests that in this case code-switching calls into play the social meaning of the two codes in the repertoire. The pattern of double switching often occurs in conventionalised exchanges (e.g. public offices, shops, etc.), where Italian can be considered the unmarked choice.[5] In this respect, the speaker who uses the code which is marked for that given type of interaction, i.e. dialect, feels a stronger pressure to accommodate to the interlocutor's unmarked code, i.e. Italian. This shows speakers' awareness of norms of situational adequacy. On the other hand, the occurrence of an immediately following diverging switch in the opposite direction neutralises, as it were, the tendency toward accommodation to the unmarked choice, thus revealing that these norms are not too highly binding. At least they do not stop speakers from violating them in favour of partially divergent language choices, in which each one uses his or her own preferred code. And this happens even in conventionalised exchanges where speakers are aware that their own preferred code does not coincide with what they consider to be more appropriate. As a consequence, divergent language choices cannot be considered a marked form of behaviour in the situation under study. From this point of view, Sicily represents a borderline case between communities which strongly orient to a preference for talking the same language, and others in which such a preference is entirely absent (Auer 1990). In our community, when the interacting participants have different linguistic preferences, each of them will on the whole insist on his or her own choice. At the same time he or she will produce frequent, if only momentary, converging switches toward a common language of interaction, especially when the interlocutor's code is recognised as unmarked.

3.2 Reformulations

The social attributes of the codes are also relevant in another group of switches, which will be called *reformulations* here. Reformulations belong to a broader conversational repair mechanism which in this case specifically aims at correcting the use of the 'wrong' code.[6] Speakers use them in order to correct the code which they consider as marked in a given situation, but which they have almost inadvertently used. This type of switching generally occurs in conventionalised exchanges for which an unmarked choice is clearly discernible. Direction, therefore, is also relevant here and will generally be from dialect into Italian, thus showing that reformulations call into play the social meaning of the two codes. Indeed the switching here highlights a conflict between norms of situational appropriateness and spontaneity of linguistic usage. It therefore provides indirect cues about the speaker's individual preferences and competences and also about the sociolinguistic evaluation of the two languages.

An example of reformulation is given in example 3, drawn from a set of interviews on the taxation system in Italy. Here a housewife, who speaks Italian during the interview – a situation type which clearly calls for Italian as the unmarked choice – all of a sudden introduces the dialect word *spisi* ('expenses') into her speech. But she immediately interrupts herself and, after the lexical correction marker *cioè* ('that is'), translates the word into Italian. The co-occurrence of these three elements – self-interruption, correction marker and translation – allows us to draw inferences about the speaker's perception of the situation, as it shows that this is not just a mixing of a lexical item. In such a case 'speakers orient to the other language character

of the transferred item and treat its use as an "inappropriate" verbal activity
– one that calls for repair' (Auer 1984: 60). In the migrant situation analysed
by Auer, this phenomenon points to a momentary lack of competence in
the abandoned language and a better knowledge of the vocabulary of the
other. In our community instead it is rather to be interpreted as a sign of
self-censorship toward the use of the dialect in a very formal situation.

EXAMPLE 3: INTERVIEWS

A   Forse sarebbe sarebbe più giusto invece di non fare, cioè di non fare
trattenute dallo stipendio e fare un'assicurazione a vita cioè su di noi.
Se abbiamo *spis*- cioè spese per il medico, per i medicinali che ce li
paghiamo da noi stessi.

A   Perhaps it would be it would be fairer instead to make, that is to make
no deductions from our salary and to take out life insurance, that is on
us. If we have *expense*- that is expenses for the doctor, for medicines,
we'll pay for them ourselves.

---

4 Conversational code-switching in which the direction of switching does *not* matter

Up to now examples of code-switching have been discussed in which the
values and social meanings attached to the two languages in the repertoire
seem to be called into play and in which therefore the function of the
switching largely depends on its direction. These, however, represent only
a minority of the cases found out in our data. In the majority, instead, direction seems to be largely irrelevant because the same conversational function
can be carried out by a switch in both directions. What really matters is
the contrast created by the mere juxtaposition of the two different codes.
This contrast, together with other contextualisation cues, can be part of the
'reframing process' in which participants 'over the course of their speaking
constantly change their footing' (Goffman 1979: 5). In particular, code-
switching can be exploited to cope with the several tasks related to the
organisation of conversation itself, as will be shown in the following sections.

4.1 Self-repair

Code-switching, for example, can work as a self-repair technique, as an
alternative or together with the other techniques normally used in monolingual discourse, like self-interruption, vowel lengthening, hesitation pauses,
repetition, etc. Contrary to reformulations, the direction of switching is not
relevant here but depends only on the code of the reparandum which the

code-switched utterance aims at repairing. The reparandum can be a proper mistake, as in example 4: Mr R, who does not remember exactly where his cousin works, first gives a wrong answer and then, after a hesitation pause, he switches into dialect in correcting the name of the hospital.

EXAMPLE 4: THE SALE OF A BILLIARDS HALL

R   Questa persona è un infermiere. E' mio cugino ... L'incarico gliel'ho dato a lui. Lavora lui all'ospedale.

G   Dove lavora? Al:

→ R   Al Garibaddi ... *ô Vittoriu mi pari ca è.*

R   This person is a male nurse. He's my cousin ... I gave him this commission. He works in a hospital.

G   Where does he work? At

R   At the Garibaddi ... *at the Vittoriu I think he is.*

The reparandum can also be a problem of some sort, such as the search for the right word, as in example 5, drawn from a conversation between two shop assistants in a department store. V and C are talking about a mutual friend, whose problems according to C, but contrary to V's opinion, only depend on her bad relationship with her husband. In order to convince V and get her solidarity, C uses a strategy consisting of a sort of declaration of affection toward her, where she is positively compared first to a sister and then to a mother. At this point, C clearly has difficulty in mentioning somebody who can be considered dearer than a mother. She therefore interrupts herself. A hesitation pause follows, during which C looks for an appropriate word to complete the comparative construction, as is explicitly stated in the question *Comu si rici?* ('How do you say?'). Once she finds one, she utters it in Italian, while the surrounding stretch of talk is entirely in dialect. Code-switching therefore signals the solution of the search problem, as it marks the conclusive segment of the self-repair activity carried out by the speaker.

EXAMPLE 5: IN A DEPARTMENT STORE

C   *A mmia non m'u leva nuddu râ testa, tu mi po riri tuttu chiddu ca voi, non su affari mei, ma iù ... ppi mmia tu sì mmègghiu di na soru, mègghiu di na mamma e mmègghiu di ... comu si rici? Una cosa mia ... E iù a idda mi visti quannu stava mali ... Ppi mmia a cuppa è di iddu.*

C   *Nobody will get it out of my head, you can say whatever you like, it's not my business, and yet I ... to me you are better than a sister, better*

---

than a mother and better than . . . how do you say? A thing of my own
*. . . And it was her who took care of me when I was ill . . . I think it's
his fault.*

Code-switching can also be used together with other repair mechanisms
to solve problems arising from violation of the rules governing turn allocation, which generates simultaneous talk. In this case, the speaker often
switches in recycling a turn component made indistinct by an overlapping
utterance. This is what happens in example 6, drawn from the same conversation as example 5: V is telling C about a visit paid to their mutual friend
who was ill. At a possible transition-relevance place – i.e. after V has quoted
the answer given to her friend – C takes the turn to suggest a remedy for
their friend's illness (*Iavi bbisognu* 'She needs'). But, as V continues her
story, saying what she did next, C's and V's talk overlaps for a while, until
the repair device comes into play: V stops her story, while C goes on, after
recycling the overlapped utterance (*Intanto ha bisogno. . .* 'Anyhow she
needs. . .'). In doing so she switches into Italian, maintaining this language
for the rest of her current turn but going back to her preferred code in her
following turn.

EXAMPLE 6: IN A DEPARTMENT STORE

V	*Aieri cci ìi (ca cci appi a ddiarrìa).* 'Il riso non mi piace.' *Cci rissi: 'E mmanciatillu ppi mmia, si non ti piaci a ttia'.* [*Allura cci passài a viddura, cci calài u risu*
→C 5	[*Iavi bbisognu . . .* Intanto ha bisogno di una bella cura d'inizioni per tirarsi su.
V	*Sì, s'i fici.* Se n'è fatta una sola. Certo.
C	*Na sula gnizioni?*
V	*Yesterday I went to her place (as she had diarrhoea)* 'I don't like rice'. *I said 'Eat it for my sake, if you don't like it'.* [*Then I strained some vegetables, I cooked some rice*
C	[*She needs . . .* Anyhow she needs a course of injections to pull round.
V	*Yes, she had some.* She only had one. Sure.
C	*Only one injection?*

4.2 Pre-closings and sequential subordination

Code-switching may also work as a device to mark the internal structuring
of conversation into constitutive sequences. The contrastive juxtaposition of
the two codes may be used, in fact, to contextualise side sequences, opening

and closing sequences, or also pre-closings, as we can see in example 7. Four shop assistants in a big department store are vivaciously discussing a misunderstanding which caused a lot of tension and disagreement among them: a negative remark made by B on a dress on sale in the shop where they work was interpreted by C as a lack of respect toward the seller. C condemns B's behaviour, whereas the others defend it. Although in this kind of speech event participants do not need to stop the conversation by means of greetings or other terminal exchanges, as they are 'in a continuing state of incipient talk' (Schegloff and Sacks 1973: 325), they do have to solve the problem of temporarily interrupting the ongoing interaction and coordinating the suspension of the turn-taking mechanism, which is normally done by means of pre-closings. In example 7, the co-participants use an additional device, as each of them produces a code-switched utterance to contextualise the intention to bring the verbal exchange to a close, marked by the contrastive use of dialect.

EXAMPLE 7: IN A DEPARTMENT STORE

	B	Anzi ora che tu me l'hai detto, lo dirò invece di fronte a chi dico io.
	C	No, senti. . . [uno che ci vende della merce
	B	[Te lo giuro. Ma non è che. . . Io a te ti ti ammiro,
5		perché si vede che sei amica. Però devi capire il mio punto di vista, che io ora . . . *Unn'è stu vistitu?* ((all laugh except C))
→ A		*Quannu mi nni vàiu ddabbanna, prima c'agghionnu supra i pacchi.*
	C	Non tutti possono accettare quello che lei sta dicendo. Non sono
10 →		tutti che lo possono accettare. *Ccu cchistu chiuru e mmi nni vàiu a ttravagghiari.*
→ D		*Mi nni sta' iennu, bbasta!*
	B	Ma che cosa mi può succedere a me? Niente. Che io qua sopra non ci salgo più. Ma è questo lo scopo. *Fossi ancora non l'a ccaputu.* ((laughs)) Scusa, *l'ai'a ddiri a vvuc'i testa?* Non ho capito . . .
15		Secondo te è sbagliato quello che dico io?
		[. . .]
	A	Resta qua un attimo.
→ B		*Ni nn'am'a gghiri. Appoi quannu tunnamu rô bbar.*
	A	Un a:ttimo!
20	?	Ma *chiddu pròpriu* è stato!
	B	Faglielo vedere. Io in quel momento ho deciso cosa dovevo fare. ((they go away laughing))
	B	On the contrary, now that you've told me, I'll say it in front of somebody I know.

189

C   No, listen ... [he sells us the goods

B   [I swear. But it isn't that ... I admire you, because one can see you're a friend. But you have to understand my point

5   of view, that now I ... *Where is this dress?*

((all laugh except C))

A   *I'd better go now, otherwise I'll wake up among all the parcels.*

C   Not everybody can accept what she's saying. It's not everybody

10   who can accept it. *With this I'll close and get back to work.*

D   *That will do: I'm off!*

B   But what can happen to me? Nothing. I won't come up here again. But that's precisely my intention. *Perhaps you haven't got it yet.* ((laughs)) Sorry, *shall I shout it?* I don't understand ... Do you

15   think what I'm saying is wrong?

[. . .]

A   Please, wait a moment!

B   *We have to go now. Later on, when we come back from the bar.*

A   Just a moment!

20 ?   But *that* was *just* ...

B   Show it ((the dress)) to her. At that moment I decided what I had to do.

Contextualising the closing activity in a conversation can also be achieved by means of a switch in the opposite direction, i.e. from dialect into Italian, as happens in example 8: here Italian is introduced by Mr R in the pre-closing utterance which starts the closing sequence (*Va bene, signora* 'That's all right, madam'), it is accepted by the co-participant and then consistently maintained until the end of the speech event.

EXAMPLE 8: THE SALE OF A BILLIARDS HALL

R   *Iù àiu cinquant'anni. Pecciò m'u pozzu m'u pozzu pemmèttiri u lussu di stari ddà, appuntamenti (. . . . .)*

M   Cetto!

G   Badare, certo.

5 M   Badare, così. Voi ci state.

[*Nuàutri ama statu*

→R   [Va bene, signora. Io ... vediamo come viene lui farò ... il mezzo possibile. In ogni caso dico 'Signora ... questi ho questi ci posso dare questi::' ... (. . . . .)

10 M   Ecco ... Qualsiasi cosa quanto noi sappiamo una come si deve regolare.

R   Per questo, signora, immancabimmente lei entro matteddì mi vedrà personalmente.

190

M   Ecco, va bene!
15 R   Pazienza vi disturberò . . . un'altra volta.
G   [No
M   [Niente, niente. Con tanto piacere.
R   Signora! . . . Di nuovo, piacere di averla co- rivista.
M   Arrivederla!
20   ((They shake hands))

R   *I'm fifty. Therefore I can afford the luxury of staying there, appoint-*
ments (. . . . .)
M   Sure!
G   To look after, sure!
5 M   To look after, and so on. You stay there.
[*We've been*
R   [That's all right, madam. I . . . let's see when he comes I'll do . . .
my best. In any case I say 'Madam . . . I've got this I can give you
this . . . (. . . . .)
10 M   That's all right . . . Anything provided that we know what to do.
R   As for this, madam, you'll see me personally by Tuesday, without
fail.
M   That's all right!
R   Oh well, I'll have to disturb you . . . once more.
15 G   [No
M   [Never mind. It's a pleasure.
R   Madam! . . . Again, nice to m- see you again.
M   Good bye!

In side sequences or side remarks, speakers have to solve the problem of
signalling a momentary interruption of the main discourse, first, and then
of going back to it. Besides the devices normally used in monolingual
discourse, like repair-initiators and continuation or resumption techniques,
bilingual speakers can exploit the contrastive juxtaposition of the two codes.
This is what happens in example 9, where code-switching signals both the
beginning and the end of a side sequence, which is therefore entirely
produced in a different code than the main ongoing sequence. Two shop
assistants are speaking ill of a colleague of theirs, who is envious of one
of them because she has been promoted head of their department. In her
second turn Y starts a side sequence by means of a repair-initiatior and a
switch into Italian (*Sì, ma quanto?* 'Yes, but how much?'). A few turns
follow in which Italian is maintained by both participants, until Y goes back
to the main sequence using a continuation device and a switch into dialect
(*Ma ppoi idda cchi penza* 'But then does she think'), thus restoring the
language choice of the whole conversation.

EXAMPLE 9: IN A DEPARTMENT STORE

	X	*Aviss'a ffari trìrici. O mi nni vàiu n penzioni (opuru) si nni va macari idda.*
	Y	*Tu ommai n'a viri cchiù a idda.*
5	X	Cetto, cetto! *Iù mi nn'a ffari n'àutri sett'anni. Fossi idda cchiu nnica è.*
→	Y	Sì, ma quanto? Sai che può essere? Cosa più cosa meno.
	X	Ma ommai, ommai ... ma loro due speranze non ne ha:::nno.
	Y	Completamente!
	X	Completame:::nte!
10 →	Y	*Ma poi idda cchi ppenza ca na vota ca ti nni vai tu, faranno a idda ca ppoi a stari ddui tri anni?*

	X	*She'd need to win the pools. Either I would have to retire or she would go.*
	Y	*You by now are far ahead of her.*
5	X	Sure, sure! *I've still got seven years left to work. Maybe she's younger.*
	Y	Yes, but how much? Do you know how much younger she is? Not a lot.
	X	But by now, by now ... but the two of them haven't got any chance.
	Y	Not at all!
	X	Not at all!
10	Y	*But then does she think that once you retire, they* will *promote her? She's only got two or three years left.*

Example 10 is an example of a side remark marked by a switch in the opposite direction. M is talking on the phone with a friend about computers. As he realises that the computer alarm-clock fails to go off at the established time, he abruptly interrupts what he was saying to remark on this fact. In doing so, he produces a code-switched utterance in dialect, thus linguistically signalling its marginality for the content of the ongoing turn, which afterward goes on in Italian.

EXAMPLE 10: TELEPHONE CONVERSATION

	M	Fintanto che non c'è questo ... bisogna utilizzare quello là. Però io non è che a quelli mm ho dato il disco rigido ... che che può supportare il Word quattro e:: ... e tutte queste cose qua. Perciò:: praticamente ci andrò- *Ma comu mai non sunò ccà stu cazzu ri*
5		*sveglia?* ... Non ha suonato! ... E io praticamente poi ci andrò di pomeriggio quando devo stampare.

M   Until we get that one . . . we'll have to use this one. But I didn't
give them a hard disk . . . which which can support Word four
and . . . all the rest. So:: practically I'll go there- *But why on earth*
5   *didn't that fucking alarm-clock go off?* . . . It didn't go off! . . .
And practically I'll go there in the afternoon, when I need to print.

4.3 Story-telling

Code-switching can also be used to signal the main changes in footing
connected with story-telling in conversation. First of all, a story requires
that the speakers remove themselves from the usual alignment in ordinary
conversation and maintain the footing of the narrator, 'whose extended
pauses and utterance completion are not to be understood as signals that he
is now ready to give up the floor' (Goffman 1979: 22). And indeed code-
switching often occurs in utterances which serve as story prefaces, in which
the would-be teller projects a forthcoming story, thus trying to ensure himself
a stretch of uninterrupted talk. In example 11, for instance, the beauty
specialist, who wants to tell her client about an odd telephone call that she
has just received, shifts to dialect in announcing her narrative, so the story
is contextualised both by a preface and a switch.

EXAMPLE 11: BEAUTY SPECIALIST

((C answers the phone. A few minutes of conversation follow. Then she
hangs up and, addressing her client, she comments on the queerness of the
telephone call))

→ C Ma cose di pazzi! *Prima era n masculu, senti chista*
   G Al telefono
   C Prima era un uomo. Allora lui mi ha detto, dice 'Sono un amico della
      signora C., sua cliente'. [. . .]

   C What a crazy thing! *It was a man at first, listen to this*
   G On the phone
   C It was a man at first. And he said to me, he says 'I'm a friend of Mrs
      C., your client'. [. . .]

In stories introduced as topically coherent next utterances with a version
of the once-upon-a-time-format (Jefferson 1978: 222), code-switching can
mark temporal locators serving as entry-devices, as in the following example,
drawn from a conversation between strangers at a bus stop. The traffic is
paralysed because of an accident involving a motor-cycle and a van. An
elderly couple waiting for the bus complain about the long wait and talk
about the danger of driving too fast in town. The sight of the accident at

the crossroads reminds the man of another accident that he witnessed some time previously. He therefore starts to tell about it, without announcing his story by means of a preface, but simply introducing it with a temporal locator marked by a switch into Italian. This variety will be abandoned immediately afterwards, as the man goes back to his preferred code, i.e. dialect.

EXAMPLE 12: AT THE BUS STOP

   F   *Quantu stanu femmi i filobbussi, ora (. . . . .).*

   M   *(Cchi ccurriti?) Curriti a ttrenta, quaranta ntâ città . . . sta velocità!*
       ((pause))

→M   L'altro gionno, l'altro gionno, nel mese di febbraio . . . qua al

5   corso Italia . . . *c'è a via Cervignano unni si po ppassari cchê màchini.* [. . .]

   F   *How long will the buses keep still, now (. . . . .).*

   M   *(Why do you drive so fast?) Why don't you drive at thirty, forty in town . . . Such a speed!*
       ((pause))

5 M   The other day, the other day, in the month of February . . . here in corso Italia . . . *there is via Cervignano where you can drive along.* [. . .]

The same function – i.e. introducing a tale in conversation – can therefore be carried out by switching either from Italian to dialect (example 11) or in the opposite direction (example 12).

Code-switching may also occur in utterances which contain commentaries, repetitions, expansions of the story, all serving as story-telling ending devices (Moerman 1973; Jefferson 1978), by means of which the teller tries to elicit recipient talk in order to solve the problem of leaving the story and re-engaging turn-by-turn talk. Code-switched utterances in the latter case have the advantage of clearly signalling the end of the story, as in example 13, where G switches into dialect in the last utterance of a story about the reason why she was not able that afternoon to go and see a film she very much wanted to see.

EXAMPLE 13: TELEPHONE CONVERSATION

   S   Ma io ti ho telefonato per dirti ma pe- come l'hai detto che hanno tolto il Nuovo Cinema Paradiso?

   G   L'hanno rimesso ((laughs))

S   L'hanno rimesso?

5 G   Sì

S   E perché non te lo vai a vedere?

G   Perché oggi avevo appuntamento con T per andare al cinema. Ci sentiamo alle quattro, allora dico::: 'A che ora è?', dico, 'alle sei?', ci dovevamo andare alle sei, 'O alle sei e mezzo?' Dice 'Aspetta

10 →   che vedo'. Va a vedere sul giornale 'Mercoledì chiusura'. *E nni fregàu*! ((laughs))

S   Ma speriamo che lo rifanno:: giovedì

G   No, penso … spero, infatti siamo rimasti che domani se lo fanno immancabilmente perché, guarda, se ci scappa ora

15 S   No no, non lo pigliate più.

S   I phoned to tell you but why- what do you mean, Nuovo Cinema Paradiso is not on any more?

G   It's on again ((laughs))

S   It's on again?

5 G   Yes

S   And why don't you go and see it?

G   Because this afternoon I had an arrangement with T to go to the cinema. I spoke to her on the phone at four, and I says 'What time is it on?', I says, 'at six?', we arranged to go at six, 'or at six

10   thirty?' She says 'Just a moment, I'll check'. She checked in the paper 'Closed on Wednesdays'. *What a drag*! ((laughs))

S   Let's hope it will be on again on Thursday

G   No, I think … I hope, in fact we planned that tomorrow if it's on we'll definitely, because, look, if we miss it now

15 S   No no, you won't get it again.

The contrastive function of code-switching may also be exploited to enact other changes in footing that occur during story-telling: for example to underline the climax of a story, to set off the setting from the events, to report the utterances of the characters in the story, to frame comments, to differentiate narrative from evaluative talk, and so on. See, for instance, example 14, where a nurse is telling a story about her jealous husband, who once during a Carnival party took her back home once he had noticed she wasn't wearing a bra.

EXAMPLE 14: NURSE

A   Na volta, di carnevale, avevo diciotto anni, *non è ca rici era vecchia*, e m'aveva comprato, mia mamma me l'aveva regalato, un vestito. Era bellissimo, però era molto scollato di dietro, davanti no. [. . .] *Pecciò iù rissi 'non mi nni mettu' picchì si vireva dda striscia di*

5   *reggipettu. Rissi 'Non mi nni mettu'. Rissi 'non ci rugnu a ssèntiri*
nenti'. Ni nni emu a bballari. Tannu èrumu, unni èrumu? â Pedara.
Insomma, era un bel locale. *Tutti, me cugnati, amici, cosi. Lei cci*
criri? mentri ca èrumu ddà, ficimu u primu bballu . . . u secunnu
. . . si nn'accuggìu!

A   Once, it was Carnival, I was 18, *you can't say I was old*, and I
had bought myself, my mother had given it to me as a present, a
dress. It was wonderful, but it was very low cut at the back, not
at the front. [. . .] *So I said to myself 'I'm not wearing a bra'*
because you could see a strip of the bra. I said 'I'm not wearing
5   *one'. I said 'I won't let him know'. We went dancing. That time*
we were, where were we? At Pedara. Anyway, it was a nice night-
club. *Everybody, my sisters and brothers-in law, my friends,*
everyone. Would you believe it? While we were there, we had one
dance . . . then another . . . then he noticed!

The story is introduced by a conventional temporal locating device,
followed by some information on the setting, in Italian. Then C switches
into dialect in giving an evaluative comment on her age at the time of the
events being told, so that objective information (*avevo diciotto anni* 'I was
18') and personal evaluation (*non è ca rici era vecchia* 'you can't say I
was old') are differentiated by the contrast between the two codes. Later
on in the story, a second comment – in which C positively evaluates the
night-club where they had decided to go dancing (*Insomma, era un bel*
locale 'Anyway, it was a nice night-club') – is again marked by a switch.
But meanwhile the base language of the narrative has changed: it has shifted
from Italian into dialect in coincidence with the beginning of the telling of
the events (*Pecciò iù rissi* 'So I said to myself'), which is thus marked
against the setting, which was described in Italian. The switch occurring in
the second comment is therefore in the opposite direction: i.e. from dialect
into Italian. This case clearly demonstrates that the functionality of code-
switching is essentially that of achieving a contrast, which may be exploited
to mark the internal structuring of a narrative. The direction of switching
mainly depends on the internal development of the story itself and is largely
independent of the sociolinguistic values of the codes in the repertoire.
Therefore it is not meaningful in itself, but depends on the code used in
the surrounding stretch of talk. This is a pattern which regularly occurs in
almost all the stories in the data.

This high degree of autonomy of the conversational dimension in
Italian–dialect code-switching from the sociocultural values of the two codes
can be compared with different sociolinguistic situations. We refer in particular to the migrant Italian community studied by Di Luzio (1984), where
the direction of switching is more relevant, as a more constant and stable

association seems to hold between 'the dialectal variety of Italian and the world of primary socialization which it evokes and with which the participants identify themselves' (1984: 78). This is apparent in the stories analysed by Di Luzio, where the use of dialect is strongly connected with an emotive and expressive function. These stories often focus on the conflict between the sphere of primary socialisation and the external, at times hostile, world (1984: 77). Going back to German at the end of such stories can then be interpreted as 'withdrawal' from the domestic world into the more 'neutral' sphere of the surrounding situation. On the contrary, the stories in our corpus do not have such a deep relevance for the participants' cultural and emotive identities. Generally speaking, a 'double' cultural identity is shared by most of the members of the community and is somehow taken for granted. Speakers do not often feel the necessity to assert through language their group consciousness or belonging, as opposed to an external world. Italian and dialect are strictly interwoven in almost every sphere of life, in both the private and the public one. This does not mean, of course, that dialect is not more deeply connected than Italian with 'emotive' speech activities. In our data, code-switching in jokes, funny or ironical remarks, outbursts of anger or disappointment is generally from Italian into dialect. In stories, as well, the use of dialect in the punchline or in final comments may be meant to elicit emotional responses. And yet a fundamental difference remains: speakers act in a world which is entirely without ethnic conflict, which is so strong in a migrant community. This is the main reason why one cannot easily assign to dialect and Italian the values of 'we-code' and 'they-code', and it could also account for the fact that the purely conversational dimension seems to be so richly developed and prevalent in comparison with what is usually labelled situational code-switching.

4. 4 Topic change

This is clearly shown in topic change. Within Myers-Scotton's markedness model, code-switching triggered by a shift or change in topic is said to belong to the sequential unmarked type, which is similar to Blom and Gumperz's situational code-switching (Myers-Scotton 1993: 114–15). The underlying assumption is that speakers recognise a basic congruence between certain kinds of topics and codes, and that this congruence ultimately rests on the meanings or values of the languages in the repertoire.[7] Speakers therefore switch to the code they consider more appropriate for a given topic. But although this sometimes happens, it simply fails to account for many other instances in the data. Let us take for instance example 15, drawn from a telephone call between two friends. At first T is talking about politics. All of a sudden she explicitly states that she is going to talk about something else and her statement is marked by a switch into dialect. One cannnot say that T resorts to dialect because she considers it more appropriate to the new more private subject, that is, information about a mutual friend she has not been able to get through to. The use of dialect is, in fact, confined to the utterance which serves to announce the sudden topic change, but is soon afterwards abandoned, so that the new topic is dealt with in Italian.

EXAMPLE 15: TELEPHONE CONVERSATION

T   Ma l'hai visto? Io mai l'ho vista una campagna elettorale così. Questo oggi dicevamo con A. Neppure nel quarantotto, che era il dopoguerra, che c'erano ... che c'erano proprio umori tremendi. Mai si era verificato. *N'àutra cosa t'ai'a cchièdirti,* G. Cambiamo
5   discorso. Io continuo a telefonare a M. Perché è da Pasqua che le voglio fare gli auguri, le cose. Perché non la non la trovo?

T   Have you seen? I've never seen an electoral campaign like this one. I was talking about this to A today. Not even in 1948, in the post-war period, when there were ... when there were tremendous emotions. It never happened. *I've got something else to ask you,* G.
5   Let's change topic. I keep on calling M. I've been trying to give her my wishes, and so on, since Easter. Why can't can't I find her?

The use of code-switching in this example can be better understood if we take into account that the ability to change topic in conversation involves intricate knowledge of the environments where topic changes may occur and of how they may be produced, and that the topic-changing utterances usually have certain formal and structural features (Maynard 1980: 284). Code-switching may therefore be seen as one of the devices by means of which the task of changing topic may be carried out by bilingual speakers, i.e. as a contextualisation cue used to signal a change in the conversational context, while the direction of switching itself can be largely independent of the character of the newly introduced topic. In cases like this, one might say that 'the only "meaning" the cue has is (to paraphrase Jakobson's definition of the phoneme) to "indicate otherness". The direction of the change is irrelevant' (Auer 1995: 124). Were it not so, the speaker would not only switch into dialect in the topic-changing utterance, but would go on speaking dialect as long as she discusses the new topic.

4. 5 *Setting off quotations*

The relative autonomy of conversational structuring and the contrasting function of code-switching are even more evident in quotation, a function which is present in many sociolinguistic situations, but which has only been taken into superficial consideration. And yet the use of code-switching to set off quotations is worth much deeper attention, as we will try to show.

Let us start by asking: why does one so often change code in reporting somebody else's words or even one's own words, uttered on another occasion? At first sight, the most obvious and straightforward answer would be that code-switching is due to the speaker's mimetic intention to preserve the language used by the original locutor. In fact, some cases can easily be accounted for in this way. In example 16, for instance, Mr R switches into Italian to quote the answer given to his own question by an Istrian person, who, of course, does not speak Sicilian dialect.

EXAMPLE 16: THE SALE OF A BILLIARDS HALL

R   *Cci rissi: 'Ma cchi ffa? Lei lava u locali raccussì?'* (. . . . .)
'E' pecché il locale' *rissi* 'è stato chiuso'. *Ma tanta ri acqua, raccussì!*

R   *I said to him 'But what are you doing? You scrub the floor like that?'*
(. . . . .) 'It's because the billiards room' *he said* 'has been closed'. *But so much water, right up to here!*

Looking more deeply into the problem, however, one immediately realises that such an explanation cannot be assumed as a general principle, for more than one reason.

First of all, cases will be found where just the opposite happens: the speaker modifies the language choice made by the original locutor (see also Auer 1984 and 1995). In example 17, for instance, Mr R switches into dialect in reporting what one of the two co-participants had told him during their previous meeting, a few days before. It happens that the person Mr R quotes is me and I know for sure that I only spoke Italian on the occasion he is referring to.

EXAMPLE 17: THE SALE OF A BILLIARDS HALL

R   Mi sono . . . Ho avuto il piacere di conoscere sua figlia . . . che puttroppo stava uscendo e *mi rissi 'Va be', deci minuti cci pozzu ddedicari'.* 'Grazie.' Così all'impiedi all'impiedi abbiamo discusso certe cose.

R   I am . . . I had the pleasure of meeting your daughter . . . who was unfortunately going out and *she said 'All right, I can give you ten minutes'.* 'Thanks.' And so we stood discussing certain things.

Similarly, during a telephone call with a friend, I myself once happened to report in dialect words uttered by a teacher I had met at the provincial education authority office, even though I knew for sure he had spoken to me in Italian (example 18).

EXAMPLE 18: TELEPHONE CONVERSATION

G   C'era una dopo di me, no? che è entrata subito dopo di me, che appunto c'era questo problema. Ma, dico, c'era un inferno! Uno, poveretto! Io perché mi lamentavo fuori, aspettando, cioè parlavo con quelli che aspettavano. Dico 'A me non m'hanno calcolato cinque punti'. Si volta questo, dice 'Oh!' dice *'A mmia quaranta!* ((laughs)) *Quaranta cchiu ppicca!'* Dico 'Ah! E allora siamo a posto!'

5

G   There was somebody behind me, right? who came in just after me, as there was this problem. But, I tell you, it was a mess! One man, poor thing! I as I was waiting outside, complaining, I mean, I was talking to the people who were waiting. I say 'They gave me five points less'. This man turned round and says 'Well!' he says *'I got forty!* ((laughs)) *Forty less!'* I say 'Well! everything's all right then!'

5

Second, most of the time we, as researchers, cannot state exactly if the language of the quotation coincides or not with the original one, for the simple reason that the latter is unknown to us. At most one could infer the original language, and this only on the basis of the macro-sociolinguistic conditions of use of the two codes in relation to parameters like domain, situation, category of speakers, etc. But apart from the questionable correctness of assigning to the original locutor an unmarked linguistic choice, such a methodological procedure yields contradictory results.

Thus, for instance, in the first turn of example 19, A, who is telling a story about her restless grandson, switches into Italian in reporting – both as indirect (*di non fallo bere niente* 'not to let him drink anything') and direct speech (*Se il bambino* 'If the child') – the prescriptions given by a doctor in the hospital the child had been taken to. In this particular case, one could suppose that the doctor had actually spoken Italian, because Italian would be the unmarked choice in this type of situation: the doctor is indeed a speaker with a high level of education, interacting with an unknown person in the official role-relationship of doctor–patient, during work time. In switching into Italian, therefore, A is probably preserving the original language of the quotation. And yet, later on within the same story, in her second turn, the woman switches into dialect to report some other words uttered by the same doctor, in the same situation (*Picchì ccà* 'because here'). Should one presume that the doctor himself had switched from Italian into dialect? One might, of course, but on no other grounds but the intention to preserve the validity of the mimetic hypothesis. What actually happens here is that meanwhile, in order to mark the internal structure of her second turn, A has changed the base language of the story, switching from dialect into Italian (*perché il taglio è stato molto* 'because the cut was big'). Faced with the task of reporting the doctor's speech again, she therefore switches into dialect, going back to Italian at the end of the quotation. This is thus neatly set off from the surrounding context by the use of a different code, as was precisely the case in A's first quotation, only in the opposite direction.

EXAMPLE 19: NURSE

A	*E nnenti, cci ficiru na puntura ppô tètanu, ddocu, non sàcciu ppi*
	cchi ccos'è, e: e cci rìssiru di non fallo: bere niente, manciare
	niente, almeno per un quattro ore, senza manciare e senza bere e
	poi di non fallo dommire. 'Se il bambino . . . propio qualche coccio
5	di acqua', *picchì u picciriddu è nnicu, dici* 'gliela date. Però se
	dovesse vomitare lo riportate subito'. *Picchì si scantàvunu ppi nn'e-*
	morraggia intenna.
G	Ce::rto! Questo è il pericolo.
A	Ecco! Tutto qua! *Ccà mancu punti cci rèsiru,* perché il taglio è
10	stato: molto, però non era profondo. Perciò glielo hanno chiuso bene
	bene con un cerotto. *'Picchì ccà',* rici, *'a ddàricci i punti è ppiccatu.*
	Cci arresta a cicatrici'. Siccome non era profondo, *u capìu?*[8]

A	*That was all, they gave him an injection against tetanus, there, I*
	don't know what it is for, and and they told us not to let him drink
	anything, eat anything, at least for about four hours, without eating
	and without drinking and then not to let him sleep. 'If the child
5	. . . just some drops of water' *because he is a little child, he says*
	'you can give it to him. But if he happens to vomit, bring him back
	here immediately'. *Because they feared an internal haemorrhage.*
G	Su::re! That's the danger.
A	That's all! *Here they didn't even give him any stitches,* because the
10	cut was big, but it wasn't deep. So they closed it up tight with a
	plaster. *'Because' he says 'it's a pity to put stitches in here. It*
	would leave a scar'. As it wasn't deep, *did you understand?*

Let us consider one more example. In example 20, the beauty specialist, while complaining about the crazy demands of some of her clients, switches into dialect in quoting the answer she had given one of them, who insisted on the phone on fixing an appointment, when she was already busy with someone else.

EXAMPLE 20: BEAUTY SPECIALIST

C	Mi ha telefonato una cliente 'Oggi posso venire alle sei e mezza,
	sette?' 'No', perché so- già ho due con lo stesso orario, perché a

---

una ci devo mettere: le fasce ... rassodanti, no? fasce rassodanti
sono. E nel frattempo che quella ci ha le fasce, che deve stare
5   mezz'ora, io mezz'ora mi faccio un massaggio. Dice 'Io ora:' 'Viene
alle sette e mezzo? Ce ce l'ho libero alle sette e mezzo.' Dice 'No,
ho impegni'. *'E cchi vvoli? Iù no: ... unni t'ai'a nficcari?'*
G Certo.

C A client phoned 'Can I come today at half past six or seven?' 'No',
because I know- I've already got two ((clients)) at the same time,
because I've got to give one of them skin hardening ... bandages,
haven't I? They are skin hardening bandages. And while that one
5   has got the bandages on, as she has to keep them on for half an
hour, in half an hour I can do a massage. She says 'I ((want to
come)) now' 'Can you come at half past seven? I'm free at half
past seven.' She says 'No, I'm busy'. *But what do you expect? I
... where can I possibly fit you in?'*
G Sure.

It is extremely unlikely that a beauty specialist, traditionally very keen
to give an image of refinement and politeness, would use dialect in talking
with a client on the phone. In this particular case, therefore, the language
of quotation does not correspond to the language that we can infer was
originally used, supposing this was the unmarked code in that type of interaction. The methodological principle of inferring the original language on
the basis of appropriateness conditions in the use of the two codes, and of
comparing it with the language of quotation in order to establish their coincidence, therefore proves to be rather ineffective.

A third set of examples where the mimetic explanation is even more
unsatisfactory is that of 'virtual' quotations, i.e. the quotation of speech that
the speaker imagines he or she will utter, as in example 21, or that suggests
to the interlocutor, as in example 22.

EXAMPLE 21: CONDOMINIUM MEMBERS' MEETING

AM. Difatti, difatti io chiederò. Prima dato che lo conosce, anche lo chiedo
alla signora. *Cci ricu 'Senti, ma chissu comu è ccumminatu?
Eventualmenti cci putissi nteressari?'* Vediamo un pochettino, perché
se no [...]

AM. I'll ask her indeed, indeed. First, as she knows him, I'll ask the lady.
*I'll tell her 'Listen, what is he up to, this guy? If necessary, would
he be interested?'* We'll see, because otherwise [...]

EXAMPLE 22: IN A DEPARTMENT STORE

SHOP ASS.1	*Ci parrasti?*
SHOP ASS.2	*Sì.*
SHOP ASS.1	*Cchi tti rìssinu?*
SHOP ASS.2	*Ma rici ca non s'appìzzunu.*
5 SHOP ASS.1	*Cchi è non s'appìzzunu! N'an'a ffari fari a comunicazioni. Cci a ddiri, cci a ddiri* 'All'ufficio personale vogliono la comunicazione'.

SHOP ASS.1	*Did you talk to them?*
SHOP ASS.2	*Yes, I did.*
SHOP ASS.1	*What did they say?*
SHOP ASS.2	*They said the goods will not get spoiled.*
5 SHOP ASS.1	*What do you mean the goods will not get spoiled! They have to inform us. You have to tell them, you have to tell them* 'The personnel department wants to be informed'.

The same applies to impersonal remarks expressed in the form of a direct quote by an unidentified locutor. See for instance example 23, in which during the condominium members' meeting a lawyer switches into dialect to mark what he thinks might be a possible objection to his words, raised by an impersonal or not-specified speaker.

EXAMPLE 23: CONDOMINIUM MEMBERS' MEETING

AM. E allora l'optimum l'optimum quale dovrebbe essere? . . . Quello che il condominio in proprio gestisca, anche se ci ha un costo superiore, che poi non non è superiore, la eventuale retribuzione del prestatore d'opera, assoggettandola a contributi, ferie, inden-
5   nità di liquidazione e tutto. D'altra parte il costo, *non è ca rici 'Sa, ma cci sù i contribbuti'.* E' tutto proporzionale [. . .]

AM. Well, then what would be best? . . . That the owners should directly provide, even at a higher cost, but it is not really any higher, the salary of the hired person, along with social-insurance taxes, paid holidays, retirement bonus and everything. After all, *one can't*
5   *say 'But there are social-insurance taxes, you know'.* It's all proportional [. . .]

In all these cases there is no original language to be preserved, as the reported speech has not actually taken place. And yet very often code-switching does occur.

In impersonal quotations code-switching can also be a strategy to say something but at the same time distance oneself from what is being said. The use of a different language allows the speaker to depersonalise his or her point of view, assigning it to an off-screen voice. And this can also be done in order to mitigate a possible conflict or disagreement with the co-participant, as seems to happen in example 24, drawn from the conversation in which the two shop assistants talk about the unhappiness of a mutual friend. While V thinks that this is because of her too many children, C tries to suggest a different explanation, i.e. the operation that their friend has recently undergone (*Va bene, dici, ha subito un . . . lieve intervento* 'Well, one might say, she did have a . . . minor operation'). In doing so, she switches into Italian. The use of a code she has not been using so far, together with the verb of saying in the third person, might be meant by C to let V think that what she said is not her personal opinion, but rather somebody else's, which she is just reporting without necessarily agreeing upon it. C hopes in this way not to hurt the feelings of her co-participant, whom she knows to have a different opinion on this point, as one can clearly see in the turns immediately following the impersonal quotation.

EXAMPLE 24: IN A DEPARTMENT STORE

	V	*Non è ca una . . . na pessona picchì avi n caràttiri ci rici. . . Ommai chiddu stancàu macari di riraccillu. Picchì prima era cchiù* (. . . . .)
	C	*Matri! Mi pari (accussì nfilici), sta carusa.*
5	V	*Cchi ssàcciu si è nfilici, non . . . Ma tutti pari* (. . . . .). *Quattru figghi avi.*
→C		Va bene, *dici*, ha subito un . . . lieve intervento.
	V	*No, gioia! Ma si idda . . . Senti, tu a mmèttiri quattru figghi.* Quattru bambini! *E n neonatu.*
10	C	*E appuntu! E di cui è a cuppa?*
	V	*Di tutt'e due. E cchi cci ll'aveva (iddu) a cuppa?*
	V	*It's not that just because a . . . a person has a certain character you can say . . . He's tired of telling her. Because before she was more* (. . . . .)
	C	*God! That girl seems so unhappy.*
5	V	*I don't know whether she's unhappy, not . . . But everybody* (. . . . .). *She's got four children.*
	C	Well, *one might say*, she did have a . . . minor operation.
	V	*No, my dear! But if she . . . listen, you've got to remember the four children.* Four children! *And a baby.*
10	C	*Precisely! And whose fault is that?*
	V	Of both of them. *Why, is he the only one to be blamed?*

What all these examples clearly demonstrate is that the direction of switching in reported speech is not automatically determined by the language in which the original utterance was spoken, as assumed for instance by Gal (1979: 109), Myers-Scotton (1993: 117) and Sornicola (1977: 133). This is too simplistic and deterministic an explanation, which tries to link a change in code to a change in some features of the situational context. For instance, according to Myers-Scotton, switching in quotations belongs to the sequential unmarked type, because 'the code used in the reported speech is unmarked for the RO set for the earlier conversation'. As we have tried to show, this is not always the case. Moreover such an explanation would deprive code-switching of its stylistic and conversational relevance. That is probably why Myers-Scotton thinks that 'such CS is not especially remarkable' (1993: 117). She admits that occasionally switching in quotations may not be due to the purpose of preserving the original language. Code-switching in such cases would represent a marked choice achieving an aesthetic effect (1993: 139). But within the markedness model this only happens because each code is associated with a definite set of rights and obligations and with certain social attributes. As a consequence, Myers-Scotton's theory cannot adequately explain the use of code-switching in quotations in communities like the Italian one, where codes are not very sharply differentiated on the functional level and not loaded with strong cultural and ethnic connotations, as they are instead in Kenya or in other colonial settings.

The Italian case – and probably others as well – can be better understood if, following Goffman (1979: 22), one sees code-switching as one of the possible devices used to mark the change of footing which occurs whenever speakers shift 'from saying something' themselves 'to reporting what someone else said'. In other words, code-switching works as a conversational resource by means of which bilingual speakers can express the polyphony of discourse more effectively (see Lüdi and Py 1986: 158). In the *mise-en-scène* set up by the speaker in conversation, the transition from one character to another can be signalled in several ways: by the use of mimicry, tone of voice, imitation of personal ways of talking, different verbs of saying and, last but not least, by different languages assigned to the different 'voices' taking part in this communicative performance.[9] What really matters, then, is not fidelity towards the original language, or the social and cultural attributes of the codes in the repertoire, but the contrast between what the current speaker says and what 'someone *else* said, someone present or absent, someone human or mythical' (Goffman 1979: 21), someone virtual or impersonal. This is clearly shown in those cases where, as the verb of saying is missing, code-switching is the only way to mark the beginning of a quotation, as in example 25.

EXAMPLE 25: NURSE

A   *Mi pari ca fu ô sabbatu. Me figghia . . . era:: cuccata ancora. Sònanu â potta . . . Scinni ccô picciriddu. Iddu è n coppu a scappari. Me figghia appress'i iddu.* 'Aspetta, non aprire' *picchì era ancora in pigiama a carusa.*

A   *I think it was on Saturday. My daughter . . . was still in bed. The door bell rang . . . She went downstairs with her child. All of a sudden he ran ahead. My daughter after him.* 'Wait, don't open' *because she was still wearing her pyjamas.*

Another case in point is that of quotations embedded in another quotation and not introduced by any other signal, as for instance in example 26. P is talking of a visit paid to his father in a nursing home. He reports first the nurse's words and then the answer of an old lady, who tries to explain to the nurse the reasons why the old people there are tired of life. Within the old lady's reported speech, we find another quotation, as the old lady – who is being quoted – herself reports the prescriptions constantly given by doctors to ill people. The embedded quotation is only signalled by the contrast between Italian and dialect.

EXAMPLE 26: WHOLESALER'S

P   *A nfimmera*, sai, s'arrabbiò. 'Tutti stamattina state facendo questo ragionamento, però poi nessuno volete morire.' 'No', *rici*, 'non è vero!' Gli ha risposto l'altra vecchietta, poveretta. 'Non è vero, perché siamo stanchi . . . Stanchi di essere: . . . tormentati . . . iniezioni

5   *"e cchissu e ppìgghiati a pìllula e ppìgghiati a cumpressa e:"* '

P   *The nurse*, you know, got angry. 'Everybody this morning is talking like that, and yet nobody wants to die.' 'No', said she, 'that's not true!' the other old lady replied, poor thing. 'That's not true, because we are tired . . . tired of being . . . tormented . . . injections *"and*

5   *this and that, and take your pill and take your tablet and"* '

In many cases of quotations in the corpus, only the verb of saying is marked by a switch, while the quotation itself is in the base language of the turn. In a few others, the switch of the quotation is anticipated in the verb of saying (see examples 17 and 23 above).[10] In other words, it seems that the speaker can choose among a range of possibilities to set off a quotation, among which there is also code-switching, either of the whole quote or of the verb only, or even of both the verb and the quote (for details, see Alfonzetti 1992b).

What we have tried to demonstrate here does not entirely exclude the possibility that the direction of switching in setting off quotations can be partially meaningful. Indeed it can occasionally be motivated by a mimetic purpose, by the unmarked use of the two codes or by its intentional violation. Yet speakers seem to assign a priority to the contrastive potentiality of code-switching, in order to differentiate the plurality of voices taking part in discourse. And they can do this up to the point of modifying the original speaker's linguistic choice or of violating rules of sociolinguistic appropriateness. This amounts to saying that the polyphony principle provides a more general explanation, able to subsume other partial motivations, whereas the mimetic hypothesis and the markedness theory leave out many cases, which would therefore remain unaccounted for.

5 Concluding remarks

We have tried to show that, contrary to a widespread assumption, code-switching as an unmarked choice can be dealt with in terms of conversation analysis. Such an analysis enables us to discover the wide range of local functions of code-switching, which, even if not socially meaningful, do have communicative relevance.

In particular, the analysis carried out in Catania shows that code-switching – far from being caused by an insufficient competence in one of the two languages, and besides expressing a double cultural identity – works as a communicative strategy used for a variety of purposes, related either to the negotiation of the language of interaction or to the organisation of conversational activities (see Auer 1984 and 1995). In both cases, it can be viewed as a contextualisation cue, which effectively contributes to the interpretation of utterances in context. As Gumperz (1984) and Auer (1984, 1988, 1990, 1995) have already suggested, the notion of contextualisation seems to be a most promising element in the construction of a theoretical model of conversational code-switching.

In most of the local functions of code-switching between Italian and dialect, a high degree of reversibility in the direction of switching has been noted: the same conversational function can be carried out by a switch in both directions. This means that the functionality of code-switching rests largely on the contrast achieved by the juxtaposition of the two codes. It also implies that it is partly independent of the social meaning of the two codes in the sociolinguistic repertoire of the community. It is not possible therefore to assign to each code a semantic value, like for instance that of 'we-code' and 'they-code', at least not in a straightforward way. And this is probably due to the fact that, in the Italian case, bilingual speakers belong to a monocultural community, within which there are no strong feelings of separateness and cultural or ethnic conflict, as researchers in different geographical areas of Italy have already pointed out (see Berruto 1985 and 1990; Giacalone Ramat 1991 and 1995; Sobrero 1992).

On a more general level, our analysis shows that it is possible to identify conversational structures and principles which seem to be recurrent in different communities, thus showing the relative autonomy of a conversational component from the sociolinguistic situation. On the other hand, pointing out certain peculiarities in the way code-switching carries out its communicative and pragmatic functions, our study can also hopefully provide an opportunity to analyse some macro-social influences on micro-level structures and functions, by a wider comparison of data from different speech communities.

Notes

1 Dialects therefore are neither regional or social varieties of Italian, nor deviations from the standard language, as for instance in France or in Britain. They have a history going back through the centuries to Vulgar Latin. According to Trumper (1989: 36) 'what divides dialects from "written" ~ "spoken" standard is hence structural, genetic, typological, historical; what divides regional varieties from standard is functional'; see also Giacalone Ramat (1991 and 1995) and Mioni (1979). As Berruto (1989: 9) points out, although it may be difficult to draw clear-cut boundaries in the continuum between the two extreme poles of the linguistic repertoire – i.e. standard Italian and local dialect – Italian and dialect are undeniably kept apart not only 'in the linguistic data as they appear to the linguist', but also 'in the consciousness of the speakers themselves'. This results clearly from a recent survey carried out within the project of the *Atlante Linguistico della Sicilia* (ALS), elaborated in Palermo by the Centro di Studi Filologici e Linguistici Siciliani (see Ruffino 1995): almost all of the forty-nine interviewees recognised the mixed character of an oral text which they had listened to and were even able to distinguish the dialectal stretches from the Italian ones (Alfonzetti 1995).
2 For simplicity's sake the label *Italian* will be used here, as if it were an entity opposed to dialect. In actual speech, a particular variety of Italian and of dialect is used, according to geographical, social and situational parameters. The term *standard Italian* will be avoided completely because, as we have already said, such a variety is never found in spontaneous spoken language.
3 For a description of the sociolinguistic situation in contemporary Sicily, see Lo Piparo (1990) and D'Agostino and Pennisi (1995). On regional Italian in Sicily see Tropea (1976), Leone (1982) and Sgroi (1990), who carried out a structural analysis of contact phenomena between Italian and dialect from an enriched version of Weinreich's theoretical framework. A historical study of the relationships between the national language and the Sicilian dialect is provided by Alfieri (1992) .
4 In the extracts italic type is used to mark dialect. Other conventions are:

-	break off/unfinished words
. . .	a long pause within a turn
[. . .]	omitted sections
:, ::, :::	lengthened vowels
[	overlapping utterances
(. . . . .)	unintelligible stretches of talk
(( ))	transcriber's insertions

5 According to the statistical data provided by the OLS enquiry, 85.9 per cent of the interviewees in Catania use only or prevalently Italian in public offices and 59.6 per cent in shops (Lo Piparo 1990: 249–50).
6 In section 4.1 a different type of repair switching will be discussed, where the reparandum is not the code itself but a proper mistake or some other kind of conversational problem.
7 See also Blom and Gumperz (1972), Myers-Scotton (1976), and Sornicola (1977).
8 The variety of Italian spoken by A represents what in section 2 we called *uneducated regional Italian* or *popular Italian.*
9 See *Slovo v romane* in Bakhtin (1976), Mortara Garavelli (1985) and Simone (1990).
10 This phenomenon might depend on a mechanism similar to the anticipatory triggering described by Clyne (1969: 345), according to which 'switching occurs not only in consequence but also in anticipation of a trigger-word'.

Bibliography

Alfieri, G. (1992) 'La Sicilia', in F. Bruni (ed.) *L'italiano nelle regioni. Lingua nazionale e identità regionali,* Turin: Utet, 798–860.

Alfonzetti, G. (1992a) 'Neutrality conditions in Italian-dialect code switching', in *Papers for the Code-Switching Summer School,* Pavia, 9–12 September 1992, Strasbourg: European Science Foundation, 93–107.

—— (1992b) *Il discorso bilingue. Italiano e dialetto a Catania,* Milan: FrancoAngeli.

—— (1995) 'Code switching e code mixing nell'Atlante Linguistico della Sicilia', in M. T. Romanello and I. Tempesta (eds) *Dialetti e lingue nazionali, Atti del XXVII Congresso della Società di Linguistica Italiana,* Rome: Bulzoni, 413–31.

Auer, P. (1984) *Bilingual Conversation,* Amsterdam: Benjamins.

—— (1988) 'A conversation analytic approach to code-switching and transfer', in M. Heller (ed.), *Code-switching: Anthropological and Sociolinguistic Perspectives,* Berlin: Mouton de Gruyter, 187–214.

—— (1990), 'A discussion paper on code alternation', in *Papers for the Workshop on Concepts, Methodology and Data,* Basel, 12–13 January 1990, Strasbourg: European Science Foundation, 69–91.

—— (1995) 'The pragmatics of code-switching', in L. Milroy and P. Muysken, (eds) *One Speaker, Two Languages: Cross-Disciplinary Perspectives on Code-Switching,* Cambridge: Cambridge University Press, 115–35.

Auer, P. and Di Luzio, A. (eds) (1984) *Interpretive Sociolinguistics,* Tübingen: Narr.

Bakhtin, M. (1976) *Voprosy literatury i estetiki,* Izdatel'stvo "Chudozestvennaja literatura", Italian translation *Estetica e Romanzo,* Turin: Einaudi [1977].

Berruto, G. (1985) ' " 'l pulman l-è nen ch-a *cammina tanto forte*". Su commutazione di codice e mescolanza dialetto-italiano', *Vox Romanica* 44: 59–76.

—— (1987) 'Lingua, dialetto, diglossia, dilalìa', in G. Holtus and J. Kramer (eds) *Romania et Slavia Adriatica,* Hamburg: Buske, 57–81.

—— (1989) 'Main topics and findings in Italian sociolinguistics', *International Journal of the Sociology of Language* 76: 7–30.

—— (1990) 'Italiano regionale, commutazione di codice e enunciati mistilingui', in M. A. Cortelazzo and A. Mioni (eds) *L'italiano regionale. Atti del XVIII Congresso della Società di Linguistica Italiana,* Rome: Bulzoni, 105–30.

Blom, J. P. and Gumperz, J. J. (1972) 'Social meaning in linguistic structure: Code-switching in Norway', in J. J. Gumperz and D. Hymes (eds) *Directions in Sociolinguistics. The Ethnography of Communication,* New York: Rinehart & Winston, 407–34.

Clyne, M. G. (1969) 'Switching between language systems', in *Actes du 10e Congrès International des Linguistes* (Bucharest 28 August–2 September 1967), 1: 343–49.

D'Agostino, M. and Pennisi, A. (1995) *Per una sociolinguistica spaziale. Modelli e rappresentazioni della variabilità linguistica nell'esperienza dell'ALS*, Materiali e ricerche 4, Palermo: Centro di Studi Filologici e Linguistici Siciliani.

Di Luzio, A. (1984) 'On the meaning of language choice for the sociocultural identity of bilingual migrant children', in P. Auer and A. Di Luzio (eds) (1984), *Interpretive Sociolinguistics*, Tübingen: Narr, 55–85.

Gal, S. (1979) *Language Shift: Social Determinants of Linguistic Change in Bilingual Austria*, New York: Academic Press.

Giacalone Ramat, A. (1991) 'Code-switching in dialectal communities: effects on language shift', in *Papers for the Workshop on Impact and Consequences/Broader Considerations*, Brussels, 22–24 November 1990, Strasbourg: European Science Foundation, 189–225.

—— (1995) 'Code-switching in the context of dialect/standard language relations', in L. Milroy and P. Muysken (eds), *One Speaker, Two Languages: Cross-Disciplinary Perspectives on Code-Switching*, Cambridge: Cambridge University Press, 45–67.

Goffman, E. (1979) 'Footing', *Semiotica* 25, 1/2: 1–29.

Gumperz, J. J. (1984) 'Ethnography in urban communication', in P. Auer and A. Di Luzio (eds) *Interpretive Sociolinguistics*, Tübingen, Germany: Narr, 1–12.

Jefferson, G. (1973) 'A case of precision timing in ordinary conversation: overlapped tag-positioned address terms in closing sequences', *Semiotica* 9, 1: 47–96.

—— (1978) 'Sequential aspects of storytelling in conversation', in J. Schenkein (ed.) *Studies in the Organization of Conversational Interaction*, New York: Academic Press, 219–48.

Heller, M. (ed.) (1988) *Code-switching: Anthropological and Sociolinguistic Perspectives,* Berlin: Mouton de Gruyter.

Leone, A. (1982) *L'italiano regionale in Sicilia*, Bologna: Il Mulino.

Lo Piparo, F. (ed.) (1990) *La Sicilia linguistica oggi. Osservatorio Linguistico Siciliano* (OLS), 1, Palermo: Centro di Studi Filologici e Linguistici Siciliani.

Lüdi, G. and Py, B. (1986) *Être bilingue*, Berne: Peter Lang.

Maynard, D. W. (1980) 'Placement of topic changes in conversation', *Semiotica* 30, 3/4: 263–90.

Milroy, L. and Muysken, P. (eds) (1995) *One Speaker, Two Languages: Cross-Disciplinary Perspectives on Code-Switching*, Cambridge: Cambridge University Press.

Mioni, A. (1979) 'La situazione sociolinguistica italiana: lingua, dialetti, italiani regionali', in A. Colombo (ed.) *Guida all'educazione linguistica*, Bologna: Zanichelli, 101–14.

Moerman, M. (1973) 'The use of precedent in natural conversation: a study in practical legal reasoning', *Semiotica* 9, 3: 93–215.

Mortara Garavelli, B. (1985) *La parola d'altri*, Palermo: Sellerio.

Myers-Scotton, C. M. (1976) 'Strategies of neutrality: language choice in uncertain situations', *Language* 52: 919–41.

—— (1988) 'Codeswitching as indexical of social negotiations', in M. Heller (ed.) (1988) *Code-switching: Anthropological and Sociolinguistic Perspectives*, Berlin: Mouton de Gruyter, 151–86.

—— (1993) *Social Motivations for Codeswitching*, Oxford: Oxford University Press.

Ruffino, G. (ed.) (1995) *Percorsi di geografia linguistica. Idee per un atlante siciliano della cultura dialettale e dell'italiano regionale*, Materiali e ricerche 1, Palermo: Centro di Studi Filologici e Linguistici Siciliani.

Schegloff, E. and Sacks, H. (1973) 'Opening up closings', *Semiotica* 7: 289–323.

Sgroi, S. C. (1990) 'Lingue in contatto, italiano regionale e italiano di Sicilia', in *Per una linguistica siciliana tra storia e struttura*, Messina: Sicania, 369–454.

—— (1994) *Diglossia, prestigio, e varietà della lingua italiana*, Enna: Il Lunario.

Simone, R. (1990) *Fondamenti di linguistica*, Bari: La Terza.

Sobrero, A. (ed.) (1992) *Il dialetto nella conversazione. Ricerche di dialettologia pragmatica*, Galatina: Congedo.

Sornicola, R. (1977) *La competenza multipla. Un'analisi micro-sociolinguistica*, Napoli: Liguori.

Tropea, G. (1976) *Italiano di Sicilia*, Palermo: Aracne.

Trumper, J. (1977) 'Ricostruzione nell'Italia settentrionale: sistemi consonantici. Considerazioni sociolinguistiche nella diacronia', in R. Simone and U. Vignuzzi (eds) *Problemi della ricostruzione in linguistica. Atti del Convegno Internazionale di Studi della Società di Linguistica Italiana*, Rome: Bulzoni, 259–310.

—— (1984) 'Language variation, code-switching, S. Chirico Raparo (Potenza)', in P. Auer and A. Di Luzio (eds) *Interpretive Sociolinguistics*, Tübingen: Narr, 29–54.

—— (1989) 'Observations on sociolinguistic behavior in two Italian regions', *International Journal of the Sociology of Language*, 76: 31–62.

Varvaro, A. (1978) *La lingua e la società*, Naples: Guida.

INTRODUCTION TO CHAPTER 9

Peter Auer

There are possibly more studies on code-switching between Spanish and English than on any other pair of languages – most of them on bilingual speakers in the USA with a Latino background (Chicanos, Puerto Ricans, etc.). In fact important earlier studies on the sociolinguistics of code-switching such as Gumperz and Hernández-Chavez (1971), McClure (1977), Pfaff (1979), Poplack (1980) or Zentella (1981) – to cite just a few – refer to this context. Gibraltar offers not only the only possibility of studying societal English–Spanish code-switching in Europe, but also one in which Spanish and English have co-existed for at least 200 years. On the basis of bilingual data from this sociolinguistic context, Melissa Moyer presents a model of conversational code-switching which takes us some steps away from a CA-type sequential analysis of code-switching towards a more ethnographically oriented approach. Her basic argument is that the sequential analysis of code-switching alone does not account for the social significance of this form of bilingual speech.

The fortress of Gibraltar (Arab. Djebel al-Tarik, together with the Djebel Musa, its African counterpart, one of the famous Columns of Hercules in antiquity) was conquered by an English–Dutch corps fighting for the Hapsburgs during the Spanish Wars of Succession in 1704. Since the treaty of Utrecht in 1713, Gibralter has been under British sovereignty (and a crown colony from 1830 to 1969) despite several Spanish attacks (1727, 1779–83) and political attempts to unite it with Spain which reached a climax in the 1960s. In 1967, 95 per cent of the citizens voted for Britain. Yet the loyalty of the Gibraltarians towards Great Britain is not undivided today. Although the educational and local political system in the former colony follows the British model (and the official language is English), cultural and social affinities of the predominantly Catholic population are often with the Spanish.

Gibraltar was deserted by its (probably Andalusian) population during the English conquest. In the eighteenth century, the area attracted above all Genoese Italians and Moroccan Sephardic Jews; the first spoke their Italian dialect, the second an archaic Spanish. Other parts of the population of

Gibraltar at that time were Portuguese and Maltese, only a small group Andalusian. It is very likely that bilingualism was already widespread at that time; thus, an eye-witness, Don Ignacio López de Ayala, writes in 1782 (373–374, cf. Kramer 1986: 53): 'Los Ginoveses . . . como los Judios hablan bien ó mal el Castellano é Ingles, i un dialecto ó jerga comun á todas las naciones, sin excluir las Africanas.' This bilingualism seems to have flourished outside the garrison itself (which was always monolingual English) through the centuries, although the Mediterranean lingua franca referred to by López de Ayala as well as the Italian and Jewish varieties disappeared in the early nineteenth century, giving way to the exclusive co-existence of English and a variety of Spanish (Yanito) in which traces of the older multi-lingualism still can be found.

In her contribution, Moyer discusses, among other data, fictitious and stylised conversations taken from the weekly newspaper *Panorama*. Although they may not depict exactly the code-switching practices of Gibraltarians today, they do demonstrate that Gibraltarians see their identity well expressed by this way of speaking. It seems to be looked upon, perhaps not as a prestigious variety, but certainly as one which fits the needs of the 'true' Gibraltarians such as 'Cynthia' and 'Cloti', who are equally competent in Spanish and English, but seem to feel more at ease switching between the two.

In order to analyse her conversational data, Moyer suggests a three-level model which roughly corresponds to the three levels of structure in code-switching as outlined in the Introduction to this book (see pp. 3–4). On the highest level, language choice for the situation is considered and, in the Gibraltarian case, said to be usually determined by external factors such as the institutional context of Moyer's example 1. Usually, it is possible to determine a base language of the interaction; in Moyer's approach (which differs in this respect from Myers-Scotton's, 1993), it is defined by the statistical preponderance of words in one language or the other. In some situations (reminiscent of Myers-Scotton's 'unmarked language choice'), there may be no base language since the two languages are used with equal frequency (as in examples 1 or 4).

Moyer's middle level is that of conversational ('sequential') structuring. In her model, it becomes meaningful only against the background of the base language, a claim which contrasts with Alfonzetti's (this volume) and weakens the autonomy of this level. Cases in which no base language can be determined would not be interactionally meaningful *qua* code juxtaposition and could be considered instances of a mixed code (as described in the Introduction, p. 15). On the lowest level of intra-turn switching, Moyer's description hinges on grammatical criteria such as the extension and the integrity of the switched constituents.

Bibliography

Gumperz, John J. and Hernández-Chávez, Eduardo (1971) 'Bilingualism bidialectalism, and classroom interaction', in A. Dil (ed.) *Language in Social Groups. Essays by John J. Gumperz*, Stanford, Calif.: Stanford University Press, 311–350.

Kramer, Johannes (1986) *English and Spanish in Gibraltar*, Hamburg: Buske.

López de Ayala, Ignacio (1782) *Historia de Gibraltar*, Madrid.

McClure, E. (1977) 'Aspects of code-switching in the discourse of bilingual Mexican-American children', in M. Saville-Troike (ed.) *Linguistics and Anthropology (GURT)*, Washington, DC: Georgetown University Press, 93–115.

Myers-Scotton, Carol (1993) *Social Motivations for Codeswitching: Evidence from Africa*, Oxford: Clarendon.

Pfaff, Carol (1979) 'Constraints on language mixing: intrasentential code-switching and borrowing in Spanish/English', *Language* 55, 2, 291–318.

Poplack, Shana (1980) 'Sometimes I'll start a sentence in Spanish Y TERMINO EN ESPAÑOL: toward a typology of code-switching', *Linguistics* 18, 581–618.

Zentella, A.C. (1981) *'"Hablamos los dos. We speak both."' Growing up bilingual in El Barrio*, Ph.D. Thesis, University of Pennsylvania.

9

BILINGUAL CONVERSATION STRATEGIES IN GIBRALTAR

Melissa G. Moyer

1 Introduction

This chapter analyses bilingual conversational activities in Gibraltar in relation to work carried out by Auer (1995) on the sequential organization of conversational code-switching, as well as by Muysken (1995a, 1995b) on proposals for a typology of sentential code-switching structures. Special attention is dedicated to the forms and meanings of English/Spanish code-switching in situated verbal interactions. The data considered were collected by Moyer from various social situations in Gibraltar between 1987 and 1992.[1] Gibraltar is an ideal language laboratory for undertaking research on conversational code-switching.[2] In this small British territory English and Spanish are used on a daily basis in almost every verbal interaction. The population has a balanced linguistic competence. The high level of proficiency in two languages explains the variety and richness of communicative strategies available to bilingual members of this community.

Bilingual conversations from Gibraltar are analysed and explained in relation to language choices at three levels of conversation organization. These choices are strategies available for communicating meaning available to speakers with a high level of proficiency in both English and Spanish. The first choice involves the selection of a main or dominant language for the entire conversation. The main language serves to frame the code-switching choices made at the other two levels of conversation organization. At an intermediate level participants can momentarily switch their language for a limited number of turns. Language negotiation between participants takes place at this level. Meanings related to inter-turn language choices are recuperated by a sequential analysis along the lines proposed by Auer (1995). At the lowest level, there are several intra-sentential switch types within a turn that a speaker fluent in English and Spanish can choose. Such structural switches function as contextualization cues for the creation of the situated meaning.

Several bilingual conversation extracts are analysed on these three levels in an effort to show how contextualization cues combine with additional textual resources such as *topic*, *alignment of speakers*, and *humour* to represent the ambivalent and multifaceted identity of Gibraltarians.

Section 2 offers background information about the community of Gibraltar together with some basic insights on the norms, values and attitudes of language use. Section 3 on conversational competence illustrates bilingual conversational competence in a simulated bilingual conversation where specific linguistic strategies are used in the creation of situated meaning. Section 4 discusses a proposal for analysing bilingual conversations in terms of language choices which are made at three distinct levels (as outlined above) of a conversational event. Section 5 on bilingual conversation strategies presents three extracts which are discussed in relation to the three-level model of language choice proposed. The last section summarises the main ideas about bilingual conversation set out in this chapter.

2 The community

Gibraltar has been a small British colony since 1713. It is located on the southern tip of Spain in the Andalusian province of Cádiz. It is four kilometres long and occupies an area of approximately 584 hectares, with a population in 1995 of 31,874 inhabitants. Gibraltar is a melting pot of peoples from different cultural backgrounds and with different languages who have settled there throughout the centuries to pursue various military, trade and commercial interests.

Nowadays, Gibraltarians in spite of their multiethnic past constitute a relatively homogenous group. They share a developed linguistic competence in both English and Spanish, as well as similar norms of language use. The language variety currently spoken in Gibraltar is referred to as *Yanito*. It consists of various patterns of code-switching with a proportionately small lexical substratum from Italian, Hebrew, Arabic and a local vernacular. This lexical substratum, compiled by Cavilla (1978) in a dictionary, is disappearing among the younger generations who prefer to use English or Spanish words. Most Gibraltarians can carry out conversations in either English or Spanish, or in both languages at the same time. Code-switching is a common phenomenon and it is used in both oral and written discourse. Patterns of language choice discussed in this chapter take into consideration the social setting and the type of structure switched, as well as the interpersonal dynamics of the verbal interaction. There are specific domains or settings in which language choice is normative. Code-switching (Spanish and English) and monolingual Spanish speech are commonly used in informal situations, with family and friends (Moyer 1992a). English, on the other hand, is reserved for formal contexts including the work place and school, and for interactions with local government officials.

Language contact in Gibraltar contrasts with the situation of other multilingual settings where members of the community do not share the same linguistic competence, attitudes or norms. Such differences often lead to social tension between different ethnic groups (as in the case of Belgium, Canada, or Catalonia) which is absent in Gibraltar.[3] The population interacts on a daily basis with the Spanish (primarily from across the border) and the British (soldiers, government representatives, as well as newly arrived immigrants) who for the most part are monolingual speakers. Social tensions arise at different times from the political policies implemented by both Spanish and British governments.

3 Conversational competence

Bilingual communicative competence in Gibraltar entails knowledge of the rules for intra-sentential code-switching as well as the norms of language use of both English and Spanish, but, in addition, this competence includes knowledge of the way two languages can be combined in a conversation. The analysis of a fictitious conversation in this section illustrates how distinct bilingual strategies such as (a) the choice not to select a main language (i.e. Spanish or English) for carrying out the conversation, (b) the negotiation or agreement by the participants to adopt the mixture of Spanish/English in their turns and (c) the frequent switching of different structure types in intra-turn and intra-sentence units contribute to the creation of meanings relevant to the portrayal of Gibraltarian identity.

Analyses of bilingual conversations typically focus on the distribution of two languages in an interaction and on the way specific bilingual strategies or cues are interpreted in situated conversation. But code-switching does not exist in isolation as a meaning-creating device; it groups together with other contextualization cues in order to jointly produce meaning inferences. Studies on conversational code-switching often ignore the way bilingual strategies interact with other linguistic and discourse devices (i.e. prosodic features, topic, reference, and alignment of speakers) in the construction of meaning. The present analysis seeks to show how some of the bilingual strategies mentioned above (a–c), as well as specific textual and linguistic devices, participate in the global organization of the interaction and in the construction of situated meaning.

The conversation selected is a fictitious exchange published in a weekly newspaper in Gibraltar called *Panorama*.[4] It is an idealized conversation which is a contribution to the newspaper column titled 'Calentita: Gibraltar's National Dish. El Telephone Talk de Cynthia y Cloti'. The text selected is an imitation of a telephone conversation between two Gibraltarian housewives. It lacks important features of natural interactions such as the presence of pauses, repetitions, reformulations, incomplete utterances, back channels and hedges. However, it has other features which include an organized system of turn-taking, adjacency pairs, and markers of orality. The text also makes use of other linguistic devices, which include topic development, alignment of the participants in the conversation, absence of a main language, humour, and several intra-turn code-switching structures that jointly contribute to the interpretation process.

The text published in the 'Calentita' column is a humorous criticism of the social and political life of Gibraltar. This conversation is representative of the sort of articles published by *Panorama* between 1988 and 1991. It was selected on the basis of its topic, which expresses the general indignation over the remodelling of the Gibraltar airport as well as with the persons responsible for this undertaking. The analysis of the conversation provides deeper insight into the verbal representation of the Gibraltarian identity in interactions between members from their own community and with members from outside.

EXAMPLE 1

Oh dear, *no nos quieren en el* so-called new air terminal, *qué pena me da.*
    ('THEY DON'T WANT US AT THE')   ('I'M SO UPSET.')
What are you saying, Cloti dear.
Mujer, que if you are a passenger you now have a bigger
('WOMAN, THAT')
departure lounge, which is well and good, *pero a los demás*
                          ('BUT FOR THE OTHER')
5 airport users *le han dao con la punta del pie*, which is not well and
              ('LIKE GIVING THEM A KICK,')
good.
You don't say . . .
I say, *y lo digo, que han quitado* all the chairs from the waiting area,
        ('AND I SAY, THAT THEY HAVE TAKEN')
and I *imaginate que hay que sentarse en el suelo*, my dear Cynthia.
              ('IMAGINE THAT YOU HAVE TO SIT ON THE FLOOR,')
10 *Vamos, que nos ha costado un millón y no hay un sillón.*
('COME ON, IT COST US A MILLION AND WE DON'T HAVE A SEAT.')
And given that our airport is famous for delays, that place is going to look like a *zoco.*
        ('ARAB MARKET')
Claro, already there were people this weekend sitting on the floor, and ('OF COURSE')
you cannot blame them. *Mi Juan, que es un* walking
           ('MY JOHN WHO IS A')
15 computer, *contó* only 16 seats, would you believe it?
           ('COUNTED')

Como que nos vamos a tener que comprar un cushion *para el pompi,*
('WE ARE GOING TO HAVE TO BUY')   ('FOR OUR BEHINDS,')
if you ask me.
And you must see the new waiting area, blimey, *es largo y estrecho*
                              ('IT'S LONG AND NARROW
como el tunel de Casemates.
LIKE THE CASEMATES TUNNEL.')

20 Really, what a brainwave, *a lo mejor se creen que en Gibraltar las*
                              ('MAYBE THEY THINK THAT IN GIBRALTAR
personas son sardinas.
PEOPLE ARE SARDINES.')
Not only that, my dear, but from what I've seen they keep it closed
until the plane lands.
What a *fandango,* my dear.
          [NAME OF A DANCE]

25 *Como que el hombre de las llaves va a termina cansao* with so many
('THE MAN WITH THE KEYS IS GOING TO END UP TIRED')
comings and goings. Can you *imaginate* the scene *si hay un*
                              ('IF THERE IS AN')
airport deal *y vienen 30 o 40* aeroplanes everyday, *el tío no va ganar*
          ('AND THIRTY OR FORTY')   ('THE GUY ISN'T GOING
para zapatos. And if you happen to be in the Silk Cut bar having a
TO EARN ENOUGH FOR SHOES.')
drink, you cannot see the arrivals and departure monitor, would you
30 believe it?
Caramba, what organization. And I *imaginate* that the acoustics remain
('GOSH')
as bad as ever?
You've hit the nail on the head, my dear. *Como hablen por el altavoz*
                    ('IF THEY TALK OVER THE LOUD SPEAKER
no se entera una de nada.
NO ONE CAN UNDERSTAND A THING.')

35 *Y quien fue el séneca que* decided to put the arrivals waiting area
('WHO WAS THE SMARTY WHO')
outside the main concourse?
Como que hace falta un concurso para enterarse.
('WE NEED A COMPETITION TO FIND OUT.')
Y dicen it can handle one million passengers!
('AND THEY SAY')
Qué comedia. Do you know that there is only room for a single
('WHAT A COMEDY.')
40 immigration officer to check all departures? *Imaginate* if one person
had to check a million passports a year!
You don't say . . .

Y lo que han hecho es poner one of those mobile tunnel-ways so that
('AND WHAT THEY HAVE DONE IS PUT')
passengers can go from the aircraft right into the terminal.
45 *En días de levanter,* they'll be blown into it as usual.
('ON THE DAYS WITH A LEVANTER WIND,')
Aquí no ha cambiado nada. Welcome to Gibraltar.
('NOTHING HAS CHANGED HERE.')

It is important to examine the way linguistic and textual devices jointly
contribute to the construction of meaning and the portrayal of a community's
identity. This instance of a fictitious conversation can be considered a form
of social practice in the sense of Fairclough (1992). The bilingual strategies
used represent the ambivalence Gibraltarians feel in real life. Different identities are presented as the topic develops throughout the conversation.

Gibraltarians have the need to reaffirm their uniqueness because of the
Spanish government who permanently exercises its claims over the territory. This often leads them to manifest their alignment and identity with
the British. However, they also need to distinguish themselves from British
colonial power and resist the second-class citizen status they sometimes are
assigned.[5] This leads to a personal and collective ambiguity regarding their
true identity: a hybrid culture and identity manifested linguistically by bilingual code-switching, a behaviour which is often viewed negatively and a
source of some joking and irony. It is also common for the population to
characterize their way of speaking in critical terms. Code-switching to many
simply elicits an inability to speak English or Spanish properly.

Topic is the central organizing principle for the construction of a coherent
exchange and its interpretation in this conversation. The code-switching
strategies, the humour generated by code-switching, and the alignment of
participants with members of the community and with the Spanish are the
main resources used to construct and reproduce the duality of the Gibraltarian
identity. The conversation reproduces the relation of a social group of
Gibraltarians (i.e. the airport users) with other in-group members of the
community who are responsible for remodelling the airport. Cloti, the first
interlocutor, is the voice of all airport users who are unhappy with the
changes which have been made. Pronominal reference to the airport users
are expressed in both English and Spanish. The inclusive first-person plural
pronoun *nos* in Spanish is used in the first sixteen lines to refer to the airport
users, who are not passengers. An important cohesive device is the co-refer-
ence of Spanish pronominal *nos* and the English pronominal referent *you*
which is ambivalent in many turns between the airport users and the interlocutor (lines 3, 14, 17, 26, 28).[6] The people responsible for renovating the
air terminal are never identified personally. Mentioning the authority who
took the decision is avoided by selecting a Spanish verb which grammatically allows for a non-expressed subject (lines 1, 8, 33, 38, 43). The only

exception is line 22 where the English verb *keep* is accompanied by a required overt subject *they* with no clearly identifiable referent. The indirectness of the criticisms and the deliberate avoidance of identifying those who undertook the renovation protects the actors and diffuses the responsibility for such a deed. At the same time this strategy avoids the polarization of public opinion and preserves the unity of Gibraltarian identity for outsiders.

Three different sectors of the society (airport users, passengers and the persons responsible for the renovation) are identified in example 1. This contrasts with other *Calentita* conversations where Gibraltarians are portrayed as a homogenous group which is counterposed to the Spanish. The representation of Gibraltarian identity thus varies according to whom they are compared. In example 1, the discussion of the airport renovation contrasts different groups and their position in relation to an issue which is controversial. The conversation is a collaborative venture where both participants, Cloti and Cynthia, avoid negotiating a main language for carrying out the conversation. However, they ratify the topic of conversation by supporting what each other says.

An account of code-switching in this fictitious telephone conversation sheds light on the ties between the general meaning of the text, the conversation structure, and the socio-political reality of Gibraltar. The frequent switching of languages is a deliberate strategy to reinforce local identities and avoid association with Spanish or British identities and modes of expression.

Code-switching in example 1 also has a humorous effect which can be associated with the two rather frivolous housewives as the main participants, the informal and intimate language of the exchange, as well as the contrast with the more serious key of the rest of the newspaper. *Panorama* is published entirely in English (except for the *Calentita* columns), and it presents local and international news in a serious and formal tone. There is a noticeable contrast in language, style, tone and topic between *Calentita* and the rest of the weekly. Humour creates ambiguity, as pointed out in Woolard's (1988) analysis of code-switching and humour in Catalonia. In the present examples it reflects the ambivalence Gibraltarians feel towards their identity. Code-switching carries a hidden prestige which is made explicit by the attitudes and evaluations expressed by Gibraltarians themselves.

Cynthia and Cloti switch languages freely between turns. While most turns also involve an important degree of internal switching, there are others which are monolingual, as in lines 2, 22, and 23. Within each turn different structural units are switched, as for example '*no nos quieren en el* so-called new air terminal, *qué pena me da*' (line 1), where the switched words do not form a full syntactic or phrasal constituent, or '*Como que nos vamos a tener que comprar un* cushion *para el pompi* if you ask me' (lines 16–17), where cushion is an insertion of a single lexical item and *if you ask me* is an instance of alternation where an entire clausal constituent is switched.

In the following sections a more detailed discussion is presented of the various bilingual strategies available to Gibraltarians.

4 Three levels of language choice

Research on the structure of conversational code-switching has improved understanding of the negotiation process, as well as the interactional rules governing the distribution of languages in bilingual exchanges. Important contributions in this area have been made by Auer (1984, 1988, 1995), who proposed four distinct sequencing patterns for code-switching within a conversation. These patterns characterize the logical combinations of two languages that can be made by one or two speakers.[7] Information about the participants and the process of language negotiation is provided within this model, as well as some facts about switch types (i.e. insertions) that do not affect language choice for the interaction. Auer's model of conversational code-switching accounts for the speech of second-generation Italian immigrant children in Constance (Germany), but requires some further elaboration to be able to account for the bilingual conversational strategies used by Gibraltarians.

The high level of proficiency in both English and Spanish of Gibraltarians gives them more bilingual communicative alternatives than are available in communities whose members have a less balanced linguistic competence. In addition to the distribution of languages between turns – a process often associated with negotiating a language for the interaction – there are other bilingual resources available such as the choice of a main language for carrying out a conversation or the use of a variety of different intra-turn and intra-sentential structures that can not be reduced to lexical insertion or pattern IV as proposed by Auer.[8]

Bilingual conversations in Gibraltar typically involve language choices at three distinct levels of conversational structuring.[9] At the *highest level* a main language can be selected for the entire conversation. At the *intermediate level* within the same conversation participants may momentarily select or negotiate the use of a different language for a limited number of turns.[10] At the *lowest level,* a speaker may choose to switch different types of structures within a turn or turn constructional unit.

The main language chosen at the *highest level* and the directionality of the code-switch in a conversational exchange is dependent on the linguistic competence of the speakers. It sets the frame for the entire exchange. In Gibraltar, where bilingual proficiency is high among members of the community, speakers have an equal option of using either English or Spanish as a main language for conversing. A speaker's choice can reflect her or his assumptions about the situation, and the alignment with a given group, as well as a given set of values or attitudes. This assessment of an exchange may or may not be ratified by the participants in the conversation. The main language of a conversation can only be determined by taking into account the wider linguistic context of the conversation or speech event. A researcher must look beyond short exchanges or extracts in an effort to determine whether or not the participants use a main or dominant language for the entire conversation. The criteria for identifying the main language can be, for example, social information about the community together with the language in which the most words and morphemes are uttered.[11] It is possible for a main language to be interrupted in a conversational exchange as a result of negotiation or accommodation among the participants.[12] Another possibility for a *Yanito* speaker is to avoid adopting a main language altogether. (This option, illustrated by example 1, involves frequent inter- and intra-sentential code-switching which can be interpreted as a 'strategy of neutrality' (Heller 1988; Alfonzetti 1992) or as an avoidance to align oneself with members of either one of the language groups).

By extending the analysis of conversation beyond limited extracts of bilingual speech, it is possible to retrieve the actual assumptions and presuppositions about the speech event that speakers make when choosing a main language for a conversation. This meaning is distinguished from the information about interpersonal relations reflected by inter-turn language negotiation, which can be recuperated from a sequential analysis at the *intermediate level of language choice*. Here, the negotiation of language can be traced through the sequential development of the exchange. But the contrast which inter-turn switching sets up is meaningful when related to the main language of the conversation and the collaborative creation of meaning in the interaction. Therefore, the negotiation of language between turns becomes meaningful only when contrasted with the main language of the conversation.[13] The main unit of analysis adopted on the intermediate level is speakers' turns. The proposal by Auer (1995) for a set of language alternation patterns in conversation takes into account this type of code-switching as well as code-switching occurring within a speaker's turn.

At the *lowest level* of the conversational hierarchy are the language choices within a speaker's turn. A speaker's turn is made up of utterances which in many instances correspond to fully fledged sentences. Within a sentence or an utterance, Muysken (Muysken 1995a) proposes three patterns of code-switching, which are defined by the size or number of elements switched, the type of switch, and whether different grammatical systems are activated, by directionality which is established from left to right or by what part of the clause is uttered first, and by syntactic constituency or whether the elements switched form a phrasal constituent with a lexical head. These patterns involve choices and they can communicate meanings on their own or jointly with other linguistic and bilingual contextual cues.

Van Hout and Muysken (1994) and Muysken (1995a, 1995b) propose a typology based on the structural relatedness of the items that can be inserted from a different language on this lowest level.[14] They distinguish three types of switching. The first type includes switches that are preceded and followed by elements from the other language. These switches can be phrasal constituents (NP or PP) or also a single word. They are referred to as *insertion*. The main feature of insertion is that an element or elements are inserted into a structure with a single base language.[15] The second type, which includes switches of entire sentences, clauses and peripheral elements, is referred to as *alternation*. Alternation involves changing to a different base language for the switched lexical items. The third type includes switches of several words which do not form one or more constituents. A process known as *congruent lexicalization* is involved. It is difficult to establish the main language in this last pattern as the grammatical relations of two languages are closely intertwined. A speaker can use one or more of these code-switching patterns as stylistic or meaning-creating devices for organizing and structuring the conversation.

In research carried out by van Hout and Muysken (1994: 303) a tentative sociolinguistic profile of the types of communities which use specific code-switching patterns is presented. Insertion predominates in neo- and ex-colonial settings as well as among recent immigrant groups. Alternation is common in stable communities with a tradition of language separation. Congruent lexicalization is a pattern that can be attributed to second-generation immigrant groups as well as to speakers of closely related language pairs who share diglossic or standard/dialect varieties.

5 Bilingual conversation strategies

Examples of different conversational strategies used in Gibraltar can be displayed and discussed in relation to the main language of the conversation, the sequential organization of English and Spanish among the participants in the interaction, and the type of intra-turn and intra-sentential code-switching structure. These three strategies available to bilingual speakers in Gibraltar are not always present in other multilingual settings where code-switching strategies are often more restricted. For example, the Chinese community in Tyneside described by Li Wei (1994) hardly uses intra-sentential code-switching in conversation. Members of the Puerto Rican community in New York only code-switch at grammatically equivalent sites in the sentence (Poplack 1980). The insertion of single lexical elements predominates in typologically different language pairs such as Tamil–English (Sankoff, Poplack and Vanniarajan 1991), Finnish–English (Poplack, Wheeler and Westwood 1989), and Arabic–French (Naït M'barek and Sankoff 1987). In Auer's (1988) study of Italian immigrant children in Constance a preference is shown for German as a main language, which can be attributed to lack of linguistic competence in Italian.

Selection of a main language is not a neutral choice in Gibraltar. It can show formality as well as the speaker's alignment with Spanish or British identities. In order to attain a full understanding of its meaning, reference must be made to the setting and the particular context, as well as the inter-personal dynamics of the verbal interaction. As Auer (1995) points out, there are some inadequacies in approaches like that of Fishman (1972), which assume that certain conversational activities constrain the use of a language in a given situation. This observation is borne out in the three examples that follow, where it is demonstrated that situation alone does not explain the language choice in bilingual conversations. Example 2 includes an exchange between the teacher (T) and one of the students (S) attending an electronics class at a local vocational training school.[16]

EXAMPLE 2

   T   But ... eventually where will that tube be used? For ...? Will it be used for a television?

   S   Uh ... No.

   T   No. Why not?

5 S   *Sí porque lo que estás diciendo es un* coiler, *un* coiler ...
      ('YES BECAUSE WHAT YOU ARE SAYING IS A')   ('A')

   T   *Sí, exacto.*   OK. That is ... That is the main difference you know.
      ('YES, EXACTLY.')
      State how the beam is deflected. Now the next one comes up. State that a beam is deflected that ... that is ... that is the ... that's the principle of the television tube. You remember as well the diffi-

10   cult display with the magnet? Just walking behind the oscilloscope making the uhm beam move.

While the choice of a main language can result from negotiation between participants, in this case it is dictated by the setting. In Gibraltar, official education is conducted entirely in English. The use of English defines the formality of the entire interaction and establishes the social distance between teacher and student. The choice of main language and the reasons why English is adopted are crucial for the further interpretation of code-switching at the sequential and the structural level. A sequential analysis of example 2 shows how this formal relation between teacher and student is cancelled in line 6. The teacher accepts the student's use of Spanish in line 5 by responding and providing feedback to the student's answer to a question previously formu-lated in English by the teacher. A sequential analysis also gives information about the roles and relations, and indicates which participant has the upper hand in establishing the main language of the interaction. In the example above, it is the teacher who recognizes and accepts the student's preference for Spanish, but he quickly switches back to English after this acknowledgment has been made. A friendly relationship between the participants can also be inferred from the teacher's acceptance, which in this context could have been a demand for the student to answer the question in English.

The Spanish forms that each one of the participants uses are embedded in the main language of the class (i.e. English), and at the same time within the sequential ordering of turns. The situated use of code-switching in conversation sheds light on the participant- and discourse-related functions of bilingual structures along the lines proposed by Auer (1984, 1988). Thus, the switch by the student in line 5 is a contextualization cue which contrasts with the rest of the discourse. It is through this contrast that inferences about the meaning and discourse function of this code-switch can be inferred.

The student within his turn (line 5, *coiler*) uses insertion, one of the code-switching forms distinguished by Muysken (1995b). The item *coiler* is a technical term taught by the teacher in English for which the student has no way of knowing the Spanish equivalent. The insertion is therefore participant-related.

In line 6, the teacher switches the two lexical elements *Sí, exacto* which are peripheral to the rest of the teacher's utterance in English and do not form a syntactic constituent. The discourse meaning of the switch can only be understood if related to the student's turn preceding it. While acknowledgment on the part of the teacher can be tied to the actual acceptance of the student's answer, the fact that the teacher responds in Spanish confirms this interpretation of acceptance of the previous turn as well as the language used by the student.

Example 3 is from an interview carried out with two nurses at a local hospital. The main language of the entire interview, which lasts for approximately ninety minutes, is Spanish, although the interviewer (M) makes it clear to nurse A and female nurse E from the start that either English or Spanish can be used. The analysis that follows takes into account the main language of the entire interaction, the sequences of turn-taking and the code-switching types, in order to understand the language choices involved in this interaction. Two different types of intra-sentential code-switching structures are present.

EXAMPLE 3

E   *Pasa como en el banco. Mi hija trabaja en el banco y vino un* ('THE SAME THING HAPPENS AT THE BANK. MY DAUGHTER WORKS IN A
jefe inglés y a lo primero he was very nice, very nice with every body. BANK AND A NEW ENGLISH BOSS CAME AND AT FIRST')
Ya le dieron un puesto, ya un poquito alto . . .
('THEY GAVE HIM A JOB PRETTY HIGH UP. . .')

A   *Ya está cambiado.*
('HE HAS CHANGED.')

5 E *... y ya está cambiado. Ahora cuando se fue otra vez a*
('... HE HAS CHANGED. NOW WHEN HE RETURNED TO
Inglaterra, ya llamaba, and he was the nicest person *¿sabes? a*
ENGLAND, 'HE WOULD CALL')   ('YOU KNOW?
LIKE
lo primero. Con que eso es lo que tienen ellos, cuando vienen aquí,
AT FIRST. SO THAT IS WHAT THEY HAVE. WHEN THEY COME
es que les ponemos tanto ...
HERE WE GIVE THEM TOO MUCH ...')

A *... tanta importancia. Nosotros tenemos la culpa.*
('... TOO MUCH IMPORTANCE. IT'S OUR FAULT.')

10 M *Sí, no ...*
('YES, NO...')

A We're to blame.

E *Pero es como en todos los lados, muy buenas personas.*
('BUT IT'S LIKE EVERYWHERE, VERY NICE PEOPLE.')

M *Sí.*
('YES.')

E *Son buenas personas.*
('THEY'RE NICE PEOPLE.')

15 A *Mira yo he trabajado con ellos en* maternity. *No es trabajar pero*
('LOOK I'VE WORKED WITH THEM IN')   ('IT WASN'T WORK
BUT
he vivido la sala y la he visto. Había dos pacientes yanitos.
I LIVED THE WARD AND I'VE SEEN IT. THERE WERE TWO YANITO
PATIENTS.')
They were going to have a baby. *Ellas prefieren que esté un* nurse
('THEY PREFERRED TO HAVE A')
con ella que es de Gibraltar o que hable su lenguaje porque
('WITH THEM FROM GIBRALTAR OR WHO CAN SPEAK THEIR
LANGUAGE BECAUSE
es más cariñosa dicen. Porque los   nurses *ingleses*
le dicen que
IT'S MORE AFFECTIONATE THEY SAY. BECAUSE THE') ('ENGLISH
20 *quiere levantar la almohada y dicen:*   'Oh, I haven't
got the time
THEY ASK THEM TO LIFT THEIR PILLOWS AND THEY SAY:')
now. Wait until later.' 'Your husband can do it for you.' They are
colder. The attitude is colder.

Example 3 belongs to a larger speech event involving a question-and-answer exchange which begins with the interviewer's question in Spanish and ends after line 22 where a different question is asked by the interviewer.[17] There are six turns preceding the extract reproduced here, five of which are entirely in Spanish and the sixth predominantly Spanish with a final embedded clause in English. The sequencing pattern of these turns preceding the extract can thus be summarized as follows: Sp.1 Sp.2 Sp.3 Sp.1 Sp.4 Sp.Eng.2.[18] (The numbers represent the participants in the order of their intervention in the interaction, i.e. M = 1, A = 2, E = 3). The main language in the example and in the entire speech event is Spanish; it is not dictated by situation or societal norms i.e. the requirement that public education be carried out in English as in example 2, but rather by the presence of the interviewer, although it was clear to the participants that either language could be used. Spanish lexical items also predominate in example 3, where in a total of 194 words only 26 per cent (51 words) are in English.

Switching between turns takes place after a general agreement has been reached among the participants to communicate primarily in Spanish.[19] This language choice reproduces one of the styles frequently used with family and friends. Spanish as a main language sets the tone, and opens the doors to more intimate topics of conversation and to more friendly interpersonal relations. The researcher, who introduced herself as a native American speaker of English, initiated the interview in Spanish with the goal of establishing an informal situation conducive to conversational code-switching. If the interview had been initiated and carried out in English, speakers A and E would have been more reluctant to switch into Spanish with an outsider, because this would have been tantamount to admitting that they were not as British as the British who just speak English. Using Spanish and switching to English lends itself to a more flexible interpretation. With switches into English, speakers are aligning themselves with a prestige variety. Their use of Spanish can be interpreted as a language of preference rather than linguistic incompetence.

The example illustrates a departure from the monolingual Spanish turns in the preceding context (except for the sixth turn). A sequential analysis of language choice is helpful for understanding the structuring of turns as well as the interpersonal alignments (reflected by inter-language choice) between the participants in the interaction.[20] The sequencing pattern of example 3 can be summarized as follows: Sp.Eng.3 Sp.2 Sp.Eng.3 Sp.2 Sp.1 Eng.2 Sp.4 Sp.1 Sp.3 Sp.Eng.2. This distribution of languages by turns shows how the interviewer (speaker 1(M)) initiates the communicative event in Spanish and continues to use the same language throughout the exchange. A different language choice is initiated by speaker 2 (A) in the last turn preceding example 3, but this same speaker uses monolingual Spanish in her next two turns and English and Spanish/English in the last two turns. Thus, there is no consistency in the language choices of speaker 2 or speaker 3 (E), who starts off with Spanish in the context preceding example 3, combines Spanish and English within a turn for her first two turns in example 3, and then returns to Spanish for her last two turns. More than negotiation between the participants, it is language choice which seems to contribute to the coherence of the conversation and the structuring of turns. Speakers are not trying to reach an agreement on a common language of interaction.

For instance, a sequential analysis allows one to establish coherence in the interaction by linking the code-switch in line 2 with the switch in line 6, both of which are uttered by the same speaker in different turns. In line 2, the new boss who came from Britain is presented as *very nice*, which is a piece of new information. The contrasting function of code-switching is precisely what gives this description of the boss saliency. Confirmation of this description is provided by a repeated reference to the boss as *very nice* through code-switching in line 6. However, a purely sequential analysis of this example would miss the fact that the participants have chosen to express themselves predominantly in Spanish rather than in English or in a more balanced use of Spanish and English, as illustrated in example 1.

On the intra-turn level, the main code-switching structures the speakers use are alternation and insertion. Both forms are illustrated in the turn of nurse A starting on line 15 by the lexical items *maternity* (line 15), *nurse* (line 17) and *nurses* (line 19). From a structural perspective, these lexical items are nested in a Spanish linguistic context which precedes and follows the inserted elements. The discourse role of these code-switched items can only be interpreted if they are placed in relation to the main language. The direction and the contrast of the code-switching structures (both the instances of insertion and alternation) in the turn of nurse A reproduces the cultural links and the way people talk about certain concepts like *maternity*, *nurse*, or *having a baby*. Speakers know the word in Spanish but they rather align themselves with British conceptions of these events. Alternation is illustrated by *they were going to have a baby*, which is a separate clause following the grammar of English (line 17), or the direct quotation of the patients in the maternity ward in English (lines 20, 21, 22).

Example 4 is taken from a spontaneous conversation between three teachers in the common room at a public high school. This conversation differs from the two previous ones in that there is no main language. Lexical items in English and Spanish are numerically balanced. Out of a total of 131 words in this text 66 are English and 65 are Spanish (50 per cent each). An additional criterion is the context and the relation between participants. This extract was obtained from a 60-minute recording which includes exchanges by different participants (teachers in all cases) who practise frequent intra-sentential switches similar to Example 1.

EXAMPLE 4

   T   *No tienen educación ¿eh? Las niñas . . .*
      ('THEY DON'T HAVE ANY MANNERS. HMM? THE GIRLS . . .')
   A   *¿Qué no tienen?*
      ('THEY DON'T HAVE WHAT?')

T   *Ha salido un lote de niñas* including fifth years, and sixth years.
    ('THERE'S A GROUP OF GIRLS')
    Both fifth years. Have stood . . . I'm holding the door. I'm holding
5   the door.
A   For them, *claro.*
            ('OF COURSE')
T   For them. And then two sixth years and a fifth year stood back and
    said come in. I was waiting for that.
E   *Pero tú te esperas que en este, en este, en este* day and age
    ('BUT DO YOU EXPECT THAT IN THIS IN THIS')
10 *que se cojan las niñas y te dejan a ti de pasar, porque te llamas /?/*
    ('THAT THE GIRLS ARE GOING TO STOP AND LET YOU PASS
    BECAUSE YOU ??')
A   Heh, heh.
E   *Vamos, porque sea el*   head of year *de aquí.*
    ('COME ON, BECAUSE YOU'RE')   (' HERE')
T   *No /?/. Además yo no soy* head of year.
    ('NO. BESIDES I'M NOT')
E   Sorry.
T   *Yo soy* year coordinator.
    ('I'M')
15 E   Sorry, sorry.
T   Now the . . . now the in word is coordinator.
E   *Yo es que creí que todo /?/.*
    ('I THOUGHT THAT EVERYTHING?')
T   *Escucha, ya hasta los* toilets *son* coordinated.
    ('LISTEN, NOW EVEN THE')   ('ARE')

The recording starts with line 1, and the communicative event in this extract ends when there is a topic shift and when different participants intervene.[21] The conversation which continues after the change in topic displays a similar distribution of languages.

This example illustrates an instance of spontaneous code-switching where there are no restrictions such as situation (see example 2) or interviewer (see example 3) strong enough to impose a main language on the exchange. There is no agreement by the participants on the language to be used in the context in which this conversation was carried out. The participants in the conversation know each other well; they are close friends, which explains the uninhibited use of code-switching. The setting may be defined as informal. As in example 2, the type of code-switching is influenced by the close ties maintained by the participants. It would be out of place for them to use English, which is normally relegated to formal contexts. Spanish/English turns predominate; only four out of fifteen turns are uttered entirely in English.

The language choices by turn sequences are summarized as follows: Sp.1 Sp.2 Sp.Eng.1 Sp.Eng.2 Eng.1 Sp.Eng.3 Laugh 2 Sp.Eng.3 Sp.Eng.1 Eng.3 Sp.Eng.1 Eng.3 Eng.1 Sp.3 Sp.Eng.1 (T = speaker 1, A = speaker 2, E = speaker 3). This sequencing is closest to Auer's pattern II. Language negotiation in this extract is dynamic and it changes as the conversation develops. T complains about the students' behaviour. A goes along with T, and demonstrates this by selecting the same language as T in lines 2 and 6. E, however, challenges T in line 9 and selects Sp.Eng.in response to his previous turn which is entirely in English. This lack of agreement is carried through for the entire extract and it is manifested by the choice of different languages. Language choice for a given speaker is not a stable choice as Auer's patterns indicate but rather involves several of the proposed patterns within the same conversation.

The three code-switching types, insertion, alternation and congruent lexicalization, proposed by Muysken (1995a, 1995b), are present. Insertion is illustrated by *head of year* (lines 12, 13), *year coordinator* (line 14), *toilets* and *coordinated* in line 15. These items consist of a single lexical item or a phrasal constituent which are embedded in an otherwise Spanish linguistic context. Congruent lexicalization is illustrated by the switches that are not a single constituent such as *day and age* in line 9. Alternation takes place between turns when one speaker uses English and the other Spanish. There is also an instance of alternation in line 3 and 4 where a whole clause in English is uttered within a turn which includes a clause from Spanish. The occurrence of these three types of code-switching structures in the sentence seems to be typical of communities with a proficient bilingual linguistic competence.

6 Conclusion

Research on conversational code-switching focuses on the form and meaning of this bilingual manifestation of communicative competence. In this chapter, attention was dedicated to both these aspects. Bilingual data from Gibraltar shed light on the rich and variable code-switching strategies that current bilingual conversation models do not fully explain. A typical conversation in Gibraltar makes use of at least three bilingual strategies: selection of a main language for the interaction, negotiation of language or languages between turns, and preference for various intra-sentential code-switching structures. The research presented observes that the three strategies discussed correspond to choices at three levels in the organization of conversation. A related concern is meaning and the way code-switching as a cue without literal meaning establishes the contrasts that permit meaning inferences to be made. The analysis of the *Calentita* text has shown how bilingual strategies work together with other textual resources such as topic, alignment of the speakers and humour to portray the ambivalence of Gibraltarian identity.

Notes

The research reported on in this chapter was carried out with support from the Spanish *Ministerio de Educación y Cultura* through grant PB93-0838.

1 The data used make up a small part of a larger corpus consisting of written texts and more than sixteen hours of oral material which has been transcribed.

2 The term 'code-switching' is used in the widest sense. It is intended to include inter-, intra-, and extra-sentential mixing of two or more languages. It is specified when reference is made to a particular type of code-switching.

3 Social tensions related to bilingual language choice are presently channelled towards reaffirming local identity and resisting Spanish political pretensions of sovereignty over Gibraltar.

4 The conversation is from an issue of *Panorama* published 17–23 September 1990.

5 Gibraltarians have the same passport as an ordinary citizen living in Britain. They also have the right to enter Britain at any time. In certain spheres, however, their second-class status is perpetuated by both the Gibraltarians themselves and the British. See the comments by the nurses in example 3, which illustrate this point.

6 An exception to the ambiguous referent *you* is elicited by Cynthia (line 2): *What are you saying, Cloti dear*.

7 The four patterns distinguished by Auer (1995) are: *Pattern Ia* A1 A2 A1 A2//B1 B2 B1 B2; *Pattern Ib* A1 A2 A1 A2 A1//B1 B2 B1 B2; *Pattern IIa* A1 B2 A1 B2 A1 B2 A1 B2; *Pattern IIb* A1 B2 A1 B2 A1//A2 A1 A2 A1; *Pattern IIIa* AB1 AB2 AB1 AB2; *Pattern IIIb* AB1// A2 A1 A2; *Pattern IV* A1 [B1] A1 (where A, B denote languages and 1, 2 speakers).

8 The term *insertion* in Auer 1995: 126 replaces his earlier term *transfer* (Auer 1984).

9 The term *choice* is adopted throughout the chapter to account for and refer to the continuous making of conscious and unconscious linguistic choices for linguistic and extra-linguistic reasons. These choices can be situated according to Verschueren *et al.* (1995) at all levels of linguistic structuring.

10 The main language of the conversation is momentarily interrupted when switching is negotiated at this intermediate level.

11 For obvious reasons of space the full 90-minute recordings can not be considered. The entire recording and the immediately preceding turns are taken as the context for establishing the main language of the exchange. For a partial transcription of these recordings see Moyer (1992a).

12 The main language in Gibraltar can often be established by the setting in the Fishman (1972) sense but also within the dynamics of the interaction.

13 If a given speaker does not choose a main language then this meaningful contrast is not present in the conversation.

14 Muysken's (1995a, 1995b) and van Hout and Muysken's (1994) proposals are characterized by a set of diagnostic features, but these criteria for distinguishing alternation, insertion and congruent lexicalization are not always clear cut.

15 'Base language' is to be distinguished from the 'main language' as used in this text. It is defined here as the language determining the grammar of the sentence.

16 In the transcriptions, the three dots '. . .' denote an unfinished utterance. The symbol between slashes '/?/' represents an unintelligible word.

17 The question asked by the interviewer in Spanish is *¿Y cómo son los ingleses, los que viven aquí?* ('And what are the English like, those who live here?').

18 The previous turns have not been included because of limitations of space.

19 Participants could have chosen to communicate primarily in English, in which case the majority of the lexical items would have been in English rather than Spanish. This choice is prior to the negotiation of language that may be taking place in example 3.

20 The negotiation of language among speakers in a conversation is more likely to reflect disagreement when participants in the conversation do not have the same degree of linguistic competence in the two languages.

21 The next turn where there is a change in topic is uttered by E, who says *Escúchame, los* toilets ... *las niñas están cagándose cantidad* ('Listen, the toilets ... the girls are shitting a lot').

Bibliography

Alfonzetti, G. (1992) 'Neutrality conditions in Italian–dialect code-switching', in *Papers for the Code-Switching Summer School*, Pavia, 9–12 September 1992, Strasbourg: European Science Foundation. 93–108.

Alvarez-Cáccamo, C. (1990) 'Rethinking conversational code-switching: Codes, speech varieties, and contextualization', in *Proceedings of the 16th Annual Meeting of the Berkeley Linguistics Society*, Ann Arbor, Mich.: Braun-Brumfield, 3–16.

Auer, P. (1984) *Bilingual Conversation*, Philadelphia: John Benjamins.

—— (1988) 'A conversation analytic approach to code-switching and transfer', in M. Heller (ed.) *Code-Switching: Anthropological and Sociolinguistic Perspectives*, Berlin: Mouton de Gruyter, 187–213.

—— (1995) 'The pragmatics of code-switching: A sequential approach', in L. Milroy and P. Muysken (eds) *One Speaker, Two Languages: Cross-Disciplinary Perspectives on Code-Switching*, Cambridge: Cambridge University Press, 115–135.

—— (1996) 'From context to contextualization', in *Links and Letters* 3: 11–28.

Backus, A. and van Hout, R. (1994) 'Distribution of code-switches in bilingual conversations', in *Summer School on Code-Switching and Language Contact*, Ljouwert, The Netherlands: Fryske Akademy, 16–28.

Cavilla, M. (1978) *Diccionario Yanito*, Gibraltar: Medsun.

Dabène, L. and Moore, D. (1995) 'Bilingual speech of migrant people', in L. Milroy and P. Muysken (eds) *One Speaker, Two Languages: Cross-Disciplinary Perspectives on Code-Switching*, Cambridge: Cambridge University Press, 15–44.

Fairclough, N. (1992) *Discourse and Social Change*, Cambridge, England: Polity Press.

Fishman, J. (1972) 'Domains and relationships between micro- and macro-sociolinguistics', in J. Gumperz and D. Hymes (eds) *Directions in Sociolinguistics: The Ethnography of Communication*, New York: Holt Rinehart and Winston, 435–453.

Gumperz, J. (1982) *Discourse Strategies*, Cambridge: Cambridge University Press.

Heller, M. (ed.) (1988) *Code-Switching: Anthropological and Sociolinguistic Perspectives*, Berlin: Mouton de Gruyter.

Kramer, J. (1986) *English and Spanish in Gibraltar*, Hamburg: Helmut Buske Verlag.

Labov, W. (1972) *Sociolinguistic Patterns*, Philadelphia: University of Pennsylvania Press.

Li Wei (1994) *Three Generations, Two Languages, One Family*, Clevedon, England: Multilingual Matters.

Martens, J. (1986) 'Gibraltar and the Gibraltarians: The social construction of ethnic and gender identities in Gibraltar', unpublished Ph.D. dissertation, School of Oriental and African Studies, University of London.

Milroy, L. (1987) *Observing and Analysing Natural Language*, Oxford: Basil Blackwell.

Moyer, M. (1992a) 'Analysis of code-switching in Gibraltar', unpublished Ph.D. dissertation, Universitat Autònoma de Barcelona.

—— (1992b) 'Spanish English code-switching in Gibraltar', in *Papers for the Code-Switching Summer School*, Pavia, 9–12 September 1992, Strasbourg: European Science Foundation, 51–68.

—— (forthcoming) 'Entre dos lenguas: Contacto de inglés y español en Gibraltar', *Foro Hispánico*.

Muysken, P. (1991) 'Needed a comparative approach', in *Papers for the Symposium on Code-Switching in Bilingual Studies: Theory, Significance and Perspectives*, Strasbourg: European Science Foundation, 253–272.

—— (1995a) 'Code-switching and grammatical theory' in L. Milroy and P. Muysken (eds) *One Speaker, Two Languages: Cross-Disciplinary Perspectives on Code-Switching*, Cambridge: Cambridge University Press, 177–198.

—— (1995b) 'Ottersum revisited: Style-shifting and code-switching', Paper presented to the Dutch Sociolinguistics Conference, mimeo.

Myers-Scotton, C. (1993) *Social Motivations for Code-switching*, Oxford: Clarendon Press.

Naït M'barek, M. and Sankoff, D. (1987) 'Le discours mixte arabe/français: des emprunts ou des alternances de langue?', *Revue Canadienne de Linguistique*.

Poplack, S. (1980) 'Sometimes I'll start a sentence in Spanish Y TERMINO EN ESPAÑOL: Towards a typology of code-switching', *Linguistics* 18: 581–618.

—— and Meechan, M. (1995) 'Patterns of language mixture: Nominal structure in Wolof–French and Fongbe–French bilingual discourse', in L. Milroy and P. Muysken (eds) *One Speaker, Two Languages: Cross-Disciplinary Perspectives on Code-Switching*, Cambridge: Cambridge University Press, 199–232.

—— Wheeler, S., and Westwood, A. (1989) 'Distinguishing language contact phenomena: Evidence from Spanish-English bilingualism', *World Englishes* 8: 389–406.

Sankoff, D., Poplack, S. and Vanniarajan, S. (1991) 'The empirical study of code-switching', in *Papers for the Symposium on Code-switching in Bilingual Studies: Theory, Significance and Perspectives*, Strasbourg: European Science Foundation, 181–206.

Schultz, E. A. (1990) *Dialogue at the Margins*, Madison: University of Wisconsin Press.

van Hout, R. and Muysken, P. (1994) 'Alternation, insertion, congruent lexicalizatons: Corpus based and structural approaches', in *Summer School on Code-switching and Language Contact*, Ljouwert: Fryske Akademy, 302–306.

Verschueren, J., Ola Östman, J. and Blommaert, J. (1995) *Handbook of Pragmatics*, Amsterdam: John Benjamins.

Woolard, K. (1988) 'Code-switching and comedy in Catalonia', in M. Heller (ed.) *Code-switching. Anthropological and Sociolinguistic Perspectives*, Berlin: Mouton de Gruyter, 53–76.

INTRODUCTION TO CHAPTER 10

Peter Auer

The Turkish work migration of the 1960s and 1970s into middle and northern Europe certainly was the largest migration the continent experienced after World War II. Although the psycholinguistic aspects of spontaneous second-language acquisition among the first-generation migrants, as well as those of their children's bilingualism, have received some attention in the research literature, the repercussions this migration has had both on the Turkish language spoken outside Turkey, and on the linguistic repertoires of the various milieus of the receiving societies with which the migrants came into contact, has remained largely unexplored. Also, little is known about the status and prestige of Turkish in Turkish and ethnically mixed communities, which in some parts of Europe – particularly in the large cities – have consolidated into social structures that have long surpassed the level of the temporary or provisional.

With respect to code-switching, we are certain that it occurs differently in the various generations of Turkish speakers (see Backus 1996), and most likely more among women than men. In addition, there is some evidence that children develop code-switching skills gradually; whereas small children switch mainly in response to gross situational shifts, particularly with shifts in participant constellations (thereby showing some kind of recipient orientation), or because of their individual preference for one language over the other, the rhetorical and more subtle discourse-related functions of code-switching so often described in the linguistic literature do not seem to appear in the European migrant communities before age 10 or 12 (see Auer 1988: 208 for some hints on the Italian case). Some further comments on developmental aspects of code-switching among migrant children may be found in Jørgensen (1992) as well as in the following chapter, which is based on a longitudinal study of Turkish children in Denmark. In fact, J. N. Jørgensen finds that between the first and fifth year of school, Turkish boys increase the frequency and the functions of code-switching between Turkish and Danish.

The notion of 'power' or 'dominance' in interaction that is central to Jørgensen's contribution is not very easy to pinpoint. Jørgensen links it to the relationship of responsive versus initiative moves in an interaction, the first indicating submission, the second power. However, in bilingual conversation, the notion becomes more ambiguous. Here, it may be said that in a minority language context, the minority language is the language of submission and the majority language that of power. This macro-sociological power then infiltrates the conversational exchange such that a speaker who uses the power language (the majority language) also exerts interactional power over his or her co-participant(s). The following chapter is above all a refutation of this simplistic notion of how macro-societal power translates into micro-interactional structures.

Jørgensen shows that the further one moves 'down' from the national level on which inequality between Danish and Turkish (and, of course, their speakers) doubtless exists, towards the level of conversational interaction between children, the more this imbalance loses its straightforward explanatory force. Thus, at the level of the community, Turkish is less clearly the language of submission (and Danish that of power) than at the national level; and at the level of conversational interaction, Jørgensen found only occasional attempts by the children to allude to the superior position of Danish on the national level for power wielding. In many other cases, code-switching assumed its potential for exerting power in its local context only. Here, sequential aspects of negotiating language choice become relevant, i.e. whether speakers accommodate another speaker's language or whether they distance themselves from it. In this way, language choice is a tool of power-wielding not so much because it borrows its status from large-scale societal inequality, but rather because it symbolically expresses convergence with and divergence from the other's code (cf. the discussion of extract 3 in the Introduction).

Bibliography

Auer, Peter (1988) 'A conversation analytic approach to code-switching and transfer', in M. Heller (ed.) *Codeswitching*, Berlin: Mouton de Gruyter, pp 187–213.

Backus, Ad. (1996) *Two in One: Bilingual Speech of Turkish Immigrants in The Netherlands*, Tilbury: University Press.

Jørgensen, J. N. (1992) 'Children's code-switching in group conversations', in European Science Foundation, Network on Code-Switching and Language Contact, *Code-Switching Summer School Pavia 9–12 September 1992*, Strasbourg, 165–182.

10

CHILDREN'S ACQUISITION OF CODE-SWITCHING FOR POWER-WIELDING

J. N. Jørgensen

1 Introduction

In interpersonal relations, power is derived from the access to resources which make it possible for one individual to change the world, influence events or attitudes, according to his or her own desires in spite of opposing desires of others. Some of these resources are related to language. Linguistically we exercise power in a wide range of ways, while we draw upon not only our structural command of one or more languages, or varieties of a language, but also our knowledge of the different values assigned to them. In face-to-face communication we can, directly or indirectly, refer to the more or less agreed-upon differences in power and status between two or more languages which are at our disposal for a particular piece of communication. This reference we can use to establish our own power base, which we can choose to employ in particular communication situations. By this measure, speakers of some languages, or varieties of language, automatically can expect to be able to wield more power than speakers of some other languages, or varieties, everything else being equal. Likewise, bilingual speakers can expect to have more success with trying to change the world using one of their languages than the other language, everything else being equal.

The power differences present in a society or a culture may thus be applied in a particular piece of communication as dominance. Dominance is the exercise of power in a particular situation involving particular interlocutors. In some specific situations the dominance of one party may be a given thing because of general societal patterns of power, for example in teacher–student dialogues or police interrogations. In other situations dominance is to a larger extent established by the linguistic strategies employed by the interlocutors.

Linell (1990) and Linell and Gustavsson (1987) describe dominance in terms of the balance between initiatives and responses in the production of each interlocutor. The powerful and dominating interlocutor's utterances will relatively often be strong initiatives (i.e. either directing, controlling or inhibiting moves, Linell 1990: 159), whereas the opposite is the case for the less powerful interlocutor. For instance, adult–child conversations are often characterized by an unbalanced distribution of initiatives and responses, as the adult asks questions (strong initiatives), and the child gives answers which yield the information asked for by the question, but the child does not offer new perspectives or suggest new topics with the answers. The child's contributions are so-called minimal responses.

Ng and Bradac (1993) distinguish between several strategies for organising conversational roles. 'Casting' is the assignment by direct or indirect means, of roles to one's interlocutors. 'Mirroring' on the other hand is the strategy by which one attempts to fill out the roles others assign to one. The third strategy, 'negotiation', is the mutual attempt to compromise on the assignment of roles. The power to assign roles to others can derive from general norms: for example a teacher has the power to assign the role of story-teller, or listener, to a child.

There is little doubt that bilinguals by some of their code-switching do relate to differences in power and status that go beyond the particular communication situation. Code-switching from the relatively powerless of two languages into the relatively powerful may have certain meanings, and switching in the opposite direction other meanings which are related to the difference in power and status between the languages (or, perhaps more precisely, between native speakers of the two languages). Differences in power and status between the speakers may, however, also relate to factors on a larger scale than the individual level without depending on their preferred language, for example if the speakers belong to a group or a class with certain linguistic rights, such as priests or – again – teachers.

Code-switching studies often distinguish between switches whose meaning relate to macro-factors, and switches which are at play within the given conversation. Gumperz (1982) distinguishes 'situational code-switching', which is related to differences in classes of activities bound to certain settings in 'a simple, almost one to one, relationship between language use and social context', from conversational code-switching, which is 'metaphorical' in relating information about how the speakers 'intend their words to be understood' (1982: 61). Situational code-switching is determined by factors outside the content of the particular interaction. Differences in power and status between (groups of speakers of) languages are some of these factors.

Myers-Scotton (1988) emphasizes the dynamics between 'a normative framework' and 'individual, interactive choices'. Code-switches are linguistic choices as 'negotiations of personal rights and obligations relative to those of other participants in a talk exchange' (1988: 178). She distinguishes between unmarked and marked language choice. The unmarked choice depends on a 'rights and obligations set associated with a particular conventionalized exchange', i.e. on situational factors similar to Gumperz's more than on immediate personal motivation, whereas the marked choice signals that 'the speaker is trying to negotiate a different rights and obligations balance'.

Both approaches distinguish between two kinds of code-switching, one in which the immediate, personally motivated communicative intent is the most salient determiner of the switch, and one in which an existing set of conventions is the more salient determiner. On the one hand we have one kind of code-switching which is basically determined by apparently relatively long-term factors outside of the particular communication undertaken by the speakers, i.e. *globally determined* switching. On the other hand we have a kind of code-switching which is basically determined by apparently relatively short-term factors within the particular piece of communication, i.e. *locally determined* switching. This distinction is of course not a geographical one, but rather the switches are locally or globally determined with respect to a particular communication situation vis-à-vis a totality of communication situations.

For linguistic minorities the difference in status between languages is indeed an important factor. What Gumperz (1982) labels the 'we-code' is, in the case of minorities, usually related to low prestige, its use restricted to private spheres, and at the same time a sign of belonging to the minority. Code-switching into the minority language may depend on a change in situational factors: a conversational item may remain 'unmarked' in spite of the code-switch, if the change establishes a minority-language situation, for example if a monolingual elderly speaker of the minority tongue enters a room in which bilingual adolescents are speaking the majority tongue. In this situation the adolescents will be expected to switch into the minority tongue; if they do not, their non-switching will be 'marked'.

On the other hand code-switching into the minority language may be a tool to express solidarity, or to rebel, or to exclude a particular conversant, and exactly because of the relatively low status of the language switched into, the conversational item may be 'marked'. The same code-switch may therefore simultaneously have locally and globally determined aspects.

Heller (1995: 171) finds that 'it is essential to link [language] practices to the ideologies which legitimate the unequal distribution of resources and the values accorded them, and to the real-world consequences they have for people's lives', and further that 'If we can use code-switching to understand processes like power and solidarity, it is because code-switching shows us how specific interactions are mediated through social institutions.'

However, we do not know well what role global power differences play in the development of the two languages of young bilinguals with respect to their contextualized pragmatic skills. In the case of children and adolescents it is not even clear what 'society', understood at a comparatively abstract level, for example on the level of 'nation' or 'community', means for the individual. 'Those who have power' are not likely to be same for children as they are for their parents. For instance, from the children's perspective the parents themselves may often be 'those who have power', even if the parents are low-income, low-prestige immigrants to a European city.

As it is, children in conversation with adults, specifically grade school students vis-à-vis teachers, are by the general norms of culture and society relatively powerless, and therefore conversations are dominated by adults. This does not mean, however, that children are unable to dominate conversations as such. In this chapter I will look at linguistic power-wielding among bilingual minority school-age children to see how strategies of domination in their mutual conversations can be understood in relation to global and local factors. I will argue that although some of their power-wielding code-switching can certainly be understood in relation to global factors, there is also power-wielding code-switching which can only be understood as being local.

I will draw on a longitudinal study of the bilingual development of Turkish-speaking children in Danish schools (Jørgensen *et al.* 1991). These children belong to the second generation of the labour migration wave which most of north-western Europe experienced around 1970. They live in Køge, about fifty kilometres south of Copenhagen.

As elsewhere, these immigrants to Denmark have suffered low prestige, high unemployment, low educational success, etc. (Jørgensen 1995b, forthcoming). In the public debate about their education there has been a strong pressure on the minorities to give up their mother tongues and replace it with Danish. This pressure has come from politicians, teachers, administrators, and even from the Ministry of Education. All this has not been wasted on the minorities, who are well aware of their status in Denmark. The parents of school-age children feel the pressure very much, a fact which has important consequences for their language attitudes and their expectations of their children. Turkish parents are generally pessimistic about the future possibilities of their children with respect to education, and although they wish their children could maintain Turkish, they do not think society will let them do so if they want to pursue education beyond the grade school (Holmen *et al.* 1995, Holmen and Jørgensen 1994). Even the attitudes of the mother-tongue teachers of Turkish are sometimes negative towards the children's Turkish, which is considered inadequate, rural and unfit for academic purposes. This attitude reflects a view of language held among many voices in a debate in Turkey itself, some of whom find that Turkish as such is not a 'modern' language (*Dil Öğretimi Dergisi* 1991).

On the national level, the difference in power and status attached to the Danish and the Turkish languages is very large. Although every individual in principle has the right to be addressed in a language he or she understands, there is no doubt that Danish is the stronger language in almost every conceivable way.

In Køge the families of Turkish origin, except for a few, live in one of two social housing quarters. Their presence there is evident in the supermarkets, the gardens and elsewhere. Turkish-speaking immigrants are by far the largest minority in the community. In one of the districts the young second-generation Turks seem to be at ease with their Danish peers, and satisfied with their living. In a study of their leisure-time acitivities, Can (1995) found that in this district the Turkish boys spend a lot of time together, but also quite a bit of time in Danish leisure-time facilities. The boys sometimes take on small jobs distributing newspapers or hauling boxes at the supermarket. The girls in general spend less time with Danish peers than the boys.

In the other district the situation is quite different. The young second-generation Turks are unhappy and not on good terms with their Danish neighbours. The boys, for instance, complain that they cannot get jobs, and that the Danes do not treat them well.

A third group, those who live in their own houses, spread across a relatively large area, spend most of their time with Danes. They say they often miss other young bilingual Turks, so that on some weekends they may seek the company of one of the groups mentioned above.

On the community level, it thus seems that the difference in power and status between Danish and Turkish is not quite as large as it is nationally, considering the place the two languages occupy for the young bilinguals in the first-mentioned district. Turkish parents in Køge are not as pessimistic or defensive about their mother tongue as they are elsewhere in Denmark (Jørgensen 1995a).

The children in our study are all from this district, and they attend a school in which the pressure to shift language has been mild compared to that in the rest of Denmark. The children are offered Turkish classes, and these classes are an integrated part of their school day. Their Turkish teachers also perform other duties at the school, and there are typically Turkish pictures on the walls as well as Danish ones. Thus the children's Turkishness is allowed some room and has a certain profile. About one-third of the children are of Turkish origin and speakers of Turkish; the rest are almost exclusively native Danish speakers.

In Danish schools there is a wide-ranging freedom for the teacher to choose methods and materials, and classes can be very different. Usually there is a mixture of teacher-centred teaching, group work and individual work. Generally the bilingual children in our study are expected by their teachers to speak Danish when they are not working on their own, but there are no strict rules (Gimbel 1994).

So on the school level the power difference between Turkish and Danish seems to be even smaller than on the community level, at least for the first five or six school years. To be clear, there is absolutely no doubt about the power difference between the languages. There is still a strong pressure to learn Danish (although not a strong pressure to give up Turkish), and there is no pressure to learn Turkish. For the speakers of Turkish, although there are opportunities for using their language without offending anybody, and there are both adults and other children to discuss problems with in Turkish, it is still easier to find opportunities to communicate in Danish.

We see that the relationship between the two languages can be defined on (at least) three different 'public' levels. The further away from the children's everyday world, the more we find hostility towards the minority tongue, the less it is considered useful or even appropriate. Closer to the children's everyday life, there is much less overt suppression or downgrading of Turkish, and it is questionable whether the children are at all aware that the pressure against their mother tongue is so strong on the national level.

It is of course a major point in sociolinguistics that global factors do in fact influence children's linguistic development. The trickling down of the global attitude through local administrators, teachers, or even parents, is bound to have an effect on the children's choice of language in different situations, and it is bound to have an effect on the motivation to develop either language. Nevertheless, the younger the children, the more effect we can expect the home to have. Apparently, Turkish homes maintain the mother tongue to a much higher extent than other immigrants in Scandinavia (Jørgensen and Holmen 1994). The Turkish parents express strong wishes that their children become bilingual. Generally they argue for the acquisition of Danish to take place in school, and their motivations are instrumental, whereas the motivations for maintaining Turkish are affective. The parents are not impressed by their children's skills in Turkish, as opposed to Danish, so by and large we can assume that the home environment of the children in our study is Turkish-dominant. It is likely that the parents will accept the children's acquisition of Danish unchallenged outside the home, but also expect them to speak Turkish at home. In this respect the 'private' level is different from the 'public' level. In Gumperz's terms Turkish is dealt with by the children's parents as their 'we-code', while Danish is the 'they-code'.

We can not be sure, however, that this is how the children see it themselves. As they grow up and reach adolescence they develop a bilingual identity which can be negotiated and refined in interaction with other bilinguals. Code-switching is one of the linguistic tools that the bilingual teenagers can use in negotiations not only of meaning, rights and obligations, but also of power and identity. Thus the 'we-code', if there is indeed one, may be code-switching itself: that is, the mixed language is at the disposal of the young bilinguals as a means to establish borders of identity, in opposition not only to all adults (who are more than likely to disapprove of language mixing, no matter how much they mix themselves), but also to the young monolinguals.

2 Children and linguistic power

In the Køge study we work with two main types of conversations involving the bilingual children. First, there are two tape-recorded face-to-face conversations between a child and an adult, one with a Turkish adult and one with a Danish adult. Second, there are two group conversations between children with no adults present, the groups consisting of three or four bilingual children and two Danish and two bilingual children, respectively. Holmen (1993) demonstrates how the children's linguistic behaviour is tuned to the differences in linguistic rights and obligations between interlocutors. For instance, in child–adult conversations, Ismail, an 8-year-old boy, reacts to the initiatives taken by his interlocutor, but is quite passive himself. He expects to be asked questions which he answers obligingly without offering particular points of view or elaborating very much on the subject discussed.

On the other hand, in group conversations with other children when there is no adult present, he is assertive and even aggressive, and he controls the conversation until the other boys call for an adult to intervene (see example 1). The boys have been asked to cut and paste some items from a warehouse catalogue onto a piece of cardboard, and they are in the middle of doing this. Heman is a Danish adult who is in the next room (but unable to hear the boys, because the door is closed)

EXAMPLE 1

MURAT	İsmail bu iyiymiş len bu iyiymiş İsmail len aha.
	('Ismail this one is good, man, this one is good, Ismail, man, here.')
ISMAIL	o koltuk pek büyük len.
	('that armchair is too big, man.')
MURAT	onuda şuraya yapıştır len.
	('then paste it over here, man.')
ISMAIL	git len büyük büyük çok büyük Murat.
	('buzz off, man, big, big, it is too big, Murat.')
5 ERDİNÇ	İsmail.
ISMAIL	ney hani.
	('what is it, where?')
MURAT	İsmail, Erdinç iyi kesmemii len getir bak getir bak biryerlerini eksik yapmış valla.
	('Ismail, Erdinç has not cut it properly, man, come here with it, come see, come here with it, come see, something is missing, by God.')
ISMAIL	yok len.
	('no, man.')
10 ERDİNÇ	*Heman.*

ISMAIL   sus len benimle.
(‘shut up, man, with me.’)
MURAT   *Heman.*
ISMAIL   sus len niye boşuna çağırıyorsunuz ama daha yeni böyle.
(‘shut up, man, why are you calling for him for nothing but
then, here is again another one like it.’)

Holmen has analysed Ismail’s Turkish conversations with respect to initiatives and responses using a simplified set of categories from Linell and Gustavsson (1987): very roughly spoken ‘initiatives’ introduce new themes or perspectives to the conversation, for instance Murat’s first utterance in the example above; ‘minimal responses’ are reactions to initiatives or elaborated responses which are sufficient in amount of content to be conversationally adequate but not more than that, for instance Leyla’s second utterance in example 2; and ‘elaborate responses’ include not only an element of response, but also an element of initiative, for instance Murat’s second utterance in the example above. In Table 10.1 we find Holmen’s figures together with the figures for Ismail’s conversations with Danes.

The distribution of initiatives and elaborated responses on the one side, and minimal responses on the other side, which we find in the conversations with adults, is almost the reverse of what we find in the group conversations. This tells us that Ismail can wield quite a bit of power over the other boys, and that this power is reduced to nothing when adults are involved. Ismail knows this, and the best move the others can use is to call on an adult. The threat is enough to force him into a compromise. Secondgraders do in other words play linguistic power games. We cannot know exactly how aware they are of this, or how well they know their own skills, but we can clearly see that power-wielding skills certainly are there as implicit knowledge.

The power differences documented here are institutional in the sense that they are found between adults and children. The adults in our study are either

Table 10.1 Ismail’s distribution of initiatives and responses as percentages of all utterances in each conversation, with Danish adult, Turkish adult, two Danish boys and two Turkish boys, respectively

	With Danish adult	*With Turkish adult*	*In mixed group*	*In bilingual group*
Initiative	0	13	44	50
Elaborated response	9	11	19	40
Minimal response	74	73	18	5
Others	17	4	19	5

Danish, or they could be said to represent Danishness because they are teachers or otherwise 'public figures', i.e. they are not recruited from the children's private circles. But there are also differences between the children, and these differences cannot be explained as institutional differences. Neither do they depend entirely on the power difference between the Danish and the Turkish language, because, as we can see in Table 10.1, Ismail is also able to exercise power when he is in company with Danish boys.

3 Linguistic power and code-switching

The bilingual children in our study use code-switches in a variety of ways (Andersen 1994), many of which have pragmatic functions, such as power-wielding. Some of these code-switches are openly related to global factors, for instance as in example 2. Four third-graders (9 years old) are working together on a task in which they are expected to find furniture in a catalogue, cut it out and glue it on a piece of cardboard. They have been asked to note the prices of the furniture they choose. Mesut is determined to buy cheap furniture; Leyla and Filiz both want to buy nice things.[1]

EXAMPLE 2

MESUT   *prøv at se der, koster noget der næsten to tusinde kroner?*
('try and look there, does anything there cost about two thousand kroner?')

FILIZ   *da nej.*
('no.')

LEYLA   *det koster i alt koster den otte tusinde, nej det skal vi ikke have.*
('it costs eight thousand all together, no we are not going to have that.')

MESUT   *det der, ikke det.*
('that one, not that one there.')

5 FILIZ   *skal vi ikke den her, eller den?*
('shouldn't we take this one, or that one?')

LEYLA   *nej.*
('no.')

MESUT   *hvor meget koster den?*
('how much does it cost?')

LEYLA   *nej den.*
('no, that one.')

MESUT   *vi kan godt købe den her, den er billig, prøv at se, skal vi*
10   *ikke købe den?*
('we can buy this one, it is cheap, try and look, shouldn't we buy this?')

245

FILIZ   *ih billigt, nej, den er lidt grim.*
      ('eh, cheap, no, it is a bit ugly.')

LEYLA   *nej.*
      ('no.')

MESUT   *det har jeg altså klippet den ud nu hvor er spejlet nu?*
      ('I have cut it out now, where is the mirror now?')

15 LEYLA   ni kavat, ih onu kullanmacakta olur kullanmıyacağız ya bu daha güzel.
      ('you pimp, eh we don't have to use it, we won't use it, this one is prettier.')

FILIZ   kapat şu bantı öyle konuş.
      ('turn off the tape recorder, and then talk like that.')

SELDA   ih Leyla.
      {giggles} ('eh Leyla.')

FILIZ   ben ne yaptım biliyon mu?
      {whispers} ('do you know what I have done?')

MESUT   *I må altså ikke snakke tyrkisk.*
      ('you must not speak Turkish.')

20 LEYLA   *og der er også nogle spejle der.*
      ('and there are also some mirrors there.')

MESUT   *jeg forstår ikke hvad I siger.*
      ('I don't understand what you are saying.')

FILIZ   *orv ja hvor du lyver.*
      ('oh how you are lying.')

LEYLA   *nå hvad så Mesut, vi tager den her spejl.*
      ('so what, Mesut we will take this mirror.')

MESUT   *nej, jeg har en fin spejl her.*
      ('no, I have a fine mirror here.')

25 FILIZ   *ih ih nej Mesut.*
      ('eh eh no, Mesut.')

LEYLA   *er den flot?*
      ('is it pretty?')

FILIZ   tabii.
      ('of course.')

LEYLA   *er han ikke.*
      ('isn't he.')

FILIZ   oy Türkçe anlamıyor.
      {whispers gigglingly} ('oh no, he doesn't understand Turkish.')

The children are trying to be well behaved and nice, so they discuss the possible solutions, and they suggest alternatives in a quiet manner – in the beginning. Everything is done in Danish. They become more agitated, and suddenly Mesut declares that he has made the decision, in his own favour, and he has already cut out the piece of furniture he wanted them to choose. Leyla immediately bursts out, in Turkish: 'you pimp'. This is a very strong derogatory word in Turkish, and the effect is immediate. Filiz suggests the tape-recorder be turned off (which they cannot do anyway), so they can talk more openly. Filiz introduces a topic to this effect, but she is halted by Mesut who maintains they must speak Danish. For a while Leyla follows him, but Filiz soon returns to Turkish, in order to tease Mesut.

In this conversation Danish is used for the 'public' content, i.e. the school-like task we have assigned to them. Turkish is used for private business and for emotional utterances. In this way, code-switching from Turkish into Danish becomes a way of changing the subject, or the attitude expressed, into the cool, student-like problem solving. Code-switching from Danish into Turkish is a way of changing the subject into something private, or to express emotions about the task, etc. This division of labour between the languages reflects the overall relationship between Danish and Turkish in the everyday lives of these children. It is only indirectly an indication of the power difference on the national level, or the community level. The children speak Danish when talking about school matters, because this is after all the domain of Danish – and they speak in Turkish about private and emotional matters, because these are Turkish domains. Danish here works as a 'they-code', and Turkish as a 'we-code'. The code-switches can be explained by factors beyond the particular conversation, which are glob-ally determined, although only indirectly by societal power differences.

However, not all code-switching among the children in our study can be explained by global factors. The following example is an extract from a group conversation between three Turkish girls in the fifth grade.

EXAMPLE 3

SEVINÇ	he Nevin konuşma istiyom eh *jeg havde ikke nogen det der* şeyim yoğdu fan – *ja fantasi ah energi* çok oynadım.
	('eh Nevin, I wanna say something too, I didn't have any of that there fan – yes fantasy ah energy, I danced a lot.')
NEVIN	*du har sgu da energi når du, du har sgu da energi når du øh Sevinç det hedder alts – det hedder altså ikke energi*, onun adı başka bir şeydi energi yaşayanlara.
	('you do bloody well have energy when you, you do bloody well have energy when you eh Sevinç, it is called –, it is not called energy, energy is about living things.')
SEVINÇ	prateinim yok işte.
	('I didn't have any protein.')
NEVIN	neyin yok?
	('you didn't have any what?')

	SEVINÇ	*protein.*
		('protein')
	NEVIN	o ne la, bilmediği bir şey söyledi.
		('what is this, she doesn't know what she's talking about.')
10	SEVINÇ	*åh du ved da heller ikke noget Nevin.*
		('you don't know anything either, Nevin.')
	NEVIN	*du ved det heller ikke.*
		('you don't know either.')
	SEVINÇ	*du ved det heller ikke.*
		('you don't know either.')
	NEVIN	*nej jeg ved det ikke jeg siger det . . . du siger bare xxx.*
		('no, I don't know, I (don't) say it . . . you just say xxx.')
	SEVINÇ	energi öğretmenim dedi ya, energi bitiyor diye.
		('the teacher has told us that the energy can run out.')
15	NEVIN	*jaja.*
		('yeah-yeah.')
	SEVINÇ	öğretmenim dedi ya çok hoplayınca enerjiniz bitiyor diye.
		('the teacher said, if you jump a lot your energy runs out.')
	NEVIN	*jeg har forstået det vi skal altså ikke snakke, er det derfor du er kommet ud her?*
		('I have understood, we are not going to talk, is that why you've come out here?')
	SEVINÇ	*ja.*
		('yes.')
20	NEVIN	*nå det kan man godt høre på dig.*
		('well that's easy to tell.')
	SEVINÇ	eyi bir daha senle konuşmayom Nevin.
		('hey I am not gonna talk with you any more, Nevin.')
	NEVIN	konuşma.
		('then don't talk.')

These girls both want to control the situation; most notably they attack each other personally. First Sevinç presents an argument for having been tired on an earlier occasion. Although her argument, seen from our perspective, is in fact right, Nevin claims the opposite so strongly that Sevinç becomes uncertain and changes her argument. Nevin senses she is on to something and pursues her success with an inquisitive *neyin yok?* ('you didn't have any what?'). This weakens Sevinç's position further, and as a result she simply escapes into the other language, in this case Danish. Nevin scores her point ('she doesn't know what she's talking about'), still in Turkish, but Sevinç continues in Danish. Having scored her point, Nevin graciously accepts this switch. Then follow a few turns of childish quarrelling in Danish, but Nevin strikes again ('I don't know, I don't say it', i.e. 'I am not one to talk about things I do not know about'). Now Sevinç once again switches, this time into Turkish. She introduces a strong argument: the teacher says so. This time Nevin does not accept the switch, but continues to speak Danish. Sevinç realizes that she is getting stronger, and therefore she repeats her argument, still in Turkish, while Nevin continues in Danish. Knowing that this is a victory, Sevinç can go back into Danish, but she falls into a trap ('that's easy to tell'). For the third time Sevinç switches. Having the upper hand again, Nevin finally follows her into Turkish.

The code-switches used by Nevin and Sevinç mark crucial points in the conversation. The girls do not code-switch according to subject or theme – a couple of times they say the same thing in both languages. Likewise, they do not code-switch according to the attitude they want to relate – they are aggressive and emotional in both languages. In fact, the girls use code-switching in order to turn the direction of the conversation, and by using code-switches to achieve this they mark these specific points in the conversation as crucial.

The girls' switching back and forth between the languages is so smooth and effortless that we can consider them to be quite advanced code-switchers. They use code-switching – *regardless of direction* – as a means of linguistic power-wielding. Except for the fact that code-switching is generally stigmatized, and at least by institutional adults often mistaken for a lack of structural resources in one or the other language, this fact cannot be seen as a result of societal differences in power and status between the languages. Rather, the bilingual adolescents employ code-switching as a marker of individual bilingual identity in opposition to adult norms or to the norms of other groups of adolescents, or both. In this sense, of course they do in a way relate to societal norms. But if so, these are not the norms regulating the relationship between the two languages, but those which demand monolingual utterances in either language and disallow mixing. The young bilinguals counter these norms, and in this process language mixing becomes their 'we-code'. The particular use of code-switching in conversations like the one we have just seen must therefore be explained by factors other than global power differences. This illustrates the need for a micro-perspective on code-switching.

4 Developing code-switching skills for power-wielding

The following example is taken from a group conversation between four bilingual boys in grade 1. They are 7 years old, and although they are raised in Denmark, they have not had any regular teaching of Danish until their school start.

EXAMPLE 4

	MURAT	bana masa lâzım bana masa bulun ya.
		('I need a table find a table for me.')
	EROL	bana ben de tuvalet eşyası arıyorum ha aa.
		('for me too, I am looking for toilet things ha ah.')
	UMIT	o zaman.
		('in that case.')
	MURAT	verdim ya sana.
		('I did give you one.')
5	EROL	onların hiç biri olmazki hangisini alacağım kocay?
		('none of them fits, which one should I take, the big one?')
	ADNAN	olur.
		('okay.')
	MURAT	bende mutfak işleri var.
		('I have got kitchen work.')
	EROL	*jeg ved det godt.*
		('I know that.')
	MURAT	aha ya tuvalet aha ya tuvalet aha ya tuvalet.
		('there is the toilet there is the toilet there is the toilet.')
10	EROL	Danimarkacada konuşun Danimarkaca tamam aa bakayım.
		('speak Danish Danish okay ah let me see.')
	UMIT	aa.
		('ah.')
	MURAT	baksana.
		('look.')
	MURAT	kocaman yerler var.
		('there are huge places.')
	UMIT	oh.
15	EROL	oh görmedim ben bunları.
		('oh I did not see them.')
	ADNAN	len *lim*inizi *låne* edeyim benimki olmuyor.
		('man let me borrow your glue mine will not.')
	EROL	bana ne vermeyiz, kendininkini al mecbursun.
		('I do not care we will not give it, take your own, you must.')
	ADNAN	pis herif.
		('dirty fellow.')
	EROL	bizimkini almak yok.
		('you cannot take ours.')
20	ADNAN	bir masa bulamadım ya.
		('I have not been able to find a table.')
	UMIT	ben de bir masa bulamadım.
		('I could not find a table either.')
	EROL	salak Abdi ne yapıyorsun sen.

('you fool what are you doing.')
MURAT   sence burda masa olur mu deli misin.
          ('did you think that there was a table here are you crazy.')

The four boys discuss, in Turkish, the problems involved in doing the task, each of them mainly concentrating on his own part. Murat and Erol are looking for pieces of furniture, Murat for the kitchen, and Erol for the toilet. They both request the help of the others, Murat pointing out that he has already given Erol what he is asking for. Erol attracts the attention of Adnan, but Murat intervenes ('I have got kitchen work'), much to the dissatisfaction of Erol who exclaims 'I know that' in Danish. He shows his irritation by using Danish, and Murat reacts by suddenly being able to help him. Erol makes his point clear by saying in Turkish 'speak Danish', and then he turns to the task again.

The next problem arises when Adnan cannot find the glue. He asks in Turkish, using Danish loanwords (in fact, the Danish noun *lim*, 'glue' with Turkish inflections, and the Danish verb *låne*, 'borrow' or 'lend' compounded with the Turkish verb *etmek*). Erol refuses to lend Adnan his glue, so Adnan complains in Turkish with a derogatory expression, 'dirty fellow'. Next both Ümit and Adnan are unable to find what they want, so Murat and Erol unite to scold them.

This example shows us four children who are involved in problem solving, and at the same time striving to gain control of the conversation. Murat and Erol are the stronger ones, Adnan and Ümit the weaker ones. Turkish dominates the conversation quantitatively, and by being used for all purposes. Danish and its status as the language of power is indeed taken into use once, but Turkish is used throughout for verbal fighting.

By and large, the children at this point in their school careers use little Danish, and the items they use either are loans or are directed to monolingual Danish speakers.

The same boys were recorded in grade 5. This time they were asked to build a Lego construction. The following example is from their conversation.

EXAMPLE 5

ADNAN   *han skal have t-shirt på.*
          ('he is going to wear a T-shirt.')
MURAT   ne nasıl düz mü olsun.
          ('what how is it going to be straight.')
EROL   *hvad for noget?*
          ('what?')
MURAT   şöyle iki ikişer tane burda.
          ('like this two double here.')

5 EROL   bu tarafa doğru gitsin xxx.
('it is going this way xxx.')

MURAT cık yok.
('no no.')

UMIT   hey ayak öyle olmasın şöyle şöyle.
('hey the leg is not going to be like that, like this like this.')

MURAT o küçük olur ya.
('but that will be too little.')

UMIT   boşver işte küçük.
('it doesn't matter how little.')

10 MURAT dur bir dur dur.
('wait a bit, wait wait.')

ADNAN *nej* küçük olmayacak ayaklar büyük olacak.
('no they are not going to be small, the legs are going to be big.')

MURAT aha bak bu ayakkabısı şimdi şurdan da şey gider.
('here look this one is the shoe, and from here goes that one.')

UMIT   he.
('yes.')

ADNAN *den skal mindst være så stor.*
('it has to be at least this big.')

15 EROL   *nå jo mand.*
('oh yes man.')

MURAT anladın mı?
('did you understand?')

EROL   *ja.*
('yes.')

MURAT bu bir ayağıxxx.
('this is one of its legs xxx.')

EROL   *nå der.*
('oh there.')

20 MURAT öteki ayağını da yapıyor.
('and he is making the other leg.')

EROL   *jeg troede den skulle være sådan her.*
('I thought it was going to be like this.')

ADNAN *nåja* hele şükür anladı.
('oh yes finally he understood.')

EROL   xxx ben siyahları buluyorum.
('xxx I'm going to find the black ones.')

MURAT tamam sen ne yapacaktın?
('okay what were you going to do?')

25 UMIT   ayak.
('legs.')

EROL	hepimiz ayak yapıyoruz şimdi, *krop* güzel olsun.
	('we are all making legs now, the body must be pretty.')
ADNAN	*krop* zor olur.
	('the body will be difficult.')
EROL	boşver *det er lige meget* güzel olsun yeter.
	('it doesn't matter it doesn't matter as long as it is pretty.')
ADNAN	güzel de olmaz, *det bliver svær krop xxx kroppen.*
	('it won't be pretty either, it will be a difficult body xxx the body.')
30 UMIT	kaç?
	('how many?')
MURAT	dur o kadar çok değil şey de olacak.
	('stop not that many, there have to be eh.')
ADNAN	*det skal ikke være tyndt, Murat, kroppen Murat, det skal ikke være tyndt det skal også være tykt.*
	('it is not going to be thin, Murat, the body Murat, it is not going to be thin it has to be thick too.')
MURAT	*ja ja.*
	('yes yes.')
35 ADNAN	*jeg skal bruge de der ellers kan jeg jo ikke se ellers jeg kan ikke blive ved.*
	('I need those or I can't see or else I can't continue.')
EROL	aman ya biraz daha uzasın ya.
	('it has to be a little longer.')
ADNAN	*ellers kan jeg ikke blive ved.*
	('or else I can't continue.')
MURAT	yo burada pantolon mu birşey olacak böyle dışarlara giden.
	('no there has to be a pair of trousers or something here that goes outside.')

Again most of the conversation revolves around the task the boys are solving, but simultaneously they are jockeying for control of the conversation. The first utterance of the example is in Danish, but Murat code-switches into Turkish. This code-switch seems to surprise Erol who asks 'what?' It turns out in Murat's answer to this that he was talking about something other than the T-shirt Adnan mentioned. Murat, Erol and Ümit continue in Turkish, discussing how the legs should be constructed. Adnan intervenes with one Danish word ('no'), and the rest in Turkish. The others do not react to his utterance, and so he repeats, in Danish, that he wants the legs to be big. Switching into Danish he is able to attract the attention of Erol who suddenly discovers that Adnan has a point ('oh yes'). Murat teasingly asks Erol in Turkish whether he has really understood, and Erol maintains in Danish that he has. Murat continues to explain anyhow, still in Turkish, and Erol realizes that he had not quite understood ('I thought it was going to be like this'). Adnan comments on this, teasing Erol. Throughout this part, Erol is under attack by the others, especially Murat who is speaking Turkish. Erol avoids defeat in this power struggle by speaking Danish, but simultaneously he does not avoid the discussion of the task – he still follows Murat and listens to him.

Once this exchange is over, Erol switches into Turkish and introduces a new theme ('I'm going to find the black ones'). Murat marks his acceptance ('okay') and continues in Turkish along this line ('what were you going to do?'). All four boys now discuss the body of the Lego man they want to build. They use the Danish word *krop* as a loan, but the rest is in Turkish until Erol underlines his point of view by saying it first in Turkish and then in Danish ('it doesn't matter'). Adnan counters this by making his next statement first in Turkish and then in Danish. Murat brings a new subject into the discussion, in Turkish ('how many?'). In the rest of this example, Erol and Murat unite against Adnan, who makes his claims in Danish while the others speak Turkish.

These boys code-switch much more in grade 5 than they did in grade 1, and the switches are used for a wider range of purposes. To be sure, Danish still lends words to the children's Turkish. Furthermore, in some cases, Danish is switched into just because it is the language of the school and therefore the language in which one can make one's claims stronger. Danish is used to repeat and underline an already uttered point of view, and in this way its greater power than Turkish becomes a power tool. In this respect, the boys' code-switching does relate to global factors.

But code-switching in itself, in one direction or the other, is also used simply as a way of countering the claims of the opposite part of a discussion. Adnan continues in Danish, while Erol and Murat continue in Turkish, as the three of them discuss the legs in the latter patter of the example. This is not because of the boys' different language preferences, because earlier on it was Erol who maintained Danish throughout an exchange, while Murat used Turkish. It is the use of the opposite language of the interlocutor which is in itself an instrument in the power struggle, and the direction of these inter-utterance code-switches is unimportant. In this respect the code-switching does not draw on global factors, but solely on the particular constellation of points of view in the particular part of the conversation. Similarly, code-switching is used to introduce new topics of discussion. For this purpose, code-switching in either direction is possible.

Between the ages of 7 and 12 children develop their linguistic skills tremendously. They acquire literacy, their linguistic awareness increases, and their pragmatic skills become steadily more refined. The same applies to code-switching (see Jørgensen 1993). Between grade 1 and grade 5 the four boys in our examples have developed code-switching into a tool which can be used with reference both to global power factors and to local factors. The more powerful boys use code-switching more often and in more advanced ways than the less powerful boys. Erol, for instance, is able to hold on to either language as it suits his needs best. This indicates that to really understand how bilingual children develop their linguistic power-wielding skills, we must understand the larger framework of power distribution between their respective languages, as well as the ways they adjust their use of one or the other language to the particular constellations of viewpoints in their conversations with other bilinguals.

5 Conclusion

The final example illustrates a case of strong dominance. Esen, a bilingual girl, is in complete control of the conversation, with especially Hans, a mono-lingual boy, and Erol, a bilingual boy, addressing her directly in most of their contributions. In fact Esen controls two simultaneous conversations. In his first utterance Erol tries to involve her in getting the scissors from Hans, but she refuses. In his next remark, Erol suggests the two of them join forces against the others, in order to be faster with the task. He uses Turkish to exclude the two monolinguals. In Gumperz's terms, he uses Turkish as the 'we-code'. Esen continues the conversation with him, including a reprimand, in Turkish. Hans also addresses Esen and asks for her advice in his first utter-ance. Esen participates in this conversation, too, but in Danish. Thus she keeps the two conversations apart, thereby avoiding conspiracy and rebellion: *divide et impera*. She controls Erol by accepting his choice of language, and then attacking him on his identity ('don't be like Hatice'), an attack that might cause a sympathetic reaction from the others, had they been able to under-stand it. She controls the others by directing them in Danish. So her language choices are certainly addressee related, but they are also determined by her short range communicative intent: to control the situation.

EXAMPLE 6

HANS	*Esen skal vi ikke have sådan en lille hund med på ferie.*	
	('Esen let's take such a nice little dog along on vacation.')	
ESEN	*åh.*	
	('oh.')	
JANE	*så klip så klip den ud.*	
	('then cut it cut it out.')	
HANS	*hej søde lille hund.*	
	('hello sweet little doggie.')	
5 EROL	*hvad skal jeg så si – skal også bruge saks.*	
	('what shall I then – I also need a pair of scissors.')	
ESEN	*jamen han må jo gerne få det.*	
	('yes but he can have it.')	

EROL   daha kesmiyor, gel bunları gecelim bunları gecelim.
('he doesn't cut any more; come on, let us do it faster than them, let's pass them.')

HANS   *skal jeg klippe det her ud skal jeg klippe det ud Esen.*
('must I cut this, must I cut this, Esen.')

ESEN   *hvis den altså må komme over og rense den.*
('only if it can cross over, and clean it.')

10 HANS   *jeg tror jeg godt du må. søde lille hund.*
('I think that's okay. sweet little doggie.')

JANE   *åh hvor den søde hund skal han skal han*
('oh where is the sweet doggie, is he, is he.')

EROL   *jeg fundet den xxx.*
('I found it xxx.')

ESEN   beklicen bizi Erol.
('wait for us, Erol.')

HANS   *puddelhunden må gerne komme med over.*
('the poodle may also come across.')

15 EROL   *saks.*
('scissors.')

JANE   *han skal også have skjorter med.*
('he must also take a shirt along.')

ESEN   bekle sende Hatice gibi olma.
('wait, don't be like Hatice.')

Esen's strategy illustrates my point: by exploiting the global factors of language choice as well as the particular constellations of interlocutors she is able to dominate and control two simultaneous conversations. Furthermore, she assigns roles to each of her interlocutors, and they try their best to mirror her expectations. The eventual outcome of the task given them by us as adult researchers is very likely to be what she wants it to be.

Summing up we can see that some children, one way or another – although it is to the best of my knowledge never taught – develop a comprehension of the global factors which give power and casting rights in conversations. They also develop skills in manipulating these factors to influence events according to their own desires. This they do in a complicated interplay of global and local factors. Code-switching as a power instrument in conversations between bilingual grade school children is the example in focus here: some of the bilingual children's code-switching does relate to global factors, but as a whole their code-switching cannot be understood if we do not involve the local conversational factors.

Note

1   In this and subsequent examples, italics are used for Danish. Other transcription conventions: curly brackets enclose transcriber's comments; 'xxx' denotes unintelligible speech; a single dot (.) denotes a break.

Bibliography

Andersen, Suzanne (1994) *Pragmatiske aspekter af kodeskift hos tosprogede børn*. Københavnerstudier i tosprogethed Køgeserien bind K2. Copenhagen: Danmarks Lærerhøjskole.

Can, Mediha (1995) 'Frihed og fritid', in J. N. Jørgensen and C. Horst (eds) *Et flerkulturelt Danmark. Festskrift til Jørgen Gimbel 22.9.1995*. Københavnerstudier i tosprogethed bind 25. Copenhagen: Danmarks Lærerhøjskole, 69–85.

Dil Öğretimi Dergisi (1991). Ankara: Ankara Üniversitesi Basımevi, 2: 35.

Gimbel, Jørgen (1994) *Undervisning af tyrkiske elever i Køge kommune*. Københavnerstudier i tosprogethed Køgeserien bind K3. Copenhagen: Danmarks Lærerhøjskole.

Gumperz, John J. (1982) *Discourse Strategies*. London: Cambridge University Press.

Heller, Monica (1995) 'Code-switching and the politics of language', in Lesley Milroy and Pieter Muysken (eds) *One Speaker, Two Languages*. Cambridge: Cambrige University Press, 158–174.

Holmen, Anne (1993) 'Conversations between bilingual schoolstarters', in Bernhard Kettemann and Wielfried Wieden (eds) *Current Issues in European Second Language Acquisition Research*. Tübingen: Gunter Narr Verlag, 337–347.

Holmen, Anne and J. N. Jørgensen (1994) 'Forældreholdninger til skole og sprogbrug', in S. Boyd, A. Holmen and J. N. Jørgensen (eds) *Sprogbrug og sprogvalg blandt indvandrere i Norden, bind 2: temaartikler*. Københavnerstudier i tosprogethed bind 23. Copenhagen: Danmarks Lærerhøjskole, 91–115.

Holmen, Anne, Sirkku Latomaa, Jørgen Gimbel, Suzanne Andersen and J. N. Jørgensen (1995) 'Parent attitudes to children's L1 maintenance: a cross-sectional study of immigrant groups in the Nordic countries', in Willem Fase, Koen Jaspaert and Sjaak Krooen (eds) *The State of Minority Languages. European Studies on Multilingualism 5*. Lisse, The Netherlands: Swets and Zeitlinger, 173–185.

Jørgensen, J. N. (1993) 'Children's code switching in group conversations', in *European Science Foundation Network on Code-Switching and Language Contact Code-Switching Summer School*, Pavia, 9–12 September 1992. Paris: European Science Foundation, 165–181.

Jørgensen, J. N. (1995a) 'Tyrkiske forældre til skolebørn', in K. E. Bugge and J. N. Jørgensen (eds) *Tre år efter. En punktvis efterundersøgelse af Folkeskolens Udviklingsråds projekter vedrørende indvandrerelever*. Københavnerstudier i tosprogethed bind 26. Copenhagen: Danmarks Lærerhøjskole, 61–82.

Jørgensen, J. N. (1995b) 'Language hierarchies, bilingualism, and minority education in the nordic countries', in J. N. Jørgensen and C. Horst (eds) *Et flerkulturelt Danmark. Festskrift til Jørgen Gimbel 22.9.1995*. Københavnerstudier i tosprogethed bind 25. Copenhagen: Danmarks Lærerhøjskole, 87–105.

Jørgensen, J. N. (1997) '"Ethnic" and "societal" factors of immigrant underachievement in the schools of the Nordic countries', in Wolfgang Wölck and A. De Houwer (eds) *Recent Studies in Contact Linguistics*. Bonn: Dümmler, 172–181.

Jørgensen, J. N. and Anne Holmen (1994) 'Sprogbrug hos tyrker i Danmark og Sverrig', in S. Boyd, A. Holmen and J. N. Jørgensen (eds) *Sprogbrug og sprogvalg blandt indvandrere i Norden. Bind 1: Gruppebeskrivelser.* Køben-havnerstudier i tosprogethed bind 22. Copenhagen: Danmarks Lærerhøjskole, 103–113.

Jørgensen, J. N., Anne Holmen, Jørgen Gimbel and Inger Nørgaard (1991) 'From Köy to Køge: a longitudinal study of the bilingual development of Turkish immigrant children in Danish schools', *Language and Education*, 4, no. 3: 215–217.

Linell, Per (1990) 'The power of dialogue dynamics', in Ivana Markov and Klaus Poppa (eds) *The Dynamics of Dialogue.* New York and London.: Harvester Wheatsheaf, 147–177.

Linell, Per and Lennart Gustavsson (1987) *Initiativ och respons. Om dialogens dynamik, dominans och koherens.* Studies in Communication 15. Linköping, Sweden: University of Linköping.

MacWhinney, Brian (1995) *The CHILDES Project: Tools for Analyzing Talk.* Second edition. Hillsdale, New Jersey: Lawrence Erlbaum Associates.

Myers-Scotton, Carol (1988) 'Codeswitching as indexical of social negotiations', in Monica Heller (ed.) *Codeswitching: Anthropological and Sociolinguistic Perspectives.* Berlin: Mouton de Gruyter, 151–186.

Ng, Sik Hung and James J. Bradac (1993) *Power in Language.* Newbury Park, Calif. and London: Sage.

INTRODUCTION TO CHAPTER 11

Peter Auer

It is common practice in bilingual studies to separate and label the languages of a bilingual group of speakers their 'we-code' and 'they-code'. At the same time, the former language is often said to be a 'minority language', the latter the 'majority language'. As the preceding chapters in this book have already shown, both dichotomies as well as their association are problematic. The notion of a 'minority language' clearly cannot be defined by reference to the number of its speakers in a given unit, usually a nation or state; for under such a definition, English would be a minority language in South Africa, India, Hong Kong and many other places, Gaelic a minority language in (the Republic of) Ireland, and Italian and French minority languages in Switzerland. It is equally difficult to define minority languages by reference to their official status (or lack of status) in the administration and legislation of a state, for some bilingual communities to which we customarily apply the term without hesitation do not suffer from such official sanctions (such as the German-speaking community in South Tyrol/Alto Adige, the Danish community in Germany (Schleswig), the German community in Denmark, etc.).

But an attitudinal definition of 'minority language' which identifies it as a bilingual community's 'we-code' will not suffice either, as the previous chapters of this book have already shown. If a mixed code has developed as in the communities studied in Chapters 3–6, it is this mixed code itself, and not one of the languages involved in its formation, that is the 'we-code' (if any). But even in the bilingual communities discussed in Part II of this book, where the 'codes' in question are kept apart and functionally opposed to each other by the bilingual participants, the language that is the minority language in quantitative terms is not necessarily the 'we-code'. For instance, in the Chinese communities in Britain (studied in ch. 7) and the Turkish communities in Denmark (studied in Chapter 10), Chinese (Cantonese) and Turkish respectively may be the 'we-code' of the first-generation speakers, but English and Danish (or the alternating use of these languages) are the 'we-code' of the children. In Gibraltar and Sicily, as demonstrated in Chapters 8 and 9, Spanish *and* English or Italian *and* Sicilian dialect are both (or neither) 'we-codes'. In all these cases, the seemingly simple and intuitively convincing equation 'we-code':'they-code'='minority':'majority language' is difficult to maintain.

The following chapter presents yet another case in which identity-related aspects clearly play a role in code-switching, but where they are once more difficult to press into the mould of the 'we-code'/'they-code' opposition. Rather, both London English and London Jamaican Creole (LJC) are 'we-codes' for the speakers of Caribbean descent investigated. It is important to know in this context that LJC is usually not the first language of its black speakers (neither, of course, of its white speakers who will play an important role in Chapter 12). Instead, as outlined in detail in Sebba (1994: 14ff.), LJC is usually a secondary variety acquired during the time of transition between childhood and adolescence. It is secondary also in the sense of a restricted competence; many of the speakers investigated by Sebba (1994) '"construct" the language they variously call Creole, Patois, black talk, bad talk or Jamaican on the basis of a collection of stereotypical features which are associated with JC as spoken in Jamaica' (1994: 18).

The prestige LJC enjoys in the youth community (among both black and white speakers) is to a considerable degree that of a youth code and supported by other features of youth culture such as reggae music, the rasta movement, etc. For this reason, it is clear that although LJC is a 'we-code' in the sense of a 'youth code' (and to a minor degree a 'race code'), the 'unmarked' language of everyday interaction among its speakers is London English. The code-switching practices described by Mark Sebba and Tony Wootton therefore differ from those found in other bilingual communities in that London English is almost always the 'ground' of a conversation against which LJC stands out as a 'figure'; or, to use different terminology, the language-of-interaction is almost always London English.

With respect to the basic question running through Part II of this book, the authors take an additive view. In the first part of their contribution, they present a sequential analysis of code-switching, roughly applying the apparatus of conversation analysis. Code-switching is shown to serve numerous discourse-related functions; it 'contextualises' various speech activities, particularly within a turn. From this analysis, a picture emerges in which LJC usually provides the 'principal message content' in an otherwise London English turn, while London English embedded within an otherwise LJC turn provides background information. It is not clear how this finding could be accounted for (let alone predicted) by calling LJC the 'we-code' and London English the 'they-code' of these speakers. (Note that according to Sebba and Wootton, code-switching for quotations is independent of the language of the original (reported) language, which parallels Alfonzetti's findings reported in Chapter 8.)

Yet this sequential approach does not explain all the switches in the data. In the second part of their contribution, Sebba and Wootton therefore link code-switching more directly to questions of identity; these identities (or 'personae', as they might be called more appropriately) are not 'brought along' into the conversation, however. Rather, Sebba and Wootton demonstrate how they are 'invoked' or 'brought about' (Hinnenkamp 1987) in interaction, that is, how a speaker comes to 'inhabit' a particular 'persona' which is selected from an inventory of possibilities within the wider cultural context but not predictable from it. Thus, rather than externalising the meaning of conversational code-switching from interaction into some kind of pre-existing speaker's identity, they 'conversationalise' identity, bringing it into the scope of interaction.

Bibliography

Hinnenkamp, Volker (1987) 'Foreigner talk, code-switching and the concept of trouble', in Knapp, K., Enninger, W. and Knapp-Potthoff, A. (eds), *Analyzing Intercultural Communication*, Berlin: Mouton-de Gruyter, p. 144f.

Sebba, Mark (1994) *London Jamaican*, London: Longman.

11

WE, THEY AND IDENTITY

Sequential versus identity-related explanation in code-switching

Mark Sebba and Tony Wootton

1 The 'we-code' and 'they-code'

The concepts of 'we-code' and 'they-code', first introduced into the literature on code-switching by Gumperz, have been used productively by many researchers. The concept of 'identity' is often invoked at the same time. Gumperz, for example, in his discussion of 'we-' and 'they-' codes, also makes a link with a notion of *group identity*:

> The tendency is for the ethnically specific, minority language to be regarded as the 'we-code' and become associated with in-group and informal activities, and for the majority language to serve as the 'they-code' associated with the more formal, stiffer and less personal out-group relations.
>
> (1982: 66)

For most users of these terms, 'we-code' and 'they-code' refer respectively to the ethnic language of a bilingual community,[1] and the language of the wider society within which that community forms a minority. The opposition of 'we-' versus 'they-' codes thus presupposes a particular relationship between monolingual and bilingual communities, as well as particular types of social relationship within the minority group.

While many researchers have subsequently made use of the 'we-code' and 'they-code' in accounts of code-switching behaviour, others have pointed to the problematic nature of this formulation, e.g. Auer (1991: 333ff.):

> The often invoked characterisation of languages as a 'they-code' and a 'we-code' tends to be used as an a priori schema imposed on code alternation data from outside. It is also too gross and too far away from participants' situated, local practices in order to be

able to capture the finer shades of social meaning attributed to the languages in a bilingual repertoire.

Gumperz himself was clear that a straightforward association between the content of an utterance and the language in which it was uttered was not what he intended, for he immediately follows the preceding quote by saying: 'But it must be emphasized that, in situations such as those discussed here, this association between communicative style and group identity is a symbolic one: it does not directly predict actual usage' (Gumperz 1982: 66).

Nevertheless, Stroud (this volume) notes that code-switching research from this perspective often 'rests on a naive social theory . . . which presents concepts such as agency, action, identity and social role as non-problematic'.

In this chapter we want to explore the notions of 'we-code', 'they-code' and 'identity', and the relations between these.

2 Who is 'we'? Problems of identifying 'we' and 'they'

Gumperz warns explicitly that the association of 'we' and 'they' with particular codes 'does not directly predict actual usage' in a given instance. Furthermore, it is by no means certain that the 'we'/'they' distinction is meaningful in all bilingual minority communities. In addition, some minority groups within a larger society may be relatively easy to identify, whether by external criteria or through their own ascription, while others are not. The complexity of the relationships between minority groups and mainstream society on the one hand, and the two (or more) languages involved on the other, mean that the 'we-' and 'they-' codes cannot be taken as given in any particular situation. In an apparently classic case of 'we' versus 'they', Cantonese in Hong Kong (where it is, of course, actually a majority language) can be seen to function as a 'we-code' for both teachers and students, in classrooms where English is learnt as a second language. The 'they-code', English, is required for the formal business of the class, but Cantonese is appropriate for informal functions. In the following example, English is the appropriate language for the greeting, but when the teacher corrects herself, she uses Cantonese (which she shares as a native language with most of her students) to 'cancel' her incorrect utterance (data from Cheung 1995):

TEACHER   good afterno . *m'hai* . {laughs} good morning class
          (Cantonese *m'hai* = 'no')
STUDENTS good morning Miss Chan

In Hong Kong, the 'foreignness' ('they-ness' if you like) of English for the ethnic Chinese population is obvious, as is the 'we-ness' of Cantonese for the majority of Hong Kong Chinese. In this case the 'we-code' is actually the *majority* language, although in the educational domain from which this example is drawn, it is English that has the higher status.

Although the boundaries of the communities and languages are relatively clear cut in the case of Hong Kong, they are not always so. For British-born Caribbeans living in London, the 'we-' and 'they-' codes are much harder to establish empirically. The language varieties used by these speakers include London English (the 'majority' language) and London Jamaican, a local variety of Jamaican Creole (see Sebba 1993). Caribbean-born members of the same family (whether of the same generation or older) may be native speakers of a Caribbean Creole (not necessarily Jamaican): informal talk in family settings thus often involves the use of London Jamaican, some Caribbean variety of Creole, London English and possibly British Standard English.

Although a simplistic equation of 'we' with ethnic minority language would suggest that London Jamaican should function as the 'we-' code for British-born Caribbean speakers, an ethnographic study of the community combined with an analysis of actual conversational practices shows that things are in fact more complicated. While London Jamaican could be seen as the ethnically exclusive code (although it is used by some white people as well,)[2] it is the ability to use *both* London English and London Jamaican which most saliently characterises the 'Black British' speaker.[3]

For the young Caribbean Londoners of this study, both London English and London Jamaican have some of the characteristics of 'we-'codes. London Jamaican is a 'we-code' because it excludes outsiders (particularly white people) and its province is the family and peer group, especially during informal conversation. But London English is also a 'we-code': it is used among family and peers in the most intimate discussions and is the preferred code for use most of the time for most of the speakers in the study. English is also a Caribbean language; although Standard English is not a 'we-code' for most first-generation Caribbeans in Britain, it is certainly not a foreign language for them or for their children.

While London Jamaican can be used to exclude outsiders – and London English cannot – we want to argue that the kinds of linguistic behaviour supporting the notion of 'we-' and 'they-' codes are of a much more complex kind than is implied by invoking contrasts in code use according to gross relevance of context. In what follows, we will try to account for code-switching observed in the data on the basis of conversation-internal criteria, and to give warrants as far as possible for code-switches on the basis of the behaviour of participants in the conversation.

3 The speakers and the data

As mentioned in section 2, the language behaviour of British-born Caribbeans is characterised by the use of two distinct varieties: the local variety of British English, popularly called 'Cockney' and here referred to as London English; and a local variety of Jamaican Creole, here referred to as 'London Jamaican'. Although Jamaican Creole draws most of its lexicon from English, and is often treated as a dialect of English, there are significant points of difference between Jamaican Creole and British English in lexicon, phonology and grammar (see Sebba 1993 for a detailed account of these differences).[4] London Jamaican is only slightly different from Jamaican Creole, but importantly, it is seldom used on its own by the speakers in the study. There is nearly always shifting between London English and London Jamaican in everyday speech among peers (other situations may call for the use of London English exclusively). Indeed, the use of London Jamaican is often very limited in terms of number of utterances; in most informal conversations London English predominates in terms of quantity. Furthermore, while all the individuals in this study seemed to have passive knowledge of the Creole, they differed in their ability to produce it consistently. London Jamaican is not necessarily a 'mother tongue' as it is usually learnt *after* London English, even by speakers with Jamaican connections, and often as a 'second dialect' rather than a native language (see Sebba 1993).

For the purposes of this study, stretches of talk have been identified as 'London Jamaican' or 'London English' on the basis of a mixture of phonological, grammatical and lexical markers. Items which have stereotypical value as markers of Creole are often used by speakers in a tokenistic way, for example to mark a word which conforms to London English grammar as 'Creole' by virtue of its pronunciation. As a result, 'London Jamaican' stretches of talk may be difficult to identify from the transcription used here, which uses an adaptation of Standard English orthograpy. Throughout the transcription, therefore, italics are used to identify stretches which are marked as London Jamaican by virtue of grammar, pronunciation, lexis or a combination of these.

The data on which this chapter is based were obtained in one of two ways. Some speakers, black students in London comprehensive schools, were left in a room with a tape recorder and asked to 'talk Jamaican' while the researcher (Sebba) went out of the room. Other recordings were made by somewhat older informants in their own homes, using a tape recorder on loan from the researcher. In spite of some technical problems, both methods were successful in providing usable and interesting data. The first method provided most of the conversations initiated in London Jamaican, with code-switches into London English. The second method produced hours of London English, with occasional switches into London Jamaican for short stretches. Although in the second method the data collection is outside the control of the researcher, we believe the data collected by this method to be more reliable, as it partially eliminates the observer paradox.

4 Code-switching of black Londoners: a sequential analysis

4.1 Introduction

In this section we will show that London English (LE) and London Jamaican (LJ) are used differentially in a systematic way by speakers within the same turn in conversation. We will show that broadly speaking, participants in a conversation orientate to LJ stretches embedded in a basically LE turn as having differential status from the adjacent LE material, providing the principal message content. On the other hand, LE stretches embedded within a basically LJ turn correspond to material of secondary importance, such as speakers' comments on thematically more important material, or diversions from the main theme of the turn, for instance those involving speaker-initiated insertion sequences.

We shall only discuss a selection of all the possible kinds of code-switch here. They are classified on the basis of the direction of the switch (LE to LJ or LJ to LE) and on whether they are mid-turn or turn-final switches. 'Quotations' are dealt with as a separate category. There are other kinds of mid-turn switches, some of which seem to involve self-repair, as in example 1, where a speaker begins in one code, interrupts herself, and then switches code, expressing the semantic content ('he's moved') of the just-spoken stretch in the new code. As we are not sure what motivates switches of this sort (several examples occur in the data) we will not deal with them further.[5]

EXAMPLE 1

C   *me naa lie* (0.4) e's moved – *'im move back in wid 'im mudda*
     (2.0) *them splitup*
J   so did 'e tell you why *dem splitup*?

4.2 Switches from LJ to LE

In this section we will examine in detail some examples of switches to LE within a turn which is basically LJ, i.e. instances of LE 'framed' by an LJ utterance.

Example 2 is a case of such a switch. B is commenting on the actions of her brothers in a domino game, where they slam down a domino on the table and call out a word.[6] B signals the jocular nature of her comments at the beginning of her turn by *'ear 'im now no!* ('Just listen to him!') followed by laughter. She then comments on three players in turn – '(you) slap down, he says "pin", he slaps down, he says "needle", he slaps down he-.' All of this is done in LJ. At this point B cannot remember the word called by the third player and so initiates an insertion sequence, in LE: 'what did you say again ... what did you say?' She gets her reply from one of the players: *crablouse.* (The

266

pronunciation of this item is Jamaican, but probably no significance is to be attached to this fact, as the speaker has a Jamaican accent even when speaking English.) B then ends the insertion sequence and returns to complete her original sequence in LJ by repeating *crablouse* and so ending her turn.

EXAMPLE 2: DOMINO GAME

B   *'ear 'im now no!* **he he**
     (you) *slap down 'im say* ['pin' (0.8) *'im slap down 'im say 'nee* [*dle'*
M   [(pin) **ha ha ha**   [**ha ha ha**
B   *'im slap down i* what did you say agai [n? (0.6)
M   [**eh ha ha ha**
B   (0.8) what did you say?
?L   *crablouse*

While not all instances are as clear as this, example 2 seems to be quite typical of one class of switches to LE within a basically LJ turn. The LE sequence is a sort of sub-routine, a sequence embedded in the turn but not part of the mainstream; it does not necessarily start at a syntactic clause completion point (witness line 2, where it begins after a subject pronoun) and its purpose is to elicit or check on information, to make it possible for the speaker to complete the current turn.

These characteristics are again exemplified in example 3, where C wants to tell J that 'Johnny' was the one who told C about a particular party which she was not invited to. C's turn is constructed to require a name following *she invite* ('she invited'), but C is not sure whether J knows Johnny or not, so she performs a check on this, resulting in a short insertion sequence in LE: *you know Johnny? – yeah.* C then immediately returns to LJ, to say what she had to say about Johnny: *him tell me* (where the use of *him* as subject pronoun, and the lack of a past tense marker on *tell*, clearly marks this as LJ). C then switches to LE with a change of topic – this is a different sort of switch from the ones under consideration here.

EXAMPLE 3: CATFORD GIRL'S POSSEE (1)

  J   (   ) *she never did invite me* (0.2) are YOU goin' ?
  C   *no she never invite me neither*
  J   's not fair
  C   *no, she invite* (0.4) um (.) you know Johnny ?
5 J   yeah
  C   *him tell me* (0.8) and my mum went to her house and she said (0.4)
      she's o- she just told 'er she's 'avin' a christenin' (0.2) *me no know
      if me a go*

So far we have seen two examples of switching involving inserted sequences of conversation, and two or more turns. They have in common the fact that the inserted sequence interrupts the flow of the turn in which it is initiated and correspondingly switches code, from the LJ of the matrix turn, to LE. Another type of switching from LJ to LE seems to have a very similar psychological motivation, but does not involve an inserted sequence of turns: the speaker simply switches to LE and then back in the course of present turn. This is illustrated in example 4, where C is trying to remember the date of a party. The LJ stretch *man* (1.0) *Leonie have party* ('Leonie had a party') is followed by a pause of one second – presumably as C tries to remember the day. C interrupts this silence by asking *when*? (this could equally be LE or LJ) followed by a long pause. Now note that if J were to interpret this as a genuine request for information, she could respond, for example, *on Tuesday* or *I don't know* in LE, creating an insertion sequence like those of examples 2 or 3. Instead, C answers her own question – but true to the form established by (2) and (3) she answers in LE: *don' remember when it was* and then immediately switches back to LJ to 'link up' with the first part of her turn. The LJ sequence thus reads: *Leonie have party but she did tell all o' dem* ...

EXAMPLE 4: CATFORD GIRL'S POSSEE (2)

J	*Leonie have party?!*
C	*man* (1.0) *Leonie have party* (0.4) *when?* (1.2) *don' remember when it was but she did tell all o' dem no fi- t say not'in'* (0.6) *cau' she no wan' too much Cyatford gyal de dere* (1.0) *an' Jackie 'ave one*
5	*too*
	(0.4) *never say not'in'*

Example 4 thus shares many of the characteristics of (2) and (3) in that it involves doing a piece of talk in LE that is clearly offset from the main theme of the turn, and typically interrupts it syntactically as well. It is different mainly in that the other speaker does not participate.

A very similar example – from a speaker far removed in time and space from those of (4) – is (5). Here again, B is in the midst of a LJ stretch when she interrupts herself after the subject pronoun *me*, pauses for nearly a second and then asks *what 'appened* (clearly distinct from LJ *wh'ap'm*, which is a frequently used expression). After the hesitation form *um* and a short pause she answers her own question, starting with *yeah* (which could belong to either code) and continuing in LJ to describe what she did next. Example 5 is different from (4) in that in (5), B's response *yeah* to her own question merely serves to introduce the continuation of her story in LJ, while in (4) the LE sequence actually provides additional information relevant to the narrative, namely that C cannot remember the date of the party.

EXAMPLE 5: THE PHONE CALL

  B   Na:h (0.6) (up) (0.4) Tuesday e told whasisname
      (t) *come – come phone me right* (0.2) *So me me –*
→   (0.8) what 'appened u:m (0.2) yeah,
      so a phone Winston and tell Win- and tell Winston
      (and) 'e goes to me 'e wants to go out (0.6)

Yet another kind of switching is illustrated by example 6, which involves the same speaker, B, as in (5). The LJ part of B's turn *da? is a halfcaste ... an im stone black* is interrupted by her own laughter and the interpolation *you know what I mean* in LE.

EXAMPLE 6

  B   cause some of them you see, (.) outside the street, (.)
       right, [and you say *da? is a halfcaste*
?L   [an' you don' know you can't (   )
→B   [*an im stone black* he he you know what I mean?
5 F   [e::: yeah yeah
→B   *stone black*

The tag *you know what I mean* here functions as a kind of commentary on the surrounding LJ material, and is clearly offset from it, being in LE.[7] This code difference seems to correspond to a difference between information-carrying parts of the turn (in LJ) and 'comment' (in LE).

4.3 Switches from LE to LJ

While instances of long LJ stretches are relatively rare in our corpus, long stretches of LE are common. However, it is also common to find short stretches of LJ within a turn, 'framed' by LE on either side, or at the end of a turn, immediately following an LE stretch. We will look at some examples of each type.

LJ stretches 'framed' by LE on either side usually correspond to a part of the message regarded by the speaker as most salient, either in that the LJ stretch contains the most important information, or else because it is central to the theme of the turn. Example 7 illustrates an LJ stretch which carries the most important information. To understand this it is necessary to set the extract in its context. B is talking with her friends about an incident at a party. Someone had told a boy that B wanted him. Emboldened by this, he had gone straight up to her and said that he had heard she had called him and wanted him. B tells her friends that she was shocked and responded by saying coldly *did I really?* Her friends support her action and the discussion continues for a minute or so to the point where the extract begins. In her turn B goes on to recount what happened after she rebuffed the boy in question. She agreed to dance with him because, she says, – switching to LJ at this point – *me know say, me no 'ave nothin' inna my mind(but to dance)* – 'I knew I had nothing in my mind but to dance' – i.e. from her point of view it was all innocent and involved nothing more serious than dancing. This is really the key statement of B's turn as it gives her explanation of why she agreed to dance with a man whose initial approach had shocked her and led her to respond coolly to him.

The LJ stretch *me no 'ave nothin' inna my mind* is distinguished from the rest of the turn structurally as well as in terms of its code. B's turn is structured as a telling of a series of events which followed the initial exchange between her and the boy: *then I just laughed, and then 'e just pulled me for a dance . . . and then we started to talk*. The sequence beginning with *I didn't mind* and ending with *but to dance* disrupts this pattern and is thus set off from the rest of the turn. It strikes us as most interesting that this part of B's turn begins and ends in LE, although the most essential part of it, the portion which describes B's state of mind, is in LJ. It is as though B 'works up' to the LJ portion and then 'comes down' to LE afterwards.

EXAMPLE 7

	B	if the guy will come up to you and say 'I hear say you want me'
	?	YEAH
	B	he must've got the impression that you were running you were
		{MOCK PANTING} 'oh (you) (god) 'e's nice yeah, I wan' ['im' ( )
5	?	[YEAH
	B	you know that shi?ries?[8]
	?	that's the so [rt of (pushy man) ( )
	?	[(so) I had to say 'did I really?' (0.6) I
		[did I really?
10	J	[yeah (.) and that is the right way to be
		(0.8)
	?	mmm
	J	[( )
	B	[then I just laughed (0.6) and then 'e – 'e just pulled me for a
15		dance – I didn't mind dancin' wiv 'im
		['cause *me know say, me no 'ave nothin' inna my mind*
	J	[yeah
	B	[but to dance, and then we star?ed to talk and all the rest of it
	J	[yeah
20	B	[and tha?'s it
	J	[yeah

270

```
      B   [full stop!
      J   [yeah
          (2.0)
 25   J   'e was a nice guy, but differently, right
```

Another example where a switch to LJ from LE appears to upgrade the LJ stretch in importance is (8). B and her friends are discussing the length of time it takes to get over a relationship and J has said that she has only had one boyfriend in the last four years. The central theme of this part of the conversation is time: the length of time between relationships. B's turn also has 'time' as its central theme – but the *only* reference to time in the turn is made in LJ, and the reference to time is the *only* LJ portion of the turn. The theme of time is again picked up by J's response to B, *Look how long it's been with me* ... The recurrent references to length of time, and the way J responds to B's turn as being 'about' a length of time, provide independent evidence of the importance of *a whole heap o' mont's* to the conversation. This phrase also happens to be the only one in LJ in B's turn – in fact, the only LJ in this part of the conversation. This suggests that LJ plays a significant role in 'upgrading' or 'highlighting' an important part of the conversation.

EXAMPLE 8

```
      J   I mean it does take time ge??in' to kn- find the right person
      B   Le? me tell you now, wiv every guy I've been out wiv,
          it's been a?- a whole heap o' mont's before I move with the next
          one
  5   J   NEXT one, yeah!
          (1.8)
      J   Look how long it's been with me though Brenda
```

4.4 Turn-final switches

A somewhat different phenomenon is a turn-final switch to LJ from LE. In this case, the last part of a turn is in LJ and the immediately preceding part of it in LE. One such example is (9), where B and her friends are discussing the length of time it takes to get to know a man. The last sentence of B's turn begins in LE: *I can't find all that*, and then switches to LJ for the last part: *shi??eries in a day!* This last sentence is the part of B's turn which the other participants respond to with an echoing chorus of *you can't*, followed by J's response to the explicit time reference in the LJ part of B's turn: *I tell you, sometimes it takes years*. This provides independent evidence of the saliency of B's last sentence, and in particular for the LJ final part of it, which is also somewhat louder and raised overall in pitch.

271

EXAMPLE 9

	B	I wanna guy (0.4) my guy (.) ('as) – I've gotta
		see that guy (.) 'e mus' 'ave ambition, (0.2)
		I must see that me 'n' 'im can work togevver, [right (.)
	?	[yeah
5	B	an' – (1.0) build fings
	?	yeah (0.2)
	B	build fings togevver you know what I me [an I wanna know say,
	?	[yeah
	B	this guy is an impen – independent g[uy
10	?	[yeah
	B	who can do fings on 'is own, I can't find
→		I can't find all that *shi??eries in a day*!
	J	you can't
	?	no you can't
15	J	you can't know one man in (.) I tell you s- (it)
		sometimes it takes years

A second type of example is (10), where the turn-final LJ portion 'reinforces' something said immediately before in LE. The conversation is about how to respond to an invitation to 'step outside' at a party: the gist of B's turn is that if someone were to ask her to go outside for 'fresh air' at a party, she would not want to go outside for fresh air, and would not go. The way the turn is constructed is interesting. B begins by offering her view as something which should be of interest to the others: *I'll tell you now.* (She had made several previous attempts to interrupt with *let me tell you.*) Next she places her story in the realm of the hypothetical: *(if) anybody goes to me* ... The next part is a quotation of what the hypothetical invitation would sound like, and is characterised by a Creole pronunciation of the vowels in *go* and *outside*, though the phrase as a whole (*go outside for fresh air*) is not clearly marked as LJ.

Next B states, in London English, her attitude to all such propositions: *I don't wanna go outside for fresh air, right* – and now switches to LJ to echo her own words, but more emphatically: not only would she not want to go, she will not: *me na a go outside for no fresh air*: 'I'm not going outside (ever) for any fresh air'. The strengthened assertion (*won't* versus *wouldn't want to*) and the build-up to a climax are already there in B's turn even without the code-switch from London English to LJ: 'fresh air' is mentioned three times, each time with greater prominence than before, and the overall impression is of a crescendo which reaches its climax with the final 'fresh air'. The Creole gives an added emphasis to the last part of the turn and marks its imminent end; this is shown by the reaction of the other speakers. J starts to speak in overlap with B as soon as B has spoken the main part of her LJ 'echo' sentence, *me na a go outside*. This is in contrast with switches framed on both sides by LE, such as in example 7, which, as we pointed out, are not interrupted because of the importance of their message. In examples like (10) the LJ seems to provide emphasis as a sort of narrative device, rather than marking out the most important material of the turn.

EXAMPLE 10

B   'ang on a minute (   ) I'll tell you now [(   ) (anybody)
?   [it's wrong though
B   goes to me, right, go outside for (   ) fresh air I don't wanna go outside for fresh air, right, *me na a go outside* [*for no fresh air*
J   [even if you do go out for fresh air it don't mean you're gonna have sex outside there

---

4.5 Quotations

Code-switching is a frequent correlate of reported speech in conversation. As we shall mention below, the direction of the switch is not always significant, and the code used for the quotation is not necessarily that of the actual speech being reported. However, in example 11 we have a nice illustration of a code-switch in mid-turn being used to create a 'persona' for an individual whose speech is being reported. B and J are talking about a particular man who had impressed B by his industriousness and drive. B begins her enthusiastic description of his virtues in LE: *now 'e 'ad everyfing if you was to sit down an' 'ear that guy speak*. At this point she is interrupted with a repeated *'e was nice*, spoken three times in overlap by J and an unidentified speaker. Meanwhile B continues by describing the man's plans, beginning in LE *('e was going) to Jamaica, 'e was going to*. Now J switches to LJ: *build 'is place, 'im a build 'is business* and then returns to LE for *an it's the type of guy like that ... I want*.

EXAMPLE 11

B   now 'e ad everyfing if you was to sit down an 'ear that guy speak
    (.)   ['e (was going) to Jamaica
J   ['e was ni:ce (0.8) 'e was ni:ce
B   'e was going to *build 'is place* (0.6)
5   [*'im a build 'is business* (1.0)
?   [ye:h 'e was NI:CE man
B   an' it's the type of guy like that (0.6) I [want
?   [yeah

```
      (0.6)
10 B  [know what I mean? But there again, those things didn't even
   ?  [(    )
   B  [enter my mind turaatid!⁹
   ?  [(    ) last night
```

B's turn is constructed interestingly, as a list of the man's attributes; this is achieved by the device of repeating key phrases, namely *'e was going* and *build 'is,* each repeated once. The switch to LJ occurs before the first instance of *build 'is* (phonetically [bɪlɪz], compare LE [bɪɫdɪz], and this could be taken as a direct quotation of the man's words, rendered in LJ because he is apparently a Jamaican; cf. B's *if you was to sit down an' 'ear that guy speak.* More interestingly, however, this switch somehow indexes a culture for which this goal stands as an ideal: building your own place is a plausible goal in Caribbean culture but very unusual in Britain. In a sense, B's list reflects through code the progressive 'Jamaicanising' of the person talked about: he 'goes to Jamaica' in LE, he becomes a participant in Jamaican culture in LJ. Finally B's conclusion – *it's the type of guy like that ... I want* returns to LE (after a long 1.0-second pause). Thus 'quotation' is rather complex and involves additional phenomena apart from a simple switch to mark a quotation. We have discussed it at length because it is an interesting example of how complex factors can be involved in code-switching.

Finally, we have some examples where the difference between codes, rather than the direction of the change, seems to be what is important. It is common for speakers to switch codes when they quote (directly or indirectly) something said by someone else. The code used for the quotation does not necessarily correspond to the code actually used by the original speaker – rather, the change of codes seems to be a narrative device used to offset the quotation from the matrix in which it is embedded. A clear example of this is (12), where the indirect quote *you was going to see it* is framed by the LJ *I t'ink you did say* before, and *dough* ('though') after. This is especially striking since the speaker switches twice, the second time just for the single word *dough* which ends her turn.

EXAMPLE 12: PRIVATE LESSONS

```
   A  wha? was 'private lessons' like?
      (1.8)
   B  (nah) de boy experience [he::
   A                          [eheh: experience what?
 5 B  (      ) start now
      (4.0)
```

A *I t'ink you did say* you was going to see it *dough*
   (0.6)

B yeah, but we didn't *catch out* (2.8) you know 'cause *I was sick an'
   t'ing you know?

4.6 *Code-switching of black Londoners: some conclusions*

We have seen in this section how a switch from LJ to LE corresponds in a broad sense to a change from the main theme of the conversation to some kind of 'sub-routine' or secondary material: a check on shared information, a search for a missing name or date, a comment indicating how the material should be interpreted. On the other hand, a switch to LJ is generally associated with an 'upgrading' of the LJ material: either it is an additional way of marking it as salient in the discourse, or it gives an added emphasis, especially when it is turn-final.

We noted in section 2 that at first sight, both LE and LJ could be 'we-' codes for the young black Londoners of this study. Both languages are used at home, and in intimate talk. However, the differential uses of the codes in conversation suggest that the 'we' versus 'they' distinction is present in the way that Gumperz's theory might predict. The more salient, more consequential material is spoken in LJ, while LE is used in the midst of an LJ stretch to 'downgrade' the importance of the LE part. In fact, the idea that 'creole' or 'patois' is used for emphasis is familiar to code-switching speakers and is almost a folk linguistic notion.

In the next section we will go on to examine the links between code and identity.

5 Code and identity: bilingual and monolingual perspectives

In the examples of the previous section, it was London English – the outgroup language for the Caribbean community in Britain – which was used to mark parts of the conversation which had less salience, such as asides and interruptions. However, in the Cantonese/English example of section 2, the in-group language, Cantonese, was used for the same purpose. In Gal's study of Oberwart, Austria, German – the code associated with prestige and authority – functioned as a 'topper' in escalating arguments for ethnically Hungarian bilinguals, 'a last word that was not outdone' (1979: 117). But for London Jamaican/London English bilinguals, it is London Jamaican, the in-group or 'ethnic' language, that apparently has this function (see 4.4 above).

All this indicates that although speakers may systematically differentiate the codes in conversational practice, it is not possible to make a priori assumptions about which code carries the putative 'we' functions and which the putative 'they' functions. This can only be decided by looking at the functions which the codes serve, which may vary from situation to situation and cannot be treated as given.

As pointed out in section 1, where terms like 'we-code' and 'they-code' are invoked, some notion of individual, group or social identity is usually explicitly or implicitly used as well. For example, Gumperz, in the quote given in section 1, talks of an 'association between communicative style and group identity'. A similar kind of association can be found in the work of Le Page and Tabouret-Keller (1985), who conceive of a speaker's behaviour as a series of 'acts of identity'. Starting from a description of the variation in behaviour of one of their Belizean speakers, the 'old lady', they write:

> The old lady ... shares with those in her community a capacity for more Spanish-like or more Creole-like or more American-like behaviour; she can shift her identity according to her company and she and her friends vary from one to the other according to the degree to which they are prepared to shift in any particular direction to proclaim their political and cultural identity. Here we introduce, then, the concept which is the theme of this book, that of linguistic behaviour as a set of *acts of identity* in which people reveal both their personal identity and their search for social roles.
> (Le Page and Tabouret-Keller, 1985: 14; emphasis in original)

For Le Page and Tabouret-Keller, linguistic behaviour involves 'shifts of identity' on the part of the speaker, through which she or he 'proclaims' her identity. Inherent in the work of Le Page and Tabouret-Keller is the notion that social groups are constructs of individuals who choose to identify themselves, or not, with particular groups (as identified by that individual) from time to time. 'Shifting identities' in talk, then, means affiliating with or disaffiliating from particular groups in whom the speaker has identified a particular type of linguistic behaviour. Le Page and Tabouret-Keller in their work seem to conceive of this social action being performed linguistically, for example through choice of lexis, grammar or pronunciation (broadly speaking, stylistic choices within one language variety) or by choice of language (as defined by the speaker, rather than by a linguist). Although their work concentrates on speakers in multilingual environments, in particular the Caribbean, it seems unlikely that only bi- or multilinguals (or bidialectal speakers) have the possibility of proclaiming their identity through speech. What seems often to be overlooked is the fact that so-called 'monolinguals' can also perform 'acts of identity' through talk, though using different resources.

Antaki, Condor and Levine, on the basis of a study of monolingual talk in English (by anonymous, but apparently British, speakers), conclude that social identity is a 'flexible resource in the dynamics of interaction' (Antaki *et al.* 1996: abstract). Identities, they say,

> never just appear, they are always *used*; they only make sense as part of an *interactional structure* (like a story or argument), and ... they are *highly flexible*. The participants use their identities as warrants or authority for a variety of claims they make and challenge, and the identities they invoke change as they are deployed to meet changing conversational demands.
>
> (emphasis in original)

Their point is that at any given juncture, a participant may assume, or be attributed with, a single identity; but in the course of a dynamic interaction, several different identities are likely to be active. In their detailed example, one participant, a recently qualified doctor, can be seen to invoke various identities in the course of story-telling and argument. Although there is talk of medical matters, the word *doctor* – and, the authors argue, the social identity which goes with it – is not used until turn 279 of the conversation. In the meantime, this speaker has used and has been attributed with other identities such as 'recently-qualified-medical-student' and 'recently-qualified-medical-student-with aspirations-to-continue-in-his-career', which fit the current collaborative purposes of the participants in the conversation – which the identity 'doctor', up to point where it is invoked, does not.

This example shows that for monolinguals, social identities are made relevant, are *used*, in talk. We must assume that bilinguals can and do use social identities in exactly the same way, except that they can draw on a more varied range of linguistic attributes – and through these, the extralinguistic structures which they symbolise – in the creation of those identities.

Let us now look at some further extracts from a conversation involving London English/London Jamaican bilinguals. Examples 7–11 in section 4 were all taken from this rather long conversation, in the course of which the participants, a mixed-gender group in their late teens or early twenties, display markedly differing gendered attitudes on the topic of casual sex. The men are in favour, and cannot see any reason for refusing an opportunity. The women are opposed. (This conversation took place in 1983 before AIDS was widely known about.) During the discussion, much of the conversational work done by B (who was taping the session, though not secretly), involves rejecting arguments put to her by her male interlocutors, and defending her position that she would always say 'no'.

In the course of this conversation, in which London English overwhelmingly predominates, there are frequent short switches to LJ, mostly by the speaker B. In examples 7 and 8, we saw that LJ highlighted the key statement of B's turn, while in (9) and (10) the speaker's turn was so structured as to make the most important point at the end of the turn, coinciding with a switch from LE to LJ. We were able thus to give a sequential account of a number of the switches. The account we gave of example 11 was somewhat different: here, LJ was used to create a 'persona' associated with an individual being talked *about* but not participating in the conversation. This was not linked strictly to sequentiality. With this in mind, let us examine some later occasions in the same conversation where B switches from LE to LJ.

EXAMPLE 13

(approximately 50 turns after example 10)

```
    P    same way like they can eat the kebab after the party
         they can get some'n uh (.)
    B    no:::!=
   ?M    =he he he
 5  B    I don't [no way eat the kebab after the party ]
    J           [no: (        )                        ]
         you know wha' I mean=
    P    =you don't always but one time you could eat one you know wha'
         I mean you could eat one in the wrong direction you know wha'
10       I mean
    B    hear [him now noh!
              ('JUST LISTEN TO HIM NOW!'10)
   ?S        [I mean (.) no you couldn't
    B    no I couldn't
         (1.0)
15  P    anybody could (0.4) anybody could [(0.4) anyone
    B                                      [BOY let me tell you now when
         me eat it come from (mh) it goh from my mout' whe y'a try tell me
                                      ('WHAT ARE YOU
         TRYING TO TELL ME?')
         (1.0)
20  P    yeah but it'll go any [direction
    B                          [no I don't business no
                               ('I DON'T CARE!')
         it couldn't (0.6) [an' 'e know seh me no nyam
                           ('HE KNOWS THAT I WON'T EAT'11)
   ?M                 [(        )
    B    whatever you tink you (could) [nyam
25 ?S                                  [(YOU KNOW) you gotta mind
         that ah=
    B    =you might nyam   [(0.6) it
   ?S                      [ah
```

In Example 13, where casual sex becomes euphemistically 'eating the kebab after the party', B's first response to P's *they can eat the kebab after the party* is in LE: *I don't no way eat the kebab after the party.* Her next response is a mocking *hear him now noh!* ('Just listen to him now!') in LJ. However, her most forceful responses to P are also in LJ: the angry *BOY let me tell you . . .* which meets with a one-second silence, and *'e know seh me no nyam whatever you tink you (could) nyam* ('and he knows that (*seh*) I won't eat (*nyam*) whatever you think you (could) eat'), which has the force of a 'topper'. Although the argument goes on, the theme of 'eating the kebab after the party' is now dropped. The discussion about casual sex, however, continues. How shall we account for the LJ in example 13? Whereas in earlier examples, B switches from LE to LJ in mid-turn, here B has constructed some turns entirely in LE (line 5) and others entirely in LJ (turns beginning lines 15 and 20). We can find other examples of this:

EXAMPLE 14

(approximately 60 turns after example 13; some of the intervening talk is not transcribable)

	B	'ang on a minute 'ang on a minute 'ang on a minute listen *somebody tell me to goh see see see see one brick wall dere, hh r(h)un frough it noh*
		('GO ON, RUN THROUGH IT')
5		you know your own mind
		[you know *you nah goh run frough dis damn brick wall*
	P	[na: na: tha's stupid tha's stupid
	??	[( )
	B	[I don't **business**
10	P	that is stupid=
	B	=NO: IT ISN'T STUPID

In this example, B's conversational management *'ang on a minute listen* is done in LE, but the rest of her turn consists of an 'if . . . then' structure in LJ: 'if somebody says to me, see that brick wall there, run through it! – you're not going to run through this damn brick wall!' (the LE *you know your own mind* which interrupts the stretch of LJ is an 'echo' of an LE phrase which has been used several times in the talk just prior to this).

We could try to explain each of B's switches to LJ – in a long conversation which is overwhelmingly in LE – purely on the basis of sequentiality (e.g. 'turn-final switch') or function ('adding emphasis'). However, it is apparent from a comparison of B's use of LJ in these examples and elsewhere in the conversation that she is not simply using LJ as a vehicle for emphasis or anger; elsewhere LE carries out this function, as we will see below. A purely sequential account seems to be sufficient to explain some but not all of B's switches to LJ. How can we account for the rest?

An alternative account for B's code-switching behaviour is to apply the notion of 'social identities within the framework of a conversation', developed by Antaki *et al.* (1996) for monolingual speakers. If instead of examining where code-switching occurs in a purely local context, we look at the conversation *as a whole* we can see that one of the social identities which B takes on is that of 'a woman who rejects casual sex'. Within the interactional structure of the continuing argument, it is *this* identity which seems to be invoked and relevant at each point where B uses LJ to construct all or part of her turn. Other identities, meanwhile, are associated with LE: for example, B as 'manager of the conversation' (a role she seems to have adopted, as keeper of the tape recorder), and B as the person in whose room the conversation is taking place. Notice her angry reaction (in LE) in the following example when someone knocks over an ashtray earlier in the conversation.

EXAMPLE 15

	P	and I catch ('er now) y'know but I see it 'appen
	J	I dunno I dunno
	B	it could'n happen
	J	no::
5		{noise of something falling}
		hhhh
→B		ah FUCKIN' HELL man
		(2.0) {laughter from one male}
		now you lot gonna have to tidy up my room I'm sorry
10	B	[I don't care]
	B	[I did-] I didn't do that (Isaac) did it

In example 15, B's anger is real, not feigned. Yet no part of her turns is in LJ. By way of contrast, let us look at example 16.

EXAMPLE 16

(approximately half-way between examples 13 and 14)

	B	=I don't care (0.2) put it this way (.)
		if I was [( )
	J	[American girls

```
   B    if I was to go to   [Jamaica Germany
5  J                        [(German) girls
   B    I don't business where, right, I'd ch- (right) same over here, I chat
        to anybody (0.6) same over there
        [me chat to anybody but anybody come tell me about sleep
  ?F    [ye::s
   B    wid dem s:: [same day when you (buck up) wid a STRANGER
  ?F                [na: (        ) (        ) (        )
  ?G                [(        )
```

In this example we see B, still responding to the suggestion that 'a chat' might lead to sex, building up to a rejection of promiscuous behaviour. This example is quite similarly structured to example 10, beginning with a number of conditional possibilities expressed in LE (*if I was ...*), and ending with the main act of avowal in LJ: 'I chat to anybody but if anybody suggests I sleep with them the same day when you (meet up) with a stranger ...!!' The apodosis is left unstated. In between her initial rejection of a male participant's suggestion with LE, *I don't care*, and her climactic LJ *when you (buck up) wid a STRANGER*, which ends her turn, B moves through a series of stages: from the 'pure' LE *if I was to go to Jamaica, Germany* to the stereotypically LJ expression *I don't business* ('I don't care') which, however, has Standard English grammar in *I don't* (Jamaican Creole *me don'* /mi duon/), together with London English phonology; through the phonologically LJ, but grammatically Standard English *same over here, I chat to anybody (0.6) same over there*; and from there to *me chat to anybody,* where both phonology *and* grammar are now marked as LJ. As B's language moves by stages from LE to LJ, we can see how by stages she comes to 'inhabit' her LJ persona of 'a woman who rejects casual sex'.

Why should LJ rather than LE be associated with this social identity for B? There is evidence elsewhere in the London Jamaican data that for women, Creole has associations with a robust and assertive, but morally conservative, female persona.[12] There is no space here to develop this hypothesis further; but what is important is that such an explanation is independent of given notions of 'we-code' and 'they-code'. Rather, such an account relies on *ethnographic* information revealing the values put by users on the codes they use. Evidence from the London Jamaican data suggests that in addition to local, sequential explanations of code-switching, it is also necessary to look at the interaction as a whole, as well as the wider context in which it is located. This does not exclude the possibility of interpretations in terms of 'we-code' and 'they-code'; however, such interpretations must take into account the shifting and negotiated nature of social identities within talk as well as the values attached to the different codes by their speakers.

6 'We' and 'they' in narrative

In the reported speech of narratives and arguments we can find evidence both of how identity is attributed by speakers and of the symbolic value of the different codes. In two separate examples, Alvarez-Cáccamo (1996) shows how 'we-' and 'they-' codes in reported speech may be relative to the act of reporting itself. Within one interaction, Spanish characterises a reported exchange which took place many years previously, while Galizan characterises the here-and-now, the language of the narrator in the current interaction. In this interaction, according to Alvarez-Cáccamo, social conflict is recreated through 'the opposition between the Galizan-speaking "we" of the reporting episode, and the Spanish-speaking "they" of the reported events'. He states: 'The power of linguistic choices here works for the construction of positive interactional face through strategic self-identification (1996: 53).' In another of Alvarez-Cáccamo's examples, a student leader in a public debate on a contentious matter switches from Spanish to Galizan to quote, ironically, the patronising words of an imaginary member of the 'compliant' Galizan elite towards the students. Here, 'social information about the managers of official Galizanhood (the Galizan-speaking political elites) is integrated and symbolically contrasted with information about a "resistant", Spanish-speaking "we" in a single discursive unit which subsumes the reporter's view of socio-ideological conflict' (1996: 39). In both of these cases the narrators were Galizans reporting the speech of other Galizans. In the second, the *actual* language of the original utterance (or, in the second case, the utterance attributed ironically to an imaginary speaker) is less relevant than the language *assigned* to it by the narrator who reports it. The 'we' and the 'they' are thus not fixed in a particular bilingual situation, but are also flexible, and can be seen as indices of shifting social identities which are themselves negotiated, manipulated and constructed in the course of talk.

In the following narration (the text is from Sebba 1993: 119–120), a young British-born Caribbean describes an incident in the shop where he works to his classmate at school – also a British-born Caribbean.

EXAMPLE 17

F   yeah man, I was on the till on Saturday (1.2) and this this black man *come* in (1.0) and (0.6) you know our shop, right, (0.6) they u:m (0.2) give (.) refund on (0.3) Lucozade bottles (0.4)

G   m:

5 F   a black man *come in an' 'im b(h)u::y a bottle* (.) of *Lucozade* while 'e was in the shop [an'

G   [free p- e's e got free pee off is it?

F   yeah

```
    G    small ones or big ones?
10  F    big ones and 'e drank the bottle in fron? of us an then ask(d) for
         the money back (see man) me want me money now
    G    [heheh
    F    [he goes (pnk) (I'm on) the till guy (.) hhh (I jus ) (0.6) I jus' look
         round at 'im (0.6) I said well you can't 'ave it (1.9) I said I 'ave
15       to open the till (w) wait till the next customer comes (1.0) 'now!
         open it now and gi' me de money' (1.0) I said I can't (0.8) the man
         just thump 'is fist down an'(screw up dis for me) (.) (s no man)
         the manager just comes (.) 'would you leave the shop before I call
         the security' hh the man jus' take the bottle an' fling it at me an
20       (I) jus' catch it at the (ground)
```

In this narrative, the narrator (F) switches frequently between LE and LJ.
Throughout, LE characterises F's own actions and speech (*I was on the till
on Saturday, I said I 'ave to open the till* etc.) while the unpleasant customer's
actions and speech are narrated in LJ (e.g *'im b(h)u::y a bottle (.) of
Lucozade, me want me money now*). The match is not perfect, as some of
the customer's actions are described in LE. However, no part of F's actions
or speech are given in LJ.

F describes the customer on first mentioning him as *this black man* – a
rare example of ethnic labelling in this data – which seems to be intended
to distance himself from the customer. However, the narrator of the story
and his audience, are *also* 'black' (African-Caribbean.) *This black man*
might, therefore, be taken to designate 'one of us'. That it clearly is not
intended in this way is shown by the way that LJ – the 'ethnic language'
or putative 'we-code' of all three persons involved – is actually used to
distinguish and distance the customer described, to create his 'otherness'.
Meanwhile at the start of his story the narrator F identifies himself as the
'person on the till' (*I was on the till on Saturday*), an identity subsequently
associated with LE throughout the narrative. In using LE he sets himself
off from the customer, but he also preserves the 'we-ness' of himself and
his interlocutor of the here-and-now, G, as most of their preceding chat has
been in LE without switching.

It is also clear in example 17 that the location of code-switches is not
sequentially determined, by their position within F's turn, but rather depends
on which of the interactants in the story is being personated at the time.

In reported speech, the creation of identities for actors is a necessary part
of the narrative strategy. At the same time, the narrator of a story creates
his or her *own* identities, often contrasting the narrator's character with that
of others talked about, and showing him or herself in a positive light (see
Tate 1993). The above examples show how the contrast between codes
can be used to construct 'we's and 'they's along with other more specific
identities in talk.

7 Conclusions

Social identities can be seen to be flexible constructs, created, negotiated and constantly changed in the course of interaction. There is no one-to-one mapping between these and 'group identities'. The linguistic medium by means of which social identities are constructed may itself be a part of the identity, but we cannot assume a fixed relationship between a social identity and the language of the utterance that evokes (or invokes) it; rather, such relationships are themselves negotiated and constructed in the interaction, drawing on cultural resources located both inside and outside the interaction itself. The notions of 'we' and 'they' can now be seen to be subsumed within more local, and changeable, social identities which are made salient from time to time within a conversation. Social identities are made manifest through *talk*, not just through the actual language or 'code' used but also through the content and context. The language or languages of an utterance may be relevant to the social identity evoked, as in examples above, or may not be (see Gafaranga 1996); and where it is relevant, it is not the only factor. If there are only two or three distinct codes available but a multiplicity (in theory, infinitely many) of social identities to be evoked and manipulated, the relationship between code and identity is necessarily much more complex than one-to-one.

In conclusion, we may say that the notion of 'identities' as constructs within talk usefully combines a focus on conversational interaction with an acceptance that code choice cannot be accounted for solely by factors within the conversation.

Notes

Parts of this chapter, in particular the last part of section 2 and sections 3 and 4, form a slightly revised version of Sebba and Wootton 1984, which has not previously appeared in print.

1 In Blom and Gumperz's classic study (1972), switching was between a local dialect of Norwegian and the national language. However, their study still exemplifies the minority language/majority language distinction.

2 See Hewitt 1986 and Sebba 1993 for more detailed discussion of white speakers of Creole, and Rampton (this volume) for a discussion of 'language crossing'.

3 See Meeuwis and Blommaert (this volume) for a 'monolectal view' of code-switching where the 'overall code-switched variant used by speakers is seen . . . as *one code in its own right*'.

4 For example, the initial consonant of *thing*, RP /θ/, is typically /f/ in London English, /t/ in Jamaican; final /l/ (e.g. in *well*) in a London pronunciation is velarized [ł], while in Jamaican Creole it is clear, [l]. Many short and long vowels and diphthongs also have different values in LE and LJ. The most common grammatical markers of LJ in the examples given here are: use of the Standard English object pronoun forms (*me, him, them*) as subjects; past tense verbs either unmarked or marked by preverbal *did* where this would not be used in Standard English; preverbal negation using *no*, sometimes combined with the aspect marker *a* as *naa*.

5 Transcription conventions used in the examples:

italics	London Jamaican (Creole)
normal print	London English
bold print	laughter
CAPITALS	loudness, emphasis
[ ]	start/end of overlap
= =	latching (i.e. no interval between adjacent turns)
(text)	insecure transcription
( )	unintelligible syllable(s)
(.)	micro-pause
–	pause
(*n*)	silence of length *n* seconds.
-	break off/unfinished word
{ }	transcriber's insertion
:	lengthened vowel

6 The exact significance of these words is not known. They may be codes for communicating with partners who cannot see one's pieces.

7 The pragmatics of *you know what I mean* in LE and LJ is dealt with in Sebba and Tate 1986.

8 'Shitteries': junk, nonsense.

9 A commonly used swear word.

10 This is a fairly common LJ expression used in playful mockery. The words have Jamaican pronunciation.

11 *seh* = 'that', *nyam* = 'eat'.

12 Take for example the following conversation recorded in another part of London with different speakers. This was clearly a 'performance' where two girls, aged around 15, took on the persona of women of their mothers' generation, pretending shock and horror at the way girls dress:

C *Joan de other day y'know me see dis gyal a walk down de street* (0.6) *she have on one piece o' mini y'see* (if for) *tell you how much I cyaant stand dem tings deh* **hhh** *dem a show off dem leg* (0.2) *no:h shame* (0.6) *dem does put black people to shame bwoy I tell you any time I see dem gyal deh I feel like slap dem inna dem face and say go put on clothes*

J *I can just imagine her twist-up leg dem*

C *Yes man!* (0.4) *Not a slip and ting y'know!*

J *Not a* [*slip!* {feigned/overdone shock}

C   [*No* [*star*
                  ('friend')

J   [*Most o' we black gyal* brought up to wear a slip under our clothes ain't it

C *Seen!* (0.4) *Me dear!* (0.4) *De gyal not have a slip upon she!* (0.6)

J I say wou – that woman mus' (0.4) *no:h if me did come up to my house* (an') *my mamma* would drag me back in and tell me to *put on clothes!*

C She'd drag me by *de* skirt an' *fling* me in the bedroom (0.2) *change it* she would say to me!

Bibliography

Alvarez-Cáccamo, C. (1996) 'The power of reflexive language(s): code displacement in reported speech', *Journal of Pragmatics* 25, 1: 33–59.

Antaki, C., Condor, S. and Levine, M. (1996) 'Social identities in talk: speakers' own orientations', *British Journal of Social Psychology*, 35, 473–492.

Auer, P. (1991) 'Bilingualism in/as social action: a sequential approach to code-switching', in *Papers for the Symposium on Code-switching in Bilingual Studies: Theory, Significance and Perspectives*, Strasbourg: European Science Foundation, Network on Code-Switching and Language Contact, 319–352.

Blom, J.P. and Gumperz, J.J. (1972) 'Social meaning in linguistic structures', in Gumperz, J. J. and Hymes, D. (eds), *Directions in Sociolinguistics*, New York: Holt, Rinehart and Winston, 407–434.

Cheung, Cindy Mei-Yan (1995) '"Jing yu jaa jiu, gwong dung waa jaa jiu." Codeswitching practices in two bilingual classrooms in Hong Kong', unpublished MA dissertation, Lancaster University.

Gafaranga, J. (1996) 'Rwandese identity in French or French identity in Kinyarwanda: Kinyarwanda–French Code-Switching', paper given at conference 'Identités et Politiques Linguistiques en France et dans le Monde Francophone', University of Surrey, 8–9 June 1996.

Gal, S. (1979) *Language Shift*, New York: Academic Press.

Gumperz, J.J. (1982) *Discourse Strategies*, Cambridge: Cambridge University Press.

Hewitt, R. (1986) *White Talk, Black Talk*, Cambridge: Cambridge University Press.

Le Page, R.B. and Tabouret-Keller, A. (1985) *Acts of Identity*, Cambridge: Cambridge University Press.

Sebba, M. (1993) *London Jamaican: Language Systems in Interaction,* London: Longman.

Sebba, M. and Tate, S. (1986) 'You know what I mean? Agreement marking in British Black English', *Journal of Pragmatics* 10: 163–172.

Sebba, M. and Wootton, A. J. (1984) 'Conversational code-switching in London Jamaican', paper presented at Sociolinguistics Symposium 5, Liverpool.

Tate, S. (1993) 'Constructing heroines and villains: the use of reported speech in troubles telling', unpublished MS.

INTRODUCTION TO CHAPTER 12

Peter Auer

The following chapter deals with code-switching of a certainly non-prototypical kind (see Franceschini, Chapter 3), and therefore one that has hardly been mentioned in the existing linguistic literature. 'Crossing', the use of a minority variety by speakers of the majority in socially and communicatively 'liminoid' cases, is not only a case of switching into a non-legitimate language (Bourdieu 1982), but also a case of non-legitimate switching, since the switchers do not have unproblematic access to this variety, a point that was first made by Hewitt in his pace-setting study of Creole usage among white British adolescents (Hewitt 1986). In fact, as Rampton has shown elsewhere in detail (Rampton 1995), the British adolescents who use (usually a small set of expressions or features of) varieties such as Punjabi, stylised Asian English or Creole cross both a linguistic border and a group border, i.e. that of their ethnic group. At the same time, the use of the others' 'we-code' may be seen as an attempt to allude to an identity which the adolescents have in common despite their different cultural and racial backgrounds. It is an attempt to create a transracial and transethnic common ground, or, as Ben Rampton puts it, 'the use of an out-group language [can] be cross-ethnically "we-coded"' (1995: 59).

Since 'crossing' refers to an inter-group practice of language use, Rampton's study also touches on the question of 'inter-cultural communication'. However, this inter-culturality is of a special kind, again representing a non-prototypical case when seen against the background of the bulk of publications on this subject. As Rampton describes it,

interactional sociolinguistic studies of interethnic communication in Britain have been generally concerned 1. with workplace interactions involving adults, who 2. have been brought up both inside and outside Britain, who 3. are unfamiliar with one another, and who 4. occupy different positions of institutional power. The gist of these studies is to show how, 5. despite initial good will, hidden differences in participants' communicative resources disrupt 6. straight discussion, generate negative social categorisations, and 7.

result in the reproduction of racism. In contrast, my concern is a) with the recreational interaction of b) British-born adolescents, who c) know each other well, and d) whose institutional positions are roughly similar. These young people e) recognise and even exaggerate the differences in their communicative repertoires f) in a set of stylised and often playful interactions that up to a point at least, g) constitute a form of antiracism.

(1995: 21)

Rampton's analysis is based on a larger study in a 'high stress' housing area of a middle-sized town situated in the South Midlands of England. In this town, as in Britain in general, immigration from the West Indies, from India and from Pakistan was strong in the 1960s, while in the 1970s immigration was dominantly from Bangladesh and East Africa. In the particular state middle school of the neighbourhood investigated by Rampton, 9 per cent of the pupils were Afro-Caribbean, 12 per cent Bangladeshi, 28 per cent Indian, 28 per cent Pakistani and 20 per cent Anglo (Rampton 1995: 26). Among the ethnic minority groups, there was a stratification in terms of economic success with the Indians ranking on top, followed by Afro-Carribeans and Pakistanis, with the Bangladeshis in the worst position.

The data on Creole usage by white adolescents presented and discussed by Rampton in the following chapter may be compared with those on Creole usage by black adolescents in Sebba and Wootton's contribution (see the previous chapter). From such a comparison, it appears that code-switching is a marginal phenomenon in inter-racial interaction, not only in quantitative terms, but also because of its restriction to what Rampton calls 'liminoid' speech activities and interactional contexts (i.e. activities/contexts 'at the margin' of focused interaction). This restriction, however, should not be taken to imply that an analysis of 'crossing' cannot provide important insights into the construction of meaning in code-switching practices in general. The opposite is the case.

Rampton proposes to combine conversation-based micro-analyses of interactional exchanges with an analysis of their wider ethnographically recoverable setting. His particular theoretical approach owes much to two scholars. On the one hand, he takes up John Gumperz's distinction between situational and metaphorical switching, which already played an important role in the preceding chapter by Sebba and Wootton (see p. 000–000). Rampton widens Gumperz's notion of situational switching in order to make it comprise all 'relatively routine contextualisation cues', while metaphorical switching (which is to be applied to crossing) 'denies the recipient an easy footing for subsequent interaction'. Metaphorical switching (which he renames 'figurative switching') thus requires more interpretive work by the recipient and, possibly, it does not enable participants to arrive at a shared interpretation of the code-switch at all (and therefore remains 'ambiguous'; cf. in a similar vein, Stroud's analysis in Chapter 13).

On the other hand, Rampton applies Bakhtin/Voloshinov's notion of polyphony to 'crossing', taking up Bakhtin's idea of double-voicing which was conceived in order to deal with the various ways in which reported speech (*čužaja reč*) may be incorporated into the speech of the self (or the narrator). Rampton distinguishes uni-directional double-voicing, in which the original voice is largely preserved, from vari-directional double-voicing, in which the original voice is ironically subverted. He assigns the first to crossing into Creole, and the second to crossing into Punjabi and stylised Asian English, the codes which are less prestigious for the adolescents.

Bibliography

Bourdieu, Pierre (1982) *Ce que parler veux dire*, Paris: Fayard.
Hewitt, Roger (1986) *White Talk Black Talk*, Cambridge: Cambridge University Press.
Rampton, Ben (1995) *Crossing: Language and Ethnicity Among Adolescents*, London: Longman.

12

LANGUAGE CROSSING AND THE REDEFINITION OF REALITY

Ben Rampton

1 Introduction

In this chapter, I shall first give an account of 'language crossing', a verbal practice that has not been very widely recognised in sociolinguistics (cf. Rampton 1995a). Then, with a description in place, I shall consider some of crossing's more general implications for research on code-switching. More specifically, I will suggest that:

1   By focusing overwhelmingly on bilingual ingroups, research has traditionally tended to neglect the emergence of new plural ethnicities, built in an *acceptance* of old ones (Hall 1988).

2   To gain any purchase on the exploration and/or renegotiation of reality – in my research, a reality of race stratification and division – full recognition needs to be given to Gumperz's notion of metaphorical code-switching, though this needs some further clarification, perhaps most profitably by being drawn into close association with Bakhtin's notion of double-voicing (1984: 181–204).

3   For the same reason, it would be helpful if code-switching research relaxed its commitment to discovering coherence and systematicity in code-switching, and attended more closely to incongruity and contradiction. In the process, a clearer view would emerge of the (not infrequent) local occasions when code alternation no longer functions adequately as a contextualisation cue and instead becomes part of the 'main action', an object of explicit political dispute (cf. Goffman 1974: ch. 7; Hewitt 1986: 169, 181).

4   To respond adequately to all three of these points, the notion of conversation used in code-switching research needs to be a very broad one, and it is also essential to attend to the representations of code-switching and language difference in artful performance and the public media.

I would like to begin with the account of language crossing, starting with a preliminary definition.

2 Language crossing: a preliminary definition

The term 'language crossing' (or 'code-crossing') refers to the use of a language which isn't generally thought to 'belong' to the speaker. Language crossing involves a sense of movement across quite sharply felt social or ethnic boundaries, and it raises issues of legitimacy that participants need to reckon with in the course of their encounter. In line with this, in the adolescent friendship groups where I studied it (Rampton 1995a), crossing either occasioned, or was occasioned by, moments and activities in which the constraints of ordinary social order were relaxed and normal social relations couldn't be taken for granted.

3 Some examples

The examples of crossing that follow come from a research project which used the methodologies of ethnographic and interactional sociolinguistics to examine four closely interrelated dimensions of socio-cultural organisation: language, seen both as a central element in social action and as a form of knowledge differentially distributed across individuals and groups; the 'inter-action order' mapped out by Erving Goffman; institutional organisation, encompassing domains, networks, activity types, social roles and normative expectations; and social knowledge specifically as this relates to race and ethnicity. Two years of fieldwork focused on one neighbourhood of the South Midlands of England, with twenty-three 11 to 13 year olds of Indian, Pakistani, African Caribbean and Anglo descent in 1984, and approximately sixty-four 14 to 16 year olds in 1987. Methods of data-collection included radio-microphone recording, participant observation, interviewing, and retro-spective participant commentary on extracts of recorded interaction. The analysis was based on about 68 incidents of Panjabi crossing, about 160 exchanges involving stylised Asian English, and more than 250 episodes where a Creole influence was clearly detectable, and three significantly different contexts for language crossing were identified: interaction with adults, interaction with peers, and performance art.

Here is the first example:

EXAMPLE 1

Participants: Ray (13 years old, male, of Anglo/African-Caribbean descent; wearing radio-mike), Ian (12, male, Anglo descent), Hanif (12, male, Bangladeshi descent), others.

Setting: 1984. Coming out of lessons into the playground at break. Ian and Ray are best friends. Stevie Wonder is a singer whose song 'I just called to say I love you' was very famous. Ray has a bad foot (see line 17).[1]

	RAY	IA::N::
	HANIF	( )
	IAN	((from afar)) RAY THE COO:L RAY THE COO:L
	HANIF	yeh Stevie Wonder YAAA ((laughs loudly))
5	RAY	[it's worser than that
	IAN	((singing)): [I just called to say
	HANIF	ha (let's) sing (him) a song
	IAN	I hate you
	HANIF	((loud laughs))
10	ANON	((coming up)) ( ) are you running for the school (.)
	RAY	huh
	ANON	are [you running for the school=
	RAY	[no
	ANON	=[I am
15	IAN	[he couldn't run for th- he couldn't [run for the school
	RAY	[SHUT UP=
	RAY	=I couldn- I don wan- [I can't run anyway
	HANIF	[right we're wasting our [time=
	IAN	[I did=
20	HANIF	=[come on (we're) wasting our time=
	IAN	[you come last ( )
	HANIF	=[[mʌmʌmʌ:]
	ANON	[I came second
	IAN	((singing)) I just called to say [I got] a big=
25	RAY	[I hate you]
	IAN	=[lʊlla:]
		((Panjabi for 'willy'))
	HANIF AND	((loud laughter))
	OTHERS	
	RAY	((continuing Ian's song)) so's Ian Hinks (1.5)
		((Ray laughs)) no you haven't you got a tiny one (.)
30		you've only got (a arse)

In this extract, Ian directs some Panjabi abuse at his good friend Ray, and among other things, the formulaic use of song helps to ensure that it is understood as ritual and jocular, not personal and serious (cf. Labov 1972; Goodwin and Goodwin 1987).[2] When he starts out in lines 6 and 8, he seems to be identifying himself with the first person expressed in the song, but when he repeats it in lines 24 and 26, it looks as though he's putting the words in Ray's mouth rather than claiming the 'I' for himself – certainly,

Ray's retaliation in line 28 suggests that it's him that has been attributed the item in Panjabi, not Ian. Whatever, Ian comes off best in their brief exchange of ritual abuse: Ian's [lʊlla:] upstages Ray's effort to preempt him in line 25; it is Ian who wins an enthusiastic response from third parties in line 27; and in lines 29 and 30, Ray evidently judges his own immediate retort (line 28) as itself rather weak.

Here is a somewhat different example of Panjabi crossing, this time centred around *bhangra*, a form of Panjabi music which was a major youth cultural force in the neighbourhood (cf. Rampton 1995a: ch. 10).

EXAMPLE 2

Participants: Sally (15 years old, female, Anglo descent; wearing radio-mike), Gurmit (15, female, Indian descent), Lorraine (15, female, Anglo descent), Anon.A (female, Anglo), Anon.P (female, Panjabi).
Setting: 1987; dinnertime, sitting outside. One of the girls has a cassette player and is listening to *bhangra* on headphones. These headphones are fairly inefficient and the music can be overheard by everyone. During the interaction, there seems to be some play about who the *bhangra* cassette actually belongs to – cf. lines 1–8.

	SALLY	((high pitch)) cor who's song's this can I listen
	?	((odd laugh))
	GURMIT	((laughing lightly)) Lorraine's
	ANON.P	((?light laugh?))
5	SALLY	is it Lorraine's
	GURMIT	((laughing lightly)) yeh
	ANON.A	(no it isn't)
	SALLY	((calling out)) OH LORRAINE [EH LORRAINE HAS IT GOT=
10	?	[( )
	?	[you want the other side
	SALLY	=((f)) [*kenu mɪnu*] ON it
		((words from a Panjabi song meaning 'she said to me'))
	?	((the cassette is changed over to the other side, and after this, music can be faintly heard on my recording until end of extract))
	ANON.A	it's got ((singing)) [*hәʊli hәʊli*]
	SALLY	((sings)) [*ɒ kennu mennu*] I love –
	ANON.	HELLO
15	GURMIT	oh that
	SALLY	((speaking)) my favourite song that is you know
	GURMIT	((p)) it's from Heera ((a very popular *bhangra* group)) (.)
	SALLY	is it on here (1.0)

```
20  GURMIT    no not on here (1.0)
    SALLY     ((sings pp)) [uər tʃəti he] ((speaking)) ((p)) that's a good
              'un as well (.)
              Imran likes that one (.)
              ((louder:)) what's on that side (2.5)
              ((overhearing a song)) I LIKE THIS ONE
25  ANON.A    let me listen (1.0) what is it
    SALLY     ((very quietly)) go on (2.0)
    GURMIT    I [better have a check (.)
    ANON.A      [oh this is the one I like (.) Gurmit (.)
              ((quietly, at a high pitch)) ( )
30  ANON.A    ((short half laugh)) (2.5)
    SALLY     Imran's got this (2.0)
    ?         ((p)) aah aah (5.0)
```

Both from interview data and from a close analysis of this discussion in its entirety, it was clear that Panjabi adolescents were generally unenthusiastic when white youngsters displayed an interest in *bhangra*, and in this example, this is intimated by their refusal to produce second assessments to Sally's positive evaluations in lines 17, 21 and 22 (Pomerantz 1984).[3] In fact, how was it that Sally managed to continue her discussion of *bhangra* for another forty turns or so, sporadically repeating the positive assessments and getting comparable non-responses?[4]

Up to a point, she may have been sustained in her discussion by elements of both agreement and competition between her and the other white girl, Anon.A. But the activity type that they were engaged in – listening to music – was also important. Listening to music, talk could be rather desultory, with only a rather loose interpersonal focus. Goffman's description of 'open states of talk' fits with this activity:

> [when] an open state of talk [develops], participants [have] the right but not the obligation to initiate a little flurry of talk, then relapse back into silence, all this with no apparent ritual marking, as though adding but another interchange to a chronic conversation in progress.
>
> (1981: 134–135)

In open states of talk, there is less pressure to attend to what other people say and minimal or non-responses can seem less offensive. In example 2, the primary participation framework sometimes consisted of the recorded musicians and each girl attending separately,[5] and this could soften any offence when Sally and Anon.A's evaluations failed to meet with affiliative second assessments – there were other activities going on (the songs) that also had a legitimate hold on the attention of their interlocutors.[6]

Listening to music also provided an opportunity for response cries and self-talk, in which participants produced utterances that could be taken as merely auditing the music's development. As Goffman (1981) makes clear, response cries and self-talk are actually styled to be overheard in a gathering, they are often adjusted to their audience's sensitivities, and they can provide bystanders with a licence to start interacting verbally (1981: 97–98). But on the surface at least, they don't seem to be recipient-directed, they are sequentially non-implicative, and as such, they were a convenient vehicle for tentative Panjabi crossing. Unlike the first part of an adjacency pair, self-talk didn't force any show of bilingual acceptance or rejection, and so the failure to elicit a response didn't need to entail any loss of face. Sally and Anon.A's utterances in lines 28–32 could certainly be taken as music-focused response cries and self-talk.

The third example of language crossing involves Creole.

EXAMPLE 3

Participants: Asif (15, male, Pakistani descent, wearing the radio-micro-phone), Alan (15, male, Anglo descent), Ms Jameson (25+, female, Anglo descent), and in the background, Mr Chambers (25+, male, Anglo descent). *Setting:* 1987. Asif and Alan are in detention for Ms Jameson, who was herself a little late for it. She is explaining why she didn't arrive on time, and now she wants to go and fetch her lunch.

	MS J	I had to go and see the headmaster
	ASIF	why
	MS J	( ) (.) none of your business
	ALAN	a- about us ( )
5	MS J	((p)) no I'll be [back
	ASIF	[((f)) hey how can you see the=
		=headmaster when he was in dinner (.)
	MS J	((quietly)) that's precisely why I didn't see him
	ASIF	what (.)
10	MS J	I'll be back in a second with my lunch [( )
	ASIF	[((ff)) NO [|]=[7]
		=((f)) dat's sad man (.) (I'll b)=
		=I [had to miss my play right I've gotta go
	ALAN	[(with mine)
15		(2.5) ((Ms J must now have left the room))
	ASIF	((Creole influenced)) ((f)) *l::unch* (.) you don't need no=
		([l::ʌntʃ])
		=lunch [*not'n* grow anyway ((laughs))
		([natʔn gɹəʊ])
	ALAN	[((laughs))
	ASIF	have you eat your lunch Alan

Lines 1–9 involve a verbal tussle in which Asif and Alan use questions to undermine the positions that Ms Jameson stakes out in what she says. Asif's question in line 2 treats the account she gives of her late arrival as inadequate; she rebutts his inquiry as illegimate in line 3 but this is then undermined by Alan in lines 4 and 5; and in lines 6–8, Ms Jameson is delayed in the departure she announced in line 5 by a question that upgrades the query over her initial excuse into an explicit challenge. All this time, she has been locked into the interaction by the adjacency structures set up by the boys' questions, but at line 10, she breaks out of this pattern, ignores Asif's line 9 repair initiation, again announces her departure and leaves without saying anything more. With the cooperative exchange structure now disrupted and Ms Jameson apparently disattending to him, Asif launches into some 'muttering' 'afterburn':

> Afterburn . . . is . . . a remonstrance conveyed collusively by virtue of the fact that its targets are in the process of leaving the field . . . when one individual finds that others are conducting themselves offensively in their current dealings with him, he can wait until they have closed out the interchange with him and turned from the encounter, and *then* he can express what he 'really' feels about them . . . he may turn to a member of his encounter and flood into directed expression.
>
> (Goffman 1971: 152–153)

> In muttering we convey that although we are now going along with the line established by the speaker (and authority), our spirit has not been won over, and compliance is not to be counted on.
>
> (Goffman 1981: 93)

In this refusal to submit to the unjust Miss Jameson, Asif uses some Creole/ Black English. Admittedly, it can sometimes be hard trying to distinguish Creole from the local multiracial vernacular, and Asif's stopped / θ / in *dat's sad man* is ambiguous. But in lines 16 and 17, he uses a characteristically Creole unrounded front open vowel in *not* (cf. Wells 1982: 576; Sebba 1993: 153–154), and the stretched [l] in his first 'lunch' maybe connects with a black speech feature noted by Hewitt in south London (1986: 134).

The last example of crossing also relates to a breach of conduct, though here the putative offender is a younger pupil and the language used is a variety I've called stylised Asian English.

EXAMPLE 4

Participants and setting: At the start of the school year, Mohan (15 years, male, Indian descent, wearing radio-microphone), Jagdish (15, male, Indian descent) and Sukhbir (15, male, Indian descent) are in the bicycle sheds looking at bicycles at the start of the new academic year. Some new pupils run past them.

SUKH	STOP RUNNING AROUND YOU GAYS (.)
SUKH	[((laughs))
MOH	[*EH (.) THIS IS NOT MIDD(LE SCHOOL)* no more (1.0)
	([aɪ dɪs ɪz n̪ɐtʰ mɪd̪ nəʊ mɔ:])
	ˌthis is a re ˌspective (2.0) (school)
	([dɪs ɪz ə ɹəspektɪv])
5 MOH	school (.) yes (.) took the words out my mouth (4.5)

In this extract, Mohan was claiming that the norms of conduct appropriate to secondary pupils during breaktime had been broken, and here, Goffman's account of remedial interchanges (1971: 95–187) helps to explain the way that stylised Asian English (SAE) figured in the episode. Goffman argues that two kinds of issue arise when infractions occur. One of these is 'substantive', relating to practical matters such as the offender making amends and the offended showing that they are not going to accept the way they have been treated. The other kind of issue is ritual, which in contrast is concerned with the way in which participants display their more general respect and regard for social norms and personal preserves (Goffman 1971: 95–98, 100, 116) – here the concern is with 'indicating a relationship, not compensating a loss' (1971: 118).

In line 1, the initial noticing of the infraction was announced by a normal vernacular English 'prime' – an attempt to get the (putative) offender to provide a remedy which they might do by desisting, apologising and/or giving an explanation (Goffman 1971: 154ff., 109–114). Propositionally, the utterance in line 3 only reminded the (disappearing) addressee that old rules of conduct no longer applied, but the switch to stylised Asian English made a symbolic proclamation about the transgression's relation to a wider social order. In switching away from his normal voice to SAE, Mohan aligned the offence with a more general social type, so that the offending act was now cast as a symptom. SAE was stereotypically associated with limited linguistic and cultural competence (Rampton 1995a: chs 2.3, 3 and 6) and the switch implicitly explained the transgression by imputing diminished control and responsibility to the offender. In doing so, it achieved the same effect as a sanction: 'the significance of . . . rewards and penalties is not meant to lie in their intrinsic worth but in what they proclaim about the [actor's] moral status . . . and [their] compliance with or deviation from rules in general' (Goffman 1971: 95, 98).

4 Crossing: the definition elaborated

Two things seem to run through all four of these examples (as well as many more). First, the speakers moved outside the language varieties they normally used, and they briefly adopted codes which they didn't have full and easy access to. Admittedly, there were important differences in the extent to which they incorporated these other varieties into their habitual speech. But acts of this kind were frequently commented on (with varying degrees of both enthusiasm and disapproval), and constraints on the use of both Creole and SAE were evident in the fact that white and Panjabi youngsters generally avoided Creole in the company of black peers, while white and black peers hardly ever used SAE to target Panjabis.

Second, these appropriations occurred in moments and activities when 'the world of daily life known in common with others and with others taken for granted' (Garfinkel 1984: 35) was problematised or partially suspended. These interruptions to the routine flow of normal social order took a wide range of different forms, and varied very considerably in their scale and duration (see Rampton 1995a for comprehensive exemplification). Crossing occurred:

- in the vicinity of interactional breaches, delicts and transgressions (examples 3 and 4);
- in ritual abuse, which works by suspending considerations of truth and falsity (cf. Labov 1972; Goodwin and Goodwin 1987; example 1);
- in open states of talk, self-talk and response cries, which constitute time away from the full demands of respectful interpersonal conduct (Goffman 1981: 81, 85, 99; example 2);
- at the boundaries of interactional enclosure, when the roles and identities for ensuing interaction were still relatively indeterminate (Goffman 1971: ch. 7; Laver 1975, 1981; Rampton 1995a: ch. 3.3);
- in games, where there was an agreed relaxation of routine interaction's rules and constraints (Turner 1982: 56; Sutton-Smith 1982; Rampton 1995a: chs 6.7, 7.2);
- in the context of performance art (cf. Gilroy 1987: 210–216; Rampton 1995a: Part III);
- and in cross-sex interaction, which in a setting where everyday recreation was single-sex and where many parents discouraged unmonitored contact between adolescent girls and boys, itself seemed special, unusually vested with both risk and promise (Shuman 1993: 146; Rampton 1995a: chs 7.7, 10.8).

We can summarise this relationship with moments and events in which the hold of routine assumptions about social reality was temporarily loosened by saying that crossing was intricately connected with what Turner calls 'liminality' and the 'liminoid'.[8]

These two points support each other and permit at least two inferences. First, the intimate association with liminality meant that crossing never actually claimed that the speaker was 'really' black or Asian – it didn't finally imply that the crosser could move unproblematically in and out of the friends' heritage language in any new kind of open bicultural code-switching. Second, crossing's location in the liminoid margins of interactional and institutional space implied that in the social structures which were dominant and which adolescents finally treated as *normal*, the boundaries round ethnicity were relatively fixed.

Even so, these boundaries weren't inviolable, and quite plainly, adolescents didn't submit reverentially to absolutist ideas about ethnicity being fixed at birth or during the early years of socialisation. Language crossing cannot be seen as a runaway deconstruction of ethnicity, emptying it of all meaning, but its influence wasn't left unquestioned, invisibly and incontrovertibly pervading common sense. Crossing was an established interactional practice that foregrounded inherited ethnicity itself, and in doing so, it at least partially destabilised it. In Bourdieu's terms, crossing can be seen as a form of 'heretical discourse' which broke the doxic authority of the idea that ethnically, you are what you're born and brought up (1977: 168–70; 1990: 129). As such, crossing warrants close attention in sociological discussion of the emergence of 'new ethnicities of the margins', multiracial ethnicities 'predicated on difference and diversity' (Hall 1988).[9]

But what relevance does crossing have for sociolinguistic research on code-switching? I would like to make four points.

5 Crossing's relevance to research on code-switching

5.1 From switching between one's own languages to switching into other people's

As the previous section tried to make plain, language crossing seemed to be poised at the juncture of two competing notions of group belonging. On the one hand, crossing was a significant practice in the negotiation of an emergent sense of multiracial youth community. But at the same time, this sense of multiracial adolescent community was itself fragile, set around by ethnic absolutism, a powerful common sense in which Creole was Caribbean and Panjabi Panjabi, and it seemed to be this tension that generated the feeling of anomaly in language crossing, pressing it into the liminal margins of everyday interactional practice.

Interpreted in this way, language crossing represents a cultural dynamic that merits rather more attention in code-switching research than it has perhaps hitherto received.

In the past, studies of code-switching have generally tended to focus on the conduct of groups in which the use of two or more languages is a routine

expectation, either because people have grown up with a multilingual inheritance, or because they have moved into areas or institutions where the use
of additional languages is an unremarked necessity (e.g. Blom and Gumperz
1972; Gal 1989; Duran 1981; Grosjean 1983; Auer 1988; Romaine 1988;
cf. Woolard 1988: 69–70). Because of this emphasis on languages which
are unexceptional within the in-group, code-switching research has often
provided a rather restricted notion of ethnic processes, tending to focus only
on variation in the salience and cultural contents of ethnic categories, not
on ethnic *recategorisation*, on the exploration or adoption of alternative or
competing ethnicities. In a great deal of code-switching research (as indeed
in a lot of research on intercultural communication), participants are seen
as having a rather limited choice: (a) they can maintain and/or embrace and
cultivate the ethnicity they have inherited, or (b) they can de-emphasise or
abandon it, so that ethnicity drops from the repertoire of identities available
and meaningful to them. The study of language crossing throws light on a
further option: exploring other people's ethnicities, embracing them and/or
creating new ones (cf. Rampton 1995a: ch. 11.6; 1995b).

Although it isn't a major thematic interest in code-switching research,
there is in fact a growing number of studies which suggest that this third
kind of inter-ethnic process is very far from rare. Hewitt's (1986) study of
white Creole users in south London was an important precedent for my own
research, and in cultural studies and anthropology, it has also now been
followed by Jones (1988) and Back (1996). Elsewhere, broadly comparable
accounts of the intricate sociolinguistics of social and/or ethnic redefinition
have been produced by the Hills on Nahuatl and Spanish in Mexico (Hill
and Hill 1986; Hill and Coombs 1982), by Heller on French and English
in Canada (1988, 1992), by Woolard on Castilian and Catalan in Catalonia
(1988, 1989), and by Cheshire and Moser on English and French in
Switzerland (1994) (see also Haarmann 1989; Eastman and Stein 1993).
Many of the language practices involved in these inter-ethnic dynamics
are broadly aspirational, with the participants moving towards codes and
identities that are prestigious and powerful, at least within one or two sociolinguistic domains. But as in the data presented in section 2 above, the
multivalent processes of socio-symbolic repositioning involved in other-
language use extend much further than this, encompassing aversive
caricature, as in Secondary Foreigner Talk (Ferguson 1975; Valdman 1981;
Hinnenkamp 1984, 1987; Hill 1993, 1995), as well perhaps as the use of
varieties which people feel that they are losing in situations of advanced
language shift (cf. Mertz 1989 on Gaelic in Nova Scotia). The sense of
anomaly that I have proposed as a defining feature of language crossing
can also give rise to very different strategies of socio-symbolic alignment:
'passing', in which a person fabricates claims to a natural inheritance of
the language they are adopting (e.g. Hewitt 1986: 165, 195; Trosset 1986:
187–189 on second-language learners of Welsh; also Garfinkel 1984: 125,

300

136–137); 'refusal', in which people try to reject any involvement with a language close at hand (Hinnenkamp 1980; Heller 1992: 130–133); and also a great deal of meta-linguistic debate, play and commentary (e.g. Hill and Coombs 1982).

Indeed, there is one area of linguistic study where the empirical processes surrounding language crossing are absolutely central: Second Language Acquisition (SLA) research. There are however major differences between SLA and code-switching research in terms of perspective and analytic idiom, and before it could be brought to bear in any subtle and sensitive analysis of inter-ethnic processes, basic concepts and approaches in SLA research would need to be quite extensively refurbished. Generally speaking, SLA research is experimental, not ethnographic; it is concerned with acquisition, not socialisation (cf. Cook-Gumperz 1986: 55); and it focuses on assimiliation into dominant cultures, not resistance or the spread of minority ones.[10] The effect of any attempt to reconceptualise SLA along the lines of language crossing would be to place social boundary negotiation right at the heart of the second language learning process, and this would require analysis of the relationship between the groups on either side of a boundary, the boundary's strength and character, the wider processes maintaining or diminishing the boundaries, the bridge-building resources, the interests of participants in either getting to the other side or just peering across, and finally of course, the interactional practices with which this sensitivity to boundaries was inextricably entwined. The methodologies developed in code-switching research would be a vital resource in this endeavour, and Auer's descriptive apparatus looks like an especially valuable opening (1988). The practical outcomes from a reconfiguration of this kind could also be quite significant. As I have elaborated at some length, it seemed easiest for adolescents to use other languages in liminal moments when the hold of everyday assumptions was relaxed. How does this square with Communicative Language Teaching, which is still probably the prevailing orthodoxy in second-language pedagogy? The Communicative approach stresses the importance of authentic settings, real tasks, real audiences, and language functions drawn from everyday life – in other words, precisely the conditions that led adolescents to *avoid* the use of other languages in the peer group I investigated.

Those then are some observations which point to and advocate an extension in the empirical agenda of code-switching research, together with some (rather expansionist!) comments on SLA, a research paradigm that studies processes similar to language crossing through very different lenses. Rather than looking at or beyond the current boundaries of research on code-switching, the next three points address issues of conceptualisation within its heartlands.

5.2 The importance of 'metaphorical code-switching' (or 'double-voicing')

Language crossing clearly demonstrates the value of Gumperz's early distinction between situational and metaphorical code-switching (Blom and Gumperz 1972), and it allows the latter to be elaborated in terms of Bakhtin's notion of double-voicing.

The distinction between situational and metaphorical code-switching has been glossed in a number of ways. On the one hand, metaphorical switches have been characterised as typically brief and intra-sentential, initiating or 'bringing about' new contexts, while on the other, situational switches are often seen as larger, longer and responsively tied to contexts that are relatively fixed and 'brought along'. There are, however, at least three significant problems with these attempts to define the difference.

First, the recognition that *all* contexts are socio-cognitive constructs accomplished or at least ratified in interaction has been one major source of difficulty, since in one version of the distinction, only metaphorical switches are negotiated in interaction (cf. Auer 1984: 90–91). Second, the distinction between switches that initiate a new context and those that simply respond to prior changes in the situation (e.g. Bell 1984: 182–183) is difficult to maintain if proxemic communication is considered, since this often operates as a prelude to verbal action, 'enabling participants to both project and negotiate what is about to happen' (Duranti and Goodwin 1992: 7). In this context, a purely verbal recording can be misleading, and what looks like an initiation on audio-tape may actually be responding to contexts proposed on another semiotic level (cf. Auer 1992: 4–21). Third, the temptation to regard any brief, intra-sentential language switch as metaphorical (e.g. Fishman 1972: 42; Genishi 1981: 137; McLure 1981: 70; Gumperz 1982: 60–62, 98; Breitborde 1983: 10) ignores the fact that there are many occasions when the co-occurrence expectations constituting our sense of everyday reality are collectively suspended for quite substantial periods, and during these times the double-vision characteristic of metaphorical switching (see below) can be collaboratively sustained and elaborated by a number of participants. Indeed it may well be that certain groups of speakers participate in these kinds of 'metaphorical situation' more than others – adolescents being a case in point.

In view of difficulties such as these, Gumperz's earlier distinction has fallen into some disuse, being replaced instead by the catch-all term 'conversational code-switching' (Gumperz 1982: ch. 4; Auer 1984). Coming from the data on crossing, however, this seems premature, and in attempting to provide a more coherent account capable of rehabilitating the metaphorical/situational dichotomy, we can begin with the notion of violated co-occurrence expectations.

The notion of violated co-occurrence expectations does in fact already feature in Gumperz's definition of metaphorical code-switching (1982: 98), although there is at least one way in which it leaves the dichotomy equally opaque. In so far as all code-alternation involves a switch, establishing 'a contrast and thereby indicat[ing] that something new is going to come' (Auer 1992: 32), metaphorical and situational code-switching both involve a disruption of co-occurrence expectations. But if we shift our focus away from the code juxtaposition itself to the inferences that it generates, the notions of metaphor and violated expectation take us to the heart of language crossing.

In most of the cases that Auer describes, code-alternation would appear to elicit only rather limited amounts of inferential work. Once they have resolved the initial interruption to the contextual frames prevailing hitherto, participants find little to contradict their basic assumptions about orderly conduct. Recipients reconcile themselves to switches through the kinds of 'discourse-' and 'participant-related' interpretation that Auer proposes (1988), a new footing is initiated and the flow of unexceptional co-occurrence patterns can continue, albeit now in a slightly different gear. In contrast, language crossing involved a more fundamental contravention of routine expectations – it entailed a disjunction between speaker and code that couldn't be readily accommodated as a normal part of ordinary social reality (cf. section 4), and as such, it didn't allow participants to settle into the newly introduced contextual frame as an easy basis for routine interaction.

These cases allow us, then, to reformulate the situational/metaphorical code-switching distinction as follows:

- 'Situational' code-switching can be seen as a relatively routine contex-tualisation cue, in which speakers introduce (and recipients accept) a new but fairly familiar and accessible definition of the situation. In contrast,
- Metaphorical code-switching denies the recipient an easy footing for subsequent interaction. Like figurative language generally, it involves a violation of co-occurrence expectations which makes it difficult for recipients to end their search for meaning in the relatively neat solutions normally achieved with ordinary discourse; it instead requires them to run through a much more extensive set of possible inferences (Sperber 1975; Levinson 1983: 109), and it provides the recipient with no simple answer to the question 'What next?' (Auer 1988).

Language crossing's frequent contradiction of the 'world of daily life known in common with others and with others taken for granted' (Garfinkel 1984: 35) makes it primarily a form of metaphorical code-switching. Admittedly, using this dichotomy to classify empirical instances may well be difficult, but this is in fact no more than you would expect. As studies of dead and 'sleeping' metaphor make plain (e.g. Leech 1969; Lakoff and Johnson 1980), the distinction between the literal and the figurative, between the ordinary and the exceptional, is highly variable and often ambiguous. Seen as a form of metaphorical/figurative code-alternation, this was certainly the case with language crossing, especially with crossing into Creole.

While speaker and voice were quite easily differentiated with stylised Asian English (see the paragraph on vari-directional double-voicing below), this was often much harder when Creole was used, and here crossing looked much more towards their fusion into a new identity capable of holding an uncontested place in quotidian reality. A range of factors affected the extent to which crossers were able to project Creole as an authentic expression of their identity in acts of serious self-contextualisation – who the speaker and recipients were, what their relationship was, the degree of their involvement with black culture, the particular occasion, the specific contours of the character being claimed, and so forth (see Hewitt 1986: ch. 5; Rampton 1995a: chs 5, 8 and 9). In some exchanges, Creole only occurred in actions that were offered and taken as joking, while in others the same acts might be taken for real. But what was clear was that social reality, and the speaker's position within this, were the focus for some degree of interactional renegotiation, and if code-switching research is to address the potentially creative explorations of social order in which speakers sometimes engage, it needs to work with some version of a situational versus metaphorical distinction.

In fact, the contrast between Asian English and Creole suggests that Bakhtin's notion of double-voicing may be a useful way of starting to elaborate on the different forms that 'metaphorical' code-switching can take (cf. also Hill and Hill 1986). Double-voicing is a term that Bakhtin uses to describe the effect on the utterance of a plurality of often competing languages, discourses and voices. With double-voicing, speakers use someone else's discourse (or language) for their own purposes, 'inserting a new semantic intention into a discourse which already has ... an intention of its own. Such a discourse ... must be seen as belonging to someone else. In one discourse, two semantic intentions appear, two voices' (Bakhtin 1984: 189).

There are several kinds of double-voicing, and one of these is described as *uni-directional*. With uni-directional double-voicing, the speaker uses someone else's discourse 'in the direction of its own particular intentions' (1984: 193). Speakers themselves go along with the momentum of the second voice, though it generally retains an element of otherness which makes the appropriation conditional and introduces some reservation into the speaker's use of it. But at the same time, the boundary between the speaker and the voice they are adopting can diminish, to the extent that there is a 'fusion of voices'. When that happens, discourse ceases to be double-voiced, and instead becomes 'direct, unmediated discourse' (1984: 199).

Double-voicing in Creole generally seemed to be uni-directional. Creole was much more extensively integrated into multiracial peer group recreation than either stylised Asian English or Panjabi: it had no place in the school curriculum and it was used much more by members of ethnic out-groups. Creole symbolised an excitement and an excellence in youth culture that many adolescents aspired to, and it was even referred to as 'future language'. For a great deal of the time, there was certainly some reservation in the way Creole was used by whites and Asians, and this was most noticeable in the way that they generally avoided it in the presence of black peers. Even so, crossers tended to use Creole to lend emphasis to evaluations that synchronised with the identities they maintained in their ordinary speech, and in line with this, as Hewitt underlines, their Creole was often hard to disentangle from their local multiracial vernacular (Hewitt 1986: 148, 151). In Bakhtin's terms, crossing in Creole came close to the point where uni-directional double-voicing shifted over into direct unmediated discourse (for an illustration, see example 3 and the commentary that accompanies it).

The opposite of uni-directional double-voicing is *vari-directional* double-voicing, in which the speaker 'again speaks in someone else's discourse, but ... introduces into that discourse a semantic intention directly opposed to the original one'. In vari-directional double-voicing, the two voices are much more clearly demarcated, and they are not only distant but also opposed (Bakhtin 1984: 193). This often seemed to be the case with stylised Asian English. From interviews and other evidence, it was clear that Asian English stood for a stage of historical transition that most adolescents felt they were leaving behind, and in one way or another it consistently symbolised distance from the main currents of adolescent life. In line with this, stylised Asian English was often used as what Goffman calls a 'say-for' (1974: 535) – a voice not being claimed as part of the speaker's own identity but one that was relevant to the identity of the person being addressed or targetted (see example 4 and Rampton 1995a for many other examples).

Returning to Gumperz's work, it looks as though the uni-directional versus vari-directional distinction might actually be quite a useful way of distinguishing different kinds of metaphorical code-switching, although terminologically this comparison suggests (a) that it might be worth using 'figurative code-switching' as a broad label to contrast with 'situational switching', and then (b) using 'metaphorical' switching as a subdivision within 'figurative' switching.

According to Leech (1969), when people process metaphors, they work on the assumption that the figurative meaning is somehow complementary to the literal meaning. In contrast, the interpretation of irony works on the assumption that figurative and literal meaning are somehow in contrast/ opposition. Shifting over to bilingual language use, the element of complementarity in metaphor aligns it with uni-directional double-voicing, while the dimension of contrast in irony links into the vari-directional type. In sum, if one wanted to use the term metaphor in relation to code-switching, it might be best to regard it as a subtype of figurative code-switching, as in the following scheme:

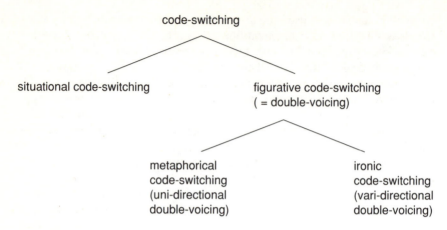

In this subsection and the last (5.1 and 5.2), I have suggested a need to repair two areas of relative neglect in code-switching research: first, an under-emphasis on cross-ethnic switching into out-group languages, and second, a movement away from metaphorical switching as an analytic concept. These two tendencies may in fact be linked. Both of them stress anomaly, incongruity and contradiction as central issues, and in doing so they perhaps don't fit in very easily with what has probably been the prevailing ethos in code-switching research.

5.3 Beyond competence, coherence and contextualisation

For the last twenty years or so, research on code-switching has waged war on deficit models of bilingualism and on pejorative views of syncretic language use by insisting on the integrity of language mixing and by examining it for its grammatical systematicity and pragmatic coherence. Achieving this emphasis on the integrity of code-switching has (a) required some explicit self-distancing from research on second-language acquisition, which is always likely to construe code-alternation as interference and incompetence (Gumperz 1982: 64–65). It has also been accomplished (particularly in work influenced by Gumperz) by (b) locating linguistic systems within a larger context of the semiotic resources and the sense-making procedures that interlocutors use in interaction: whether or not it conforms to the grammatical rules of some extra-linguistically defined community, 'there must be some regularities and shared perceptions' if code-switching operates smoothly in fluent conversation (Gumperz 1982: 70).

There is much to be said for both of these strategies in the understanding and legitimation of code-switching – as well as being morally worthwhile, they have been very well supported by empirical evidence. Nevertheless, the data on language crossing looks like something of a complication, and up to a point at least, it runs against the grain of both of these stances.

In the first place, language crossing frequently foregrounded second-language learning as an issue of active concern to participants themselves, both in the stereotype of a linguistically incompetent speaker of English quite often projected in stylised Asian English, and also in the play between instruction and deceit that constituted a lot of the pleasure in inter-group Panjabi in the playground.

In playground interaction among boys in early adolescence, for example, it was quite common for Panjabi bilinguals to invite monolingual friends of Anglo and African Caribbean descent either to say things in Panjabi, or to respond to Panjabi questions. These invitations to use another language normally contained elements which lay just beyond the learner's grasp, and the fact that an important element of what was being said to the second-language learner was incomprehensible to them was crucial, generating a great deal of the entertainment (see Rampton 1991: 230–234; 1995a: ch. 7). Learners had to operate just beyond the limits of their linguistic competence, and playfully speaking, their reputations depended on their performance. Here is an example.

EXAMPLE 5

Participants: Mohan (male 13 years, Indian descent, wearing a radio-microphone), Sukhbir (male, 13 years, Indian descent), Jagdish (male, 13, Indian), David (male, 12, African Caribbean), Pritam (male, Indian), others.
Setting: Breaktime outside. Mohan, Jagdish and David are best friends

---

	JAGDISH	((turning to David, speaking in Panjabi))
		[ə tu lɔrə di bʊn mʌregə]
		('DO YOU WANT TO BUM LAURA?')
	SUKHBIR	[ha ha ha ha ha
	OTHERS	[((laughter for about three seconds))
5	DAVID	no I don't think so
	JAGDISH	DAVID (.) no I said that- that means that you're-
		are you going to beat Laura up
	DAVID	no=
	SUKHBIR	=yeh it does, [it does (it does)
10	DAVID	((smile voice)) [that- that means [h] are you
		going to make her pregnant=
	SUKHBIR	=NO:: [( )
	MOHAN	[no

((a few moments later))

21	JAGDISH	SAY IT TO HIM (.) say it to him say it to him
		[say it to him [meɾi mãdi] ( )

('MY MUM'S FANNY')

```
        OTHERS    [((laughter))
        ANON      go on
25      DAVID     I [don't want to say that
        JAGDISH   [NO SAY IT TO HIM GO ON say it to him
        ANON      ha [ha ha ha ha
        ANON         [go on
        DAVID        [(it says- your go- )
30                it means that [MY mum's got a-
        JAGDISH                 [eh?
                  no say ((. . . the 'elicitations' continue))
```

Here, a minimal and unconfident knowledge of Panjabi was drawn into traditional playground practice, in variations on the verbal routines which the Opies describe as 'incrimination traps' (Opie and Opie 1959: ch. 4). Placed in situations of this kind, a number of strategies were available to an L2 Panjabi speaker aware of the insufficiency of their linguistic knowledge, and in this extract David's could be characterised as a knowing refusal. Another commonly used tactic was to ask a friend:

> 'my friend, you know, he swears in Panjabi to English girls, and they go and ask an Indian boy they know, and he tells them and tells them other words and they come and say it to us.'

Consultations of this kind were very commonly construed in pupil–teacher terms ('if they're our friends, we teach them it'), although as illustrated in the episode above, you'd be foolish to trust too much in the instruction that these provided:

> 'like Ishfaq tells . . . you know Alan Timms, if Alan Timms says "teach me some dirty words", Ishfaq makes him say swear words to himself ((laughs)), so he's saying it to hims . . . he goes up to Asif and he says it and Asif starts laughing.'

Particularly among 11 to 13 year old white and black boys, a high level of incompetence in Panjabi generated a range of entertaining recreational activities, and when asked, they said they wouldn't be interested in attending any formal Panjabi classes. They didn't want to improve their proficiency in Panjabi, and were evidently quite happy to remain permanently as pre-elementary language learners. The rudimentary Panjabi L2 learner was a significant and enjoyable local identity.

Following on from the way in which second-language learning was taken up as a salient issue for participants themselves, the evidence of language crossing also often controverted the way in which code-switching is most commonly seen as being coherently integrated into the communicative flow (see (b), p. 306). In the account given by Gumperz and Auer, code-switching contributes to the production and interpretation of meaning as a contextualisation cue, making relevant, maintaining, revising or cancelling any aspect of context which, in turn, is responsible for the interpretation of an utterance in its particular locus of occurrence (Auer 1992: 4). Here code-switching is closely integrated into the production of meaning, and it is one of a number of auxiliary elements skilfully but unobtrusively regulating the way in which the main content of an exchange is understood. Language crossing sometimes operated like this in what Goffman calls the 'directional track' (1974: ch. 7), but its position here was generally insecure – see Hewitt (1986: ch. 5), for example, on how white adolescents trying to use Creole sometimes had black peers 'laugh in their face' (1986: 169, 181). Instead, crossing often made code-switching a part of the 'main action' itself, an official focus of attention (see extract 5). Indeed, hauling code selection out of the directional track into the 'main action' was central to the denaturalisation of ethnicity that I've attributed to language crossing (sections 4 and 5.1 above). Rather than leaving ethnic resources as contextualisation cues shaping interaction doxically off-record and out-of-frame, crossing frequently turned ethnicity into a focal object of play, contemplation and dispute. This leads into the final point.

5.4 Not just conversation

Both to do justice to a great deal of empirical data and to help refute ideas about its oddity and deficiency, there has been a lot of emphasis on code-switching as a routine practice in everyday conversation. Increasingly, this characterisation of code-switching has been informed by Conversation Analysis (CA), itself an enormously valuable resource, making available techniques of analysis with an outstanding record in the discovery of order and skill in phenomena rejected by traditional linguistics. It is very important in code-switching research, however, to ensure that the governing notion of conversation is a broad one, encompassing not just 'politeness' (or preference organisation) but also play, ritualisation, and the interruption and suspension of routine reality production and maintenance. In the past, CA has been criticised for celebrating common sense and overemphasising harmonious cooperation (Thompson 1984: 115–118; Fairclough 1992: 19), and while there are now quite good grounds for questioning the validity of this characterisation,[11] it is vital that code-switching research operates with a notion of conversation that can accommodate a wide range of activities, including contradiction, deception and ideology critique.

From the perspective of research on language crossing, it seems particularly important not to conceptualise conversation as a genre distinct from stylisation and artful performance. As Bauman and Briggs stress, 'performances are not simply artful uses of language that stand apart both from

day-to-day life', and indeed, crucially, 'performances move the use of hetero-geneous stylistic resources, context-sensitive meanings, and conflicting ideologies into a reflexive arena where they can be examined critically . . ..
Performance . . . provides a frame that invites critical reflection on commu-nicative processes' (Bauman and Briggs 1990: 60).

All this seemed true in the performance of language crossing. First, crossing was often set off from ordinary talk with only the lightest change of 'key' (Goffman 1974: ch. 3), arising in spontaneous interaction in, for example, small-scale speech acts such as response cries, or in the vicinity of minor transgressions (see examples 3 and 4 above). And second, in the analysis sketched out in section 3 above, crossing also constituted a 'heretical' challenge to dominant notions of ethnolinguistic identity and inheritance (for elaborations, see Hewitt 1992; Rampton 1995a: ch. 12; 1995b).

With a refurbished notion of metaphorical code-switching (perhaps re-designated 'figurative'), and with a recognition that code changes can shift from simply being contextualisation cues to becoming the central focus of interaction, it seems unlikely that code-switching research will be impeded by a restricted view of conversation as routine. But to engage properly with the politics of language choice, to understand the ways in which code-switching might disrupt common-sense realities and initiate alternatives, it will also be necessary to look closely at genres which are at some points really quite far removed from everyday talk.

According to Bourdieu, if they are to be effective, challenges to dominant ways of seeing the world need to operate in more than local conversation:

> Heretical discourse must not only help to sever the adherence to the world of common sense by publicly proclaiming a break with the ordinary order, it must also produce a new common sense and integrate within it the previously tacit and repressed practices and experiences of an entire group, *investing them with the legiti-macy conferred by public expression and collective recognition.*
> (Bourdieu 1990: 129; emphases added)

As I pointed out in section 5.1, there is now a growing number of studies which show received ethnic categories being questioned and changed within local communities (Hewitt 1986; Gilroy 1987; Jones 1988; Back 1996), and in some cases this includes analysis of the micro-politics of daily interaction in terms that very obviously connect with my own account of language crossing. But in all of these studies, as well as in others (e.g. Woolard 1988, 1989), newly emergent inter-ethnic sensibilities gain crucial sustenance from artful public performances, particularly in popular music.[12]

Of course, code-switching performances to a large public need not lend their support only to new mixed communities. They can just as easily endorse race stratification and promote narrow and exclusive notions of ethnicity, as is evidenced in the literature on Secondary Foreigner Talk (see section 5.1 above). And in just the same way that positive models in the public media can impact on (broadly) conversational activity, negative representations generated by this kind of mass media code-switching can also interact with local practice in a variety of highly complex and unpredictable ways (cf. Rampton 1995a on stylised Asian English).

For code-switching research to overlook all these media representations and their interaction with everyday practice would be to risk an account that is as partial as those analyses of media discourse that neglect issues of local reception (Richardson 1994; Rampton 1996: 97–98). In the end, an exclusive dedication to conversation as the only empirical terrain could produce an analytic parochialism ill-tuned to the diaspora multilingualisms currently emerging in urban areas at the intersection of global and local (cf. Hewitt 1995; Hannerz 1989, 1990). With its eyes glued *only* to the properties of talk, research might end up waving an antiquated banner of holistic coherence at precisely the moment when the crucial values became transition and hybridity. Perhaps that is something of an overstatement, but at the very least, if academic research seeks to fulfil its potential as a way of helping to de-stigmatise vernacular practices, it needs to reckon with the forms of public legitimation and abuse that are most readily recognised by the people it is studying. Conversation is important, but it is not the only thing that people listen to.

Notes

I am very grateful to Peter Auer and the participants of the 1995 Hamburg Workshop on Conversational Code-Switching for valuable comments on an earlier draft of this chapter. The research reported here was generously supported by the Economic and Social Research Council (Grant no 00232390), the Leverhulme Trust and the British Association for Applied Linguistics.

1 In the ensuing extracts, transcription conventions are as follows:

[ ]	IPA phonetic transcription (1989 revision)
'	high stress
ˌ	low stress
،	low rise
:	lengthening
[	overlapping turns
=	two utterances closely connected without a noticeable overlap, or different parts of the single speaker's turn
(.)	pause of less than one second
-	break-off/unfinished word
(1.5)	approximate length of pause in seconds
p	piano/quietly
pp	very quietly
f	forte/loudly

ff	very loudly
CAPITALS	loud
(( ))	'stage directions', or comments
( )	speech inaudible
(text)	speech hard to discern, analyst's guess
italics	instance of crossing of central interest in discussion

Names have been altered.

2 In this peer group, ritual abuse was called 'blowing'.

3 According to Pomerantz, when speakers introduce an assessment into a conversation, there is an implicit invitation for recipients to respond with evaluations
of their own: 'A recipient of an initial assessment turns his or her attention to
that which was just assessed and proffers his or her own assessment of this
referent' (Pomerantz 1984: 62). In general, second assessments that agree

> are performed with a minimization of gap between the prior turn's
> completion and the agreement turn's initiation; disagreement compo-
> nents are frequently delayed within a turn or over a series of turns
> ... Absences of forthcoming agreements or disagreements by recip-
> ients, [absences realised with] gaps, requests for clarification and the
> like, are interpretable as instances of unstated, or as-yet-unstated,
> disagreements.
>
> (Pomerantz 1984: 65)

In lines 21 and 22, Sally makes a positive assessment of a Panjabi song (here
[uərtʃəti he]). But she elicits no response (marked by the micro-pause) and elaborates the evaluation on her own (*that's a good 'un as well (.) Imran likes that
one*). In fact, though, 'disagreement' doesn't adequately capture the way Gurmit
participates in this extract. In lines 3 and 18, Gurmit responds to Sally's first
(first) assessment by providing some information about the songs in question,
in a noticeably unenthusiastic lowered voice (*it's from Heera*). Here, she acts
as a source of knowledge rather than as a fellow *bhangra* fan, and her self-
positioning as an authority placed above the commitment of Sally and Anon.A
is made clearer in line 28 (*I better have a check*). Without (deigning to make)
any elaborate show of it, Gurmit also indicates her superior knowledge in line
20, and in combination with her refusal to engage in agreement, or indeed
explicit disagreement, her style of interaction continually suggests that her knowledge of *bhangra* places her own tastes in a different league from Sally and
Anon.A's, making it impossible for her to engage in any meaningful discussion
about likes and dislikes.

4 For example:

SALLY   that's a good 'un, that's a good 'un (.)
?   ((short quiet laugh)) (6.0)

SALLY   I love that tape (.) he brings it round my house and I listen to it

SALLY   it sounds English don' it (3.0)
ANON.A ( ) (.)
SALLY   it does dunnit a bit (.)

5 This certainly seemed to be the case in some of the longer pauses (e.g. line
32), and more generally, the girls' orientation to the music was clearly evidenced
in the way they used exophorically deictic *this* in lines 24, 28 and 31.

6 Sally's relatively hushed utterances in line 21 could be taken as an acceptance of these other claims on their involvement.

7 The symbol [ǀ] denotes the dental click.

8 'Liminality' is a concept developed by Victor Turner in particular, drawing on anthropological studies of initiation rites in tribal and agrarian societies. These rites have three phases: separation, in which initiands leave their childhood life behind; transition; and then incorporation, in which they are returned to new, relatively stable and well-defined positions in society, now a stage further on in life's cycle (Turner 1982: 24). Turner concentrates on the transitional middle phase, which he calls 'liminal':

> During the intervening phase of transition . . . the ritual subjects pass through a period and area of ambiguity, a sort of social limbo which has few . . . of the attributes of either the preceding or subsequent social statuses or cultural states . . . In liminality, [everyday] social relations may be discontinued, former rights and obligations are suspended, the social order may seem to have been turned upside down.
>
> (Turner 1982: 24, 27)

It is not possible to argue directly from this account of traditional ritual to the kinds of urban social relationship addressed in my own research. But Turner extends the notion of liminality into a form that fits more easily with practices common in industrial society, and he calls these 'liminoid' ('-oid' meaning 'like', 'resembling' but not identical). The distinction between liminal and liminoid can be hard to draw, but while, for example, liminal practices tend to contribute to the smooth functioning of social systems, liminoid practices are often creative, containing social critiques and exposing wrongs in mainstream structures and organisation (1982: 45). Similarly, liminality tends to involve symbols with common intellectual and emotional meaning for all members of the group, while 'liminoid phenomena tend to be more idiosyncratic, quirky, to be generated by specific named individuals and in particular groups' (1982: 54). For fuller discussion in the context of language crossing, see Rampton 1995a: ch. 7.9; in the context of 'new ethnicities', cf. Back 1996.

9 'We are beginning to see constructions of . . . a new conception of ethnicity: a new cultural politics which engages rather than suppresses difference and which depends, in part, on the cultural construction of new ethnic identities . . . What is involved is the splitting of the notion of ethnicity between, on the one hand the dominant notion which connects it to nation and "race" and on the other hand what I think is the beginning of a positive conception of the ethnicity of the margins, of the periphery . . . this is not an ethnicity which is doomed to survive, as Englishness was, only by marginalising, dispossessing, displacing and forgetting other ethnicities. This precisely is the ethnicity predicated on difference and diversity' (Hall 1988: 29).

10 The case against SLA research as it is most commonly practised requires much more elaboration than I can give it here. For further discussion, see Rampton 1987; 1991; 1995a: ch. 11.5; 1997; 1997b.

11 See Goodwin 1990 in particular. In fact, one can quite easily argue the converse case – that ideological discourse analyses need CA – and this can be seen even in a masterly study like Hill and Hill's account of Mexicano (1986). When Hill and Hill use the notion of double-voicing, they suggest that hesitations and dysfluencies around code-mixing reflect the fact that the utterance has become 'a translinguistic battlefield upon which two ways of speaking struggle for dominance' (1986: 392–393). It sounds here as though the speaker is an empty vessel,

and his or her strategic management of the relationship with the interlocutors is rather neglected. A more fully interactional account would need to consider the extent to which, for example, hesitations and dysfluency were in fact influenced by preference organisation – rather than being at the mercy of conflicting voices, these patterns might actually reflect the speaker's fully controlled display of the dispreferred status of the code-selection coming next.

12 In Britain, there are now a number of accounts of music which involves cross-ethnic code-switching between Creole, local vernacular English, Black American Vernacular, and/or Panjabi – see for example Gilroy 1987: 194–197; Hebdige 1987: 149–152; Jones 1988: 54–56; Back 1995, 1996: ch. 8. See also Rampton 1995a: Part IV.

Bibliography

Aalund, A. and Granqvist, R. (eds) (1995) *Negotiating Identities*, Amsterdam: Rodopi.

Alexander, J. (ed.) (1988) *Durkheimian Sociology: Cultural Studies,* Cambridge: Cambridge University Press.

Atkinson, M. and Heritage, J. (1984) *Structures of Social Action*, Cambridge: Cambridge University Press.

Auer, P. (1984) 'On the meaning of conversational code-switching', in Auer P. and di Luzio, A. (eds) *Interpretive Sociolinguistics: Migrants, Children, Migrant Children*, Tübingen, Germany: Gunter Narr Verlag: 87–112.

Auer, P. (1988) 'A conversation analytic approach to code-switching and transfer', in Heller, M. (ed.) *Code-switching: Anthropological and Sociolinguistic Perspectives*, Berlin: Mouton de Gruyter: 187–213.

Auer, P. (1992) 'Introduction: John Gumperz' approach to contextualisation', in Auer, P. and di Luzio, A. (eds) *The Contextualisation of Language*, Amsterdam: John Benjamins, 1–37.

Back, L. (1995) 'X among of Sat Siri Akal: Apache Indian, Reggae music, and intermezzo culture', in Aalund, A. and Granqvist, R. (eds) *Negotiating Identities*, Amsterdam: Rodopi: 139–166.

Back, L. (1996) *New Ethnicities and Urban Culture*, London: UCL Press.

Bakhtin, M. (1981) *The Dialogic Imagination*, Austin: University of Texas Press.

Bakhtin, M. (1984) *Problems in Dostoevsky's Poetics*, Minneapolis: University of Minnesota Press.

Bauman, R. and Briggs, C. (1990) 'Poetics and performance as critical perspectives on language and social life', *Annual Review of Anthropology* 19: 59–88.

Bell, A. (1984) 'Language style as audience design', *Language in Society* 13/2: 145–204.

Bernstein, B. (1975) 'Ritual in education', in *Class Codes and Control* III, London: Routledge and Keegan Paul: 54–66.

Bloch, M. (1985) 'Religion and ritual', in Kuper, A. and Kuper, J. (eds) *The Social Science Encyclopaedia*, London: Routledge: 698–701.

Blom, J. and Gumperz, J. (1972) 'Social meaning in linguistic structure: code-switching in Norway', in Gumperz, J. and Hymes, D. (eds) *Directions in Sociolinguistics*, Cambridge: Cambridge University Press: 407–434.

Bourdieu, P. (1977) *Outline of a Theory of Practice*, Cambridge: Cambridge University Press.

Bourdieu, P. (1990) *Language and Symbolic Power,* Oxford: Polity Press.

Breitborde, L. (1983) 'Levels of analysis in sociolinguistic explanation: bilingual code-switching, social relations and domain theory', *International Journal of the Sociology of Language* 39: 5–43.

Brown, P. and Levinson, S. (1987) [1978] *Politeness*, Cambridge: Cambridge University Press.

Cheshire, J. and Moser, L.-M. (1994) 'English as a cultural symbol: the case of advertisements in French-speaking Switzerland', *Journal of Multilingual and Multicultural Development* 15/6: 451–469.

Cook-Gumperz, J. (1986) 'Caught in a web of words: some considerations on language socialisation and language acquisition', in Cook-Gumperz, J., Corsaro, W. and Streeck, J. (eds): *Children's Worlds and Children's Language*, Berlin: Mouton de Gruyter: 37–64.

Cook-Gumperz, J., Corsaro, W. and Streeck, J. (eds) (1986) *Children's Worlds and Children's Language*, Berlin: Mouton de Gruyter.

Dorian, N. (ed.) (1989) *Investigating Obsolescence*, Cambridge: Cambridge University Press.

Duran, R. (ed.) (1981) *Latino Language and Communicative Behaviour*, Norwood, NJ: Ablex.

Duranti, A. and Goodwin, C. (1992) *Rethinking Context*, Cambridge: Cambridge University Press.

Eastman, C. and Stein, R. (1993) 'Language display: authenticating claims to social identity', *Journal of Multilingual and Multicultural Development* 14: 187–202.

Fairclough, N. (1992) *Discourse and Social Change,* Oxford: Polity Press.

Ferguson, C. (1975) 'Towards a characterisation of English foreigner talk', *Anthropological Linguistics* 17: 1–14.

Fishman, J. (1972) *The Sociology of Language*, Rowley: Newbury House.

Gal, S. (1989) 'Lexical Innovation and loss: the use and value of restricted Hungarian', in Dorian, N. (ed.) *Investigating Obsolescence*, Cambridge: Cambridge University Press: 313–331.

Garfinkel, H. (1984) [1967] *Studies in Ethnomethodology*, Oxford: Polity Press.

Genishi, C. (1981) 'Code-switching in Chicano six-year-olds', in Duran, R. (ed.) *Latino Language and Communicative Behaviour*, Norwood, NJ: Ablex: 133–152.

Gilroy, P. (1987) *There Ain't no Black in the Union Jack*, London: Hutchinson.

Goffman, E. (1967) *Interaction Ritual*, Harmondsworth, England: Penguin.

Goffman, E. (1971) *Relations in Public*, London: Allen Lane.

Goffman, E. (1974) *Frame Analysis,* Harmondsworth, England: Penguin.

Goffman, E. (1981) *Forms of Talk*, Oxford: Blackwell.

Goffman, E. (1983) 'The interaction order', *American Sociological Review* 48: 1–17.

Goodwin, M. H. (1990) *He-Said-She-Said*, Bloomington: Indiana University Press.

Goodwin, M. and Goodwin, C. (1987) 'Children's arguing', in Philips, S., Steele, S. and Tanz, C. (eds) *Language, Gender and Sex in Comparative Perspective*, Cambridge: Cambridge University Press: 200–248.

Grosjean, F. (1983) *Life with Two Languages*, Cambridge, Mass.: Harvard University Press.

Gumperz, J. (1982) *Discourse Strategies*, Cambridge: Cambridge University Press.

Gumperz, J. (ed.) (1982) *Language and Social Identity*, Cambridge: Cambridge University Press.

Haarmann, H. (1989) *Symbolic Values of Foreign Language Use*, Berlin: Mouton de Gruyter.

Hall, S. (1988) 'New ethnicities', *ICA Documents* 7: 27–31.

Hannerz, U. (1989) 'Culture between centre and periphery: towards a macroanthropology', *Ethnos* 54/3 and 4: 200–216.

Hannerz, U. (1990) 'Cosmopolitans and locals in world culture', *Theory, Culture and Society* 7: 237–251.

Hebdige, D. (1987) *Cut 'n' Mix: Culture, Identity and Caribbean Music*, London: Comedia.

Heller, M. (1988) 'Strategic ambiguity: code-switching in the management of conflict', in Heller, M. (ed.) *Code-Switching: Anthropological and Sociolinguistic Perspectives*, The Hague: Mouton de Gruyter, 77–96.

Heller, M. (ed.) (1988) *Code-Switching: Anthropological and Sociolinguistic Perspectives*, The Hague: Mouton de Gruyter.

Heller, M. (1992) 'The politics of code-switching and language choice', *Journal of Multilingual and Multicultural Development* 13:1, 123–142.

Hewitt, R. (1986) *White Talk Black Talk*, Cambridge: Cambridge University Press.

Hewitt, R. (1992) 'Language, youth and the destabilisation of ethnicity', in Palmgren, C., Lovgren, K. and Bolin, G. (eds) *Ethnicity in Youth Culture*, Stockholm: Youth Culture at Stockholm University, 27–42.

Hewitt, R. (1995) 'The umbrella and the sewing machine: trans-culturalism and the definition of surrealism', in Aalund, A. and Granqvist, R. (eds) *Negotiating Identities*, Amsterdam: Rodopi, 91–104.

Hill, J. (1993) 'Hasta la vista, baby: Anglo Spanish in the American Southwest', *Critique of Anthropology* 13, 145–176.

Hill, J. (1995) 'Junk Spanish, covert racism, and the (leaky) boundary between public and private spheres', *Pragmatics* 5/2, 197–212.

Hill, J. and Coombs, D. (1982) 'The vernacular remodelling of national and international languages', *Applied Linguistics* 3, 224–234.

Hill, J. and Hill, K. (1986) *Speaking Mexicano: The Dynamics of Syncretic Language in Central Mexico*, Tucson: University of Arizona Press.

Hinnenkamp, V. (1980) 'The refusal of second language learning in interethnic contexts', in Giles, H., Robinson, P. and Smith, P. (eds) *Language: Social Psychological Perspectives*, Oxford: Pergamon, 179–184.

Hinnenkamp, V. (1984) 'Eyewitnessing pidginisation? Structural and sociolinguistic aspects of German and Turkish Foreigner Talk', *York Papers in Linguistics* 11, 153–166.

Hinnenkamp, V. (1987) 'Foreigner talk, code-switching and the concept of trouble', in Knapp, K., Enninger, W. and Knapp-Potthof, A. (eds) *Analysing Intercultural Communication*, Amsterdam: Mouton de Gruyter, 137–180.

Jones, S. (1988) *Black Culture White Youth*, Basingstoke, England: Macmillan.

Kasper, G. and Kellerman, E. (eds) (1997) *Advances in Communication Strategy Research*, London: Longman.

Labov, W. (1972) *Language in the Inner City*, Oxford: Blackwell.

Lakoff, G. and Johnson, M. (1980) *Metaphors We Live By*, Chicago, Ill.: Chicago University Press.

Laver, J. (1975) 'Communicative functions of phatic communion', in Kendon, A., Harris, R. and Key, M. R. (eds) *Organisation of Behaviour in Face-to-Face Interaction*, The Hague: Mouton, 215–238.

Laver, J. (1981) 'Linguistic routines and politeness in greeting and parting', in Coulmas, F. (ed.) *Conversational Routine*, The Hague: Mouton, 289–304.

Leech, G. (1969) *A Linguistic Guide to English Poetry*, London: Longman.

Levinson, S. (1983) *Pragmatics*, Cambridge: Cambridge University Press.

McLure, E. (1981) 'Formal and functional aspects of the code-switched discourse of bilingual children', in Duran, (ed.) *Latino Language and Communicative Behaviour*, Norwood, NJ, Ablex, 69–94

Mertz, E. (1989) 'Sociolinguistic creativity: Cape Breton Gaelic's linguistic tip', in Dorian, N. (ed.) *Investigating Obsolescence*, Cambridge: Cambridge University Press, 103–116.

Opie, I. and Opie, P. (1959) *The Lore and Language of Schoolchildren*, Oxford: Oxford University Press.

Pomerantz, A. (1984) 'Agreeing and disagreeing with assessments: some features of preferred/dispreferred turn shapes', in Atkinson, M. and Heritage, J. (eds) *Structures of Social Action*, Cambridge: Cambridge University Press: 57–101.

Rampton, B. (1987) 'Stylistic variability and not speaking "normal" English', in Ellis, R. (ed.) *Second Language Acquisition in Context,* Englewood Cliffs: Prentice Hall, 47–58.

Rampton, B. (1991) 'Second language learners in a stratified multilingual setting', *Applied Linguistics* 12/3: 229–248.

Rampton, B. (1995a) *Crossing: Language and Ethnicity among Adolescents*, London: Longman.

Rampton, B. (1995b) 'Language crossing and the problematisation of ethnicity and socialisation', *Pragmatics* 5/4, 485–514.

Rampton, B. (1996) 'Crossing: language across ethnic boundaries', in Coleman, H. and Cameron, L. (eds) *Change and Language*, Clevedon, England: Multilingual Matters: 89–102.

Rampton, B. (1997a) 'A sociolinguistic perspective on L2 communication strategies', in Kasper, G. and Kellerman, E. (eds) *Advances in Communication Strategy Research*, London: Longman, 279–303.

Rampton, B. (1997b) 'Second language learning in late modernity', *Modern Language Journal* 81, 329–33.

Richardson, K. (1994) 'Interpreting "Breadline Britain"', in Meinhof, U. and Richardson, K. (eds) *Text, Discourse and Context: Representations of Poverty in Britain*, London: Longman: 93–121.

Romaine, S. (1988) *Bilingualism*, Oxford: Blackwell.

Sebba, M. (1993) *London Jamaican: A Case Study in Language Interaction*, London: Longman.

Shuman, A. (1993) '"Get outa my face": Entitlement and authoritative discourse', in Hill, J. and Irvine, J. (eds) *Responsibility and Evidence in Oral Discourse*, Cambridge: Cambridge University Press: 135–160.

Sperber, D. (1975) *Rethinking Symbolism*, Cambridge: Cambridge University Press.

Sperber, D. and Wilson, D. (1986) *Relevance*, Oxford: Blackwell.

Sutton-Smith, B. (1982) 'A performance theory of peer relations', in Borman, K. (ed.) *The Social Life of Children in a Changing Society*, Norwood, NJ: Ablex: 65–77.

Thompson, J. (1984) *Studies in the Theory of Ideology*, Oxford: Polity Press.

Trosset, C. (1986) 'The social identity of Welsh learners', *Language in Society* 15/2: 165–192.

Turner, V. (1982) 'Liminal to liminoid in play, flow and ritual', in *From Ritual to Theatre: The Human Seriousness of Play*, New York: PAJ: 20–60.

Valdes, G. (1981) 'Code-switching as a deliberate verbal strategy: a microanalysis of direct and indirect requests among bilingual Chicano speakers', in Duran, R. (ed.) *Latino Language and Communicative Behaviour*, Norwood NJ: Ablex: 95–108.

Valdman, A. (1981) 'Sociolinguistic aspects of foreigner talk', *International Journal of the Sociology of Language* 28: 41–52.

Wells, J. (1982) *Accents of English*, 1–3, Cambridge: Cambridge University Press.

Woolard, K. (1988) 'Code-switching and comedy in Catalonia', in Heller, M. (ed.) *Code-Switching: Anthropological and Sociolinguistic Perspectives*, The Hague: Mouton de Gruyter: 53–76.

Woolard, K. (1989) *Double Talk*, Stanford, Calif.: Stanford University Press.

INTRODUCTION TO CHAPTER 13

Peter Auer

The final chapter of this volume takes us to the very periphery of our Eurocentric world, namely to Papua New Guinea, but also, as Christopher Stroud argues, to the very periphery of what can be accounted for in code-switching within Western sociolinguistic frameworks centred around notions such as 'agency, action, identity and social role' (p. 340).

The following analysis of code-switching between Tok Pisin and Taiap in a particular antagonistic speech genre, that of the *kros*, must be seen against the background of the enormous language shift which New Guinea has undergone, particularly since World War II. According to estimates by Sankoff (1980), Papua New Guinea is an area in which some 760 languages are spoken, 35 per cent of which have fewer than 500 speakers. These languages were able to co-exist for a long time not because their speakers had little or no contact with each other, but because of a linguistic ideology which fostered multilingualism and in which language was seen as 'highly salient marker of group identity' (Kulick 1992: 2). However, both multi-lingualism and linguistic divergence for boundary markers as the two main driving forces responsible for the traditional sociolinguistic situation were weakened by the emergence of Tok Pisin as the lingua franca used on the plantations that were founded in the coastal areas under German and later Australian rule. Since men from the New Guinea villages were recruited as labourers for the plantations from the turn of the century onwards, the new variety, which was generally looked upon as the language of the white people, was brought back into the villages by the returning labourers where it enjoyed the same prestige as many other artifacts of the newly encountered world of the whites.

The story of how Tok Pisin arrived in Papua New Guinea is told by Kulick (1992: 66ff.) in his fascinating book on the small village of Gapun off the northern coast. The high symbolic value of Tok Pisin in Gapun today can be explained only by its association with the traditional concept of *save*, that part of self which comprises the values of collectivism, masculinity, adultness and goodness, whereas the opposite concept of *hed*, which comprises individualism, femininity, childishness and badness, is linked to the indigenous language Taiap. Kulick (1992: 20) summarises the status of Tok Pisin and Taiap as follows:

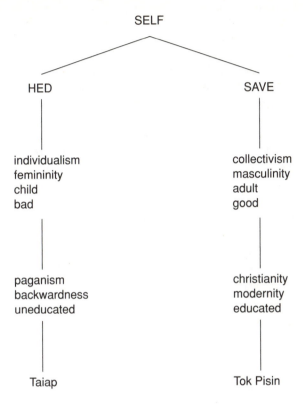

In this context of values and connotations, multilingualism tends to be replaced by monolingualism in Tok Pisin, the language of *save*, and linguistic divergence by convergence, such that the children in Gapun grow up mono-lingual in Tok Pisin. Not surprisingly, men use Tok Pisin more than women, and they are also less multilingual.

Against this background, Stroud analyses code-switching in a female speaker's *kros*. In general, code-switching in Gapun presents features well known from other bilingual contexts; in fact, the Gapuners' sensitivity to the co-participant's language preferences and their tendency to accommodate them, as well as their skilful rhetorical usage of code-switching as a resource (Kulick 1992: 74ff.) clearly place this community on the code-switching pole of the continuum outlined in the Introduction, and support a univer-salistic approach to bilingual conversational interaction. However, Stroud argues convincingly that in the monological speech genre of the *kros*, describing code-switching as discourse-related does not nearly tell the whole story.

As many other contributors to this volume, Stroud considers the we-code/they-code distinction to be 'at best a contextually specific one' (p. 335). Similar to Rampton in the previous chapter, Stroud prefers Bakhtin/ Voloshinov's notion of double-voicing/polyphony, not in the least because it allows incorporating into analysis a considerable amount of opaqueness which is central to the Gapuners' language ideology. Thus, because the speaker uses code-switching as a double-voicing technique, it remains unclear in the *kros* how much of what she says are her own words and what is an echo of others' speech. In addition, the distinction between *save* and *hed* comes into play. Since the *kros* is a genre associated with femininity (and therefore with Taiap and *hed*), the speaker's switching into Tok Pisin crosses a border: it claims for this female *kros*er the values of *save* (associated with Tok Pisin and masculinity) and breaks up traditional gender roles.

Bibliography

Kulick, Don (1992) *Language Shift and Cultural Reproduction*, Cambridge: Cambridge University Press.

Sankoff, Gillian (1980) *The Social Life of Language*, Philadelphia: University of Pennsylvania Press.

13

PERSPECTIVES ON CULTURAL VARIABILITY OF DISCOURSE AND SOME IMPLICATIONS FOR CODE-SWITCHING

Christopher Stroud

1 Introduction

In recent years, research interest in conversational code-switching has increasingly come to focus on generating accounts of the pragmatic and expressive meanings carried by switches. Although the diversity in approach and theory is enormous among those studies that have grappled with this problem, the bulk of the research can nevertheless, given a certain 'poetic license', be broken down into two main approaches. On the one hand, we find authors such as Gumperz (1982), Heller (1988) Hill and Hill (1986), and Myers-Scotton (1993). On the other hand, we find authors such as Auer (1991), Li Wei (1994) and Moerman (1988).

Characteristic for the first group of researchers is that they would all basically subscribe to some form of the view that the social meanings of conversational code-switches are carried by a set of social categories 'metaphorically symbolized by particular languages' (McConvell 1994: 8). Gumperz, for example, sees 'languages in a bilingual environment as inevitably expressing meanings of either solidarity, informality and compassion (the in-group or *we-code),* or formality, stiffness and distance (the out-group or *they-code)*' (Gumperz 1982: 66). What speakers do when they switch is to juxtapose the *we-code* and the *they-code,* and the code-switches serve to index the associations or identities linked to each code. By knowing the details of the local *we–they* situation, the intention and meanings of the switches can be extrapolated by listeners and researchers perceiving the switch (Stroud 1992: 132). The associations to each code contribute to the rhetorical and stylistic effects of the code-switch, which may range from signalling a distinction between direct and reported speech, to clarifying and emphasizing a message, to code-switched iteration, to qualifying a message or to signalling the degree of speaker involvement in the talk.

The assumption that members of bilingual speech communities attach different rights, identities and obligations to each of their languages is at the heart of the sociolinguistic accounts that Myers-Scotton, Heller, and McConvell give for conversational code-switching. For these authors, speakers who code-switch are seen as appealing to the rights, obligations and identities associated with each language. In this way, code-switching is socially meaningful. From these accounts, conversational code-switching comes across as pretty much the same animal in any cultural habitat. McConvell would claim that this 'is in line with the fundamental insight that code-switching functions similarly throughout the world' (1994: 8).

The second group of researchers, those who practice conversation analysis (CA), question the *primacy* of macrostructural or societal contributions to the social meanings of code-switching, that particular languages stand as metaphors for, and see the meanings of code-switching as emerging out of the sequential and negotiated development of conversational interaction. The meaning of any particular code-switch can only legitimately be ascertained in the context of conversational interaction, as the variety of social meanings of code-switching that interactants produce are generated *in situ*, and are 'genuine' meanings only in so far as participants attend to them structurally in their orderly co-construction of sense. In keeping with this insight, CA approaches doubt the possibility of constructing exhaustive typologies of code-switching, claiming that, like other conversational strategies, the meanings carried by code-switching are negotiated in the actual context in which they occur. Embedding code-switching in the microdynamics of conversational interaction, and asking how participants attend structurally to code-switched utterances, permits an analysis of how a *variety* of social meanings are generated by interactants in the process of an orderly linguistic co-construction of contingent social structures.

Both these accounts as they stand fall short of satisfactorily managing the ways in which code-switching may be used in (non-Western), culturally very divergent multilingual societies, and therefore also fail to account for conversational code-switching as a phenomenon. My argument is that conversational code-switching is so heavily implicated in social life that it cannot really be understood apart from an understanding of social phenomena. One implication of this is that we need to develop an approach to code-switching which integrates the analysis of language use and social action. In this chapter, I will therefore explore the role of language and code-switching as central material symbolic elements of social action in the fabrication of social orders. I will focus on how speakers through language enact, create, elaborate and reproduce culturally relevant constructs of personhood, gender, knowledge and socialization (cf. Schieffelin 1979, 1986, Ochs 1988, Merlan and Rumsey 1991), stressing how language use and patterns of code-switching both structure and are structured by indigenous cultural practices. More specifically, I will argue that attention to indigenous conceptions of action/event framed within social structures, and attention to sociocultural ideologies of language, that is, as 'mediating links between social structures and forms of talk' (Woolard 1992: 235), permit an alternative account not only of language use in general but of code-switching in particular.

The conclusion of the chapter will be that studies of conversational code-switching need to be framed within an ethnographic perspective which attends to details in how people perceive their lives, as well as in an understanding of societal dynamics. The ethnographical framing needs to be wedded to a detailed analysis of conversational microinteraction and viewed against the background of a broad notion of context. In other words, conversational code-switching is so heavily implicated in social life that it cannot be treated apart from an analysis of social phenomena.

The data which will accompany and illustrate this argument come from code-switching interactions found in the Papua New Guinean village of Gapun, in particular the speech genre *kros*. Gapun is particularly interesting in respect to issues of code-switching. Not only do villagers code-switch extensively but they do so within the framework of social structures and ethnographies radically different from those to which we are accustomed in mainstream Western discourse.

2 The sociocultural context: the village of Gapun

The village of Gapun is located about ten kilometres from the northern coast of Papua New Guinea (PNG), roughly midway between the Sepik and Ramu rivers, and has a population of between 90 and 110 inhabitants. It is a small, isolated village – even by Papuan standards embedded in rainforest and sago swamps with a negligible in- and out-migration, unruffled by the processes of accelerating urbanization and rampant industrialization otherwise characteristic of many parts of PNG. Gapuners are marginally involved in non-local market economics, and have only sporadic contact with neighbouring communities. In the late 1980s, they were more or less completely self-supporting by means of swidden agriculture, hunting and sago-processing.

Older village men and women are highly multilingual in *Tok Pisin*, the local lingua franca and one of the three national languages of PNG; *Taiap*, the local vernacular of Papuan stock; and a variety of neighbouring languages such as *Kopar*, *Adjora* and *Watam*. The generation of men and women between 14 and 20 years of age have an active, speaking mastery of Taiap and Tok Pisin only, and no village child under the age of 14 has anything but a spoken competence in Tok Pisin. The reason for this state of affairs is that Gapun is rapidly, and, considering its sociodemographic characteristics, somewhat surprisingly, undergoing a process of language shift which will soon leave Tok Pisin the only major language spoken in the village.

323

(For an extended treatment of language shift in Gapun, see Kulick 1992a.) Since it was introduced into the village at the turn of the century, Tok Pisin has increasingly come to encroach upon more and more domains and to assume functions and values traditionally associated with Papuan vernaculars. Despite this, there is as yet no single functional or social domain where talk is conducted *exclusively* in Tok Pisin, with the exception of religious discourse.[1]

Like the majority of societies on mainland New Guinea, Gapun is characterized by a social structure that is generally referred to in the anthropological literature as egalitarian. This term is usually taken to mean that societies characterized in this way are not organized into hierarchically ordered groups or classes which perpetuate themselves over time. Also, so-called egalitarian societies in Melanesia have no 'chiefs' who rule over others and pass on their power to rule to their offspring. In Gapun, there are no leaders in the ordinary sense of the word. There are *bikmen*, but such men are 'big' only in the sense that they are mature (usually over 45 years of age) and because they have esoteric knowledge and forceful personalities. There are no hereditary or structural underpinnings to the influence of these 'big men', and people listen to them only to the extent that they choose to.

Language use in the village, and the ways in which villagers discourse about language, are very much bound up with local ideologies of self, social presentation and knowledge (see Kulick 1992a). Gapuners distinguish two facets of personhood or self-conception, *hed* and *save* (cf. Kulick 1992a). In essence, *hed* is more or less equivalent to individual will, also covering notions of individualistic, selfish, stubborn, proud and anti-social aspects of personality. When villagers in certain situations emphasize their personal autonomy, it is *hed* that is being articulated. In the village, *hed* is frequently viewed negatively. It is associated with belligerent young children and aggressive and strifeful women.

Save, on the other hand, is knowledge, social knowledge, that is the ability to conduct oneself appropriately, knowledge of and sensitivity to social roles and obligations, and an awareness of the consequences of one's actions. This facet of self is continually being elaborated in village talk and action. The connotations that villagers have to *save* are, not surprisingly, connotations of maturity, maleness and solidarity. Villagers credit each other with *save* when their actions can be accounted for within a consensually derived interpretive framework, and bikmen are particularly skilled at making their actions seem to be for the general good of all. *Save* is to all intents and purposes the legitimate social construction of agency or actorhood. A person displays *hediness*, on the other hand, when his or her actions are only 'individually' motivated, perhaps even going totally against the grain of social consensus.

The negative view of the 'unsolicited' expression of personal autonomy entertained by Gapuners, and the care that villagers must take to display *save* and manage their interactions with others so as to meet with social consensus and approval, contributes significantly to how language is used in the village to structure and constrain sensitive interpersonal interactions. To lessen the potential for confrontation, conflict and provocation that the making of a request may entail, for example, Gapuners have developed the linguistic and pragmatic means of performing some speech events in ways that cannot easily be interpreted as infringements or demands. They embed their requests in a mass of talk, which emphasize that compliance is not necessary at all. Often, the requests will be 'hidden', couched discreetly 'behind' or 'underneath' words which on the surface have another meaning entirely. Because any request may be interpreted as 'giving *hed*' to another person, speakers also rely on disassociating strategies through which they distance themselves from what they are producing by continually retracting it as they develop it. And, finally, villagers are careful to use language that portrays them as non-threatening, humble and self-effacing. Importantly, requests are characteristically done in highly interactive, co-constructed sequences of utterances, containing abundant self- and other-initiated 'repairs', insertion sequences and pre-sequences. These are all conversational strategies designed to relieve the speaker of the need to be explicit, and, simultaneously, serve to co-opt the interactant into 'recognizing' the needs of the speaker and perhaps even going so far as to formulate the request himself or herself (see Besnier 1989 for a remarkably similar account of the structure of gossip in Nukalaelae).

3 A genre of anger and self assertion: the *kros*

Given the potentially explosive and highly fragile social context in which Gapuners live, the local village speech genre, the *kros*, is both a social anomaly and a natural reaction. A *kros* is a shockingly vivid and volatile genre that traffics in abuse, vulgarity and accusation. It often takes the form of a single person, frequently a lone woman, standing in her house and broadcasting across the village a stream of insults and accusations directed towards some other villager by whom she has felt wronged or provoked. The purpose of the *kros* is to publicly proclaim anger, conflict and critique, and it is the most important way for villagers to protest against what they perceive to be infringements of their autonomy. *Kroses* distribute blame, elicit sympathies and judgements from other villagers, and are occasions for legitimate self-display and assertion on behalf of the *kroser*, something which is underscored by the fact that the victim of the *kros* need not even be present at the event.

Reasons for starting a *kros* are many and diverse. What they all have in common are concerns with provocation and causality. When a Gapuner is witness to some event, action or state of affairs, she or he is not only concerned with revealing the extent of its meaningfulness or significance, but is also concerned with discovering its agency. Villagers search for explanations of changes and events by contextualizing them in all types of social relationships. The actions of other people have from the perspective of the individual

> the potential to infringe directly and potentially fatally on the self, on one's health (if my sister's son steals betel nut from an old man with knowledge of sorcery then I may be killed), one's crops (a young woman entering my newly planted garden will cause my tobacco to be devoured by insects and my yams not to grow) . . .
>
> (Kulick 1992a: 106)

A *kros*, then, is addressed to some person who the *kroser* has reason to believe has wronged him or her, and importantly the *kroser* is being *made* to *kros*, or is *obliged* to *kros*, because of the actions of the other to which the *kroser* has been subjected. In principle, the *kros* person need have no bad or egoistical intention or purpose behind the initiation of a *kros* – the *kros* itself is firmly rooted in a malevolent social relationship, not in individual *hedidness*, despite the high level of self-assertion proclaimed in the genre. In fact, it is important that the *kroser*, even in anger, asserts himself or herself as legitimately angry.

A *kros* demands a great deal of verbal skill in order to be well attuned. Although many voices may syncopate in a *kros*, they do not engage with each other. *Kroses* are performed as a (set) of monologue(s). At no point in the *kros* should the contrahents engage in any type of dialogue, unless their intention is to escalate the level of conflict to physical fighting. Comments, asides and responses that nevertheless do appear from the mouth of the *krosed* are invariably used as templates for the formulation of a sarcastic or ironic contribution which adds further insult, injury and escalation to the *kros*. Typical rhetorical strategies used in *kroses* are rhetorical questions, irony/sarcasm, repetition, contrast/contradiction and code-switching.

Kulick (1993), in an incisive exploration of how speakers use language to create gendered positions, argues that the conflict talk and oppositional moves that constitute *kroses* in Gapun serve to discursively construct gendered voices as male and female. This is accomplished through an association in village rhetoric between conflict talk and the female voice. He claims that

> . . . kroses are one of the major sites of gender negotiation in Gapun, where women define themselves, their rights and expectations by declaring publicly that these have been violated and where they assertively and artfully counter talk, often by men, that they

'shut up.' In kroses, women lay claim not only to specific female identities, but . . . women purposely counterpose those female positions with ones they assert are male.

(Kulick 1993: 512–513)

This 'interaction' between discourses of gender, affect and language is reinforced and sustained through specific linguistic practices. These practices centre around positioning men and women in different and opposing relationships to those institutions and values that everybody agrees are important, namely Christianity, modernity and civilization (Kulick 1992b: 282ff.). In this context, Kulick illustrates how the men's house oratories are significantly different from *kroses*. Even though oratories may also deal with topics of anger, this is done in co-operative sequences of talk where speakers collaboratively 'weave together their words to reframe anger as not-anger' (291), and where the resolution to the talk frequently reaches consensus. Men thus display and enact civilized and Christian values. Listing a number of dimensions that differentiate between *kroses* and oratories, Kulick summarizes thus: Women's linguistic practices for dealing with anger are in almost every way inversions of men's practices. *Kroses* are instances of self-display. *Krosers* do not seek closure or resolution; there is no format tying between turns, which are produced as monologues, no overt dialogue, and the *kros* is thick with vulgar obscenities and personal insults. Perhaps one of the most interesting claims that Kulick makes is that the links that exist in villagers' discourse between gender, the expression of anger and particular linguistic practices is one reason why Tok Pisin is rapidly ousting Taiap as the unmarked, everyday choice of language. 'Powered by its links with women and the associations bound up with stereotypes of them, it seems likely that the Taiap language itself will come to be associated with negatively valued aspects of life such as affective access, discursive irresponsibility and dangerous knowledge' (294).

In the present analysis of code-switching in *kroses*, I will take up and develop some the insights suggested by Kulick in his work. Specifically, I will argue that the genre of the *kros* is indeed a powerful discursive context for negotiation of gender roles, knowledge and affect, as Kulick proposes. However, I will also attempt to develop the point Kulick makes that women are contesting the roles assigned to them, and I will show that one subtle semiotic means whereby they are accomplishing this is by way of appropriating styles of speaking that have hitherto remained the sole prerogative of men. In other words, women are renegotiating or transforming traditional gender roles by the skilful use and juxtaposition of Taiap and Tok Pisin. In the process, they are also revalorizing language in that they are creating new gendered linkages between affect, knowledge and Tok Pisin. The following section will explore how this is accomplished in more detail.

4 Sake's *kros*

4. 1 Performing a kros

One late evening at 22.00 hours, the silence of the night was broken by
Sake, the daughter of *bikmen* Kruni, screaming out a *kros*. The *kros* seemed
to have been ignited by the incessant crying of the baby daughter of Sake's
sister Jari, and by the further vexation that Jari was nowhere to be found
when called upon to attend the child. This prime material gave rise to a
kros, in which Sake herself, the mother of Sake, Sombang, and *bikmen*
Kruni participated. What we will be specifically focusing on here is the way
in which Sake uses code-switching in this genre, and we will discuss how
code-switching functions to reproduce the gendered, social category of *kros*
in a novel way.[2]

	SAKE	*Where are you walking around looking for cock?*
		Where are you walking around looking for cock?
		It's time to sleep.
		There's no noise in the village, everyone's sleeping.
5		*Enough.*
		This manner of yours, stop it.
	SOMBANG	*I'm sick of this. not being able to sleep.*
		I'm sick of it.
	KRUNI	*If I come down* ((from the men's house)), *she's gonna*
		bugger up.
10	SAKE	Bloody idiot bastard you.
		You Jari are gonna do this, if you're gonna come here ((to
		the house))
		you better think twice when you come down.
		You're gonna get knocked down good.
		((Jari arrives))
	SOMBANG	*You don't have something?*
15		*You don't have a baby?*
		You're out walking around like you don't.
		Who are you prowling around for?
	SAKE	*I'm telling you here you're really gonna die.*
		You bring your head up this step.
20		That head of yours is gonna get broken in two.
	JARI	*We were walking around looking for something.*
		We weren't prowling around to fuck.
	KRUNI	This manner of yours
		You're doing good things.
25	SAKE	*What are you prowling around for?*
		You go and stay up there.

		You don't have a baby?
		You don't have a baby so you go and stay up there, ah?
	SOMBANG	*Why did you go and stay away?*
30	SAKE	Why did you go and stay away for such a long time up there?
		What kind of story were you telling?
	SOMBANG	*What were you up there for?*
	SAKE	*What kind of talk/story were you up there telling?*
		Bloody no good stinking nose of yours, it's rotted away.
35	SOMBANG	*Prowl around for this ((i.e. sex)).*
		I'm sick of it.
		I'm sick of it.
	KRUNI	*This kind ((of woman)), hit her upside the head.*
		When she tastes blood, she'll understand.
40	SOMBANG	*You alone ...*
		Who's wife were you walking around with? ((sarcastic)).
		Enough.
	SAKE	*Is she a child who stays at home?*
		Is she a child who stays at home?
45		*What were you prowling around for?*
	SOMBANG	*You don't have any responsibilities.*
		You, just prowl around for this ((sex)).
		Enough.
		You, I have lots of nasty words.
50		*I'm gonna start cursing at you now.*
	SAKE	*Why did you go up and stay up there? Ah?*
		Why did you go and stay up there?
	SOMBANG	Hold him ((the baby)).
		I'm sick of it.
55		Sick *of it.*
	SAKE	*Who's the woman who stays here and gets a pain in her mouth?*
		You always go away.
		My mouth pains bad from shouting for you.
		You don't have a baby?
60		You're a single woman, ah?
		You should prowl around like that?
		Mine.
		My mouth is really stinking here ((with curses)).
		I'm going to let you have it ...
65		Never mind ((pause)).
		What did you go and stay away up there for?

You stayed up there for what?

You were looking for what that you went and stayed away for so long?

JARI *Shut up.*

70 *Enough.*

SAKE *I'm gonna whip you and piss is going to bugger you up.*

KRUNI *You stay where you are.*

Stay where you are.

Tomorrow I'm gonna see the face of this kind of child.

75 You stay put.

I'm gonna sleep first.

JARI He's jealous so he's complaining.

SAKE He's jealous.

He's jealous so he's complaining here.

80 He's jealous.

You see the time?

Is it time to be out? Ah?

You see all the big men sleeping?

You got a watch?

85 Where is your watch?

You see the time?

What time is it.

Tell me then, what time is it?

It's still afternoon, ah?

90 Is everyone still out around the village?

They're all out talking?

Idiot, you're out prowling around like a pig.

You're a pig.

Do you hear?

95 You're a real pig woman.

You don't have a head.

She just stays away and stays and stays.

If you're a human being you have knowledge. ((save)) ((pause))

You don't have a baby so you go and stay away.

100 *He cries.*

If we call out to you the old one ((i.e. Kruni)) gets up and crosses us.

Is it time to be out that you go and stayaway?

SOMBANG I'm sick of this.

JARI You shut up.

105 SAKE Mm, *she'll shut up.*

Mm right.

She'll shut up for you.
You do good things so everyone is just going to shut up for you.
Yanga, your head is really good, it has a lot of fat.
(continued)

Kulick (1992a) discusses extensively how this particular *kros* exhibits many typical characteristics of its genre. First of all, the major part of the *kros* is in Taiap, although it does contain some quite substantial code-switching into Tok Pisin at certain conversational junctures. *Kroses should* in fact be performed predominantly in Taiap, as villagers consider them to be vernacular events par excellence. As we noted above, *kroses* are also highly female gendered – it is mainly women who *kros* – and this is one reason why the genre is associated foremost with Taiap.

Second, Sake makes clear that the reason for the *kros* is that Jari has encroached upon her autonomy and independence. This Jari has done not only by leaving a crying baby on Sake's hands for her to take care of, but also by subjecting her to the anger of the village men when she raises her voice in the middle of the night to shout for Jari. That Jari is promiscuous or leaves her baby alone at night are not the main problems. The real problem was the fact that such behaviour is a blatant infringement of Sake's independence and autonomy. She is therefore well within her rights initiating a public protest of such dignity.

Third, the manner in which the the *krosing* is carried out, especially the magnificence of the insults, makes this *kros* a highly typical instance of its genre. Sake insults her sister by drawing attention to Jari's ugly nose and short hair, refers to her by the name of Yanga, who is an aged, bald and unattractive man from a neighbouring village, and elaborates effectively and at length on the pig-metaphor; Jari is portrayed as an animal, snuffling around at night and bumping into the poles of houses. Sake's direct and personal attack on Jari is furthermore punctuated by threats of physical violence; Jari will be 'whipped', her 'head split' open, and Sake will 'eat' its fat; Kruni, for his part, will beat her on the head until she 'tastes blood'.

Fourth, and most interesting, are the linguistic and pragmatic strategies that formally articulate the *kros* as a genre, and at which *krosers* may be more or less accomplished at manipulating.

The current *kros* is in fact made up of three 'monologues', Kruni's, Sombang's and Sake's. They are not totally independent outpourings, however, as the contributions of each *kroser* do have a more or less explicit relation to each other. In fact, the *kros is* constructed as a collaboratively built monologue, where all three individual voices are intertwined under Sake's orchestration into a single set of complaints and abuse.

Sake is particularly good at picking up contributions made by Sombang and Kruni and incorporating these into her own speech, something that she accomplishes through repetition and/or code-switching. In effect, she seems to be building a consensus of many voices into the *kros* itself, instead of merely relying on the silent acknowledgement of the just nature of the *kros* from those who happen to hear it. For example, in lines 12 and 13 *you better think twice when you come down. You're gonna get knocked down good,* and again in 19 and 20, *You bring your head up this step, that head of yours is its going to get broken in two,* Sake spins along on the threat first made by Kruni in line 9 that Jari will receive a beating *If I come down, she's gonna bugger up.* Again, in lines 25–27, *What are you prowling around for? You go and stay up there. You don't have a baby?,* Sake reiterates the points made by Sombang a few utterances earlier, lines 14–17, *You don't have something? You don't have a baby? You're out walking around like you don't. Who are you prowling around for?* And, in line 30, *Why did you go and stay away for such a long time up there?,* Sake repeats line 29, *Why did you go and stay away?* produced by Sombang. In lines 59–63, *You don't have a baby? You're a single woman, ah? You should prowl around like that? Mine, my mouth is really stinking here,* there is a reiteration and a structural homology with Sombang's lines 46–50, *You don't have any responsibilities, you just prowl around for this. Enough. You. I have lots of nasty words. I'm gonna start cursing at you now.* The sheer number of these repetitions, both self-repetitions and other-repetitions, contribute powerfully to focusing the *kros* on these points which therefore emerge as central. Of interest is the intensive echoing or mirroring of forms between Sombang and Saki that commences in line 29 and finishes in line 33. The co-operative monologic nature of this *kros* is further underscored by the fact that there are no explicit meta-linguistic references to the speech of the other *krosers,* for example no 'reported speech', no mention of 'authorship' and no feedback signals or repairs of other types. Sake's pauses (e.g. line 98) are also very long, but there is little or no competition for a turn at *krosing.*

The use of rhetorical questions is a very prevalent linguistic strategy in this *kros,* and these serve to propel the discourse forward. In fact, the bulk of the *kros* is manifested through rhetorical questions, which serve to engage the attention of the audience on the activity of the talk at the same time as they guarantee that the speaker keeps the floor. The few contributions that are not rhetorical questions are those where the three *krosing* voices momentarily step outside of the monologic *kros*-format to engage with each other (for example, when Kruni in lines 72–76 directly addresses Sake, although he can be taken to simultaneously be addressing his contribution to Jari), or when *krosers* are reporting on their own emotional states (see lines 7–8 for Sombang), or giving threats or insults (see lines 13 and 93–96). There are very few declarative statements of fact (see line 4 about everybody sleeping). And there are hardly any directives (except those produced by Jari: see line 104, *you shut up).*

Any contributions by the victim of the *kros* risk being responded to with irony, and/or used as building blocks for insults, which is one reason why a turn-by-turn interaction risks escalating the conflict. In this context, we can note Kruni's uptake in line 24, *You're doing good things,* of Jari's lines 21–22, *We were walking around looking for something. We weren't prowling around to fuck,* and Sake's line 105–108, *Mm, she'll shut up. Mm. Right. She'll shut up for you. You do good things so everyone is just going to shut up for you,* which is a response to Jari's line 104, *You shut up,* directed to Sombang. Both rhetorical questions and the pervasive use of irony serve in this context to quash the voice of Jari under the dominant authorial voices of the *krosers.*

3.2 Code-switching in krosing

Different formal types of code-switching can be distinguished in this *kros.* On the one hand, there are switches between the contributions of the different participants in the *kros,* for example between Kruni's utterance in line 9 and Sake's code-switched contribution in line 10; or between Sombang's line 29 and Sake's code-switched repetition in line 30; or between Kruni's lines 72–76 and Jari's line 77.

Another type of code-switching in this *kros* can be characterized in relation to the syntax of the utterance design. Early on in the *kros* (lines 11–12 and 18–20), Sake encodes a threat in an 'if-then' construction, where the 'if' part is produced in Taiap and the 'then' part completed in Tok Pisin. This strategy actually permits her the option of not having to specify the prospective 'agent' behind the awful fate that will befall Jari 'if . . .' as she would have had to do had she chosen to formulate the consequent in Taiap with its ergative noun phrase marking.

By far the most common type of code-switching, however, is that which takes place within one speaker's – mainly Sake's – turn, and which involves a simultaneous repeat, utterance by utterance, of the rhetorical questions that constitute the backbone of this *kros.* In this context, it is also important to remember that the original formulation of these rhetorical points is Sombang's, although this remains unacknowledged.

Instances of conversational code-switching in this *kros* from Gapun occur in very similar structural positions to that of other communities and language environments. Code-switched utterances in relation to upcoming *end of turn* or in the context of *insertion sequences* have been found to occur in language pairs as different from Taiap–Tok Pisin as Chinese–English (Li Wei 1994), and Thai–English (Moerman 1988), and in communities as far apart from Gapun villagers as Chinese immigrants in Newcastle or Thai lawyers in Bangkok. In the search for more general principles of conversational organization that can subsume 'empirically described local structures' of code-switching, some authors have suggested that principles such as *dispre-*

ferred second can account for the social significance of *contradiction* when code-switching occurs in *insertion sequences* or *second pair parts* (Li Wei 1994). A potential interpretation of the code-switches between speakers' contributions such as in lines 9–10, or lines 29 and 30, could be one of *contrast*, serving to underscore the 'multimonologue' character of this partic- ular type of discourse. The *krosers* are not really addressing each others' contributions. Rather what we are witnessing is more along the lines of competitive self-selection. Likewise, when Sake within her turn appropri- ates the utterances of Sombang in a code-switch, these types of code-switching could be seen as conversationally dispreferred structural types; tying back to a previous contribution but diverging in language choice in the answer to a question, for example, is commonly understood to signal 'contradiction' (cf. Li Wei 1994).

However, this does not mean that everybody necessarily understands the conversational significance of these structural instances of code-switching in these ways. In Gapun, extended sequences of multiparty talk are frequently highly collaborative ventures where co-construction of discourse with many speakers contributing overlapping turns at talk is the norm. In such cases, code-switches carried by an insertion or interruptive sequence more often carry social or rhetorical meanings of support and sympathy with the main speaker than overtones of contradiction and conversational discord. In the current case, though, the monologic nature of the *krosing* genre pro- hibits an analytical approach based on the microdynamics of conversational interaction. As speakers do not orientate to each other's contributions, there is little evidence available as to how they understand these code- switches.

One interpretation of these switches which has some currency in Gapuners' local thinking about language is that they function in this context very much as what, in Bakhtin's (1984) words, can be called the *double-voiced word*, that is 'words' that orientate towards the words of another 'voice', without necessarily subjugating them to be part of the 'ideologically, controlling, monologic voice' (Hill and Hill 1986: 391). Stroud (1992) is an illustration of how conversational code-switching opens up the possibility for multiple interpretations of a men's house oratory. Oratories are speech genres where men work together to create collective fantasies of agreement in their talk, constructing polyglossic verbal accounts in which a number of different perspectives on an issue, often ones that are blatantly contradictory, are presented as equally valid and consistent. An important consequence of this type of talk is that the authorship of utterances is often indeterminable. Furthermore, the heteroglossic nature of much of the talk produced in these contexts permits interactants to choose between a variety of arguments that are presented in talk, and elaborate (through repetition, for example) those utterances that are perceived to be most conducive to interpersonal agreement.

In Sake's *kros*, we can observe language serving similar rhetorical purposes as in oratories. Her talk contains many repetitions and code-switches, which serve rhetorically to emphasize the main points of the talk and to contextualize what is said in different interpretative frameworks. Exactly what Sake is alluding to through her choice of language, however, is a matter of speculation. The two languages involved in this interaction, Tok Pisin and Taiap, have the potential to articulate a number of (locally) negotiated and overlapping metaphorical meanings, and alternative or simultaneously multivocal social meanings for any particular code-switch may be in force at any point in the *kros*. Kulick (1992a) and Stroud (1992) mention that the vernacular language Taiap has come to be associated with tradition, the land, affect, the concept of *hed* and women. Tok Pisin, on the other hand, evokes connotations to modernity, Christianity, *save*, money, schooling and men. Any of these associations may be invoked at specific points in the *kros*. In line 98, for example, Sake calls out in Tok Pisin, *If you're a human being you have knowledge*, which superficially appears to be an almost redundantly clear reference through language choice to connotations of reason and *save* carried by Tok Pisin. However, assigning metaphorical values to each language is far from an easy task, and even more problematic when having to choose whether an associative value should be conceived as in-group or out-group (cf. Gumperz 1982). Some of the values that one would have wanted to identify as traditional in-group values are essentially out-group values that are enacted locally, such as the value placed on 'hard work' and tidiness of the village of Gapun; this is a 'Catholic inspired' importation into traditional village rhetoric, especially 'harangues' by *bikmen* in the men's house. Furthermore, in-group values are continually being negotiated and contextualized within out-group frameworks. Again, in the village of Gapun, certain facets of villagers' conception of personhood are articulated in relation to Tok Pisin, and this has had consequences for the metaphorical associations to Tok Pisin, at the same time as those facets emphasized in discourses in the local vernacular have changed character (see Kulick and Stroud 1990a). In general, metaphorical associations to languages are quite likely a result of continual negotiations and on-going contestations among community members, a reflection of the fact that a speech community is not an ideologically homogeneous or amorphous structure, but composed of social groupings with very different interests. The distinction between in-group and out-group values is at best a contextually specific one, one that depends upon perspective and one that will be frequently contested.

In other words, Sake's code-switches can be read as embodying the potential for the participants in the *kros* to entertain and construct multiple interpretations of what is said. Such a use of language is quite in keeping with villagers' local ideology of speech. Gapuners' orientation to language and meaning is in important respects different from that commonly upheld among Western language users. In models of conversational code-switching, the speaker is frequently viewed as an individual, intentional actor who means something specific with his or her switch. '[F]or speakers, switching is a tool, a means of doing something. For the listener, switching is an index, a symbol of the speaker's intentions' (Myers-Scotton 1988b: 156). Myers-Scotton has, for example, proposed that the interpretation of a code-switch relies on principles of conversational inference that generate implicatures on a par with those proposed by Grice. But the significance of individual intention and agency in communication is perceived very differently by Gapuners, who frequently search for hidden meanings behind what is said and who entertain the idea that words more often hide the intentions of the speaker than they reveal them. They are very much aware that talk, events and actions may embody a significance beyond that which can be immediately apprehended, or that a person's words may not really reflect his or her intentions or motives, and talk is considered to be opaque and potentially very deceptive. Gapuners display an orientation towards the hidden meanings that may lie behind or beyond surface appearances, and village interaction is often about peeling away that which is 'apparent' in order to reveal dimensions of language that may be concealed. In *krosing*, for example, Sake uses an abundance of rhetorical questions and ironic asides; rhetorical questions are not really questions – they do not acknowledge the possibility of a response on behalf of the addressee – and irony is only perceived when the *significance* of what is said is the direct opposite of what is *said*.

Such a conception of language is quite likely instilled at an early age. Kulick (1992a) mentions the importance of the *em ia* 'look there' socialization routine that mothers use to quieten a screaming toddler. This routine attempts to draw the child's attention to some object although, as Kulick observes, 'the purpose . . . is not primarily to link an object with its name . . . since more often than not the object being pointed to and named will not actually be visible anywhere at all' (Kulick 1992a: 115).

The local sociocultural ideology of language that Gapuners entertain is reflected in a more general, and quite specifically Melanesian, orientation to significance and meaning of events and actions. Despite the fact, or perhaps because of it, that Gapuners are tucked away deep within a mangrove swamp, villagers partake in an exciting world of continual change and flux. They are strongly and positively oriented to change, which they interpret within a traditional Melanesian millenarian framework to involve the potential for a total metamorphosis of their social and physical being. Waiting for change to come about, initiating change, experiencing change, talking about it and interpreting it, frequently within discourses of a millenarian interpretation of Christianity, are highly salient features of everyday life in Gapun, and there is an emphasis on disorder and novelty in Gapuners' view of change (see Kulick 1992a). In like manner to many other Melanesian peoples, Gapuners' characteristic stance on change and flux informs their orientation to the *significance and meanings of events and actions*. To villagers' minds, change does not just come about, but is always a significant step on the way to greater changes and transformations, a 'sign of something more meaningful', an event embodying something over and above that which it superficially appears to be. This conception of significance carries implications for how meanings of events and actions are constructed/constituted, as well as for the nature of their agency or authorship.

The practice of searching for significance in patterns of events, where the significance of an action or event lies in its performative and emergent qualities (see also Merlan and Rumsey 1991), and juxtaposing facts and theories so that the secret meanings of an event can be revealed, is a fundamental constitutive dimension in how villagers view many other types of events and actions. A similar tension between that which is concealed and that which is revealed with an emphasis on the discovery of secret meaning reappears in villagers' orientation to knowledge. Strathern (1988) has dealt with this issue in conjunction with her work on traditional initiation rites among highland Papua New Guineans. She claims that these rites, which throughout Melanesia centre on the hiding, revelation and then reconcealment of sacred stories and knowledge, guide an individual through different layers of awareness.

The emergent nature of significance and meaning and Gapuners' conception of language as social action comes to the fore in the common use in village rhetoric of 'meta-languaging', that is, 'talking about talk' and the frequent use of rhetorical questions. Talking about talk is one way in which prior statements or claims are subjected to close scrutiny and critical reinterpretation in the villagers' search for the true, hidden, significance behind what was said or revealed 'by the mouth'. Talking about talk is in fact one of the main language activities to occur in men's house oratories, and is an important interactional means by which events are constituted, a discursive consciousness in Giddens' (1984) terminology (cf. Merlan and Rumsey 1991; Schieffelin 1990). This epistemological slant on meaning and significance underlies the willingness that villagers show to generate multiple, contesting and equally possible meanings for each code-switched utterance.

Perhaps the most important use of the conversational code-switching that Sake exhibits is in how she accomplishes subtle ambiguities of authorship. In the structural context of reiterating another person's words, code-switching is an echo or 'quote' of these words, at the same time as it comprises a new formulation of them. To code-switch, then, can be seen as a form of double-voiced word in the sense that a code-switched utterance is an appropriation of the words, but may also through repetition index that the ownership or authorship of the words belongs to somebody else. As it is used in this *kros*, code-switching is a means of engaging with another's voice (in this case Sombang's) without subordinating it to the authorial voice of Sake – an example of true heteroglossia – permitting an ambiguity about whose 'voice' is being heard. In using code-switching in this way, we can interpret Sake as attending to some salient cultural notions on *agency and intention*, i.e. 'the ways in which [people] formulate the possibilities of involvement and intervention in human action' (Merlan and Rumsey 1991: 90) that cross-cut both non-linguistic and linguistic 'life'. Gapuners' conceptions of intentionality and agency also find an encoding in some of the structural types found in the Taiap language and the existence of 'frames of consistency' (Whorf 1956). Following Rumsey (1990), citing Whorf (1956), the best way to study the relationship between language structure and other aspects of social life is by looking for what Whorf called fashions of speaking: global complexes of features that 'cut across the typical grammatical classifications, so that such a "fashion" may include lexical, morphological, syntactic and otherwise systematically diverse means co-ordinated in a certain frame of consistency' (Rumsey 1990: 346, citing Whorf 1956: 158). In Taiap, for example, similar functional oppositions can be argued to underlie two quite different structural areas, ergative marking of agentive noun phrases (see also Merlan and Rumsey 1989, 1991; Duranti 1994) and the formal realization of reported speech.

Ergative marking of agents is optional and is used mainly when the speaker is attributing intention, volition, and/or responsibility for an action to an agentive NP. In contexts where the attribution of agency is less of an issue, perhaps even something to be directly avoided or something to be inferred by others, no NP receives ergative marking.

Reported speech structures in a similar way are used to avoid attributing agency to talk. This is possible because in Taiap as in many other (Papuan) languages there is no formal distinction between direct and indirect speech. All reported speech is constructed in 'direct discourse', with indexical categories specified from the perspective of the reported speech situation, which therefore permits an ambiguous reading as to the authorship of an utterance.

There is yet another level of ambiguity in these code-switches. The use of Tok Pisin switches in the 'then' clause to downplay agency and *daunim hed* ('downplay *hed*') consolidates the associations that Tok Pisin stretches also carry for villagers as the language of consensus and *save*. Villagers have the option of hearing Sake modulating her voice, if they wish, relinquishing her legitimate rights as a *kros* person to pour aggression upon the victim.

In other words, Sake could be heard as subjugating the voice of Jari through her repetition of hurtful rhetorical questions and bitter irony, acknowledging the voice of Sombang in a true dialogic engagement with her words, creating an ambiguity as to what authorial responsibility she takes for what she says (or whether she is saying it *all* on behalf of Sombang), and finally spicing it all with a touch of *save* through contextualizing what she says in Tok Pisin.

Sake's code-switches, however, may hold more significance than that which is immediately apparent on the level of locally negotiated understandings of single switches. By using Tok Pisin in the context of the *kros*, Sake imports into the *kros* a dimension of *save* and consensus that had previously not been present *in this form* in the genre (but cf. Kulick 1992a for some insightful commentary on this issue). This is possible through the metaphorical relationships that Tok Pisin has with maleness and oratory, and its wider-world associations with Christian benevolence. One sense in which this 'significance' is present is through the fact that Sake seems to be trying for an air of consensus in other ways, specifically in how she structures her *kros* by 'stepping out of her monologue' to engage with the contributions of Sombang and Kruni. The use of Tok Pisin is reinforcing this contextualization of the *kros* in a framework of *save*.

On the other hand, the use of Tok Pisin in a traditional female genre can simultaneously be understood as creating the conditions for a renegotiation and revalorization of Tok Pisin and Taiap. At the present moment, Gapun is undergoing language shift, and there are clear and documented tendencies of stylistic shrinkage in Taiap; the use of the language is confined more and more to socially marked contexts, and it is increasingly becoming associated with parental anger, old men's magic chants, femaleness and *hed*. Kulick (1992a) in fact argues that the symbolic importance of Taiap for the constitution of femaleness in Gapun is linked partly to the use of this language for *krosing*, and that this is a significant mediating factor in its imminent demise (see above).

However, there are moments of 'semiotic tension' generated by Sake's use of Tok Pisin. The possibility of contesting the unique associations of Tok Pisin with oratorical consensus, maleness and *save*, and Taiap with decisive femaleness and *hed* (cf. Kulick 1992a and 1992b) that is celebrated and reinforced through endless debates in the men's house, is facilitated by the way Sake in her *kros* locks into the metaphorical discourses carried by Tok Pisin. Although we can never know her intentions, the significance of using Tok Pisin lies in how it 'recontextualizes' the meanings originally formulated in Taiap in the ways I have alluded to above. The use of Tok Pisin can be seen as 'moulding the speech situation', as working to reveal dimensions of significance through its conjuncture with Taiap.

Simultaneously, the way Sake mixes voices from different discourses is creating the foundations for a redefinition of the symbolic value of gender in Gapun. Tok Pisin has long been viewed as a possession of men, with women traditionally having little access to the language. So, as Gapuners constitute their society on a daily basis through their verbal interactions, reproducing social categories and relationships, and playing out their understandings of their world, they are introducing novel dimensions to their social reality in the process.

In order to understand the role of conversational code-switching in the reconfiguration of gender relationships, we require a broad notion of context and a reconception of how language relates to social life. Auer (1991) defines context as that which is responsible for the interpretation of an utterance in its particular locus of occurrence, and may be taken to encompass

> the larger activity that participants are engaged in (the 'speech genre'), the small scale activity (or 'speech act'), the mood (or 'key') in which the activity is performed, the topic, but also the participants' roles (the participant constellation comprising 'speaker', 'recipient', 'bystander', etc.), the social relationship between participants, the relationship between speaker and the information being conveyed by language ('modality'), etc., i.e. just those aspects of context that have been found to be related to code alternation.
>
> (Auer 1991: 334)

However, I think the current understanding of Sake's code-switches suggests working with an even broader notion of context that encompasses

> the social activities through which language or communication is produced, the way in which these activities are embedded in institutions, settings, or domains which in turn are implicated in other wider, social economic political and cultural processes [and] the ideologies, which may be linguistic or other, which guide processes of communicative production.
>
> (Grillo 1989: 15)

In the present context, these dimensions can be taken to include such phenomena as local conceptual systems, political structures, economic relationships and social organization, family and kinship systems, the wider social, political and economic processes implicated in core–periphery relations and the language shift in which these are embedded.

Furthermore, the reasoning I have presented here on the way in which code-switching is locking into novel discourses of gender requires more adequate models of social structure and understandings of how language relates to social life. Cameron (1990), Romaine (1984), Woolard (1985) and other critiques and commentators on Labovian-type sociolinguistics have pointed out that much sociolinguistics rests on a naive social theory that takes as bottom line concepts such as identity, norm, gender, etc., that are themselves in need of explication. This is also the case for sociolinguistic accounts of code-switching which present concepts such as agency, action, identity and social role as non-problematic. Bald CA approaches, although explicitly treating code-switching as social *action,* i.e. '[a specific resource] available to bilingual speakers enter[ing] into the constitution of social activities' (paraphrase of Auer 1991: 320) are not explicit on the conception of social action contained within their accounts, nor do they really propose any stand on the relation of language as social action to other, non-linguistic forms of action. An implication of this is that language is still treated as a more or less autonomous level of structure quite independent of its social uses, and only incidentally related to them.

Whatever she is doing, Sake does it skilfully. She manages to direct a multimonologue of complaint and abuse against Jari, although very little of what is said is stated as a matter of incontrovertible fact. Furthermore, not only does she manage to project a great deal of on-line sympathy and support from other villagers in how she works the contributions of Kruni and Sombang into the fabric of her *kros*, but she also comes across through code-switched repetition as possibly not being the original author of what she seems to be claiming. By threatening in Tok Pisin, she is also disguising her own agency in the punishment that may be meted out to Jari. In other words, she is being self-assertive and aggressive without really ever displaying *hed*, and without giving Jari reason for a rejoinder. Sake, always the skilful *kroser*, does not just produce an elegant *kros*, but pulls the mat away from under the option of being on the receiving end of the next one.

Just as importantly, she is sowing the seeds of a semiotic battle over the values of Tok Pisin and Taiap, and doing this through playing out gender roles in novel uses of discourse.

The 'discursive space' in which these novelties are constituted has been cleared by the 'translinguistic battlefield' (Bahktin 1984); the contesting of meanings, the discovery of hidden significance, the performative and emergent co-construction of meaning in a code-switch can be seen as one important motor for social change in Gapun.

5 Conversational code-switching, heteroglossia and polyphony

In this chapter, I have explored the social meaning(s) of code-switching within an orientation to language that emphasized the culturally significant and situated co-construction of meaning. I have focused especially on the role of sociocultural ideologies of language. By contextualizing code-switching in the *kros* within a culturally sensitive social understanding of the village that attended to questions of social change, entertained a conception of language as social action, and articulated a theory of meaning and significance built on notions of dialogicality, ambiguity, polyphony and the contesting of meanings, I have argued that insights could be gained into the culture-specific significance of code-switching.

In Gapun, meanings are sites of much contestation, and work on the production and negotiation of talk is geared towards the generation of

341

ambiguity, multivocality and vagueness. There are no single, simple meanings in the discourse of Gapuners, but a multiplicity of different layered perspectives woven into a tapestry of hidden and revealed significance. Conversational code-switching is a highly valuable motor in the discursive production of multivocality. Characteristics of code-switching such as its indexicality, non-referentiality and non-segmentability (cf. Silverstein 1976), make it well suited to the strategic linguistic needs of Gapuners.

As pointed out by Briggs (1992) for the Warao, a community's linguistic ideologies are powerful resources in the contest for social power and privilege (see also Kulick 1992b on the role of Tok Pisin and Taiap in the symbolic construction of genderedness and power in Gapun). This is definitely the case for Gapun, where the social and cultural significance of gender relationships, as defined through the genre of *krosing*, is currently in a condition of transformation. In order to understand how social change in this instance is coming about, I appealed to an analysis of code-switching. The other side of the coin is that in order to correctly understand the nature of conversational code-switching, we need to grasp the context of sociocultural change of which it is a part and which it helps restructure and transform.

Appendix: Transcription of Sake's *kros*

Transcription conventions

The transcription is phonemic, using the IPA phonetic symbols.
Italic utterances are in Taiap, non-italic are in Tok Pisin.

Line numbers correspond to the line numbering in the English translation on pp. 328–331.

Textual layout on the page is meant to correspond to the temporal placing of a contribution vis-à-vis that of other speakers.

=	signifies that the end and the beginning of two utterances are immediately adjacent
/ and ?	utterance terminal falling and terminal rising boundaries
(-)	pauses of less than one second
(1.0)	duration of pauses longer than one second
((p))	soft speech (piano)
((pp))	very soft speech
((f))	loud speech (forte)
((ff))	very loud speech
> <	encloses speech delivered very much quicker than normal
(( ))	enclose analyst's comments
:	lengthened vowel

	SAKE	*yu anaknɨ kwɛm amaikwar mbɔkŋan?*
		yu anaknɨ kwem amaikwar mbɔkŋan?
		((f)) *ŋgu taŋgar ɔrem*
		nogat nois long ples ol man i slip nambar pinis /=
5	SOMBANG	*ayata*
		ŋgume mɔrasi aŋgi ɔrɛnkurem/
	SOMBANG	*ŋa ndarakuk nimɛ tɔmbirgara aŋgwar aŋgikana/*
		ŋa mnda ida/
	KRUNI	((f)) *ŋa sirkininɛtrɛ batarkɨtakana indɛ/*
		(2.0)
10	SAKE	blari idiot ba::stard yu/
		yu Jari nda nirkɨtaka ɔkɨtaka asiŋgarɛ/
		yu mas tingting gut na yu kam daun/
		nap indai tru bai yu kirap/
		(1.0)
	SOMBANG	*yu ɔrakɔrak wakareŋankɛ?*
15		*rɔr wakareŋankɛ.*
		nimɛnda ɛkrukuk/yu ŋgan, ah, ganɔkau?
		yu aninana ɛkrukuk?
	SAKE	((p)) *ŋayi namwankuk ɛnda wasaoukɨtaka inda mɛmkɨtak*
		((f)) *nɛknɨ kɔkɨr kukukuta/k/* ((f))
20		desela hed kela bilong yu bai bruk tupela hap
	JARI	*yim ɔrakana ɛkrukuk/*
		yim indikɨnana ɛkrukaku wakare/
	KRUNI	*mɔrasi ɛŋgɔn aŋgɔ/*
		yuyi nirkwan aŋgɔ kuk/
25	SAKE	*yu ambin ɔrakana ɛkrukuk?*
		yu tutɔtaka aritak/ (. . .)
		yu rɔr wakareŋankɛ?
		yu no gat pikinini bai yu stap antap?=
	SOMBANG	=*yu ambinana mbɔka kuk?*=
30	SAKE	=bilong wanem yu go istap longpela taim olgeta long
		antap ia?
		wanem kain stori yu go wokim i stap?
		(2.0)
	SOMBANG	*ambin ɔrak aikanɨ wuriwuk?*
	SAKE	*ambinŋan nam stornɨ wurɨprukakuk?*
		(2.0)
		((p)) > blari sting nogut nus bilong yu sting olgeta pinis <
35	SOMBANG	*waiŋgar aŋgikana/*
		ŋa mnda/
		ŋa mndarakuk/
	KRUNI	*niŋan ɔrakaŋgi taou ɔtukwatan/*
		(5.0)
		and akrutakrɛ kiraoukrutak/

40 SOMBANG *yu nɛkɛr (. . .)*
ambinana animaat nɔŋor rekɨ ɛkrukuk?
ayata/

SAKE *ŋgu aŋgwarkɛ rɔr?*
ŋgu aŋgwarkɛ rɔr?

45 SOMBANG *yu ambinana ɛkrukuk?*
yu sakinɛnda?
yu ŋguŋana mɛnda ɛkrukuk/
ayata/ (. . .)
yu ŋa mɛr aprɔŋaninda/

50 *ŋa wɛkɔknɨ adɨmrɨnakana inda/*

SAKE *yu ambinana mbɔkakuk?* ah?
(3.0)

SAKE bilong wanem yu go istap antap ia?
(2.0)

SOMBANG *ɛtiŋgan/*
ŋa mnda rakuk/

55 les *utɔk mnda ida/*
(8.0)

SAKE *ŋgu ani yuwɔn sik bɨdɨgar nɔŋor aikanɨ wuk?*
(1.5)
yu wakakutakrɛ
maus bilong mi bai pen tru long singaut long yu/
((inaudible 17.0))
yu rɔr wakare?

60 yu singel meri ah?
bai yu wokabout olsem/
eh manakonde/ (. . .)
mau::s bilong mi sting nogit tru na istap/
mi laik givim yu-(. . .)

65 maski/
(10.0)
ambin ɔrakana mbɔkakukŋan?
> i stap long wanem samting?
yu painim wanem samting i go istap longpela taim <?=

JARI =((ff)) *tɔwer/*

70 ((ff))*ayata/*

SAKE ((p)) > *naɛrunaka nɔknɨ batarkɨtakana/* <=
KRUNI =((ff)) *antak/*
((f)) *ŋgɔ antak/*
((f)) *ɛpinda rarkunɛtyu nanuk niŋan rɔr inda/*
(3.0)

75 yu stap pastaim/

mi slip/
(4.0)

JARI em jeles na em i toktok/
SAKE em jeles ia/
em jeles na toktok ia/
80 em jeles/
yu tatukun ɔrɔm?
aŋgwarkɛ ɔrɔm? ah?
yu lukim ol bikpela man i slip pinis? (. . .)
>> yu hanwas?
85 *yuwɔn daramnɨ kewuk?*
yu lukim taim tu ah?
haumas tru?
yu tokim mi pastaim << (. . .) wanem taim?
(2.0)
apinyn yet ah?
(2.0)
90 ol man i stap long ples?
ol i toktok istap ah?
((p)) *babasak indɛ mbɔr bibiknɨ inda prukar ekrukuk/*
yu pik ia/
harim ah?
(1.0)
95 yu wanpela pik meri stret/
(3.0)
kokɨr wakarɛŋan aŋgi gariŋon/
istap nating istap nating istap nating/
yu man i gat save/
(22.0)
rɔr wakarɛŋanaŋgi nimɛ ɔkɨtaka akutak/
100 SAKE ((f)) *ŋi eiarakakunɛt/*
((f)) *garkɨnakrɛ lapun mɛmkɨnɛta kroskɨnɛt*
(. . .)
((f)) *ŋgu aŋgwarkɛ ɔrɔmnɨyu mbɔkakuk?*
SOMBANG *mnda*
JARI ((ff)) *yu tɔwer antak/*
105 SAKE mm/ *tɔwer akukutak/*
mm/ tru tumas/
ngu yuŋana tɔwerkɨtak/
yu wokim gutpela pasim bai ol i pasim maus long yu/
Yanga het bilong yu gutpela tru igat gris tru ia/

Notes

The thoughts contained here are the product of many talks with Don Kulick and Kenneth Hyltenstam. HSFR and the Wallenberg foundation have kindly funded work on these issues. Mikael Parkvall has also been of great help in readying transcriptions.

1   In Kulick and Stroud (1990a), mention is made of the individual variability of code-switching patterns in the village, and it is noted that such variability might be a reflex of the language shift process that the community is going through.

2   This text was audio-recorded in 1987. Don Kulick subsequently transcribed the text, with the help of a local villager, Mone. Italic passages are in Taiap; non-italic passages in Tok Pisin; transcriber's insertions are in double parentheses. The full, linguistic transcription is given in the appendix.

Bibliography

Auer, P. (1991) 'Bilingualism in/as social action: A sequential approach to code-switching', in *Papers for the Symposium on Code-Switching in Bilingual Studies: Theory, Significance and Perspectives (Network on Code-Switching and Language Contact, Vol. 2)*. Strasbourg: European Science Foundation, pp. 319–352.

Bakhtin, M. (1984) *Problems of Dostoevsky's Poetics*. Manchester: Manchester University Press.

Besnier, N. (1989) 'Information withholding as a manipulative and collusive strategy in Nukulaelae gossip', *Language in Society* 18: 315–342.

Briggs, C. L. (1992) 'Linguistic ideologies and the naturalization of power in Warao discourse', *Pragmatics* 2: 387–404.

Cameron, D. (1990) 'Demythologizing sociolinguistics: Why language does not reflect society', in J. E. Joseph and T. J. Taylor (eds) *Ideologies of Language*. London: Routledge, pp. 79–93.

Dorian, N. (ed.) (1989) *Investigating Obsolescence: Studies in Language Contraction and Death*. Cambridge: Cambridge University Press.

Duranti, A. (1994) *From Grammar to Politics: Linguistic Anthropology in a Western Samoan Village*. Berkeley and Los Angeles: University of California Press.

Gal, S. (1988) 'The political economy of code-choice', in M. Heller (ed.) *Code-Switching: Anthropological and Sociolinguistic Perspectives*. Amsterdam: Mouton de Gruyter, pp. 245–264.

Gell, A. (1975) *Metamorphosis of the Cassowaries*. London: Athlone Press.

Giddens, A. (1984) *The Constitution of Society*. Berkeley and Los Angeles: University of California Press.

Grillo, R. (1989) 'Anthropology, language and politics', in R. Grillo (ed.) *Social Anthropology and the Politics of Language*. Sociological Review Monographs No. 76, p. 15.

Gumperz, J. (1982) *Discourse Strategies*. Cambridge: Cambridge University Press.

Heller, M. (ed.) (1988) *Code-Switching: Anthropological and Sociolinguistic Perspectives*. Amsterdam: Mouton de Gruyter.

Hill, J. and Hill, K. (1986) *Speaking Mexicano: Dynamics of Syncretic Language in Central Mexico*. Tucson: University of Arizona Press.

Kulick, D. (1992a) *Language Shift and Cultural Reproduction: Socialization, Self and Syncretism in a Papua New Guinean Village*. Cambridge: Cambridge University Press.

Kulick, D. (1992b) 'Anger, gender, language shift and the politics of revelation in a Papua New Guinean village', *Pragmatics* 2: 281–296.

Kulick, D. (1993) 'Speaking as a woman: Structure and gender in domestic arguments in a New Guinea village', *Cultural Anthropology* 8: 510–541.

Kulick, D. and Stroud, C. (1990a) 'Code-switching in Gapun: Social and linguistic aspects of language use in a language shifting community', in J. Verhaar (ed.) *Melanesian Pidgin and Tok Pisin*. Amsterdam: John Benjamins, pp. 205–234.

Kulick, D. and Stroud, C. (1990b) 'Christianity, cargo and ideas of self: Patterns of literacy in a Papua New Guinean village', *Man* 25: 286–303.

Li Wei (1994) *Three Generations, Two Languages, One Family: Language Choice and Language Shift in a Chinese Community in Britain,* Clevedon, England: Multilingual Matters.

Lowenberg, P. (ed.) (1988) *Language Spread and Language Policy: Issues, Implications and Case Studies*. Washington, DC: Georgetown University Press.

McConvell, P. (1988) 'Mix-im-up: Aboriginal code-switching, old and new', in M. Heller (ed.) *Code-Switching: Anthropological and Sociolinguistic Perspectives*. Amsterdam: Mouton de Gruyter, pp. 97–150.

McConvell, P. (1994) 'Code-switching as discourse framework in Gurundji narrative', unpublished MS.

Merlan, F. and Rumsey, A. (1989) 'Aspects of reported speech and clause structure in Ku Waru', unpublished MS.

Merlan, F. and Rumsey, A. (1991) *Ku Waru: Language and Segmentary Politics in the Western Nebilyer Valley, Papua New Guinea*. Cambridge: Cambridge University Press.

Mertz, E. (1989) 'Sociolinguistic creativity: Cape Breton Gaelic's linguistic "tip"', in N. Dorian (ed.) *Investigating Obsolescence: Studies in Language Contraction and Death*. Cambridge: Cambridge University Press, pp. 103–116.

Moerman, M. (1988) *Talking Culture: Ethnography and Cultural Analysis*. Philadelphia: University of Pennsylvania Press.

Myers-Scotton, C. (1988a) 'Code-switching and types of multilingual communities', in P. H. Lowenberg (ed.) *Language Spread and Language Policy: Issues, Implications and Case Studies*. Washington, DC: Georgetown University Press, pp. 61–82.

Myers-Scotton, C. (1988b) 'Code-switching as indexical of social negotiations', in M. Heller (ed.) *Code-Switching: Anthropological and Sociolinguistic Perspectives*. Amsterdam: Mouton de Gruyter, pp. 151–186.

Myers-Scotton, C. (1993) *Social Motivations for Codeswitching: Evidence from Africa*. New York: Oxford University Press.

Ochs, E. (1988) *Culture and Language Development: Language Acquisition and Language Socialization in a Samoan Village*. Cambridge: Cambridge University Press.

Ochs, E. and Schieffelin, B. (eds) (1979) *Developmental Pragmatics*. New York: Academic Press.

Romaine, S. (1984) 'The status of sociological models and categories in explaining linguistic variation', *Linguistische Berichte* 90: 25–38.

Rumsey, A. (1990) 'Wording, meaning and linguistic ideology', *American Anthropologist* 92: 346–361.

Schieffelin, B. (1979) 'Getting it together: An ethnographic perspective on the study of the acquisition of communicative competence', in E. Ochs and B. Schieffelin (eds) *Developmental Pragmatics*. New York: Academic Press, pp. 73–108.

Schieffelin, B. (1986) 'Teasing and shaming in Kaluli children's interactions', in B. Schieffelin and E. Ochs (eds) *Language Socialization across Cultures*. New York: Cambridge University Press, pp. 165–181.

Schieffelin, B. (1990) *The Give and Take of Everyday Life: Language Socialization of Kaluli Children*, New York: Cambridge University Press.

347

Schieffelin, B. and Ochs, E. (eds) (1986) *Language Socialization across Cultures.* New York: Cambridge University Press.

Silverstein, Michael (1976) 'Shifters, linguistic categories and cultural description', in K. Basso (ed.) *Meaning in Anthropology.* Albuquerque: University of New Mexico Press, pp. 11–56.

Strathern, M. (1988) *The Gender of the Gift.* Berkeley: University of California Press.

Stroud, C. (1992) 'The problem of intention and meaning in code-switching', *Text* 12: 127–155.

Whorf, B. (1956) *Language, Thought and Reality.* Cambridge, Mass.: MIT Press.

Woolard, K. (1985) 'Language variation and cultural hegemony: Towards an integration of linguistic and sociolinguistic theory', *American Ethnologist* 12: 738–748.

Woolard, K. (1992) 'Language ideology: Issues and approaches', *Pragmatics* 2: 235–250.

INDEX